PCs made easy

STAGE 2

A PRACTICAL COURSE

caps
lock

PCs made easy

STAGE 2

A PRACTICAL COURSE

PUBLISHED BY THE READER'S DIGEST ASSOCIATION LIMITED
LONDON NEW YORK SYDNEY MONTREAL

PCS MADE EASY
A PRACTICAL COURSE – STAGE 2

Published by the Reader's Digest Association Limited, 2000

Reprinted with amendments, 2001

The Reader's Digest Association Limited
11 Westferry Circus, Canary Wharf, London E14 4HE
www.readersdigest.co.uk

We are committed to both the quality of our products and the service we provide to our customers, so please feel free to contact us on 08705 113366, or by email at cust_service@readersdigest.co.uk
If you have any comments about the content of our books, you can contact us at gbeditorial@readersdigest.co.uk

For Reader's Digest
Series Editor: Christine Noble
Art Editor: Julie Bennett
Assistant Editor: Caroline Boucher

Reader's Digest General Books
Editorial Director: Cortina Butler
Art Director: Nick Clark

PCs made easy was created and produced for The Reader's Digest Association Limited by De Agostini UK Ltd, from material originally published as the Partwork *Computer Success Plus*.

Printing and binding: Printer Industria Gráfica S.A., Barcelona

ISBN 0 276 42500 6

CONTENTS

6

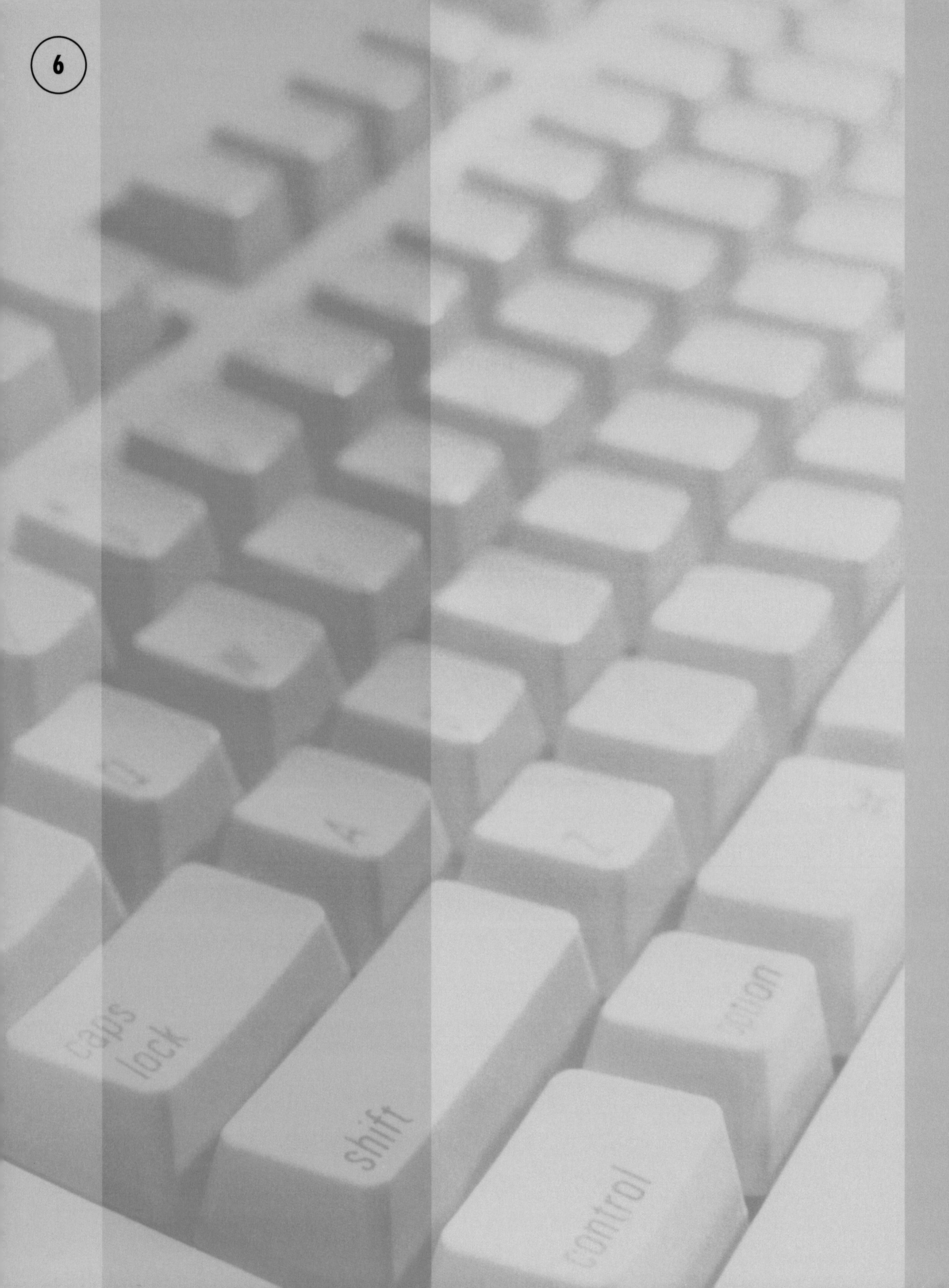

Windows

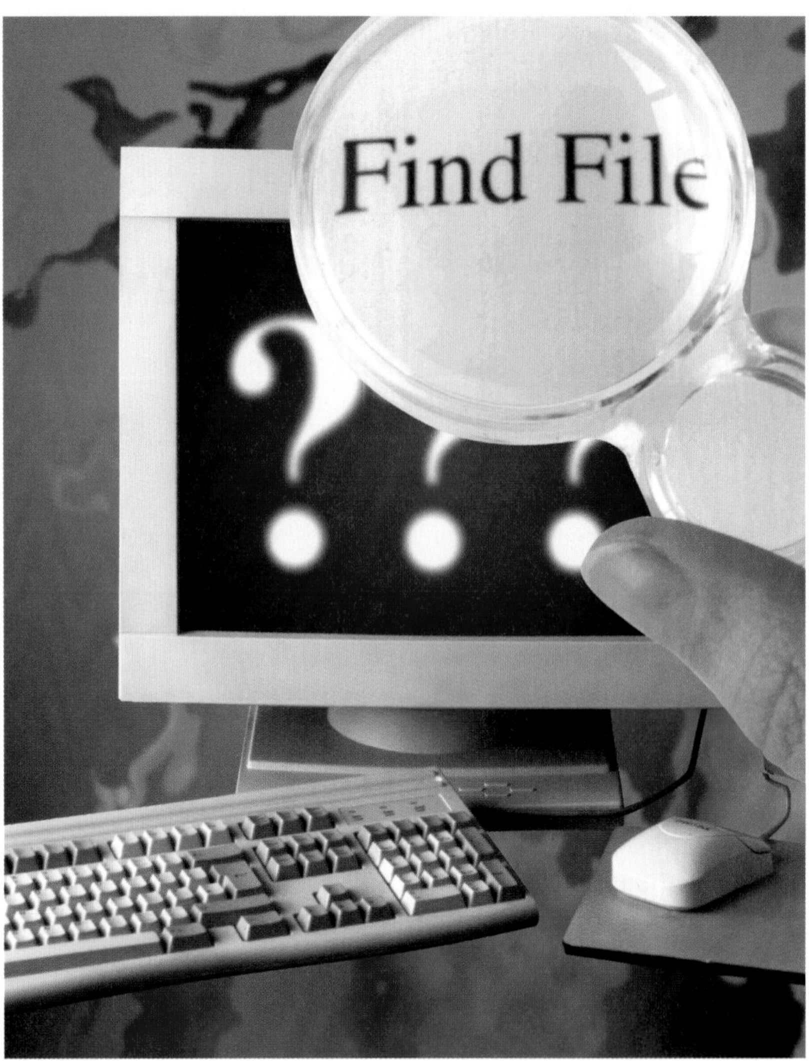

Finding files

Modern computers have huge storage capacities and can hold thousands of files. If an individual file is 'lost' on your PC, Windows' Find command can soon locate it.

When several people share a single computer, document storage can easily become messy. In the same way that things get moved around and mislaid in your house, so files can easily get lost on your computer's drives.

Whether this is because someone else has tried to be helpful and tidied up your folders or because you've accidentally saved a document in the wrong area, the result is the same: you can't find what you're looking for. Whatever the reason for losing your files, Windows can help you find them again.

The Windows Find facility is a handy built-in file retriever that quickly searches through your computer's hard disk to locate missing files. It will work whether you know the file's entire name, a part of it or just a few words of text that the file contains. All you need to do is to give the Find command as much information about the file as you have and then leave it to do the rest.

● First aid for the forgetful

It's worth bearing in mind that Windows searches for exactly what you type in, so typing in 'programme' won't find a file called 'program'. This can also be a problem if you aren't sure of what, exactly, the file was called. So what happens if you can't find the file name or the file itself doesn't contain any text that you can search for (such as an image created using Microsoft Paint, for example)?

Don't worry; you will still be able to track it down despite your forgetfulness. Windows' Find command will locate files that were altered between specific dates or a specified number of days previously. Providing you can recall roughly the last time you worked on it, you should have no trouble in retrieving the file.

Another problem that often occurs on crowded computers is that two or more files might have the same name, either because you have accidentally forgotten what you called the first one or because someone else has had the same idea. When this happens, Find will track down the name everywhere it occurs on your computer. But how do you know which of the files is the one you're looking for? Again, Find can help (see PC Tips box, left).

All in all, with the help of Find, there is no reason why any of your files should prove impossible to track down.

PC TIPS

Same-name files

Windows will not let you give the same name to two files in the same folder. But, as the amount of files on your computer grows, it is likely that you will accidentally repeat file names, perhaps having a file called 'letter1.doc' in a folder of personal letters and another 'letter1.doc' in a folder of bank correspondence. The Find command can be a boon in such cases. It tells you where each file is located and the date it was last modified – both clues to help you find your file.

Searching by name

The simplest type of search is when you can remember a file's name but just can't remember where you put it.

1 Click on the Start button and select Find from the pop-up menu. A sub-menu appears to the right. Select the Files or Folders option and release the mouse button. A window entitled Find: All Files now opens (below).

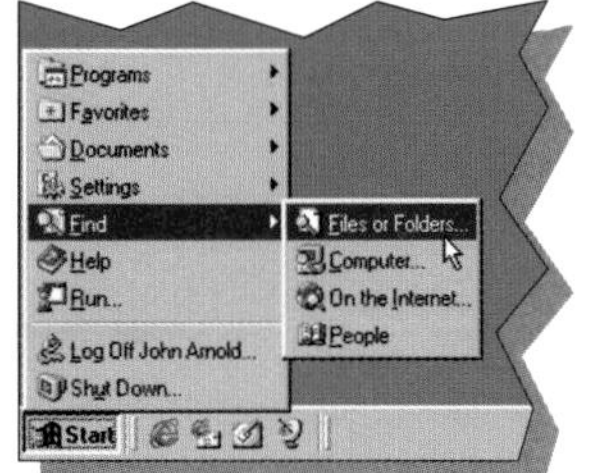

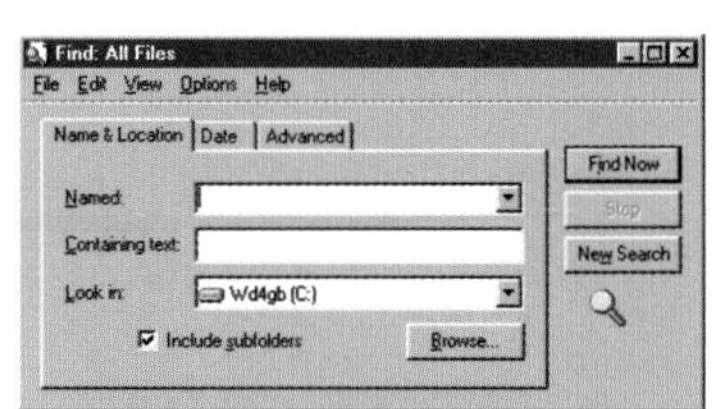

2 For the simplest search, you need only type in the name of the file you want. We've used 'ding.wav' – this is a file that many Windows computers contain on their hard disks. Press the Find Now button to get Windows working on your search.

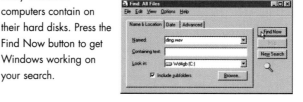

3 Windows shows the files it has found in a panel at the bottom of the dialog box. You can see a file's name, together with other information about it, including its size and its location on your hard disk. Note that the window's Title bar changes to reflect the search details.

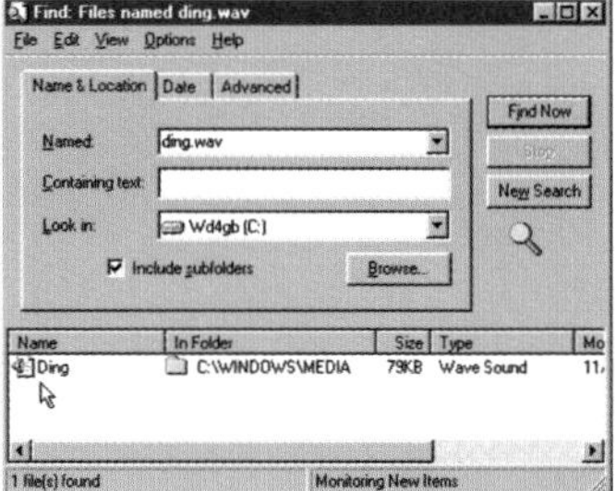

4 If you want to open the 'ding.wav' document, simply double-click on the name and Windows will open your file. In this case, it's a Windows sound file. Providing your PC has a sound card and speakers, you will be able to hear the sound file through the speakers.

Searching by date and file contents

Find will help you search for files when you are unsure about what they are called.

WHAT IT MEANS

STRING

This describes a sequence of letters and numbers. Most of the time a string is simply a word, such as 'disposal'. You're not limited to searching for complete words, however. Search for the string 'dispos', and Windows will locate files which contain any of these words: disposal, indisposed, disposing, disposition and so on. The ability to search on a string is much more powerful than just being able to search on whole words.

1 To find files by date, click on the Date tab in the Find: All Files window. Select Find all files, then the Created or Modified option, followed by the Between option. Enter two dates between which you modified (or created) the file and then click on Find Now to trace all files modified (or created) between the specified dates.

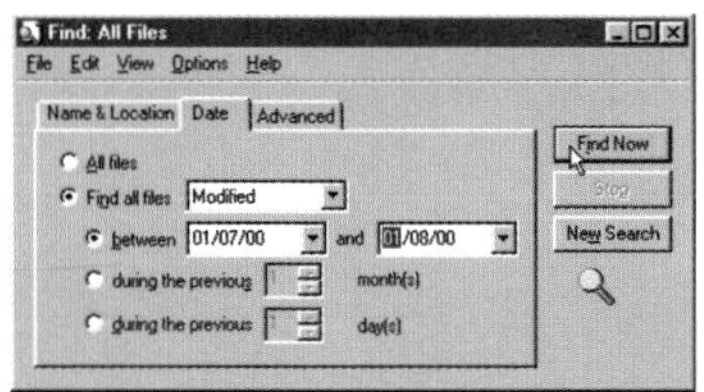

2 Depending on the dates you have chosen and how many files you have used, you may find a lot of files match your search criteria. Scroll down the list until you find the one you want. If you double-click on it, Windows will open the program you used to create it and will then open the document you want.

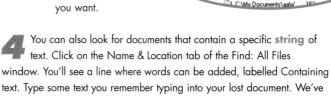

3 You can use either of the other two date search options to find files you've worked on recently. Just select the appropriate option and then click on the up arrow to select the number of months or days you want Windows to search through. Then, press the Find Now button.

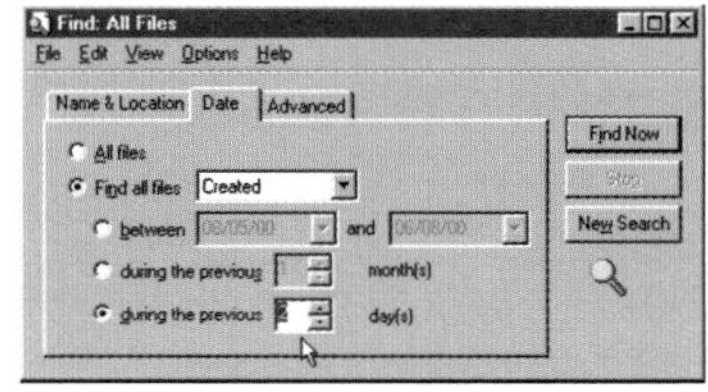

4 You can also look for documents that contain a specific **string** of text. Click on the Name & Location tab of the Find: All Files window. You'll see a line where words can be added, labelled Containing text. Type some text you remember typing into your lost document. We've entered the phrase 'offered the job' – this will help us locate the acceptance letter we created in the first Word exercise (see Stage 1, pages 32–33). Click on the Find Now button and the window Title bar changes to reflect the text entered. Windows will then give you a list of all the files which contained the phrase.

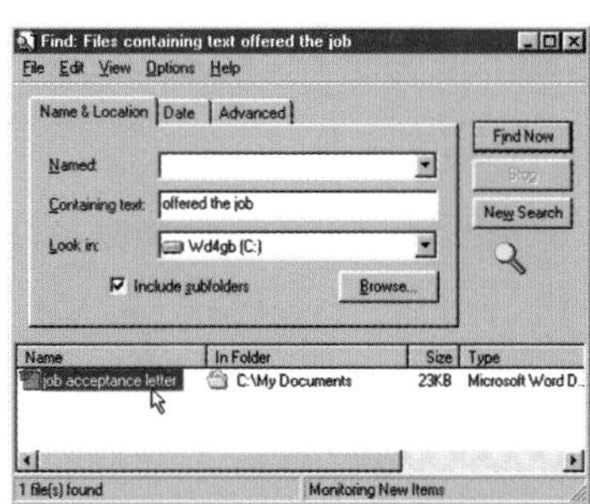

There's no reason why you should have to put up with your Windows Desktop being the same boring colours all the time. Here's how you can spice things up in a matter of minutes.

Customizing your Desktop

The first time you switch on your PC, the chances are you'll be greeted by a rather sober Windows Desktop in shades of dark blue, grey, black and white. While this might be suitable for an office environment, it's no fun for your computer at home. So what can you do to liven things up a bit?

The answer is customization. Almost all the colours and fonts of the things that make up your Windows Desktop can be changed. It's easy to do and Windows even gives you a headstart for ideas by including some ready-made colour schemes.

● Keeping up appearances

We've already found out how to use Paint to create your own Windows background and apply it to your Desktop (see Stage 1, pages 68–69). Other customization changes can be applied in almost exactly the same way. Start by clicking the right mouse button over any part of your Desktop background and select Properties from the pop-up menu to make the Display Properties window appear. We're interested in the way things look, so click on the Appearance tab and you'll see a preview of your current colour scheme. Underneath are a set of buttons and drop-down lists that you can use to modify almost any of the objects shown in the preview.

Let's start by changing the scheme to one of the ready-made ones included with Windows. Click on the down arrow at the right end of the Scheme text box and select Brick from the list that appears. Notice how the preview changes to show you this colour scheme. Now click on the Apply button to change your Desktop to this scheme.

● Do it yourself

You don't have to use Windows' ready-made schemes. Instead, you can customize individual elements of the Desktop to create your own unique set-up. To do this, click on the down arrow at the right end of the Item text box and choose the element you want to customize from the list. For example, let's change the border colour of an active window to red. To do this, select Active Window Border from the Item drop-down list, click on the colour button and choose red from the palette that appears. The preview is updated immediately to reflect the change you've made and, if you click on the Apply button, this change will be made to the whole Desktop.

You can make as many of these changes as you like. You can also change the size, colour and font of text items and the size of icons. You can even save your own customizations and add them to the Windows schemes.

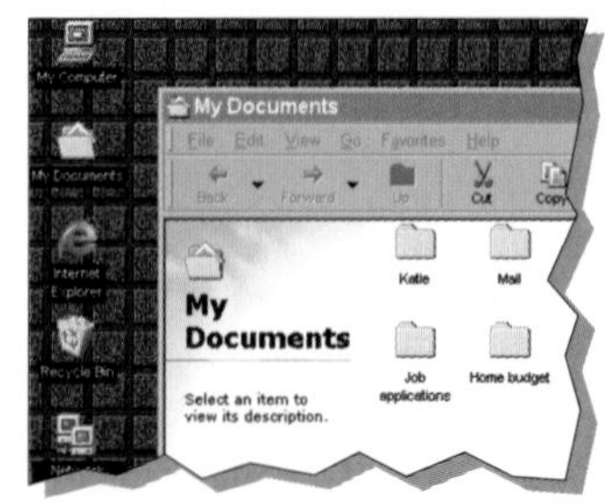

By the time you have changed your background (see Stage 1, pages 68–69) and implemented the Desktop customization techniques shown here, your computer could look very different from the standard Windows set-up!

Customize your Windows

If you wanted, you could make your Windows Desktop match your curtains! That's probably going a bit too far, but you can still easily individualize the Desktop by following our simple steps.

1 The first time you switch on your PC, the Windows Desktop probably looks a lot like the illustration below. If you don't like this standard colour scheme, you can change it by right-clicking anywhere on the Desktop and selecting the Properties option from the menu that appears.

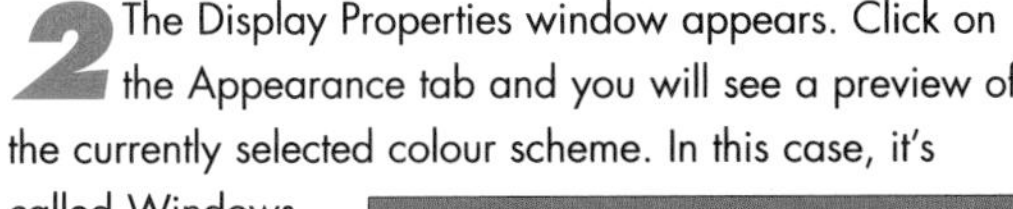

2 The Display Properties window appears. Click on the Appearance tab and you will see a preview of the currently selected colour scheme. In this case, it's called Windows Standard and is made up of a turquoise background and shades of dark blue, grey, black and white for the windows.

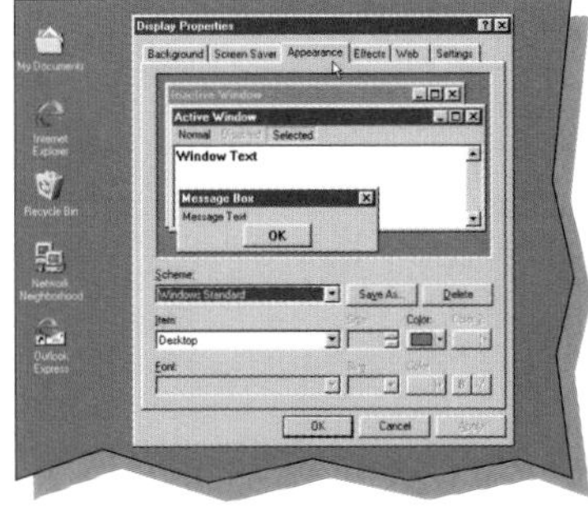

3 Windows Standard is just one of many ready-made colour schemes. Click on the down arrow at the right end of the Scheme text box and you'll see a list of alternative schemes. Here we've chosen Rose and you can see what it's like in the preview window.

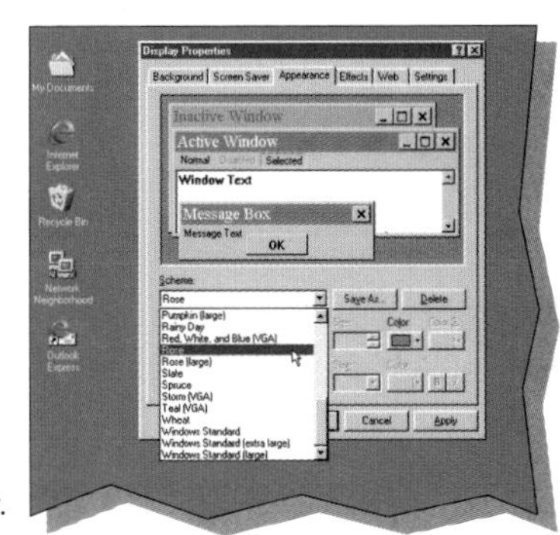

4 The preview gives you some idea of what a different colour scheme would look like, but the best way to test it out properly is to change the whole Desktop. Once you've chosen a ready-made scheme you like from the list, just click on the Apply button to see it in place.

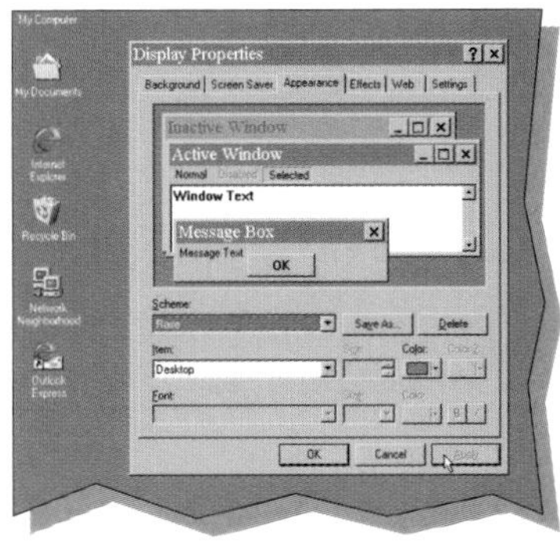

5 You can build your own scheme from scratch. Choose the Maple scheme by selecting it from the Scheme drop-down list and clicking on the Apply button (this makes your background go black). Now let's use it as the starting point for our own colour scheme.

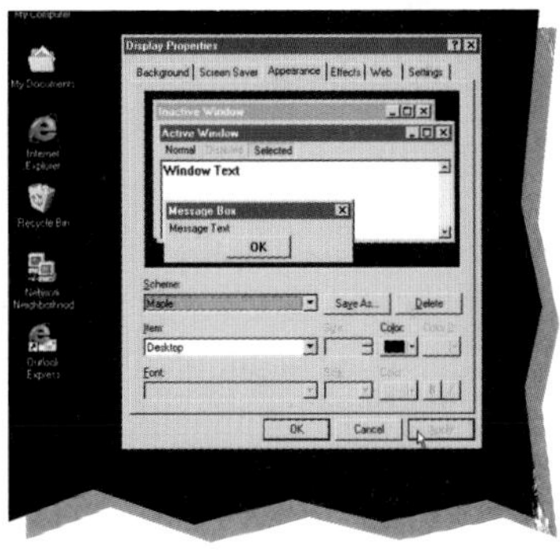

6 Click on the arrow at the right of the Item text box. Now you can see a list of all the parts of a scheme that you can customize. Select Active Title Bar and the colour on the Color button changes to that of the Title bar on an active window.

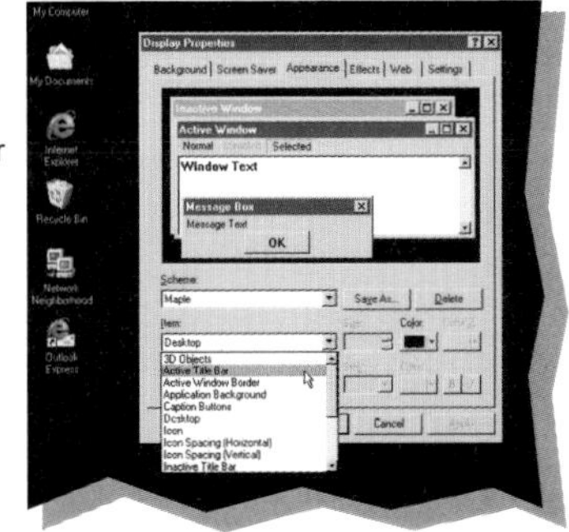

7 Now click the down arrow beside the Color button and select red from the palette that appears. Notice how the preview of the scheme is updated to reflect the change you've made. Click on the Apply button to make this change the whole Desktop.

8 Now you can experiment by customizing as many different elements as you like from the Item list. Why not try experimenting with the fonts? You can add your finished scheme to the ready-made ones by clicking the Save As button, typing in a name and clicking OK. Remember that if you decide the changes you make are no improvement on the original, it's easy to restore the original scheme (see Back To Basics, left).

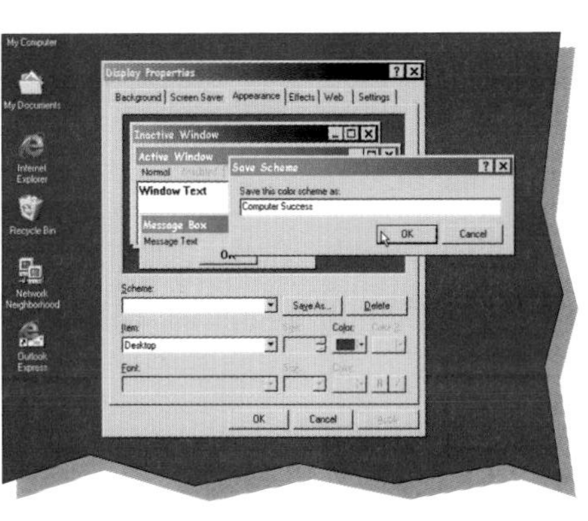

BACK TO BASICS

When you are altering the display settings, nothing serious or permanent can go wrong. Windows will simply reset itself if it can't work with your new settings. If you set up a colour scheme that you later hate even more than the original, it is easy to go back to square one. Simply select Windows Standard in the Scheme box to restore the original settings.

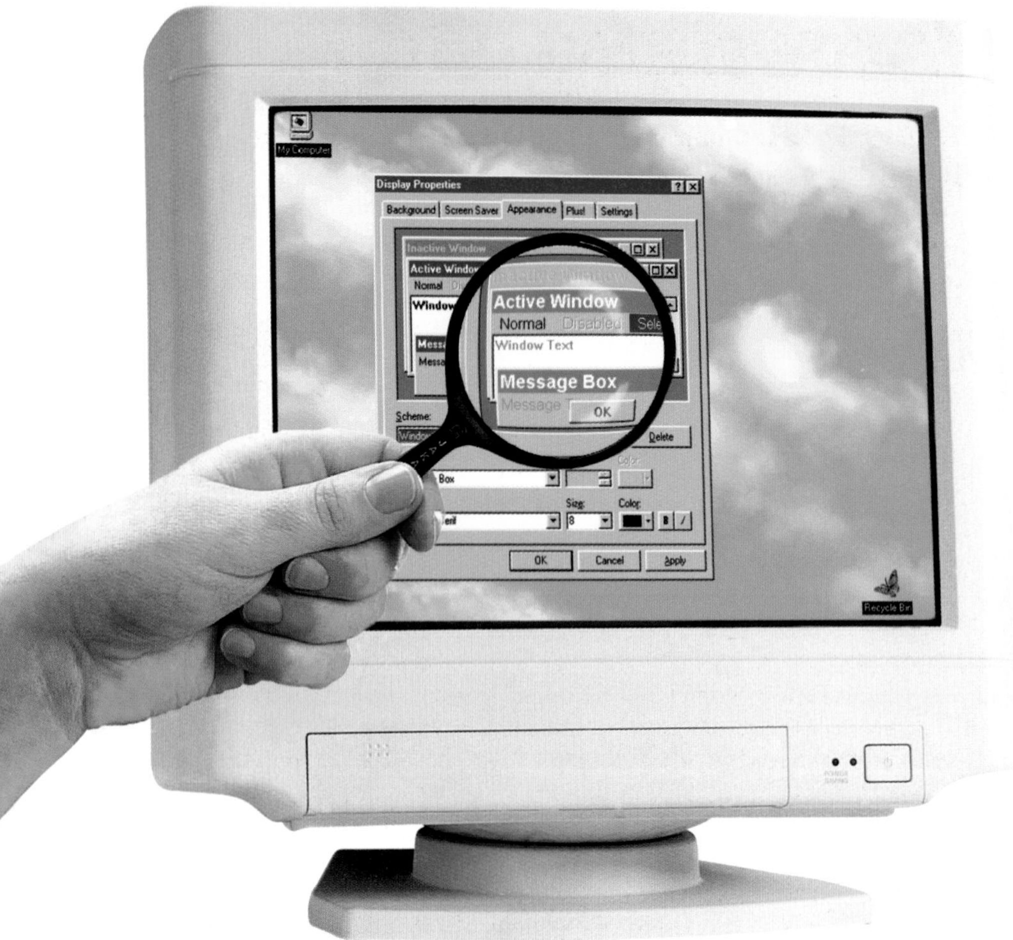

Windows gives you the tools to control how the Desktop is displayed on your monitor. Here's a guide to show you how simple it is for you to make adjustments to these display settings.

Personalize your Windows settings by making a few simple changes to the way it is displayed on your monitor.

Change your view of Windows

On pages 10–11, you saw some of the techniques to customize the way your Windows Desktop looks.

There is also another level of control over the way your Desktop is displayed on your monitor, which involves changing the display settings. There are two main display settings you can control: the display resolution and the number of colours that can be shown on screen at any one time.

The resolution is the most important display setting that you can change. This tells Windows how many pixels (or dots) to use to form the image on the computer monitor. By using more pixels to make up the picture, the more detail you will see. The limitation here is the computer monitor – some cannot display high resolutions. For example, you might find that Windows lets you try, say, 1280 x 1024 pixels, but the screen image then appears garbled and you can't see anything at all. If this happens, don't worry: Windows will switch back to your old setting automatically after a few seconds.

● Number of colours

The other important display setting is the number of colours used to display the image. The more colours used, the more memory used on your computer's graphics adaptor, so you might find that you can have a high resolution, or lots of colours, but not both.

WHAT IT MEANS

GRAPHICS ADAPTOR

The display adaptor is a device inside your computer that takes commands from Windows about what your Desktop should look like. It then converts the commands into a signal your monitor can understand. The more memory your PC's display adaptor has, the more colours and greater resolution that can be displayed on your monitor.

The easy way to change display settings

There are subtle ways of adjusting the Windows Desktop to suit your own tastes. Here we show how you can make Windows look smarter and work better on your computer at the same time.

1 The place to go to control how Windows looks on screen is the Display Properties window. This is available by clicking on the Start menu, then Settings, then Control Panel and Display. However, the quickest way is to right-click on any free part of your Desktop and choose Properties from the menu that appears.

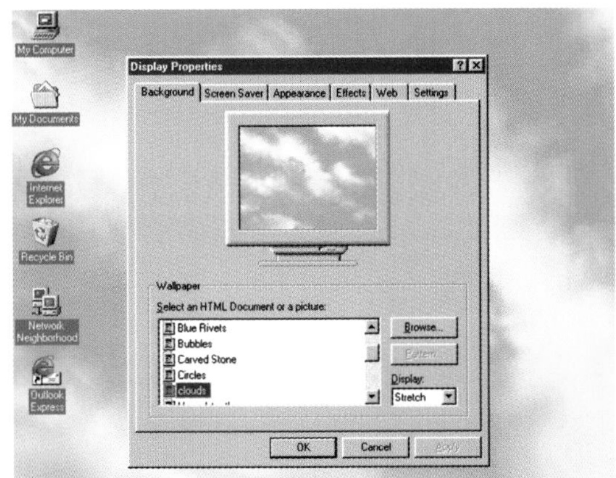

2 The settings for your display are controlled from the Settings tab of the Display Properties window. Click on the Settings tab and you'll see the sorts of things over which you have control: you can alter the number of colours used, the size of the Desktop area and the size of text on the Desktop.

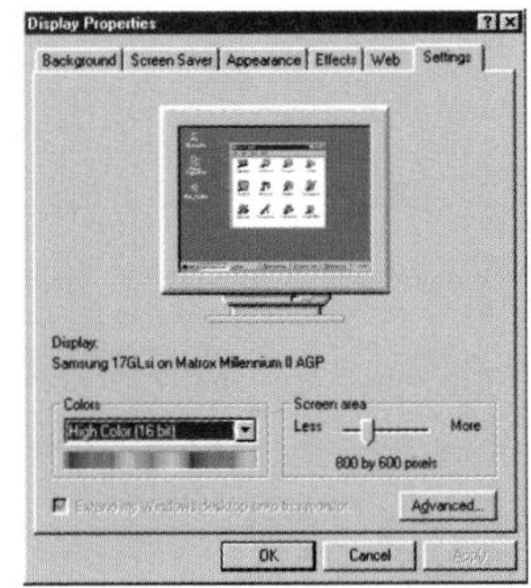

3 The Colors option controls how many colours Windows can display on the screen at once. Click on the down arrow at the right end of the Colors text box and select True Color (32 bit). Windows has only a limited amount of memory available to store the on-screen display, so you might have to compromise (see step 4).

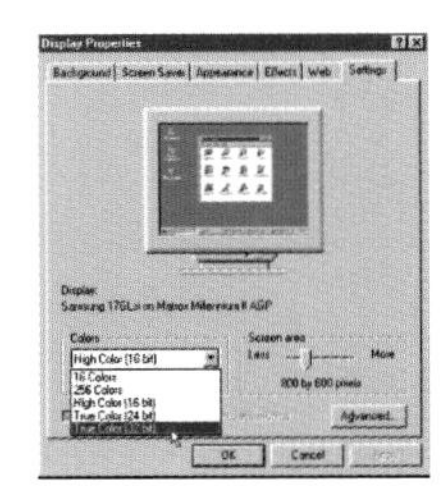

4 If you choose to display more colours, you might have to settle for a Desktop with less pixels. In step 3, before we chose True Color (32 bit), Windows was set up to use 800 x 600 pixels for the Desktop, but it has now reduced this to 640 x 480 pixels.

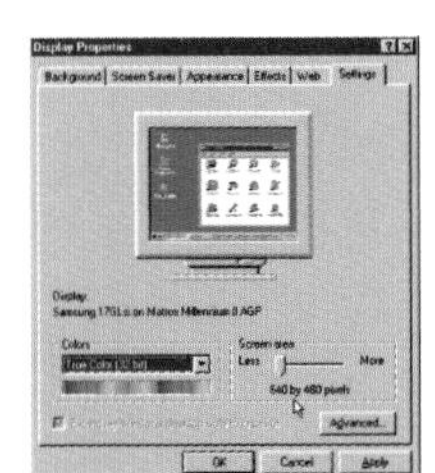

5 If the number of pixels is more important to you than the number of colours, you can use the Screen area slider to increase it. We've simply used the mouse to drag the slider back up to 800 x 600 pixels.

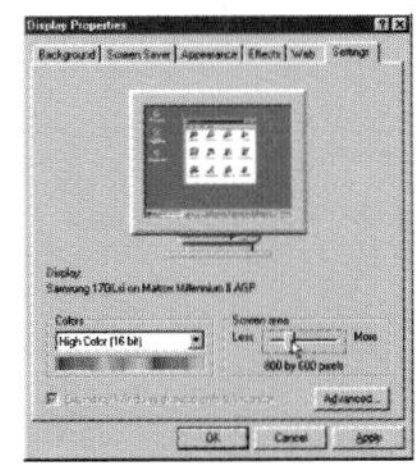

PC TIPS

Colour choice

The maximum colour display for most PCs is, theoretically, up to 4,294,967,296 colours, courtesy of something called True Color (or 32 or 24 bit colour). Some older computers can't cope with this amount, as the more colours you have, the more memory your PC needs to work out what tone each pixel is. If you select too high a number of colours, Windows will compensate by simply reducing the number of pixels that can be on display.

6 Windows also lets you control text size on the Desktop (for example, the labels beneath icons). First, click the Advanced button. A choice is offered from the Font Size drop-down list. Click on the down arrow at the right end of the text box and select the size you prefer.

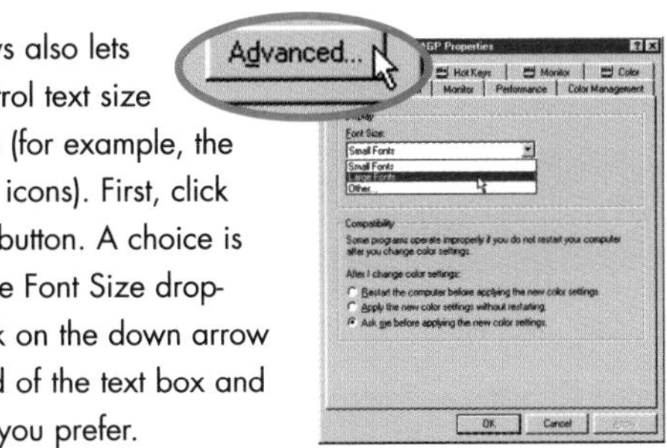

7 You can control the font size more precisely by selecting the Other option. Now you can drag and drop the ruler to change the font size by an exact percentage and see what it looks like. You can keep adjusting the font size until you're happy with it, at which point click the OK button.

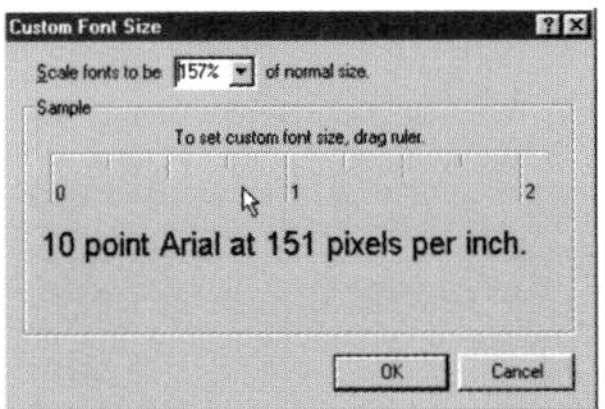

8 When you've finished making changes to your display settings, you can click the OK button or the Apply button to see what your new Desktop looks like. Sometimes Windows will need to restart your computer to make the changes happen, so don't be surprised if you see a message asking you if you want to restart.

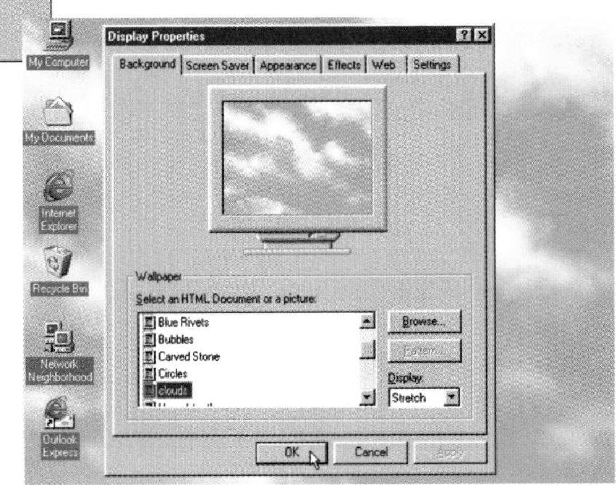

9 The reason for the restart message is that some of your software might not work properly during your present session, as it might still think your computer is displaying its windows in the same way it was before you changed the settings. As soon as you restart, the new settings will take effect.

Customizing the Taskbar and Start menu

As you make so much use of the Windows Taskbar and Start menu, it's a good idea to set them up to suit your own needs and preferences.

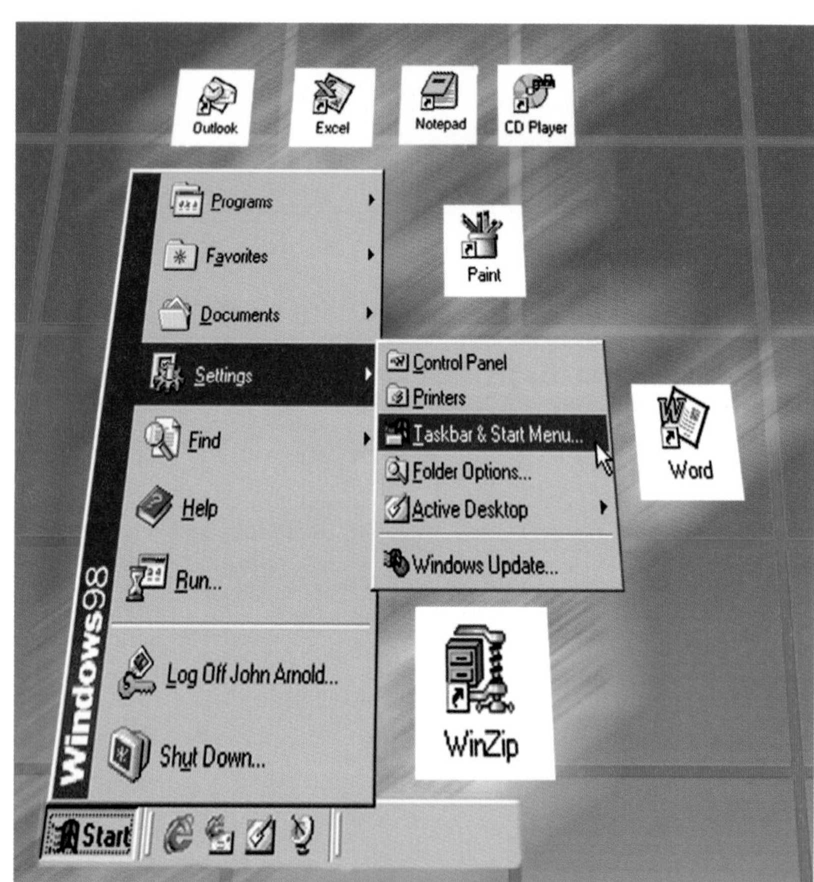

Located at the bottom of your screen, the Windows Taskbar is your main route to opening and managing programs. Windows is installed with a number of standard settings and, although these work perfectly well, as you use your computer more you will develop preferences about the way things should look and operate. Fortunately, Windows gives you plenty of flexibility to alter both the Taskbar and the Start menu.

● Taskbar options

The simplest change you might want to make is to the way the Taskbar is displayed. The default is that the Taskbar always appears on top of other items and so is always visible. Other default settings include large icons in the Start menu and the time displayed at the end of the Taskbar.

All these settings can be altered. For example, the Always on top setting means that some screen space is always taken up and not available for other programs to use. If you have a small screen or simply do not want to see the Taskbar all the time, you can easily hide it so that it appears only when you need it. The step-by-step exercise opposite (Changing the Taskbar options) shows how to change this and other Taskbar settings.

● Start menu options

Just as you can set up the Taskbar to suit your needs, so you can customize the Start menu to suit the particular way you work and make it easier to run the programs you use. The most common use for this is to make it quicker to start programs you use a great deal. If, for example, you frequently use Microsoft Paint, it can become rather tedious to have to click on Start, then Programs, then Accessories every time you want to start the program. The solution is to move Paint – or, of course, any other software you use a lot – up a few levels within the Start menu to make it quicker for you to reach. You could, for example, decide to move Paint from Accessories to Programs, saving one step, or move it right on to the Start menu itself, where it will be immediately accessible.

● Keep your options open

None of these changes needs to be permanent. You can easily change the Taskbar settings back to the default again or move programs around the Start menu if your needs change again in the future.

PC TIPS

You can move the Taskbar from the bottom of the screen to any of the other edges very easily. Click the left mouse button anywhere on the empty space on the Taskbar, hold it down and move the mouse up, left or right. You will see the Taskbar switch position. Release the button when it is in the right position.

Changing the Taskbar options

The four basic Taskbar settings can all be altered in moments, making it easy to experiment and find out what suits you best.

1 Click on the Start button and move your cursor up to Settings. Then choose Taskbar & Start Menu from the sub-menu that appears.

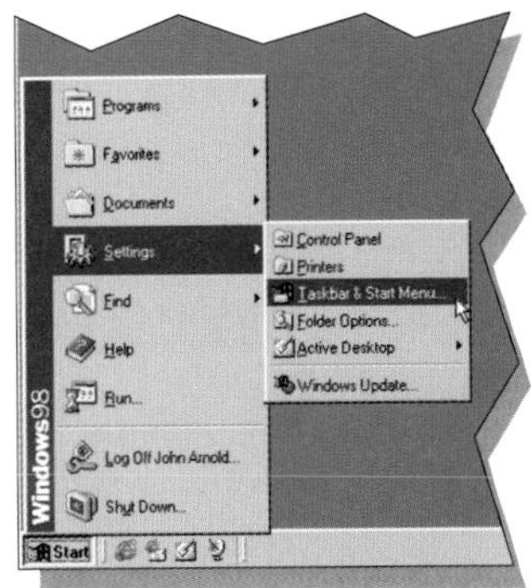

2 The Taskbar Properties window appears. On the first tab, Taskbar Options, there's a preview picture that represents your Taskbar, together with a number of check boxes. When you select or deselect these check boxes, the preview picture displaying the Taskbar will change to show what effect your changes will have. The other tab, Start Menu Programs, allows you to specify which of the programs stored on your computer appear in your computer's Start menu lists (see page 16).

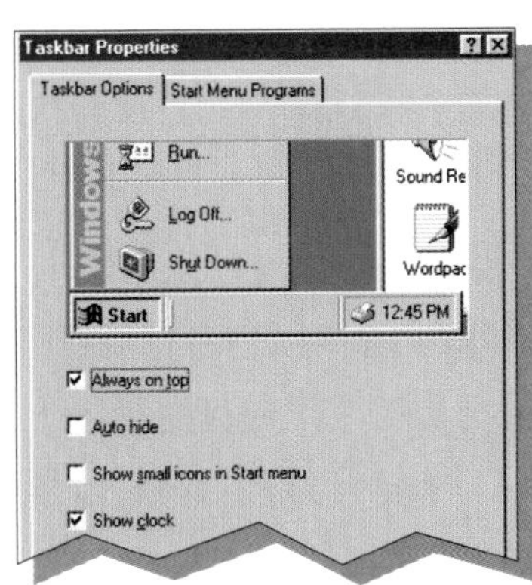

3 The first check box on the Taskbar Options tab is Always on top. This ensures that the Taskbar is always visible on the screen. If you turn this option off (click on the tick to make it disappear), the Taskbar drops behind the window in the picture. Now, when you load a program – Word, for example – and maximize the window to fit the screen, you'll see that the Taskbar is not visible. It's still there, but underneath the Word screen. You will see it if you minimize or quit from Word.

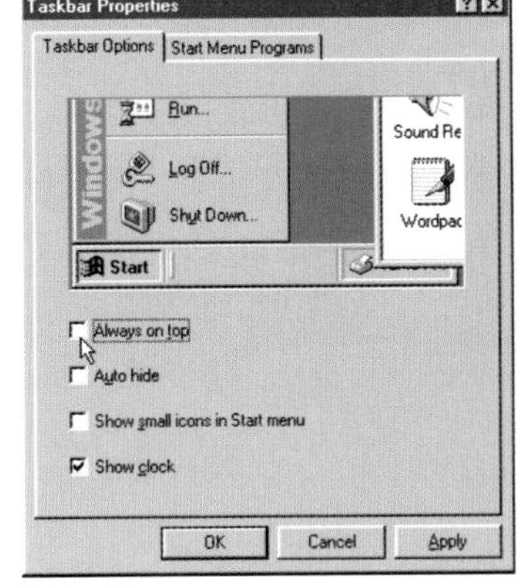

4 Go back to the Taskbar Properties window and reselect Always on top. The second box is labelled Auto hide. If you select this, the Taskbar seems to disappear (as shown in the preview picture above the check boxes) and is replaced by a dotted outline. In fact, the Taskbar is merely hidden. Press the OK button to close the dialog box. Now move your mouse to the bottom of the screen: the Taskbar pops up as you approach the edge of the screen. This is a good compromise, giving you the best of both worlds when you want more screen space and quick access to the Taskbar.

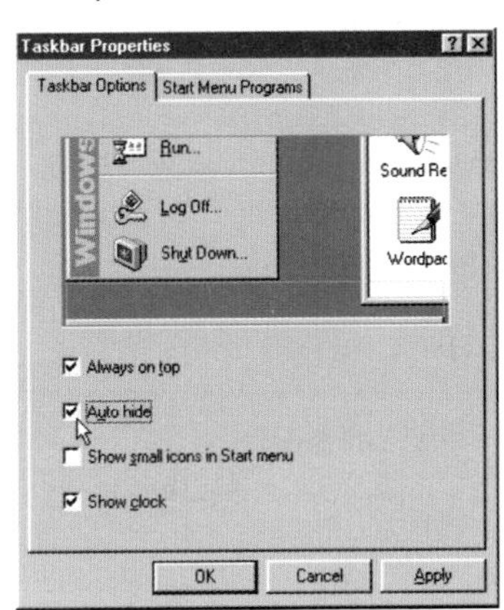

5 The third check box, labelled Show small icons in Start menu, allows you to change the normal-size icons used in the Start menu to smaller ones. Select it and you'll see the difference immediately displayed in the preview picture. As you add more programs to your Start menu (this is almost certainly a change you will want to make), these smaller icons will allow you to see more programs in a smaller amount of space.

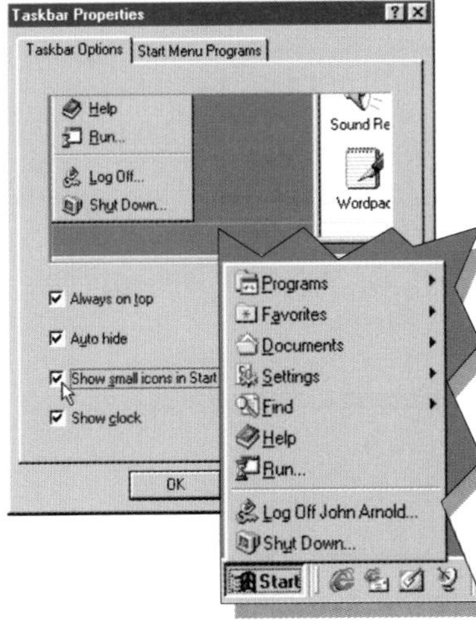

6 Show clock is the final check box. Its function is also pretty straightforward. You will probably have spotted the little digital clock display on the far right-hand side of the Taskbar and you can use this check box to turn it on or off. Don't worry if your time display also has small icons next to it, for a printer or volume control, for example, as these will remain in place.

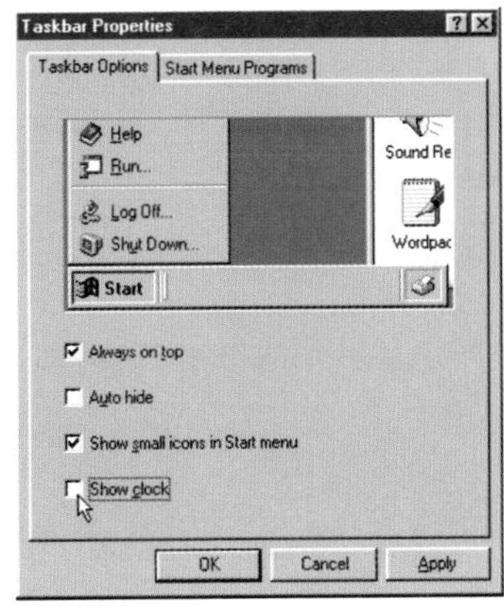

PC TIPS

Making a date

The Taskbar clock has a number of functions apart from telling the time. One of the most handy is its ability to show the date. Move the mouse pointer over the time display. If you keep the mouse pointer still for a few seconds, the date will appear in a little yellow box.

Moving programs around the Start menu

Whether or not you alter your Taskbar, you can change the way the Start menu works and which sub-menu contains what item. Here, we make Paint easier to reach by moving it from the Accessories menu to Programs.

1 Go back to the Taskbar Properties dialog box. Click on the Start Menu Programs tab. This contains four buttons that let you change the items contained in the Start menu.

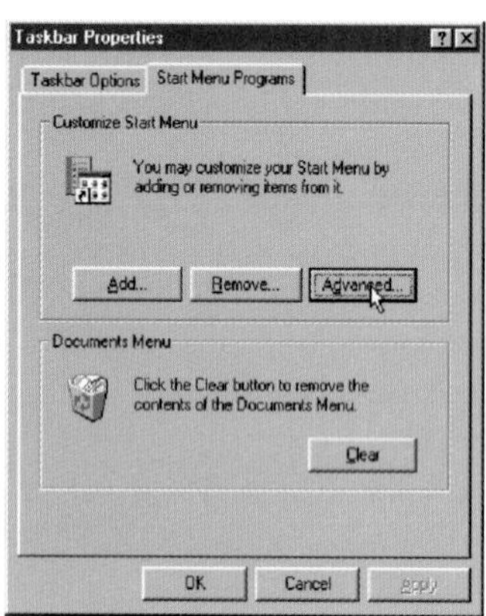

2 We're going to use the Advanced button. Don't worry, it's not difficult and it's much better for making quick changes, such as moving a program from one position in the menu to another. Click the Advanced button and Windows Explorer appears, showing the contents of the Start menu. You can see the Start Menu folder on the left and the Programs folder it contains on the right. Double-click on the Programs folder and it changes to show its contents (inset).

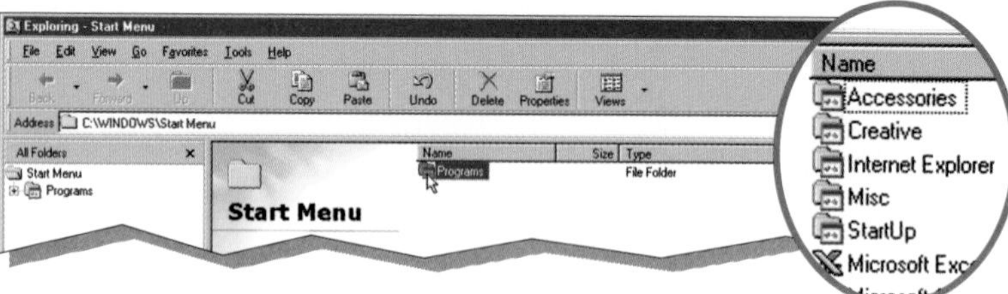

3 To move Paint from Accessories, we must look in that folder to locate the Paint program icon. Double-click on the Accessories folder in the list of items in the right-hand pane of the window. The list changes to show its contents. You should now see the Paint icon (don't worry if the other icons are slightly different to those shown here).

4 Click once to select the Paint icon, then choose Cut from the Edit menu. The Paint icon changes, becoming greyed (inset). This indicates that when you paste it to another location, it will disappear from this location (if you had selected Copy from the Edit menu, it would stay in this location when you pasted it elsewhere).

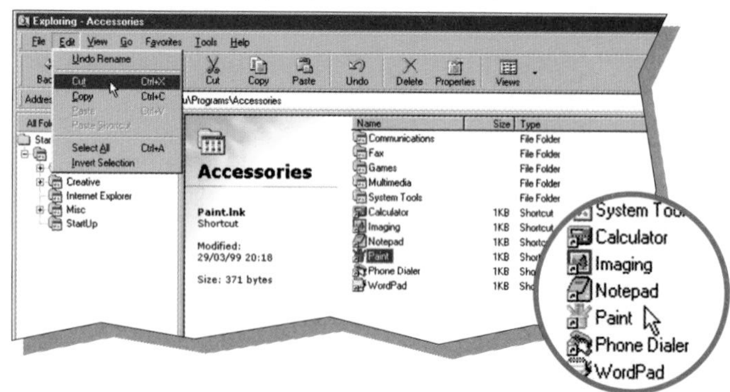

5 Double-click on the Programs folder on the left of the window to make it the current folder (notice how the folder opens).

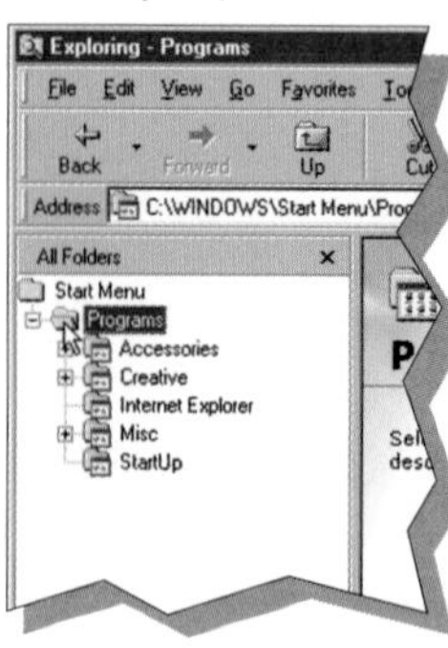

6 Now click on the Edit menu and select the Paste option. You will see the Paint icon appear in the list of items inside the Programs folder (inset).

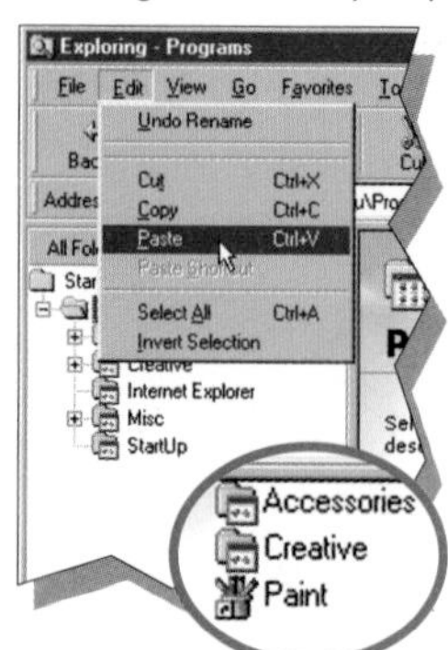

7 Close the Explorer window by clicking on the X in the top right-hand corner. Press OK on the Taskbar Properties window to close that window too.

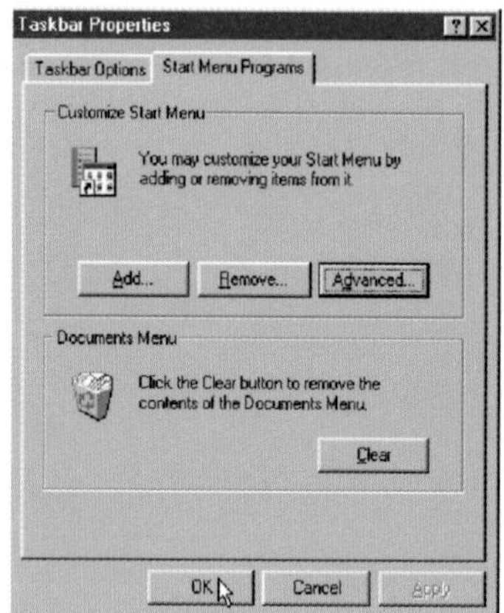

8 To check that everything has worked, press the Start button and click on the Programs sub-menu. You will now see that the Paint program appears here. You no longer need to click through several levels of menu to get to the Accessories folder to start the program. We've shown how to move a simple Windows program, but you can do this with any program.

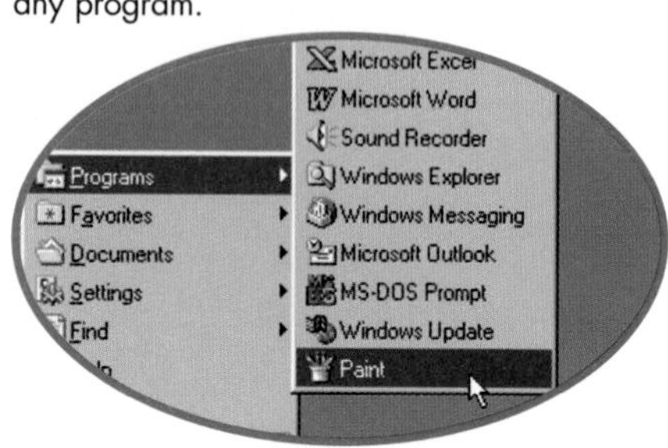

Faster access to your favourites

You can get even faster access to your favourite programs by moving them to the top level of the Start menu. Also, you can make them quicker to launch by renaming them.

1 Click on the Start button and then click on the Programs folder. Use the mouse to drag the Paint entry to the Start menu, moving the mouse pointer to just above the Programs text. When it is located in the right position, release the button.

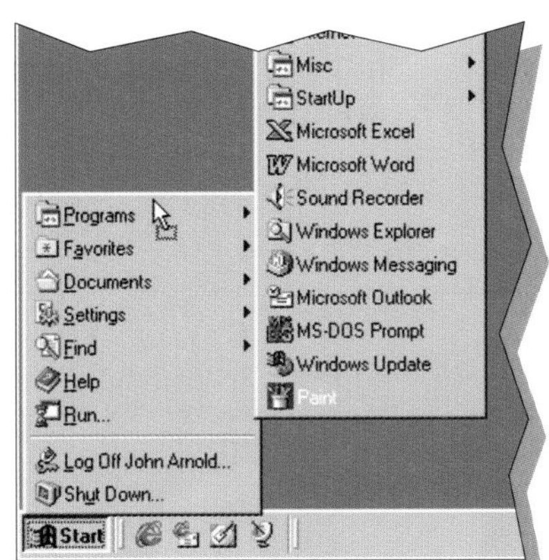

2 The Paint entry has moved to the new position. This fast way of rearranging your Start menu items was introduced with Windows 98. If you're using Windows 95, you can use the Cut and Paste method shown on the opposite page.

SHORTCUTS

Most common functions in Windows, and in the programs themselves, have keyboard shortcuts. These are very popular with advanced Windows users because it can be quicker to press a combination of keys rather than move the mouse to select options from the menus.

One of the more useful shortcuts is for the Start menu button, which is particularly handy if you don't have a keyboard with a Windows button. Just press [Ctrl] + [Esc] together and the Start menu pops up immediately. What's more, it will appear even if the Taskbar itself is hidden from view.

3 Drag other entries for each of your favourite programs. As you do, the Start menu gets larger.

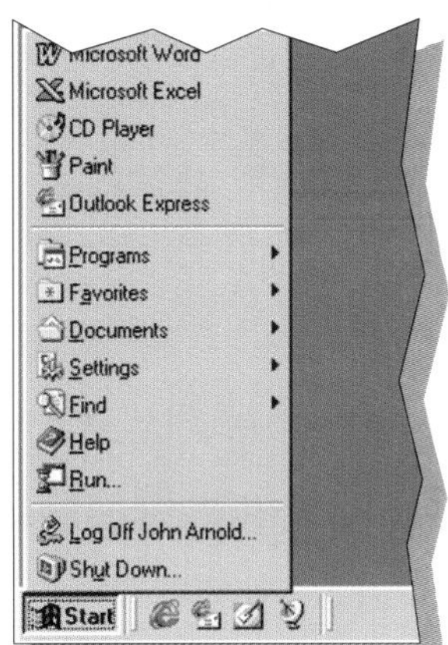

4 Follow steps 1 and 2 from the exercise on the opposite page to explore the Start menu. You can see your programs listed, one under the other. Select the topmost one and then select Rename from the File menu. Add a 1 and a space prefix to the name (inset).

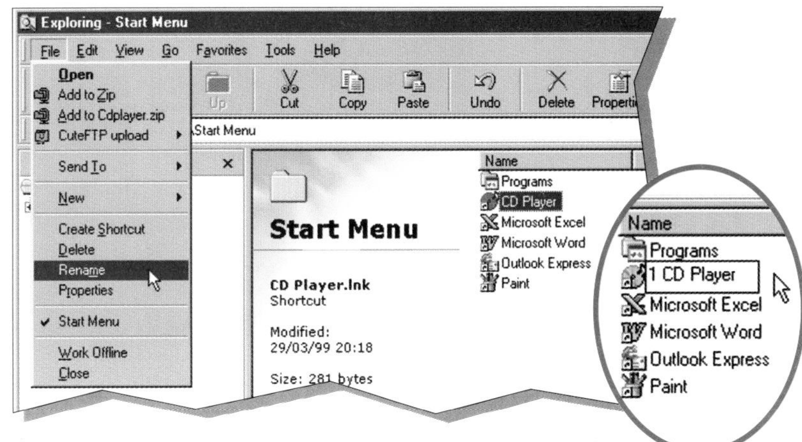

5 Do the same for the other programs you have moved, increasing the number in the prefix as you go.

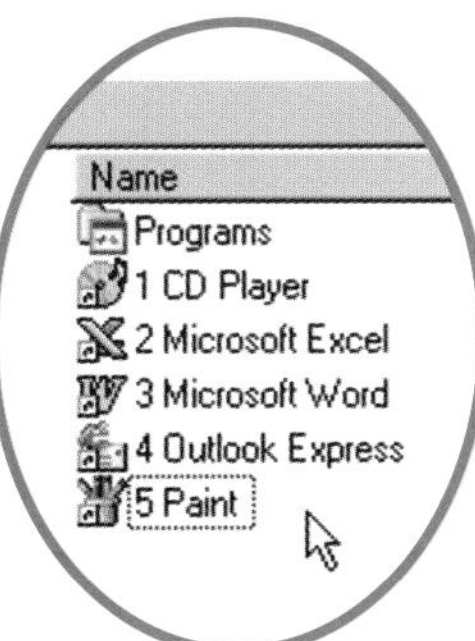

6 Now your Start menu should look something like this, making your favourite programs easier to find. However, you can now also start these programs with a keyboard shortcut (see Shortcuts, left). To load any of these programs, press [Ctrl]+[Esc], then the appropriate number – 1, 2, 3 and so on. The program will load immediately – without any mousing at all!

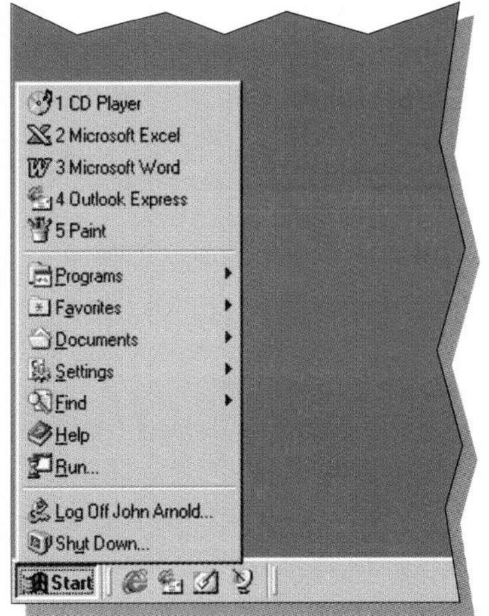

Arranging your Desktop icons

It might seem trivial to worry about the state of your computer Desktop, but the way you manage this important part of your PC can significantly affect the way you work.

It's easy to place what you want where you want it on the Desktop. We show you how over the next four pages.

In the office, an organized desk makes for a more efficient working environment. It's just the same on your computer, where a streamlined Desktop can make all the difference. As its name suggests, the Windows Desktop is the computerized equivalent of an office work desk. In itself it does nothing – it's merely a place where you can store all your useful equipment, work or even games.

● Close at hand

When you first install Windows, the only visible Desktop icons are My Computer, My Documents, Recycle Bin, Internet Explorer and Network Neighbourhood. However, like most home computer users, you've probably found that only the first four of these are useful. What we'd all really like is a Desktop where the programs we need frequently are close at hand. With a well-organized desk you don't have to hunt through a successive sequence of drawers, folders and envelopes just to find the stapler or calculator you need. In exactly the same way, a properly organized Windows Desktop will decrease the need for you to search through several layers of disk drives, menus, folders and files just to get to a program or file you need to use – especially when you need to use it quite often.

The key to making your Desktop work smarter and faster is to use shortcuts, and you can add a shortcut icon to your Desktop for

WASTE MANAGEMENT

There's no reason why you must stick to the way Windows arranges the icons on your Desktop. If you want to move them, simply drag and drop them into a new position. For example, why not drag the Recycle Bin away from the other icons to make its special purpose – deleting files – clearer. If you place it at the bottom right-hand corner of your screen, you are much less likely to drag and drop items into it by accident.

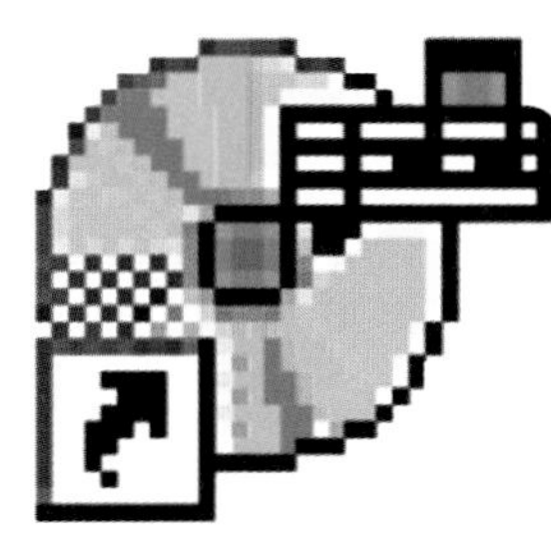

any program. By adding a strip of program shortcuts to your Desktop you'll have simple and quick point-and-click access to them. Instead of browsing through folders via the Start menu, you need only double-click on the program's Desktop shortcut to run it.

PC TIPS

When you create a shortcut, it is often called 'Shortcut to...', followed by whatever the shortcut is for. To shorten this label, use the Rename command. First use the right mouse button to click on the shortcut and choose Rename from the options that appear. You can now delete the words 'Shortcut to', or even rename the shortcut entirely.

● The choice is yours

You needn't restrict yourself to making shortcuts for programs only; you can also add shortcut icons for documents that you use frequently, such as a list of phone numbers, the novel you are working on or a simple to-do list you've created in Notepad.

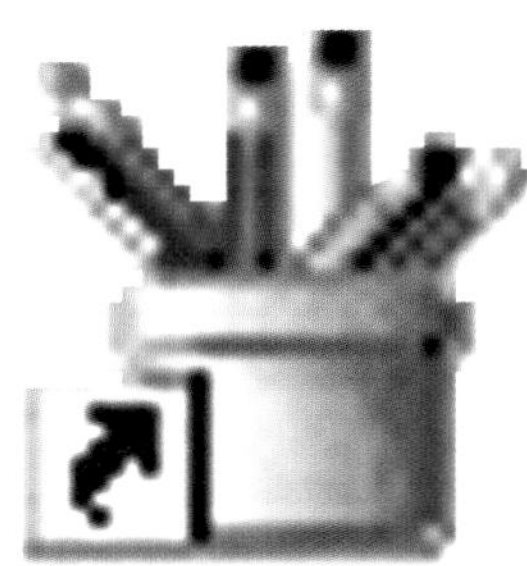

You can add as many document shortcuts as you have space for. If you don't want to clutter up your Desktop with a lot of document icons, you can create a folder for them (see Stage 1, pages 20–21). When you double-click on a document shortcut, Windows automatically starts up the program that created it with the document loaded, ready and waiting for you to work on.

● Advanced options

Once you have created Desktop shortcuts, you'll find that some new, powerful techniques will become available to you. For example, if you have created a shortcut for Microsoft Word, you can drag a text document onto it to start Word with the file ready for you to go to work on it. Things get even better if you add a shortcut for your printer to the Desktop. When you drag and drop a

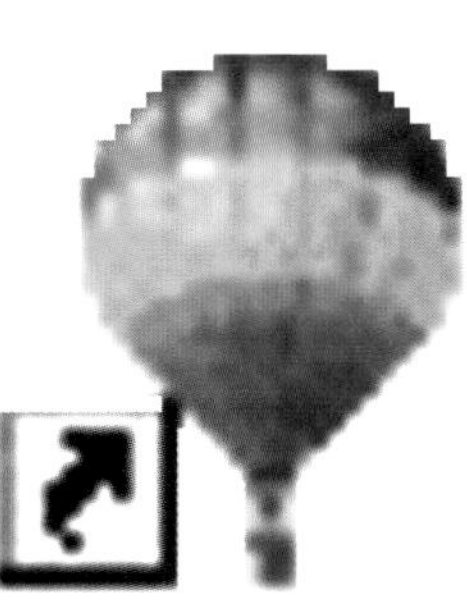

document onto the printer shortcut, Windows will immediately print it out. This means you don't have to start the program, open the document or use the File menu to print it. This is extremely handy if you want to print something quickly, or if you want to print out a number of documents at the same time.

To do so, you simply select a group of files with your mouse and drag them onto the printer shortcut as one. To select a group of files, hold down the [Shift] key and click on each file you want.

● Adding shortcuts

In the exercises that follow on the next two pages, we'll add shortcuts for programs, documents and folders to our Desktop. You will find out how to line up your Desktop items neatly and we'll also show how to add shortcuts for your computer's disk drives and printer.

Choose the ones that suit you best and you'll be amazed just how much easier your Desktop – and therefore your entire computer – will be to use.

CHECKPOINT

TOP FIVE TIPS TO IMPROVE YOUR DESKTOP

- Create Desktop shortcuts for those programs you use frequently – it'll save a lot of time compared to searching through long menus.
- Don't be afraid to add shortcuts for all sorts of items – experiment to see how much time you can save. If you find you don't need any shortcuts, you can just remove them by dragging them to Windows' Recycle Bin.
- Keep your new icons on the Desktop tidy – icons that are arranged at random don't just look untidy, they get in the way and can cause confusion. Try dragging them into groups of items that go together: programs, disk drives and documents, for example.
- If you share your computer with other members of the family, create a folder on the Desktop for each person – Mum's Favourites, Dad's Favourites, and so on – to avoid excessive clutter.
- Remember you can drag documents to a Word or printer icon to activate them almost instantly.

Creating a shortcut for Word

If you have a lot of software installed on your computer, your Start menu folders can become pretty congested. Here we make a shortcut for Word on the Desktop.

AS YOU LOAD more and more software onto your computer, the Start menu's Programs folder can become so large that it takes up two columns on screen. This can make finding the program you want to start quite difficult, particularly if you're in a hurry.

A simple way around this problem is to create some program shortcuts on the Desktop. They will appear as icons that you can double-click on to start up the relevant program. For this step-by-step exercise, we'll create a shortcut for Word by copying it from the Start menu.

1 Click on the Start button and then click on the Programs folder to reveal the list of software installed on your computer.

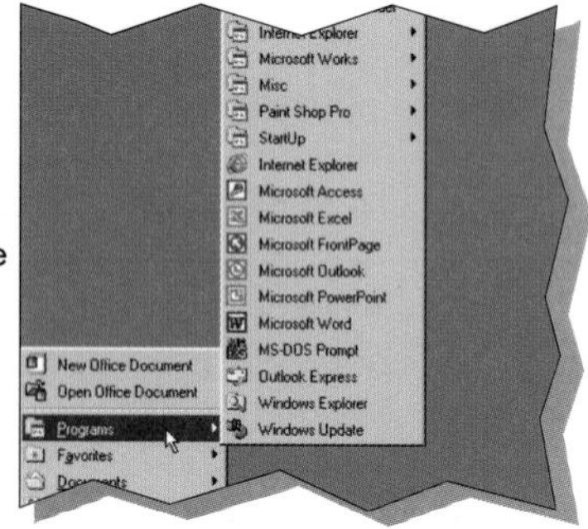

2 Locate the program you want to make a Desktop shortcut for – in this case we'll choose Microsoft Word. Using the right mouse button, click and drag the program entry onto a blank part of the Desktop.

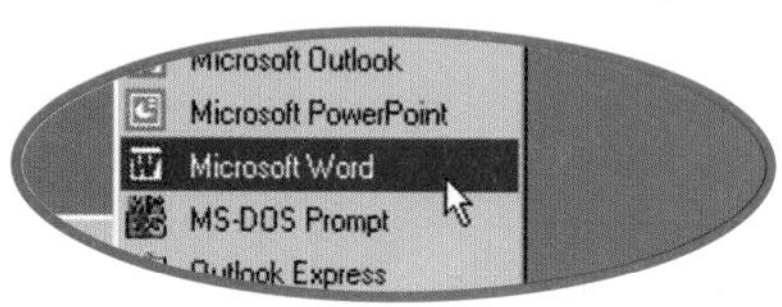

3 Release the mouse button. In the pop-up menu that appears, select the Create Shortcut(s) Here option.

4 A shortcut for Microsoft Word appears. You can move this icon around the Desktop, just like any other Desktop icon, or drag it into your Favourites folder (see opposite page).

5 Look back at the Start menu's Programs folder and you can see that the original Microsoft Word item is still in place. If you drag a program entry using the left mouse button instead of the right, Windows creates a shortcut but removes the original entry (this is useful if you want to make the menu shorter). Here we've dragged the Microsoft PowerPoint entry with the left mouse button and the program entry has been removed.

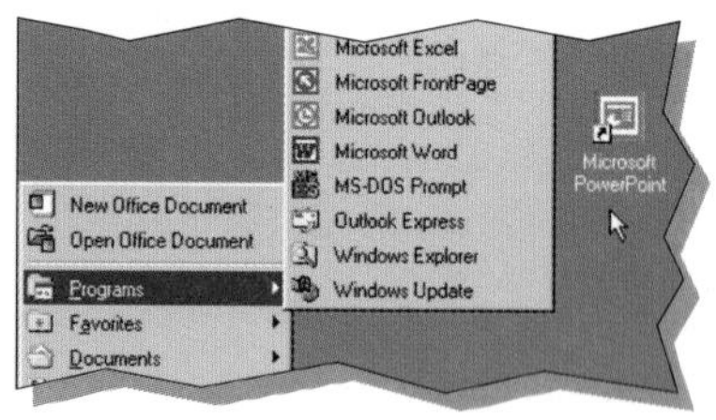

6 There's no limit to the number of shortcuts you can make for a program. If necessary, you can add a shortcut for Word – or any other program – to several folders. If you find that you're constantly working with a small number of folders, adding a shortcut for Word to each one might save you time.

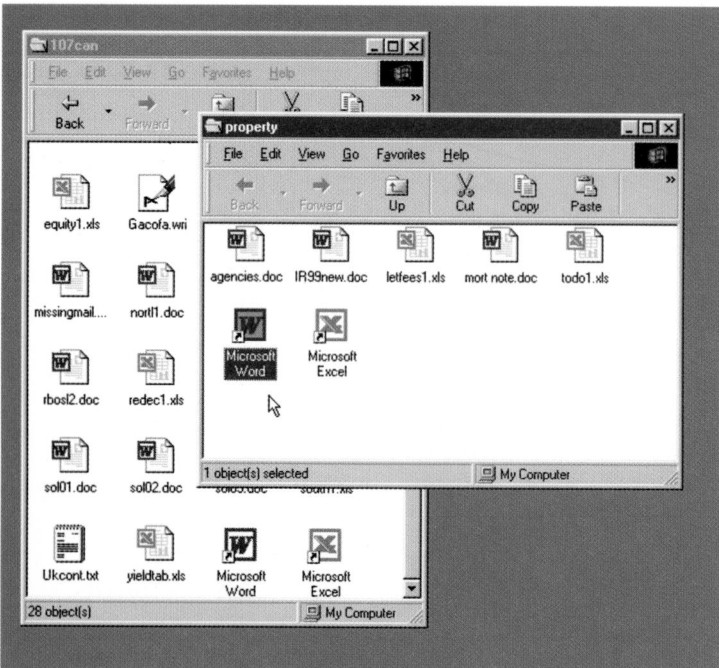

7 Once you have created your preferred arrangement of icons, you can get rid of any shortcuts that are not needed. Just drag them to the Recycle Bin.

PC TIPS

Organize your icons

After you've added a handful of shortcut icons to your Desktop, you might find that your Desktop starts to look a little disorganized. Instead of trying to line up the icons by eye, get Windows to do the work for you. Right-click on a blank area of the Desktop and select Line Up Icons from the pop-up menu.

In a second or so Windows moves any icons that are out of place and rearranges them into neat rows and columns.

Adding extra shortcuts

You can also add shortcuts for your frequently used documents and your printer. This is a really good way of speeding up the opening and printing of documents.

1 Let's imagine that we have a to-do list that we keep as a simple Notepad file stored in the My Documents folder. We use it several times a day and it's too time-consuming to keep wading through various folders several times a day when we want to open it.

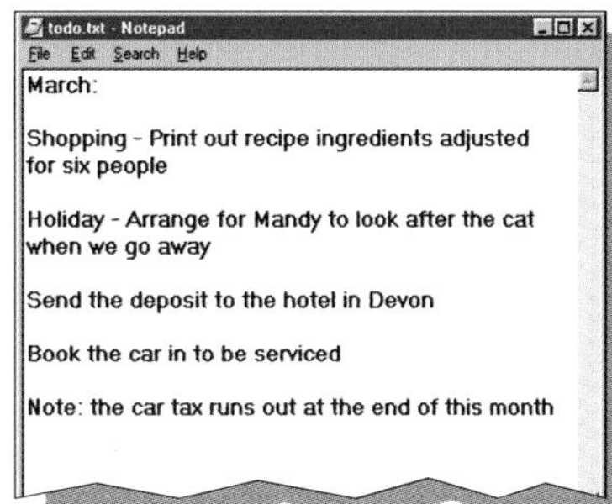

2 To add a shortcut to your Desktop for this document, double-click on the My Documents folder.

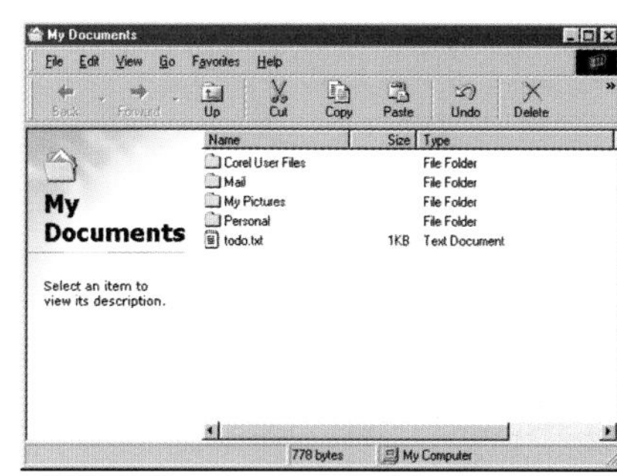

PC TIPS

Remember that you can also add shortcuts for your computer's disk drives. All you need to do is open the My Computer window, drag each disk drive icon (using the left mouse button) on to the Desktop and make sure you click the Yes button when Windows asks if you want to create a shortcut.

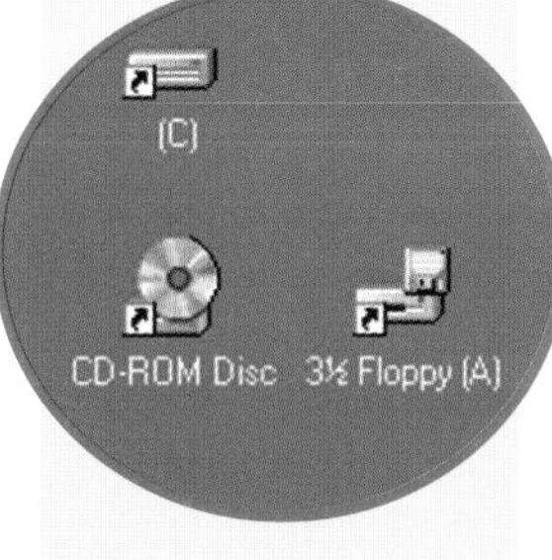

3 Use the right mouse button to drag and drop the 'todo.txt' file from the list in the panel on the right onto the Desktop. You will see an outline of the document appear as you drag it. Release it when it's roughly in position.

4 Windows asks you what you want to do. Select the Create Shortcut(s) Here option (we don't want to move the file, nor do we want to make an extra copy of the file). A new icon for the document will appear on the Desktop.

5 If you don't want lots of document icons cluttering up your Desktop, you can create a folder for your various shortcuts. Click on the Desktop with the right mouse button, select New from the pop-up menu that appears and then click on Folder from the list of options.

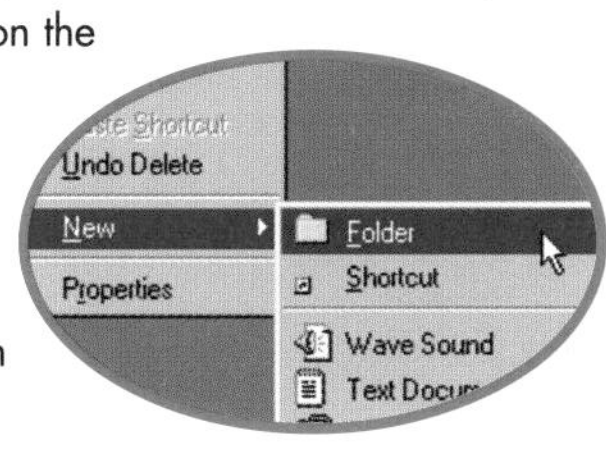

6 A New Folder icon appears on the Desktop. You can give it a new name by typing one in immediately while the title is highlighted. We've called our folder Favourites. There's no arrow at the bottom of the icon because this is a new folder, not a shortcut to another folder.

7 This folder works just like any other folder; the only difference is that it's available straight from the Desktop. You can store files and document shortcuts in it. Drag the 'todo.txt' file from its position on the Desktop into the Favourites folder.

8 Add as many shortcut icons as you like – even program and disk drive shortcuts – to your Favourites folder. That way, all the Windows items you use most often are located in one place.

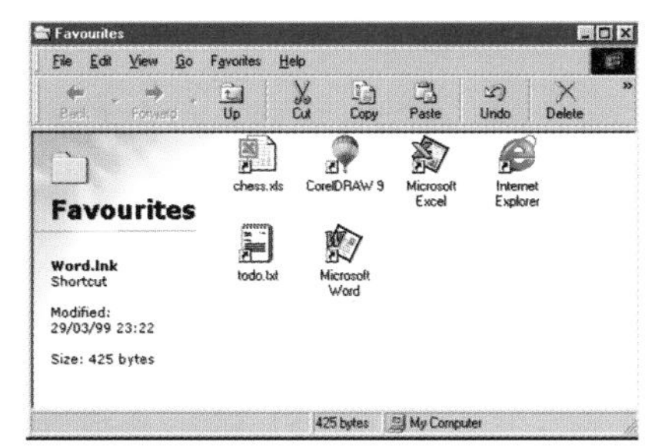

ADDING A PRINTER ICON TO THE DESKTOP

To add a shortcut for your printer to the Desktop, click on the Start button, select the Settings folder and then select the Printers option.

A window will open that already includes an icon for your printer. Click on the printer icon and drag it onto the Desktop using the left mouse button. You'll see a shortcut icon appear.

Once the printer shortcut is on the Desktop, you need only drag a file or group of files onto the icon to print them out. Windows will do all the work for you.

Using the Recycle Bin

To avoid wasting disk space, you should delete files you don't need anymore. The Recycle Bin recycles disk space and gives you a safety net if you make a mistake.

Knowing when and how to delete files and folders is an important aspect of managing your hard disk. It is also extremely useful to understand what happens when you delete a file, just in case you remove something important by mistake.

You might be wondering why you should delete files at all, if there's a risk of losing important information. The answer is that by deleting files you can prevent your carefully organized structure of folders from becoming clogged up with redundant files. Old files make it hard to find the ones you still use and they occupy valuable hard disk space that you could keep free for new files.

● How to delete files

It's very easy to delete files. All you have to do is find the file you want to remove, select it and then press the [Delete] key. Windows will ask you if you're sure you want to delete the file. Click on the Yes button if you do, or the No button if you've changed your mind or clicked on the wrong file by mistake. The same technique works for deleting other Windows objects, such as folders and Desktop shortcuts. You can also delete items by dragging them to the Desktop's Recycle Bin; it's just like moving files between folders (see Stage 1, pages 20–21).

● The safety net

You might have noticed that Windows doesn't actually ask you to confirm that you want to delete a file. It asks you to confirm that you want to send the file to the Recycle Bin.

The Recycle Bin is a special folder where Windows keeps all the files you delete. So when you delete a file, you're not really deleting it at all, just tidying it out of the way and into another folder. Windows does this as a precaution, so that you can get an important file back if you delete

it by mistake. Just as with a real wastebasket, you can reach in and retrieve something if you threw it away without thinking.

In time, your Recycle Bin will become full, and you will have to make a choice: you can increase the amount of hard disk space reserved for it or you can empty it. When you empty it, the files really will be gone for good. If you don't want to wait until the Recycle Bin is full before emptying it – for example, you might wish to ensure that private information has been permanently removed – here's an easy way how: just follow the steps below.

Working with the Recycle Bin

Sometimes you might accidentally delete the wrong document, while at other times you may need to make sure sensitive documents are destroyed immediately. Here's a step-by-step guide to using the Recycle Bin properly.

1 When you delete a file in Windows, it goes into a special folder called the Recycle Bin. You'll see its icon (right) on your Desktop. When the bin appears empty, it indicates that there are no deleted files in the Recycle Bin.

2 Let's create a dummy file in Word. We'll use this to illustrate how the Recycle Bin works. Open Word, type some text and save it as 'bintest.doc' in the My Documents folder. When you have done this, close Word.

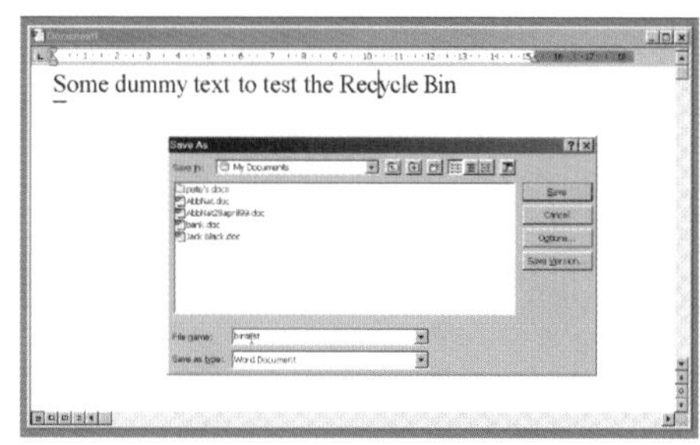

3 Open the My Documents folder and move the window so that you can also see the Recycle Bin (as shown right). Find the 'bintest.doc' file, drag it across to the Recycle Bin and drop it into the bin when the bin icon is highlighted.

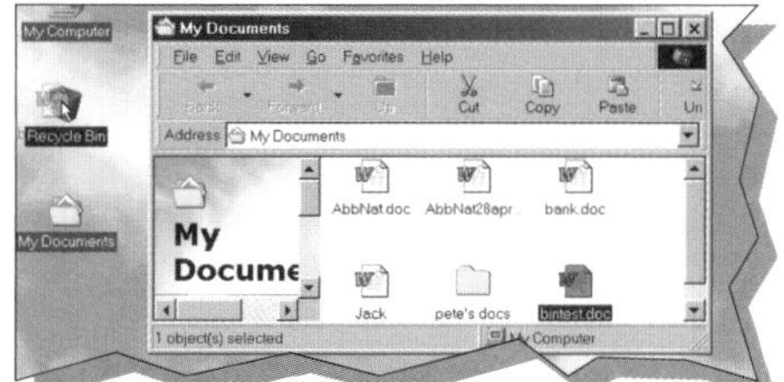

4 Windows always checks that you really want to delete the file. When it asks you to confirm your action, click on the Yes button.

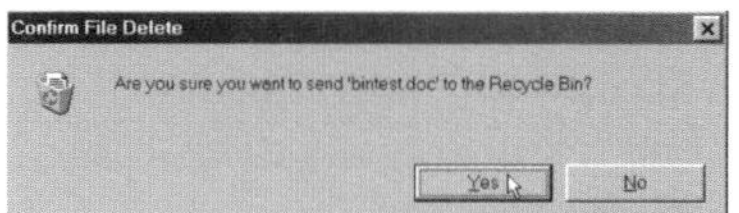

5 Notice how the Recycle Bin icon alters to show that there's now rubbish in it: the icon appears to be stuffed full of wastepaper. This serves as a reminder that you have some unwanted files in the Recycle Bin.

6 Because the Recycle Bin is really just a special type of folder, we can open it to see what files it contains. Double click on the icon and you'll see that it contains the 'bintest.doc' file you've just deleted.

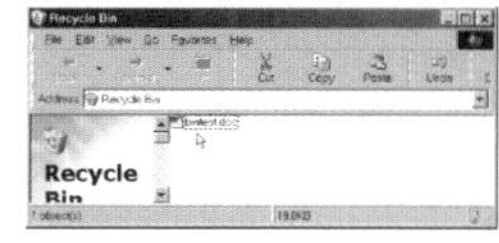

7 If you deleted this file by accident, you can get it back by clicking on the file and then clicking on Restore in the panel on the left (inset).

8 Look in the My Documents folder and you'll see that the file is back again. If you double-click on it, Word will open with the file ready for you to work on it. Now let's imagine that this file contains sensitive information – perhaps a letter to your bank manager – so you want to ensure that it is deleted permanently. First, delete the file as you did in step 3.

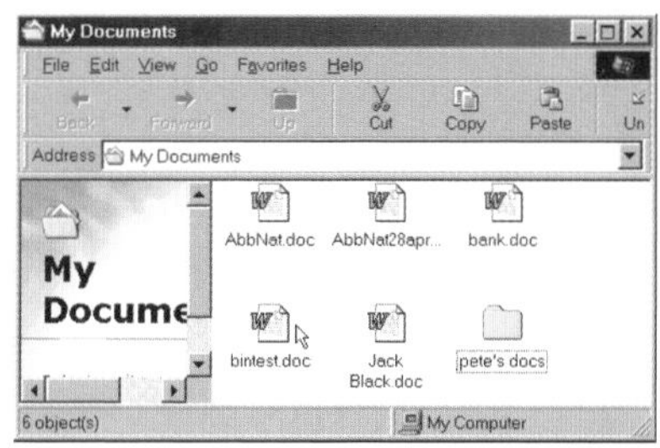

9 To remove the file permanently, double-click on the Recycle Bin, highlight the file and pick Delete from the File menu. To delete all files in the Recycle Bin, select Empty Recycle Bin from the left-hand panel.

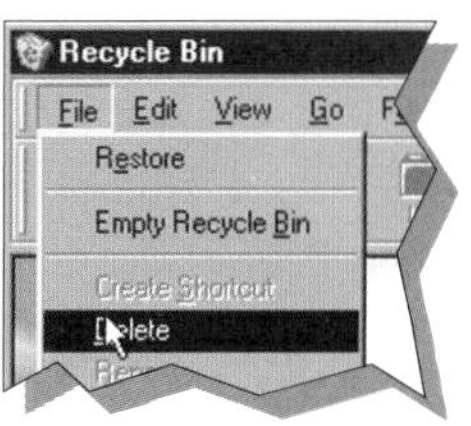

HOW BIG IS YOUR BIN?

Windows will automatically set aside part of your hard disk for the Recycle Bin. This is usually about 10 per cent of the size of your hard disk. For example, if you have a 6.4GB hard disk, you can use around 640MB for deleted files before you need to empty the Recycle Bin. This should be enough for most home users.

Backing up important documents

If your computer were to fail, it's possible that you could lose vital information from your hard disk. But if you regularly back up important files, this needn't be such a disaster.

Things can, and do, go wrong with computers – and when crashes occur, hard disks can lose data. If this happens, it can prove impossible to retrieve some files and past work can be lost.

Not only do you have to guard against computer error, but you also have to take into account possible human error. The Recycle Bin acts as a safety net to help prevent you from deleting files accidentally (see pages 22–23), but it's still possible to overwrite files accidentally. For example, if you mistakenly delete text from a Word document, then save the file, the original text is lost. Therefore, it is essential to keep copies of your important files. Keep them separately, usually on floppy disks, which can then be stored in a safe place. These copies are called back-ups.

● A good habit

Try to get into a routine of backing up important files. If you regularly change a particular document, back it up as often as possible to ensure that you have an up-to-date version. One way to do this is to copy your documents to a floppy disk using Windows' normal drag and drop method (see Stage 1, pages 14–15). However, as you are likely to accumulate a lot of documents over a period of time, it is best to use a special back-up program. Windows comes with just such a tool, called Backup. This keeps track of files and folders and backs them up automatically. It can also compress files so that they take up less space on the disks and keeps track of information about the files should you need to restore them from the floppy disk.

● What should I back up?

You will need to be selective when backing up files. They will take up a lot of room on a floppy disk and you don't want to have to use too many disks. If you can get into the habit of backing up regularly, a crash or accidental overwriting of a file becomes an annoying nuisance, rather than an irreversible disaster.

PC TIPS

You don't need to back up your programs, such as Microsoft Word, for example. You can reinstall them straight from their original disks or CD-ROMs, should the need ever arise.

Using the Backup tool

Here's how to back up information contained in the My Documents folder, from the hard disk to a floppy.

1 To access the Backup program, select Programs from the Start menu, then Accessories, followed by System Tools. Click on the Backup icon.

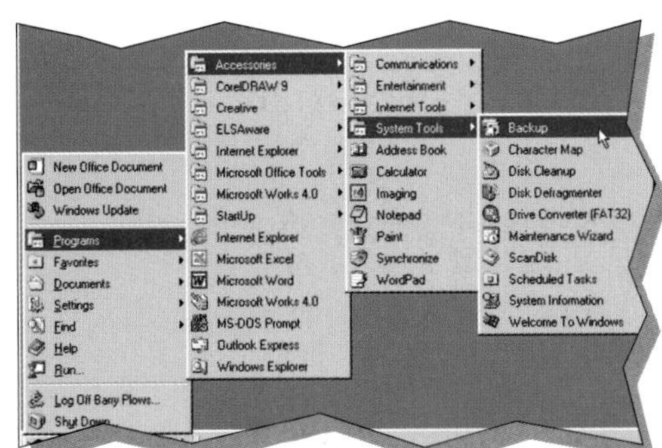

2 You'll see a succession of dialog boxes before the main Backup window appears. These cover introductory information and options for computers that have tape drives. For this exercise, just click on the OK button of each box to continue.

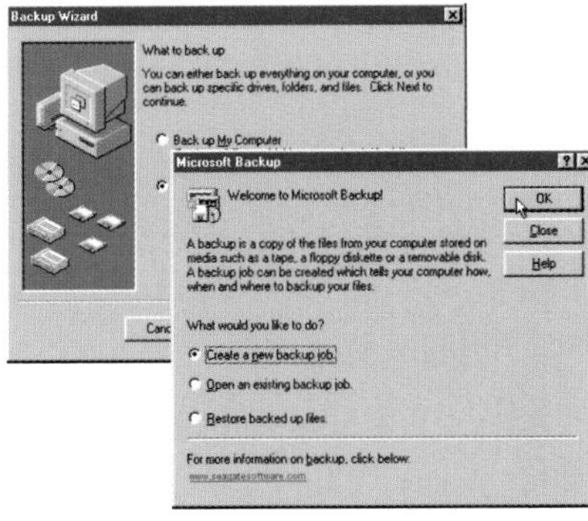

3 The Backup program has two tabs. Click on the Backup tab to be able to choose which files on what drives you want backed up.

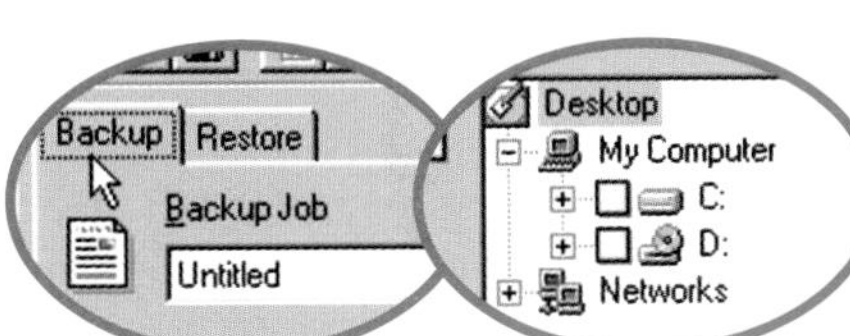

4 On the left of the dialog box is a list of items that represent the storage devices on your computer. You will almost always be backing up files from your computer's hard disk. Locate the [C:] drive and click on the small square containing a plus sign. You will see the listing of devices expand to show the contents of your hard disk.

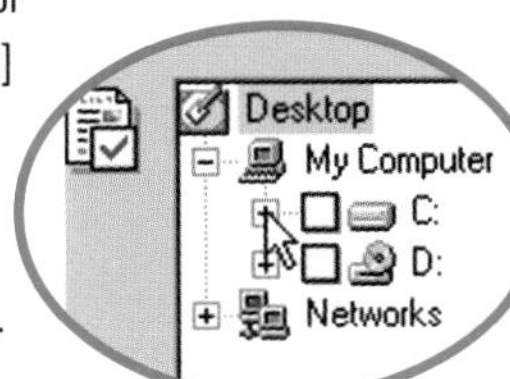

PC TIPS

If Backup isn't on your computer, you can load it from your Windows CD-ROM (this will be covered later in the course).

5 Find the My Documents folder in the list and click on the small blank square next to it. The folder is now ticked and the window on the right changes to indicate the files that are going to be backed up. Click on the ticked squares by each of the documents to remove them from the process.

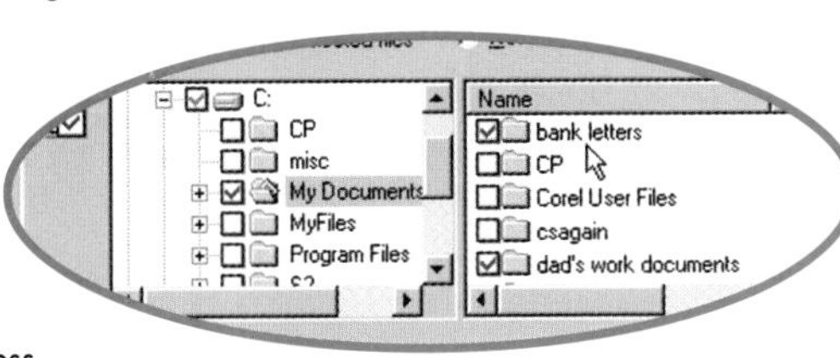

6 You also need to choose the destination for the files. Put a blank formatted floppy disk in the floppy disk drive and click on the button next to the bottom of the Backup window (below). Next, select the [A] drive in the Where to back up dialog box (right).

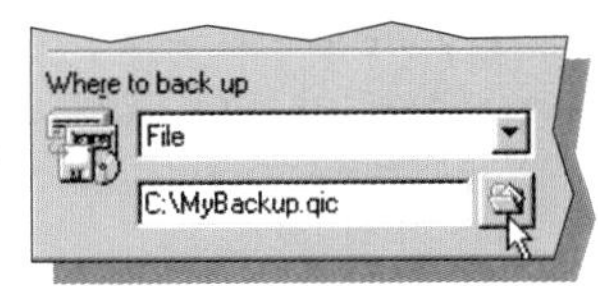

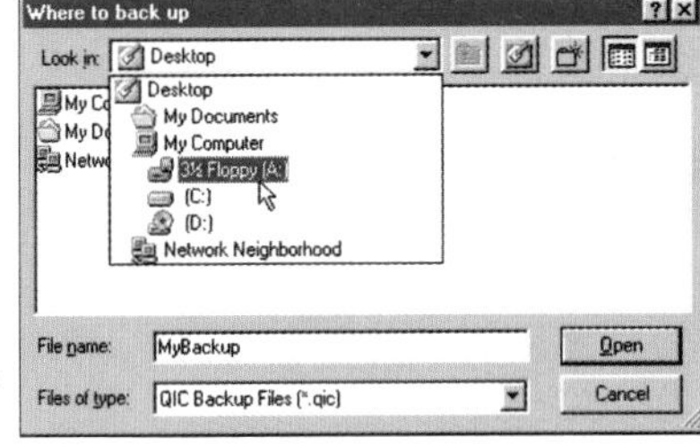

EXTENSIVE BACK-UPS

For backing up large quantities of files, it's best to buy a storage device with a bigger capacity than floppy disks. The main options are tape drives and Zip disk drives. Tape drives use special tape cassettes that store up to 2GB – equal to around 1,300 floppy disks. Zip drives work much like floppy disks, but are able to store 100MB – around 70 floppy disks.

7 Press the Start button and click Yes when asked if you want to save the job.

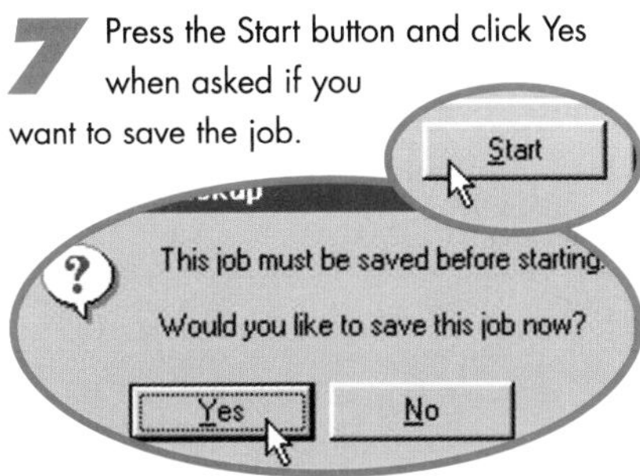

8 Once you have given your job a name, the back-up process takes only a few seconds and you can monitor progress as the files are copied. Press the OK button when the process has been completed.

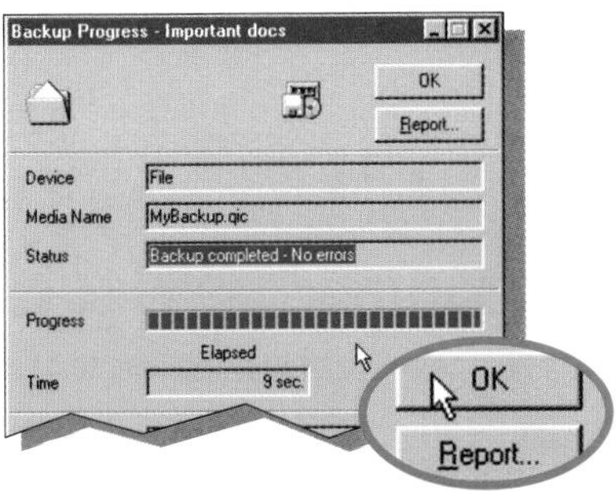

RESTORING FILES

Restoring your files after a serious crash is, hopefully, something you will never have to do. However, if you do need to retrieve data from back-up floppies, use the Restore tab of the Backup window.

Insert the back-up disk and click on the Restore tab on the main Backup window. When you select the floppy drive in the box at the top of the dialog box, you can use the panel in the centre to choose which parts of the backed-up files you want to restore. When you click the Start button, the Backup program copies the files back to the hard disk.

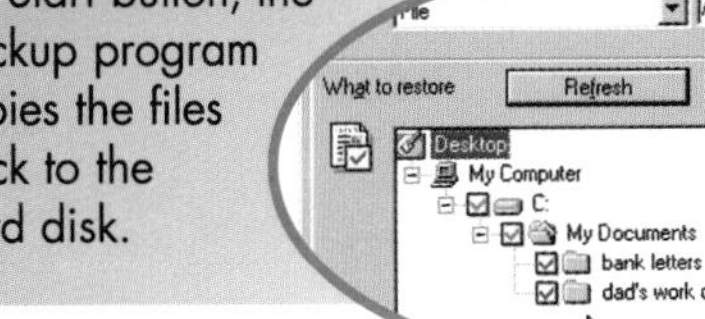

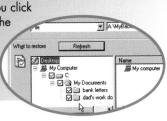

Playing music CDs

Your CD-ROM drive can play music CDs as well as run software CD-ROMs, and Windows gives you just as much control over them as your normal stereo system does.

The CD-ROM drive is actually misnamed – it isn't specific to computer CDs at all and the hardware and electronics are identical to those in most hi-fi CD players. The only real differences are the connections at the back of the drive and the buttons on the front. As a result, normal music CDs can easily be played through your computer speakers.

Your computer is able to play a music CD, but you might be wondering how to get all the standard CD player options and buttons that are available on your hi-fi onto your PC. These are actually provided by a program built into Windows called CD Player. This handy program pops up automatically when a music CD is inserted and gives you all the functions of a 'proper' CD player, and more.

Computers have more memory than hi-fi CD players and can therefore remember your favourite tracks from hundreds of CDs. You can also name each track and browse through the titles. But you don't have to take advantage of such advanced features. If you want, you can simply insert your CD and the computer will play it for you.

You can have music while you work, from a music CD in your computer. Other programs, such as Word or Excel, will run quite happily while a CD is playing.

OTHER CD PROGRAMS

Windows' built-in CD Player program isn't the only CD control program available for Windows. You might find that your PC's sound card has its own CD player, which might also have more features than the Windows version, with more complex mixing options and play lists to arrange the order of songs. For most users, though, CD Player is fine and does everything you might need.

Playing music CDs

Relax and enjoy the time you spend at your computer by playing your favourite music while you work. We show you how.

1 The quickest way of playing a music CD on your PC is simply to insert it in the CD drive and let Windows start it automatically. You will see the CD Player program appear and the music will start playing. The CD Player program will be minimized on the Taskbar.

2 The CD Player will start playing track one of the CD. To see the program's features, double-click on CD Player on the Taskbar to open the CD Player window. You'll see a number of standard CD buttons, which work in the same way as a normal hi-fi CD player. If you are not sure what they do, just keep your cursor on them for two seconds and a text bar will appear to explain them.

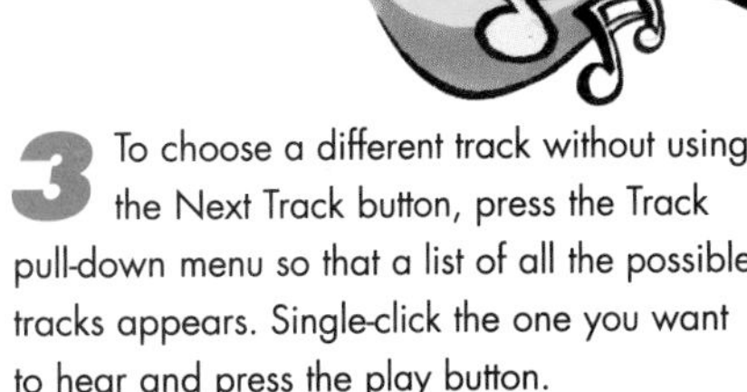

3 To choose a different track without using the Next Track button, press the Track pull-down menu so that a list of all the possible tracks appears. Single-click the one you want to hear and press the play button.

PC TIPS

Closing the CD player

When you close the CD Player, you'll notice that the music carries on playing. To stop this, pick Preferences from the Options menu and select Stop CD Playing on Exit in the dialog box.

4 The default display in the numeric window shows the amount of time, in seconds, that the current track has been playing (Track Time Elapsed). You can change this by selecting one of the two other options – Track Time Remaining or Disc Time Remaining – from the View menu.

5 As with a hi-fi CD player, you can also choose different play options for any music CD. From the Options menu, you can choose from Random Order, Continuous Play or Intro Play. The last choice plays only the first 10 seconds of each track so that you can find the one you want.

6 One of the most useful options of the CD Player program is the Play List. Windows can remember a huge number of CDs and keep a permanent record of the names of tracks and how many times, if ever, you would like to hear them. Go to the Disc menu and select the Edit Play List option.

7 A new window appears with the list of Available Tracks on the right and your Play List on the left. To remove a track from the Play List, highlight it by clicking on it and press the Remove button.

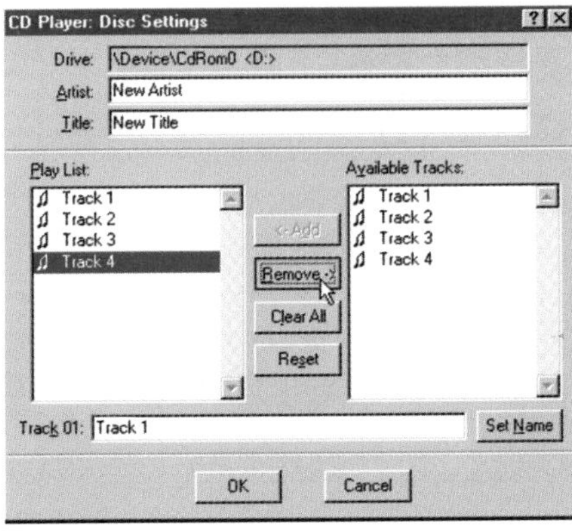

8 Do the opposite with the Add button to add a track. Using this method, you can make a track play more than once if you like. You can even completely change the order of the tracks in this way if you wish.

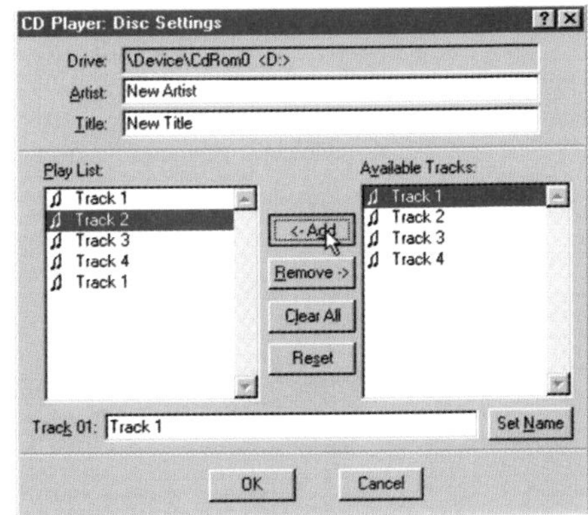

9 To set the names of tracks, just type them into the text box at the bottom and press Set Name. When you are finished with all your selections, press the OK button and all your choices will be saved.

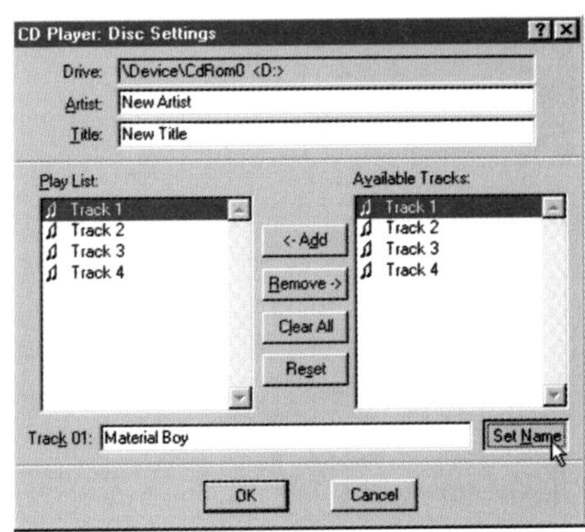

Software

Microsoft® Word

Microsoft® Excel

CorelDRAW™

Check your spelling and grammar

You won't want to spoil the effect of an attractive document by making spelling mistakes and using poor grammar. So here's how to make everything you write word perfect.

How often have you seen an excellent piece of writing spoilt by a glaring spelling error or a jarring example of poor grammar? There's no excuse for your work to suffer from problems like this because Word includes features that can detect mistakes, draw your attention to them and suggest ways to correct them. In some cases, Word will even correct things automatically while you carry on typing.

● Word's wavy lines

You might have noticed that when you're creating a document in Word, red or green wavy lines appear automatically beneath some words and phrases as you type. A red wavy line beneath text is Word's way of telling you that it thinks the word is incorrectly spelt. A green wavy line under text is Word's way of telling you that it thinks you have made a grammatical error. There are two ways to get rid of these wavy lines: you can tell Word not to display them, or you can make the corrections and they'll disappear.

There are some corrections you won't need to make yourself. For example, try deliberately misspelling the word 'the' by typing the letters in the wrong order. Watch what happens when you press the spacebar to begin the next word. The correction is made automatically by a special Word feature called AutoCorrect. Word keeps a large list of common typing mistakes like this, which extends beyond spelling mistakes to include things like missing capital letters off days of the week. You can also use AutoCorrect to make Word type repetitive phrases for you.

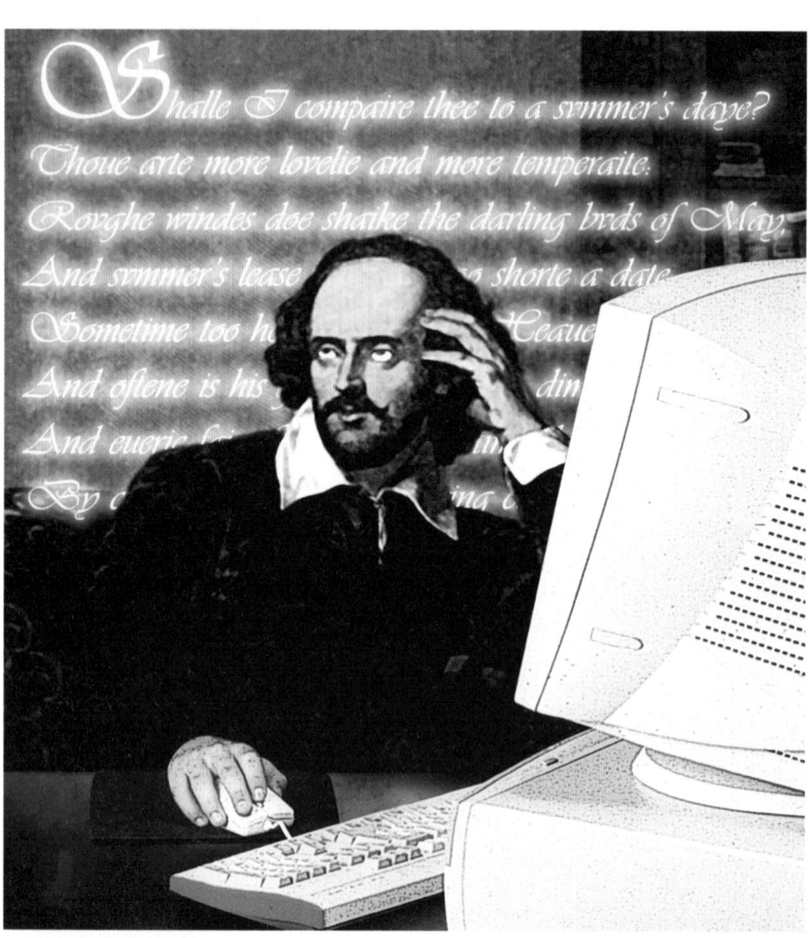

Every document you create can be a masterpiece, thanks to the power of your computer's built-in spelling and grammar tools.

● Mind your language

As part of Word's installation, the program notes the language you type in. This is so that it can install the correct dictionary, grammar and thesaurus information to check your work. To make sure your system is set to the correct language, go to Tools in the Menu bar and select Language from the drop-down menu. Then choose the Set Language option and select the language you want to use.

PC TIPS

English dialects

When checking your Word language set-up, check the country name that appears in brackets after the language. Word has nine English dialects (right). If Word makes unusual spelling suggestions, you might have it on the wrong English setting.

Correcting your spelling

Word has a huge dictionary that it uses to check your spelling as you type. You can manually check individual words or let Word go through your document word by word, drawing your attention to any mistakes it finds.

1 As you type a document, Word highlights any spelling mistakes you make by underlining them with a red wavy line. In the first paragraph of this document, for example, the words 'dokument' and 'deliburate' both need to be corrected.

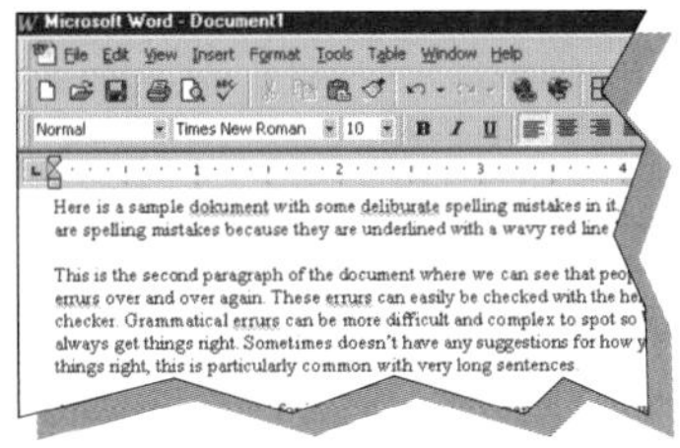

2 Let's use Word's dictionary to correct the first of these spelling mistakes. Click on the word 'dokument' with the right mouse button and a short list of options will appear. The word at the top of the list is the program's suggestion for the correct spelling. Simply click on it (in this case 'document') with the left mouse button to make the correction.

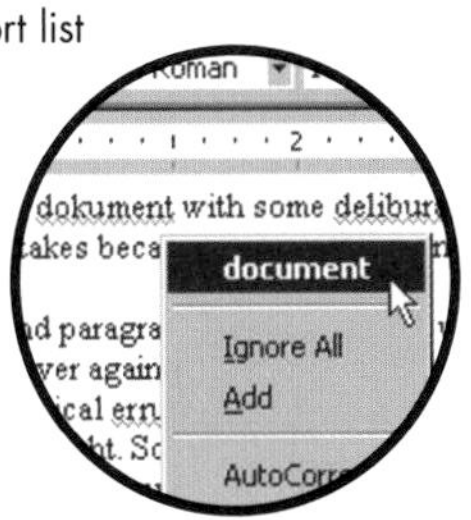

3 It would be tedious to have to correct the spelling of each individual word in a long document. Instead, we can get Word's spelling checker to work through the whole document. Position the text cursor at the start of the document and select Spelling and Grammar from the Tools menu.

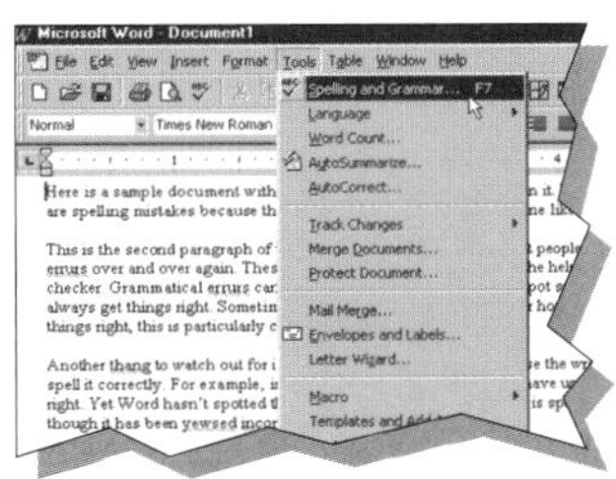

4 Notice how Word's powerful spelling checker immediately identifies the first mistake – in this example, the word 'deliburate'. The error is highlighted in red in the top box (labelled Not in Dictionary) and the program's suggested correction is shown in the bottom box. Click on the Change button to correct the spelling of the word.

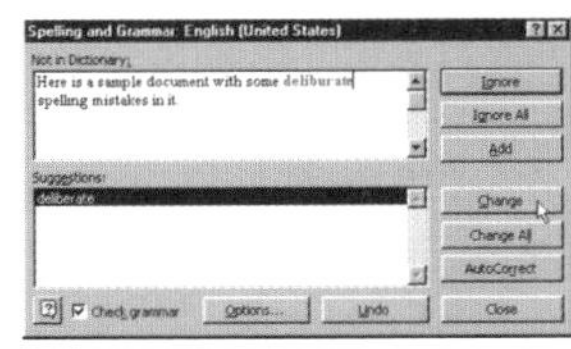

Don't forget that you can use your function keys to start the spelling checker. All you have to do is press the [F7] key. This has the same effect as taking your mouse pointer to the Tools menu and clicking on Spelling and Grammar.

5 Word's spelling checker automatically searches for the next misspelt word – this time it's the word 'thiis'. Once again, the error is highlighted in red in the top box, but in this instance the bottom box displays a variety of alternatives. Select the word 'this' and click on the Change button.

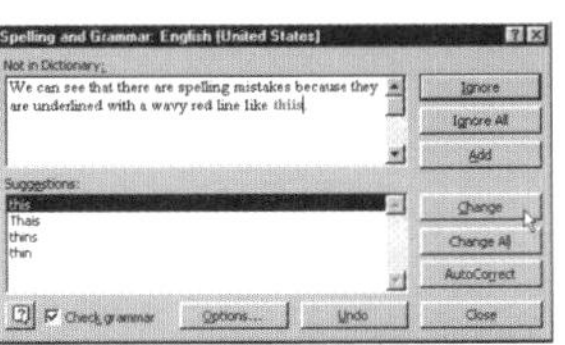

6 The next mistake the spelling checker highlights is the word 'errurs'. Again, the mistake is shown in the top box and the suggested correction appears in the bottom one. This time, the same spelling mistake occurs several times. We can fix all of these at once by clicking the Change All button.

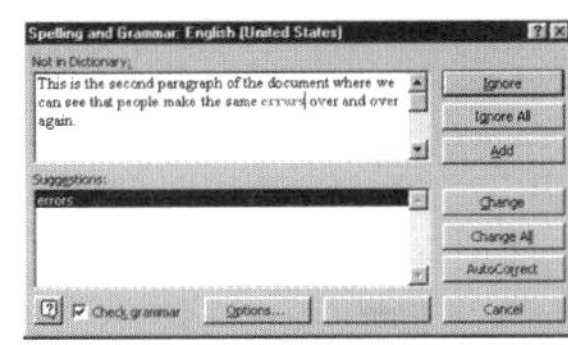

7 The spelling checker moves on to the word 'thang'. Let's assume we often type 'thang' instead of 'thing' and we'd like Word to correct it automatically in future. Make sure the word 'thing' is highlighted in the bottom box and click on the AutoCorrect button.

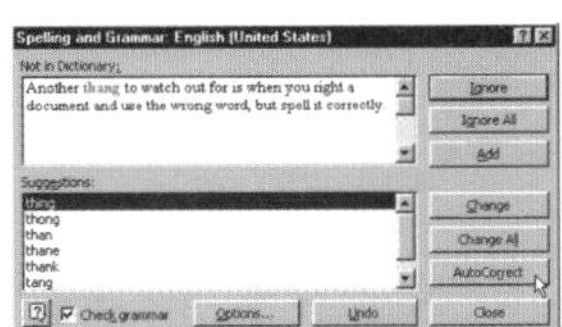

8 Now we've reached the final mistake in our document: 'yewsed'. The suggested correction is 'yews' but this is obviously wrong, it should be the word 'used'. To correct it, edit the word 'yewsed' in the top box and click the Change button to make the change in your document.

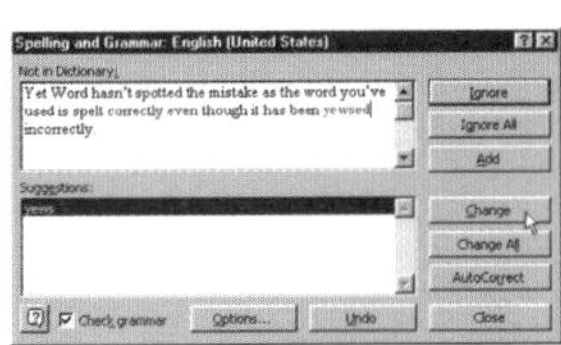

9 Now Word tells us that the spelling check is complete. Be careful, though, as the spelling checker cannot spot words spelt correctly, but used in the wrong place. Here, for example, we should have used 'write', not 'right'.

Making AutoCorrect work for you

Word can correct frequent typing and spelling mistakes automatically, leaving you free to concentrate on your writing. But you can also take advantage of the AutoCorrect feature to help minimize repetitive typing.

1 Word's AutoCorrect tool monitors what you type and automatically makes corrections if it spots one of the mistakes in its list. For example, let's see what happens when we make a mistake typing the word 'necessary' with only one 's'. Open a new document, type in 'necesary', but don't type a space afterwards. Word knows the word we've typed is misspelt and underlines it with a wavy red line.

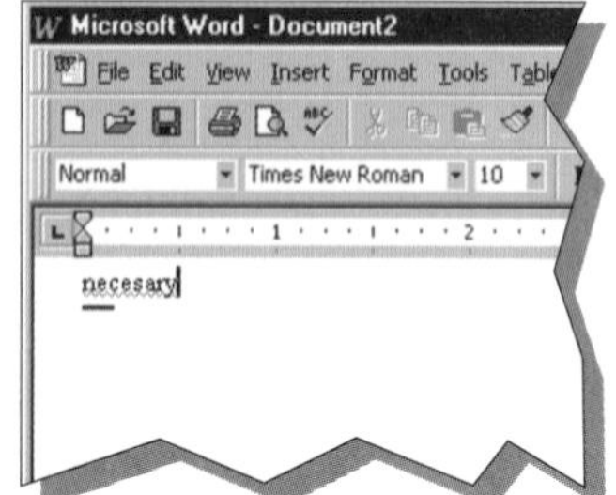

2 Next, type a space and watch what happens. Without prompting, AutoCorrect amends the spelling to 'necessary'. It also changes the first letter of the word to a capital 'N', as this letter appears to mark the start of a sentence.

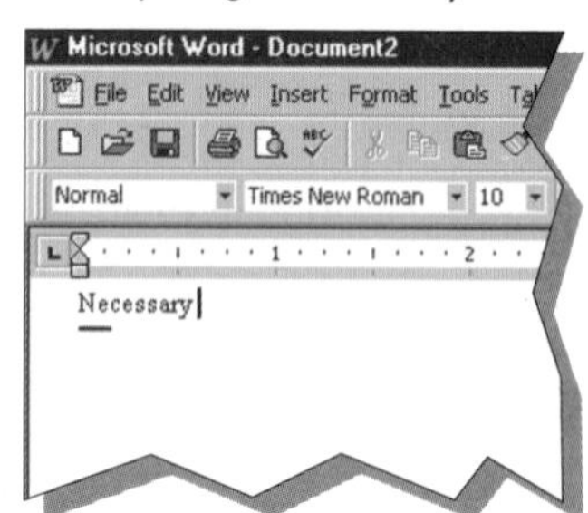

3 You can view the list of common errors that AutoCorrect looks out for by selecting AutoCorrect in the Tools menu. In this example (right), we've highlighted the mistake that was corrected in step two. You can see here that you can also choose to automatically correct other typing mistakes, such as accidental use of the [Caps Lock] key.

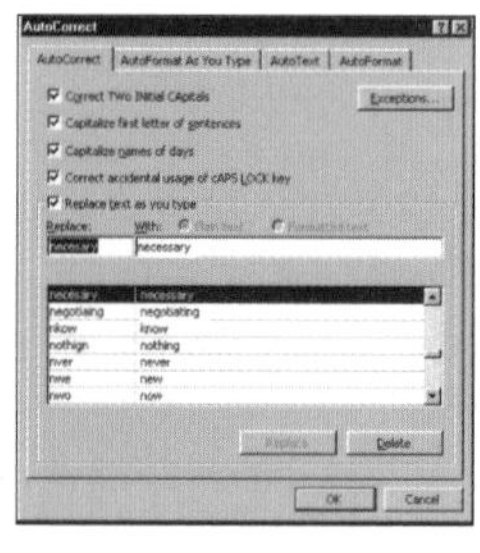

4 You can add to the list of errors that Word watches out for. Let's imagine that you frequently type 'bannana' instead of 'banana'. In the AutoCorrect dialog box, type 'bannana' in the Replace box, then type 'banana' in the With box and click on the Add button. From now on, Word will automatically correct this misspelling for you.

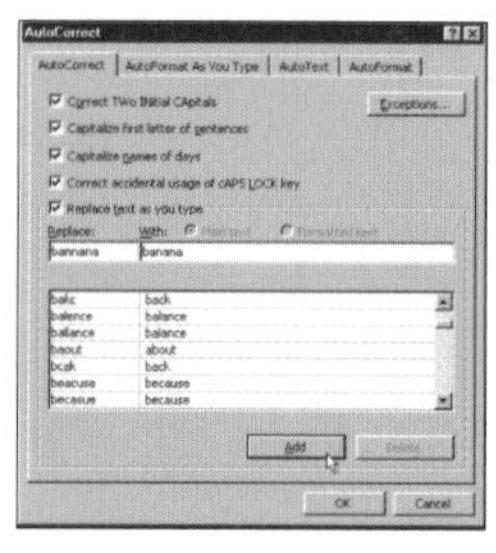

5 If you have a phrase that you use often, you can instruct AutoCorrect to automatically replace an abbreviated version of the phrase with the full one. For example, type 'mv' into the Replace box, then type 'The Merchant of Venice' in the With box and click the Add button. You have just told Word that every time you type 'mv', you want it to replace it with 'The Merchant of Venice'.

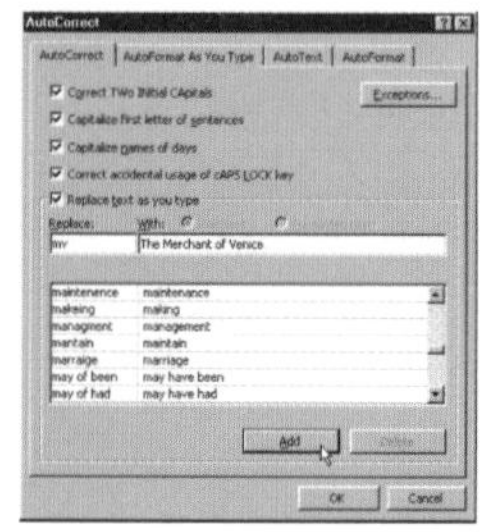

6 Now start a new document and type 'mv'. As soon as you insert a space afterwards (or a punctuation mark, such as a full stop or comma) AutoCorrect will replace it with 'The Merchant of Venice'.

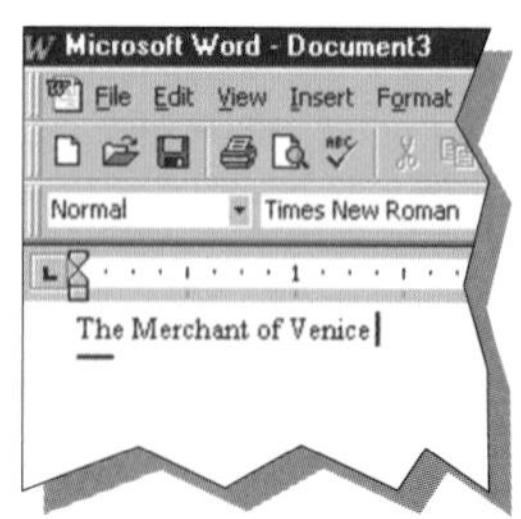

7 The AutoCorrect dialog box allows you to control other automatic changes in Word as you type. For example, if you type '1/2' (representing a half), Word will automatically replace it with a proper fraction character. Click on the AutoFormat As You Type tab to see the list of adjustments Word makes for you. You can turn these options on or off by clicking on the tick box next to each item.

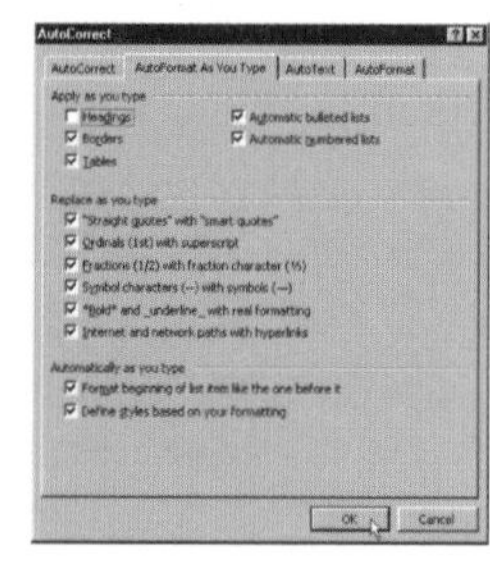

PC TIPS

AutoCorrect

AutoCorrect can take the repetition out of letter writing. If you tell it to put 'Dear Sir or Madam,' every time you type 'd' followed by [Enter], then ask it to insert 'Yours sincerely' every time you type 'y' followed by [Enter] (see step five), these two common phrases will be inserted automatically by AutoCorrect.

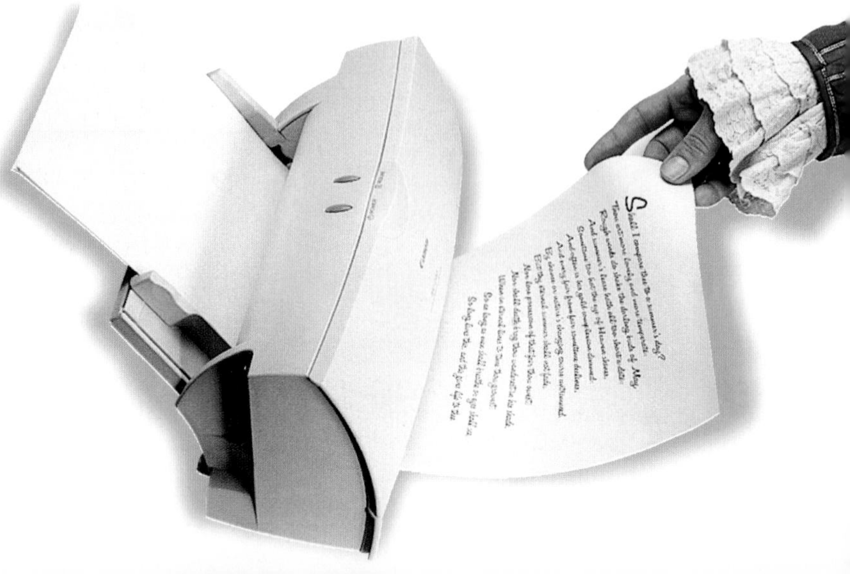

Increasing your word power

brilliant
excellent
outstanding
magnificent

Once your spelling is flawless, you can use Word's other tools to make sure your letters and documents have maximum impact.

WORD CAN do more than just check your spelling. It has a grammar checking device to help ensure that your letters and documents are grammatically faultless and well structured, plus a thesaurus of alternative words to help expand your vocabulary and avoid repetition.

Word draws your attention to anything it considers is grammatically incorrect by underlining the text with a wavy green line. By default, the sort of grammatical errors the grammar checker picks up on include possessives and plurals, passive sentences, punctuation and verb-subject agreement.

● Fussy about style

If this sounds complicated, you can alter the level of 'fussiness' to suit the type of document you're working on. Normally, Word uses an average level of grammar checking called Standard. There are other ready-made levels described as Casual, Formal and Technical. To change the setting, select Options from the Tools menu, then click on the Spelling and Grammar tab in the dialog box that appears. Next, choose a level of checking suitable for your current document from the Writing style drop-down list.

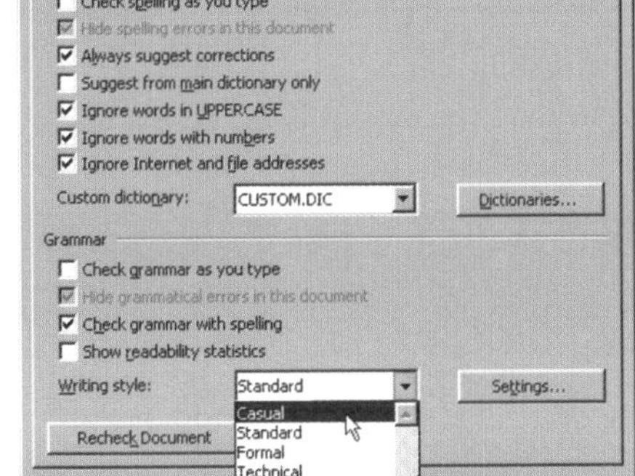

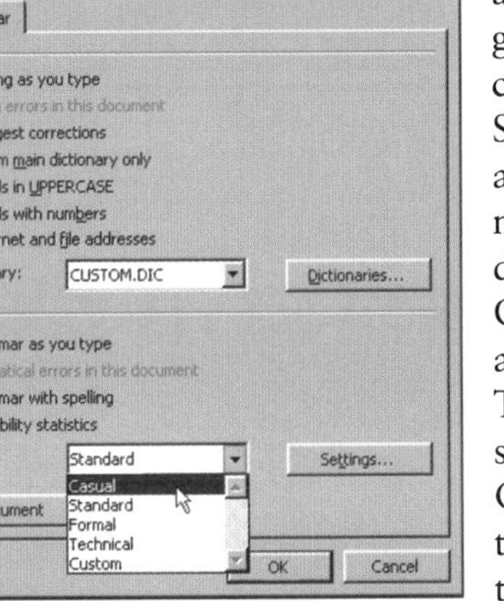

● Check out those checks

To look at the various checks Word can do, click on the Settings button. You will see a dialog box that shows the way each writing style is set up. This dialog box also gives you the opportunity to customize each style to suit your own purposes.

To change styles, simply click over the various check boxes in the scrolling list to turn particular checks on or off. You will notice that the list also includes a selection of style options. These are not strict checks for grammatical errors, but are meant to help improve the readability of your work. You can get the grammar checker to warn you about clichés, jargon and unnecessary wordiness.

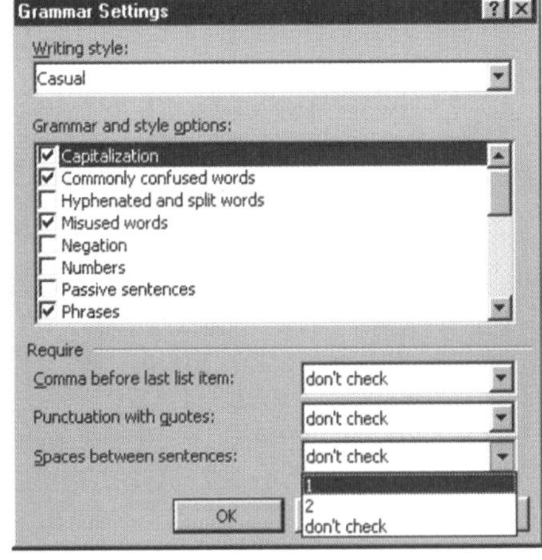

CHANGING SETTINGS

If you experiment with different grammar settings in Word then decide that you were happier with it before, don't panic! To restore the original settings, all you have to do is click the Reset button and you'll go back to square one.

PC TIPS

Thesaurus facility

To find another word for one you've already used a lot, Word's built-in thesaurus will help. Click the cursor on the word you want to look up and press the [Shift]+[F7] keys. The Thesaurus dialog box will show your word in the top left box and, below it, a selection of possible meanings. A list of synonyms or related words is given for each meaning, with the currently selected word shown above it. Use the two lists to choose the word you want and click on the Replace button to change the word in your document.

Number your pages

Almost every long printed document, book or magazine has page numbers. You can manually add page numbers to your Word documents, but there's a much smarter automatic way.

It's no coincidence that almost every printed item you see has page numbers – books, magazines and newspapers all have them because they help readers to navigate through large amounts of written material and, with an index, make it easy to find exactly the right information. So, it's a good idea to add page numbers to your Word documents – especially if you ever need to write long reports or letters.

One way to include page numbers in a document is to manually type them in at the top or bottom of every page. This has the virtue of simplicity, but it can be pretty tiresome and time-consuming because you have to do it for every single page. In addition, you will have to check that you type in the correct number for each page and position the number in the same place on every page.

The biggest problem with inserting page numbers manually comes when you decide to modify your document by adding or removing text or even whole pages. Then you'll have to go right through your document and renumber all the pages and make sure text changes haven't shunted your page numbers away from their intended positions at the top or bottom of each page.

Head and foot with ease

Word makes it easy to avoid these difficulties by creating headers and footers for documents, which offer three time-saving advantages. First, they are kept separate from the main text of your document so their position can't be altered by modifications you make to the rest of your document. Second, you only have to set up a header or footer for one page and Word will automatically apply it to all the pages in your document. And third, if the changes you make to the main document change the number of pages, Word automatically updates the page numbers in the headers and footers to cope with it.

Word gives you a toolbar to control the contents of headers and footers. You can access it by selecting Header and Footer from the View menu. Then it's a matter of typing whatever text you want to appear in the header or footer and clicking on the Close button on the toolbar.

WHAT IT MEANS

HEADERS AND FOOTERS

Headers and footers are special areas at the top and bottom of pages that are reserved for information that needs to be on every page. For example, pages often need to include the title of the current chapter or section as well as the page number.

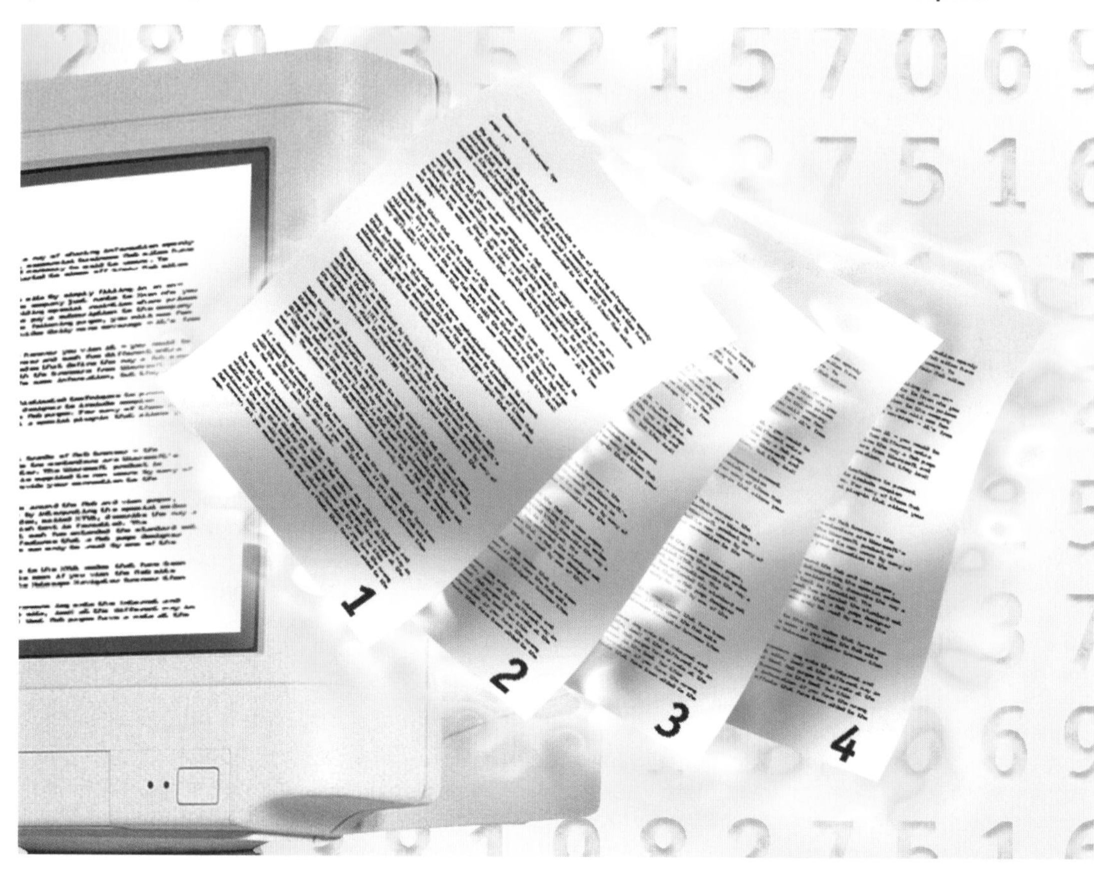

Numbering documents will help you and other readers to keep them in sequence.

Adding headers and footers

When you're working with lengthy documents, headers and footers can help you keep track of where you are and – when printed out – add professional polish to your work.

1 It's easy to add automatic page numbers to your long Word documents (our example is four pages long). First, open the Header and Footer toolbar, which controls what is inserted automatically at the top and bottom of every page in a document. To do this, go to the View menu and select the Header and Footer option.

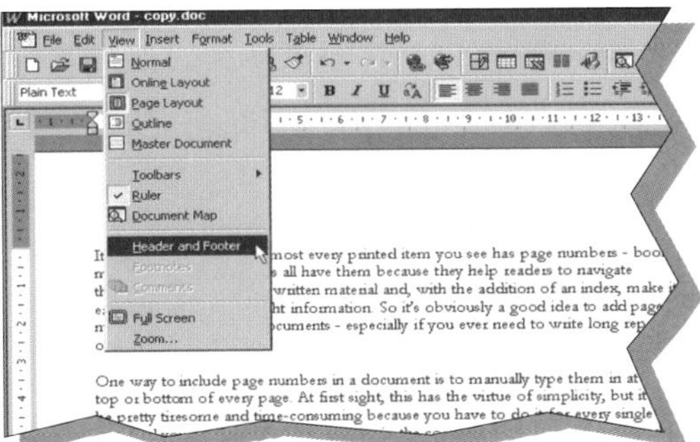

2 Now you can see the Header and Footer toolbar and a dotted rectangle that shows where the header is positioned on the page. To insert the correct page number automatically on all pages of the document, click over the Insert Page Number button (it has a # on it).

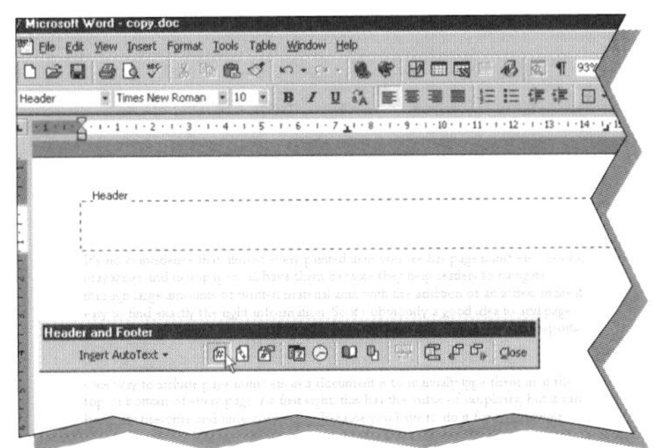

3 You can format text in the header in the same way as you format normal text in a document. Here we have centred the number '1' in the header box by clicking over the Center button in the Formatting toolbar.

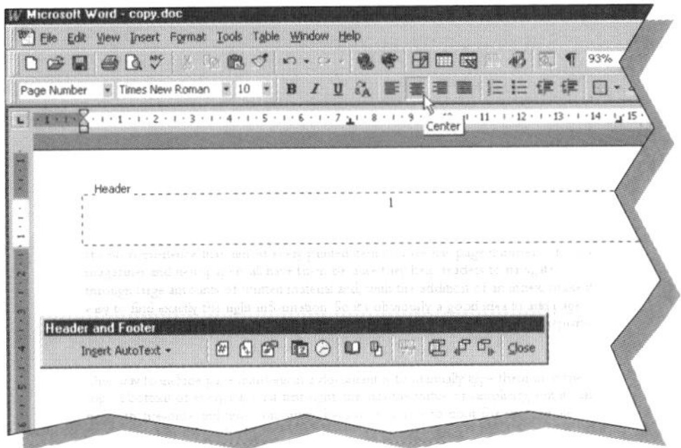

4 When you've finished work on the header, click on the Close button to close the Header and Footer toolbar and return to the Normal view. The header box disappears – it still exists, but Word has just hidden it so that it doesn't distract you.

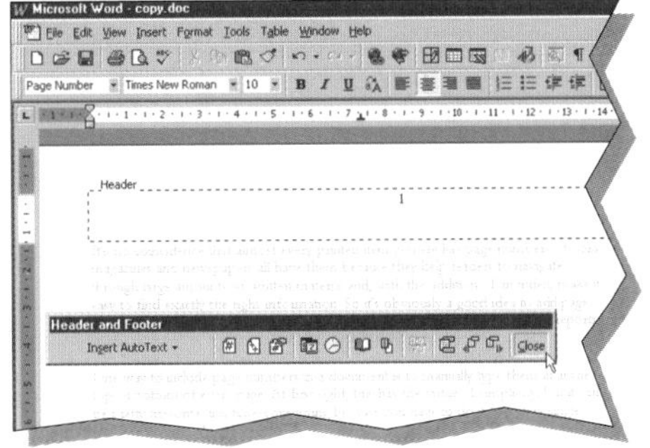

PC TIPS

Header and footer extras

Your headers and footers need not be limited to page numbers. If you click on the Insert AutoText button on the Header and Footer toolbar, you'll see a dropdown menu

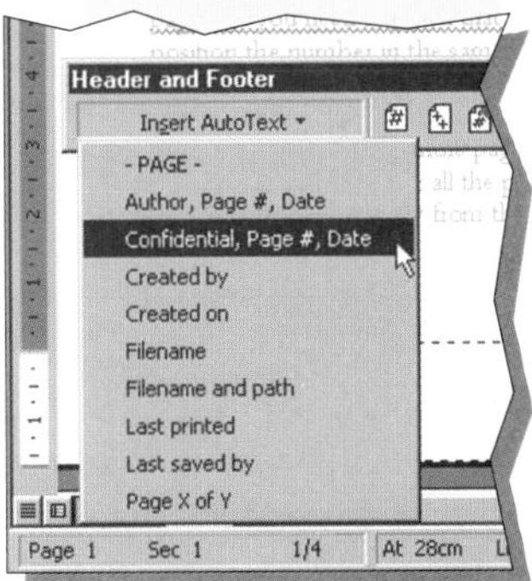

with a range of options that you can include at the head or foot of every page of your document, such as Confidential, Page #, Date.

5 To see what your finished document looks like with page numbers in place before you save or print it, select Page Layout from the View menu. Notice how the page number in the header is shown in grey.

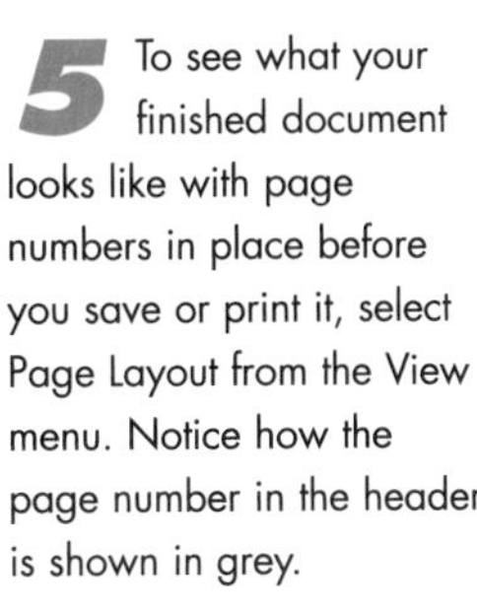

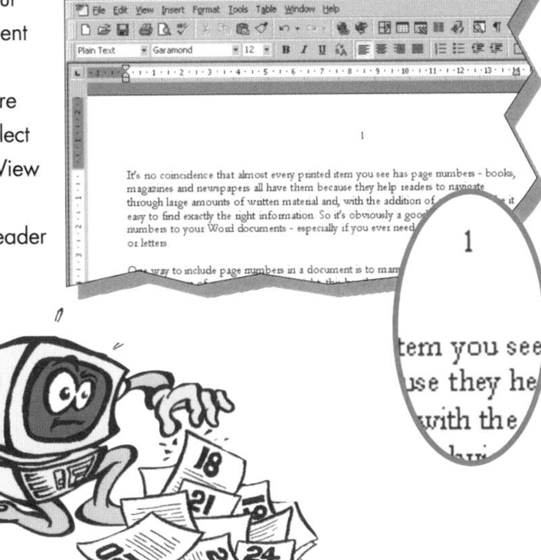

6 If you want to have the page numbers at the foot of the page instead of the head, click on the Switch Between Header and Footer icon (shown right) in the Header and Footer toolbar. You'll move to the bottom of the page and see a Footer box with the page number in place. You can format this footer in the same way as the header (see above, step 3).

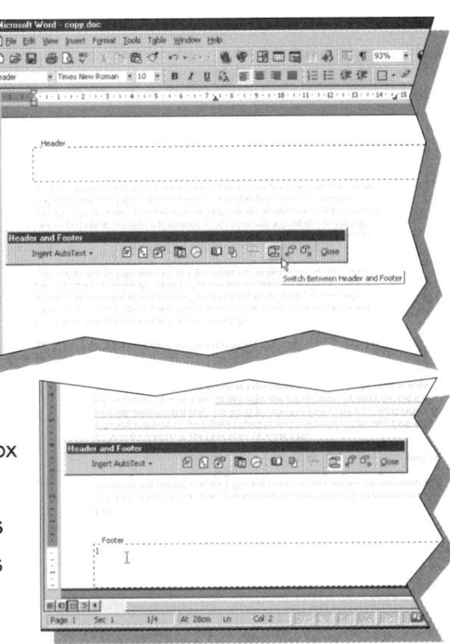

Creating tables

Many of the documents you are creating work best in table form, for example, a birthday present list or a packing checklist for going on holiday. Here we show you the easy way to set up tables in a word processing program.

Creating lists in a Word document is quite a common requirement, whether it's the shopping list, a 'to-do' list or a birthday card list. For the most basic of lists (usually those with only one column), most people simply use the [Tab] key (see Stage 1, page 32). This indents the item in the list, so that it stands out from the main body of the text. However, for more complex lists, you will need to create a table so they stay legible.

In our step-by-step examples on pages 38–39, we use the idea of compiling a list of birthday presents, using the person's name, date of birth and what present they would like. This list will illustrate most of the common steps involved in making and adjusting tables, in particular adding new rows and information. With Word tables, you can easily add something you've forgotten, in this case an extra child's or adult's birthday.

● Simplified spreadsheet

A table works much like a simplified spreadsheet. It looks similar, too, with rows and columns of cells into which you can type your information. A Word table is not as restrictive as a spreadsheet, in that the word processor doesn't mind whether you type in numbers or letters. However, it doesn't allow you to make complex maths calculations on the contents of the table in the way that Excel does. In Word, a table is more likely to be used to make your document look more professional and easy to read, rather than for calculations. As you will see from the list of birthday presents, it is easier to read and alter than a hand-written note stuck to the fridge.

● Great for lists

Although we won't explore it in detail now, Word can also do some simple mathematics with any numerical data you enter in the cells, much like a mini-spreadsheet. It is because of this versatility, combined with the ease of changing the look and format of boxes, that many people find Word's tables useful for list-based jobs. You can see from the examples opposite how anything from an order form to a business invoice can be created as a list, quickly and professionally, and still form part of a larger document or letter.

WHAT IT MEANS

CELLS

Each box in a table is called a cell. This is also the word used to describe the boxes in spreadsheets. In Word tables, each cell can be altered in size, either individually or as part of a whole column or row. To type text, select a cell by clicking on it with the mouse or by moving the text insertion point around the table with the cursor arrow keys.

Making use of tables

Tables can be used to tidy up all sorts of documents. As Word lets you include them in letters or other documents, you can use tables to make any kind of list-based information stand out.

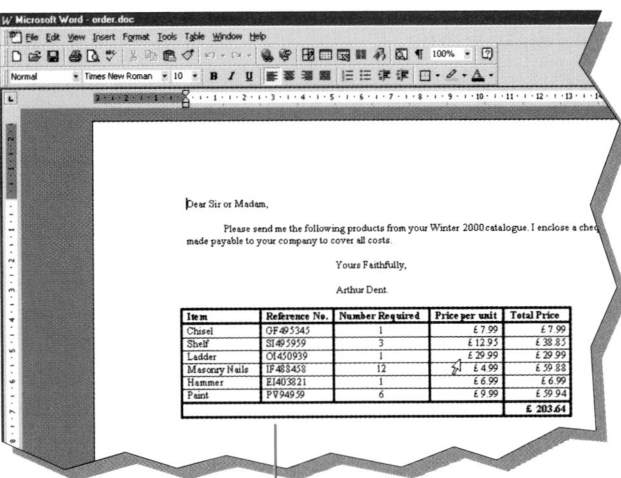
Dear Sir or Madam,

Please send me the following products from your Winter 2000 catalogue. I enclose a cheq
made payable to your company to cover all costs.

Yours Faithfully,

Arthur Dent.

Item	Reference No.	Number Required	Price per unit	Total Price
Chisel	GF495345	1	£ 7.99	£ 7.99
Shelf	SI495959	3	£ 12.95	£ 38.85
Ladder	OI450939	1	£ 29.99	£ 29.99
Masonry Nails	IF488458	12	£ 4.99	£ 59.88
Hammer	EI403821	1	£ 6.99	£ 6.99
Paint	PV94959	6	£ 9.99	£ 59.94
				£ 203.64

Order forms

Whenever you shop by mail order, it's important to make your orders clear. By compiling a five-column list containing the item required, the reference number, the number required, the price per item and the total price, you should remove any chance of misunderstanding. This example uses a simple grid to make the table easy to read, both across and down.

Travel timetables

Itemized timetables and travel arrangements are always easier to read in table form. This example uses seven columns. The headings are bold to emphasize the key information and make the table simpler to follow.

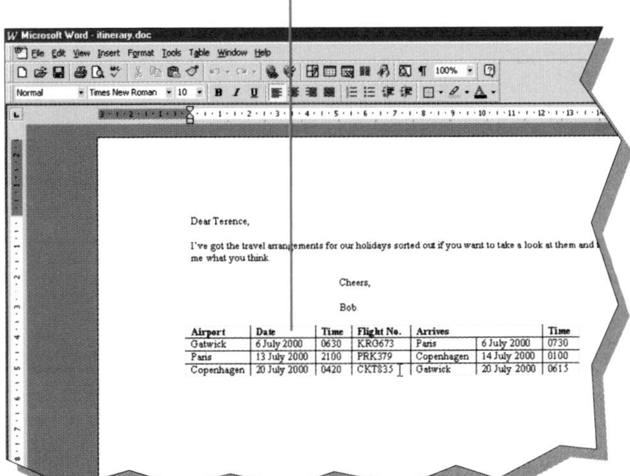
Dear Terence,

I've got the travel arrangements for our holidays sorted out if you want to take a look at them and
me what you think.

Cheers,

Bob.

Airport	Date	Time	Flight No.	Arrives		Time
Gatwick	6 July 2000	0630	KRG673	Paris	6 July 2000	0730
Paris	13 July 2000	2100	PRK379	Copenhagen	14 July 2000	0100
Copenhagen	20 July 2000	0420	CKT835	Gatwick	20 July 2000	0615

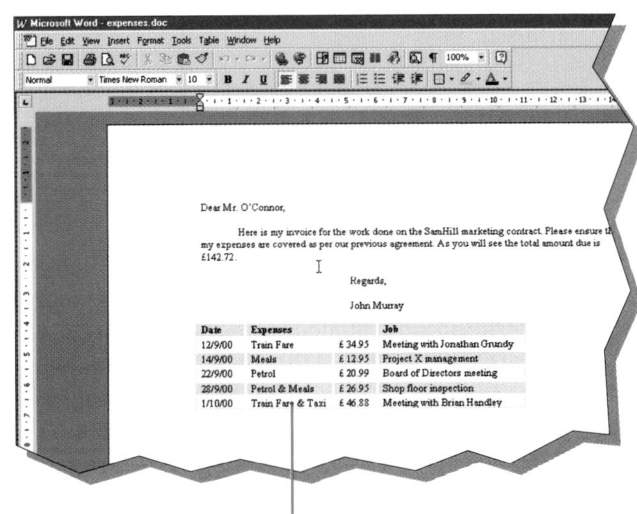
Dear Mr. O'Connor,

Here is my invoice for the work done on the SamHill marketing contract. Please ensure th
my expenses are covered as per our previous agreement. As you will see the total amount due is £142.72.

Regards,

John Murray

Date	Expenses		Job
12/9/00	Train Fare	£ 34.95	Meeting with Jonathan Grundy
14/9/00	Meals	£ 12.95	Project X management
22/9/00	Petrol	£ 20.99	Board of Directors meeting
28/9/00	Petrol & Meals	£ 26.95	Shop floor inspection
1/10/00	Train Fare & Taxi	£ 46.88	Meeting with Brian Handley

Easy-to-read invoices

For anyone running a small business or providing any sort of service, Word makes it simple to set up easy-to-read invoices. This itemized expenses bill consists of a table with four columns. Note that the third column does not need a heading. This example uses shaded backgrounds to make it easy to read across the rows.

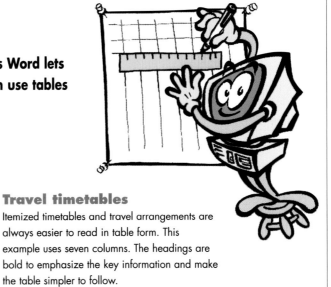

Using colours to lift lists

This reading list for a child demonstrates how using different colours makes it easier to read across the table. It also shows the benefit of using bold text in one column to emphasize the most important information – in this case, to pick out the title of the book.

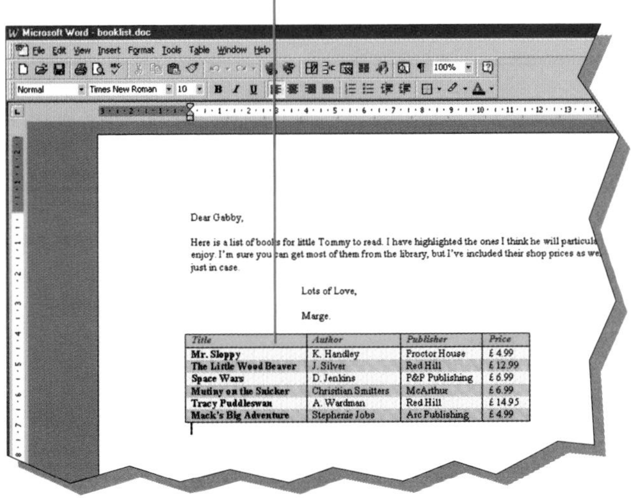
Dear Gabby,

Here is a list of books for little Tommy to read. I have highlighted the ones I think he will particul
enjoy. I'm sure you can get most of them from the library, but I've included their shop prices as we
just in case.

Lots of Love,

Marge.

Title	*Author*	*Publisher*	*Price*
Mr. Sloppy	K. Handley	Proctor House	£ 4.99
The Little Wood Beaver	J. Silver	Red Hill	£ 12.99
Space Wars	D. Jenkins	P&P Publishing	£ 6.99
Mutiny on the Snicker	Christian Smitters	McArthur	£ 6.99
Tracy Puddleswan	A. Wardman	Red Hill	£ 14.95
Mack's Big Adventure	Stephenie Jobs	Arc Publishing	£ 4.99

Creating a simple table

For this example, we'll create a short table to store information about the birthday presents given to each of seven children.

1 Position the text cursor in the document where you want the table to be. Choose Insert Table from the drop-down Table menu.

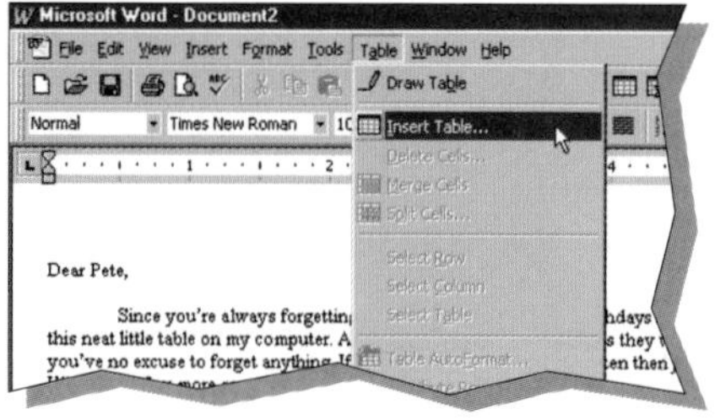

2 The table needs three columns and eight rows, so type '3' in the Number of columns box. Type '8' in the Number of rows box in the same way.

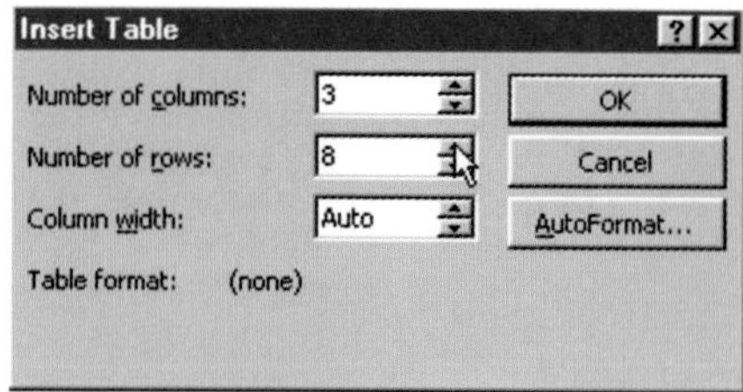

3 We need to give the width of each column to ensure it doesn't run off the edge of an A4 sheet of paper when printed. In the Column width box, type '2'. This creates a column 2cm wide. (If the width you choose turns out to be too narrow, you can alter the column width later.)

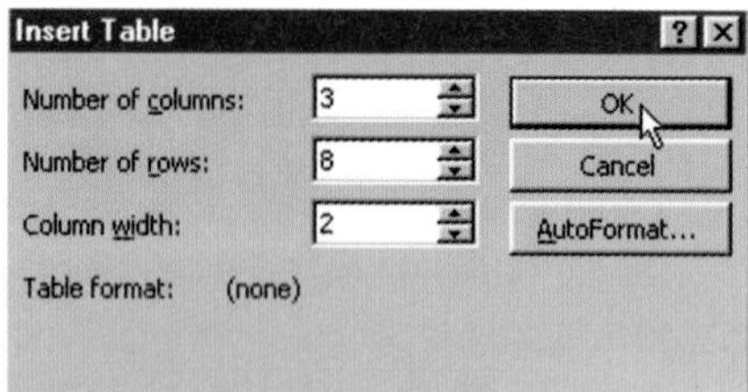

4 A blank table will appear on the screen. Click on the top left cell and type in your information. You can move around the table cells with your mouse or, if you prefer, you can use the cursor keys or even the [Tab] key.

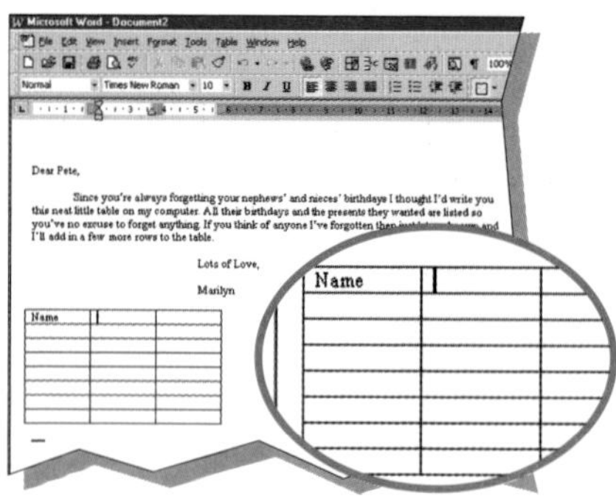

5 You can follow our example or make up your own entries. Notice how it doesn't matter if the entry is too long to fit into the width of a cell (as with 'Date of Birth' in the second cell in the top row). Word automatically puts in a second line to make room. This applies to whichever cell is affected.

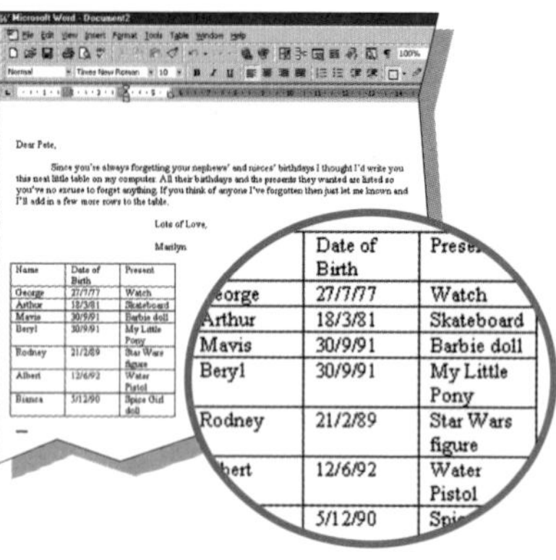

6 The normal text formatting commands work inside tables. To make all the column headings bold, place your mouse pointer to the left of the Name cell, so that it appears to point towards it at an angle (inset). Now single click and the entire top row becomes highlighted (right). If you press the Bold button in the Formatting toolbar, all the column headers will appear in bold (inset right).

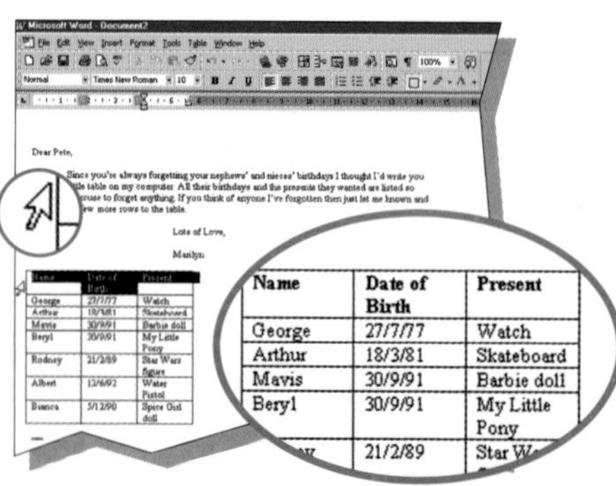

7 You can also edit individual entries. Move the pointer to the left of the 'Star Wars figure' cell; it will change to an angled pointer. Click once and this cell will be highlighted. Press the Italic button in the Formatting toolbar to italicize this text.

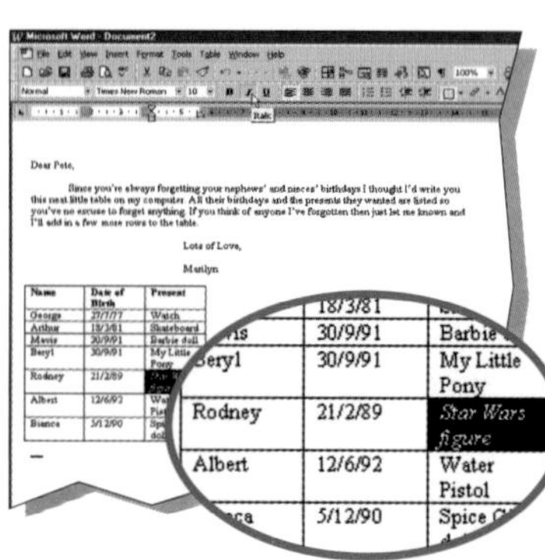

8 You can align text in columns in the same way as you would normal text. Move your mouse pointer to just above the top of the middle column. The cursor will change into a downward pointing arrow (inset left). Click once and the whole column will be highlighted. Now choose the Center button in the Formatting toolbar and the text will centre in the cells (inset right). Feel free to experiment with other columns to see how the Align Right and Justify buttons affect the look of the text in the cells. Make sure you save the table for the exercise opposite, which explores more table features.

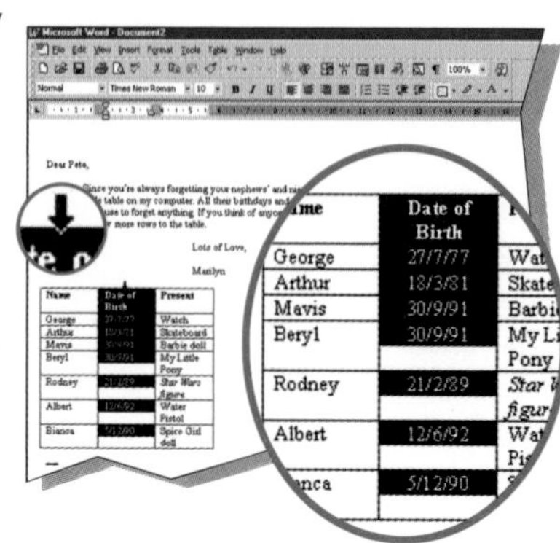

PC TIPS

If you want to draw a table quickly, there is an alternative to using the Table menu. Click the Insert Table icon on the top toolbar (right), and you will see a grid that lets you select the size and format of a table (below). Drag your mouse diagonally from the top left square to select the number of rows and columns you want. Release the mouse button. With this method, Word will automatically specify the width of columns, but you can change them once the table has been drawn.

2 x 2 Table

Fine tuning the look of your table

Here's how to modify the size of existing cells and add extra information to the table we created in the previous exercise.

1 In the example we created on the opposite page, you saw how Word increases the depth of a cell to accommodate long words or a group of words that don't fit into the width of a single cell. This can make the table look uneven and hard to read, but the width of the cells can be altered to tidy things up.

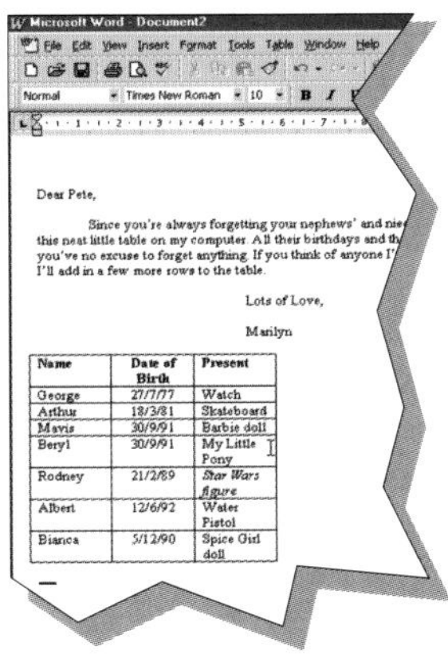

2 To alter the size of a cell, move the mouse pointer over the right border of the cell containing the long word or group of words. Your cursor will then turn into two arrowed, vertical lines. Click and hold the left mouse button. Now move your mouse to the right and a dotted line will appear to show you the new column width. When it is long enough for all the words to fit on a single line, release the mouse button.

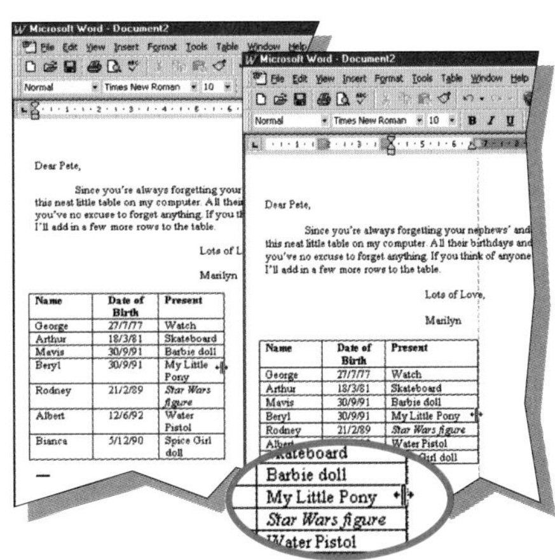

3 Sometimes, you might wish to increase the width of a single cell, perhaps to ensure that the title of a column stays on one line. Highlight the cell as before by clicking on its left edge. Now move the cursor on to the right column divider until the cursor changes, then increase the width of the cell as you did in step 2 of this exercise.

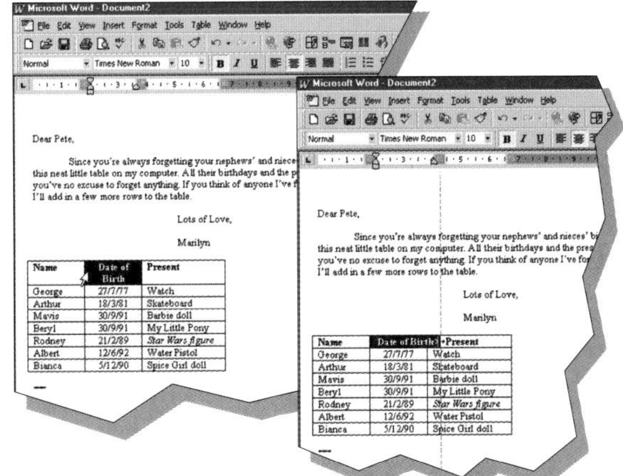

4 A common problem is needing to add extra rows of information after the table has been created. This is easy, as you can add the row at any point in the table. Highlight the row above which you want the new row to appear. Now go to the Table menu and choose Insert Rows.

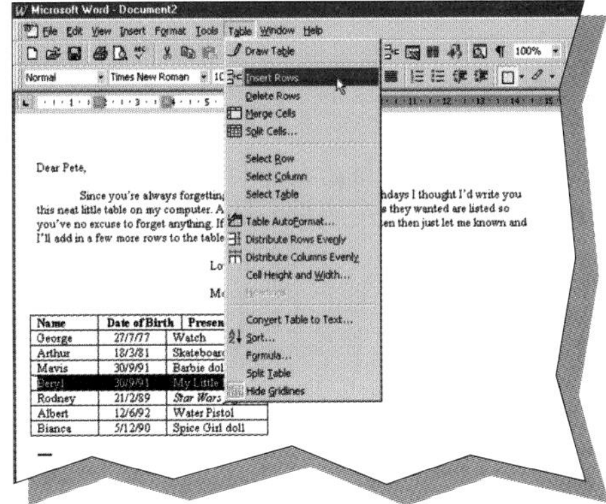

5 A blank row of highlighted cells appears. Now you can add details of another name, birthday and present, as before. You can see with the final table (below right) how these few tricks can change the look and contents of a table.

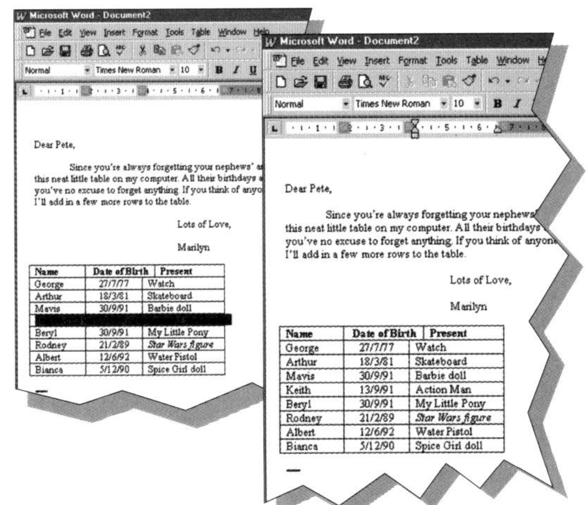

SHORT CUTS

If you want to apply the same formatting to all the text in a table, you can select it all by holding down the [Alt] key and pressing [5] on the numeric keypad (usually on the right of the keyboard). Before doing this, make sure that NumLock is switched off (see Stage 1, pages 92–93).

NUMBER COLUMNS

Text alignment is a useful tool for many different purposes, not just for making the table look neat. Often, your table will include a price column and a total price. It's useful if this can be checked or added to easily. If you align the numbers to the right, when they are entered, the prices will be oriented into pounds and pence columns aligned to the decimal point.

Price per unit	Total Price
£7.99	£7.99
£12.95	£38.85
£29.99	£29.99
£4.99	£59.88
£6.99	£6.99
£9.99	£59.94
	£ 203.64

Perfect paragraphs

Formatting can be applied to a whole paragraph in a Word document. You can also control margins, indents and spacing – and it is possible to do it all from one place, making sure each document has the best layout for its purpose.

We've already seen how you can format text in a Word document (see Stage 1, pages 30–33) to appear as you want it by controlling the size, weight, typeface and position of the text. The idea of formatting whole paragraphs is similar – you can apply a set of formatting rules to each paragraph to decide how it looks. The features you can control include the spacing above and below paragraphs, the amount of space between individual lines in a paragraph and the positions of the left and right margins.

● Visual appeal

The ability to control these aspects of paragraph formatting can come in handy, especially for longer documents or publications such as newsletters. For example, you can make a newsletter more visually appealing if you apply formatting to the paragraphs of each article within it. Also, long documents such as reports often have different sections that require different treatments (introductions, appendixes, indexes and so forth). It's just a case of thinking about what would work best for your target audience and then using the right formatting tools to achieve it.

● Reading between the lines

For example, if you were writing a play, you would want to make the script as easy as possible for the actors to follow. With this in mind, you might decide to make the left and right margins wide so that the paragraphs are narrower than on a normal document, making the lines easy to scan without losing your place.

Another example could be if you were writing a set of notes for students. You might decide to put plenty of space between the lines within each paragraph to make the information easier to follow and to provide room for the students or tutors to write in their own notes and comments.

Changes and corrections can be difficult and messy to make in handwritten work, but your PC can ensure that your documents are clear and easy to read when you use the formatting paragraphs facility.

PC TIPS

Triple-clicking

By now you'll be aware of how often you need to double-click your mouse to do certain things. For example, you can double-click to start programs in Windows; equally you can use the technique to highlight (and so select) a word in Word. Triple-clicking is a related technique where you click the mouse button three times in rapid succession to select a whole paragraph.

All the paragraph formatting options can be controlled via Word's Paragraph dialog box. First, though, you need to select the paragraph you want to format by using the drag-select technique to highlight it (or you could follow our PC Tips about triple-clicking, left). Call up the Paragraph dialog box by selecting Paragraph from the Format menu and then select the Indents and Spacing tab.

If you want to move the left and right margins, it's simply a question of using the up and down arrows to alter the values in the Left and Right text boxes found in the Indentation section. In addition, you can indent the first line of a paragraph further by using the Special text box in the Indentation section (see page 42).

● Making space

The Spacing section is used to control the spacing above and below a paragraph, as well as the spaces between the lines of a paragraph. You can use the Before and After text boxes to determine how big a space appears above and below a paragraph.

The Line Spacing text box allows you to specify how much space there should be between the lines of a paragraph. The default is one line. Word gives the options of one-and-a-half lines or double-spacing, as well as the extra flexibility to set an exact spacing distance. This spacing is measured in points (by default) and you can put whatever values you want in the At text box.

● Sneak preview

The Indents and Spacing tab in the Paragraph dialog box includes a preview facility that gives you some idea of what your paragraph formatting changes will look like before you click the OK button. The preview screen automatically changes to show the alterations you made to the settings in the dialog box.

There is no need to format each individual paragraph of a document separately – unless you want to for style reasons. To format all the text, select your whole document by choosing Select All from the Edit menu and apply the same formatting to all the paragraphs in your document at once.

WHAT IT MEANS

POINTS

A point is the most common unit of measurement in printing. A point (often shortened to pt) is 1/72 of an inch. For example, the text in this box is 8pt, the main text on this page is 10pt and the heading on page 40, 'Perfect paragraphs', is 67pt.

Your written documents will be easier to work on, easier to read and will convey a much more professional image when you format them in Word.

Changing margins and paragraph indents

Word provides a range of tools to help you improve the look of your text documents and make them more inviting for the reader. Here's our guide to margin and paragraph indents.

1 Below is the Page Layout view of the first few paragraphs of a long text document. Without paragraph formatting, the text looks daunting to the reader, so we're going to change the left and right margins for the whole document to shorten the lines.

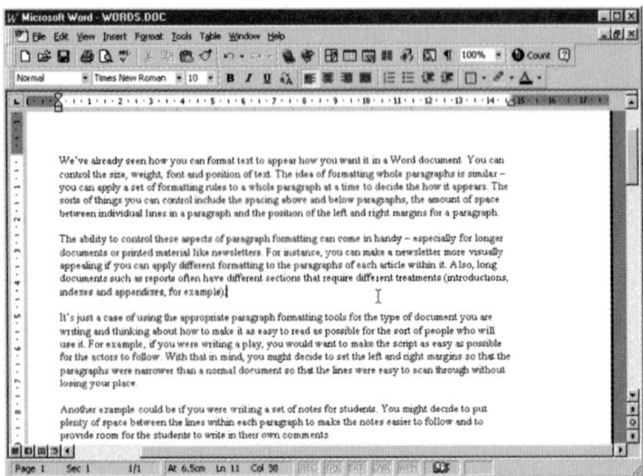

2 To do this, we first need to select all the text in the letter by going to the Edit menu and choosing the Select All option. All the selected text will be shown as white text on a black background (as in step 3).

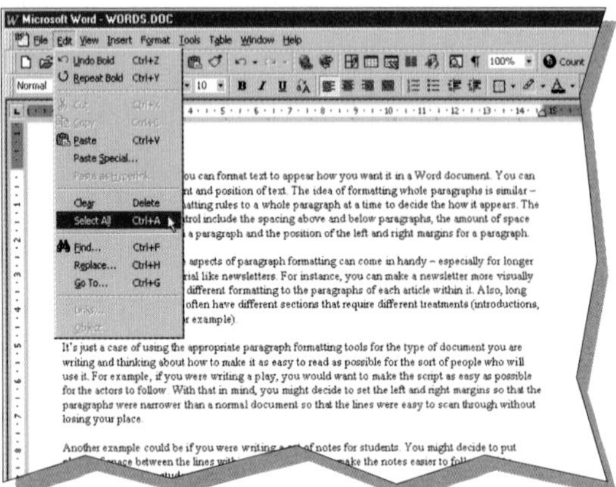

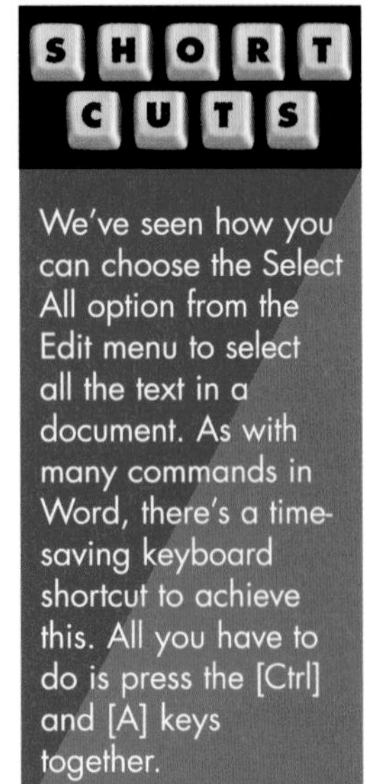

We've seen how you can choose the Select All option from the Edit menu to select all the text in a document. As with many commands in Word, there's a time-saving keyboard shortcut to achieve this. All you have to do is press the [Ctrl] and [A] keys together.

3 All the paragraph margin and indentation options are controlled via the Paragraph dialog box. To open this, go to the Format menu and click over the Paragraph option.

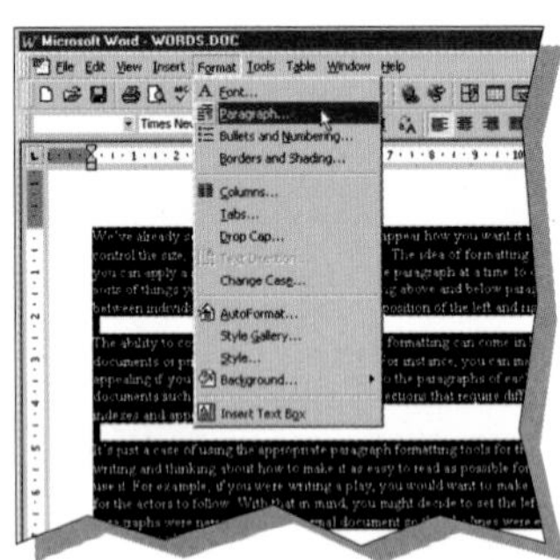

4 Click on the Indents and Spacing tab in the Paragraph dialog box. Let's start by moving the left margin in a bit. Locate the Left text box below the Indentation heading and click the up arrow to its right until the box reads 1.5cm. Notice how the bold text in the preview window moves. Now do the same for the right margin. Locate the Right text box below the Indentation heading. Click the up arrow until the box reads 1.5cm. You'll see the right end of the bold text move in the preview window.

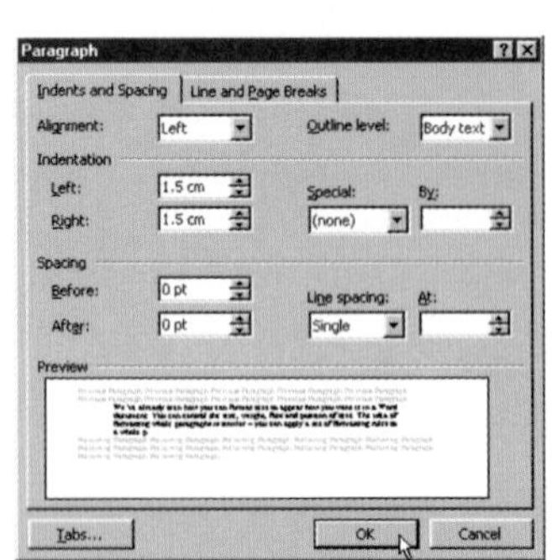

5 Click the OK button to see the changes. View the text normally by clicking once in the window to make the highlight disappear. Look at the ruler at the top of the page – you will see the two sliders showing the new positions of the margins.

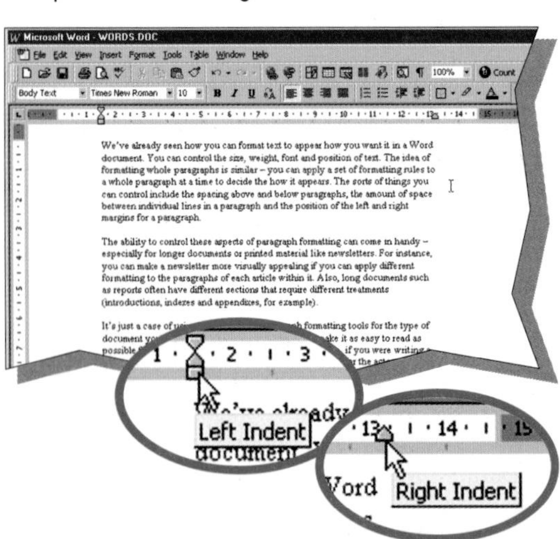

6 Now we're going to add indentations to the first line of each paragraph. First, you need to select all the text – go to the Edit menu and choose Select All. Now select Paragraph from the Format menu to open the Paragraph dialog box again. Click on the down arrow to the right of the Special text box and select First line from the list of options that appears. Notice how the measurement 1.27cm (it might be 0.3in on your PC) appears automatically in the By text box. Now click on the OK button and the result should be altogether more attractive and easier to read, as shown in the page on the right.

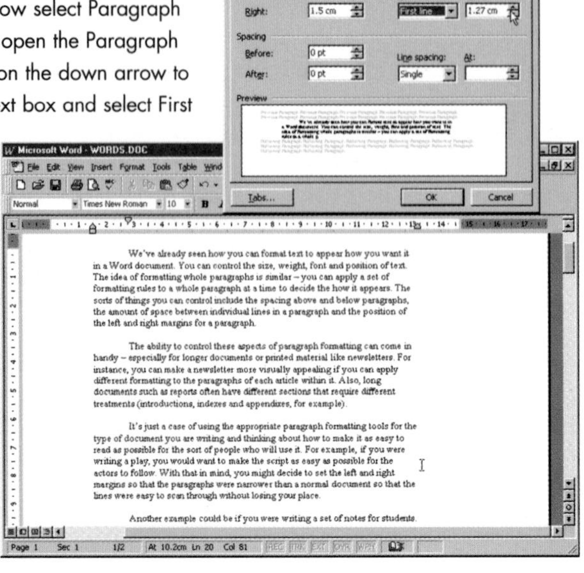

Giving your document space

Documents are often easier to read if the space between the lines of text is increased. Let's see how easy it is to do this.

1 Our document is formatted with margin and first line indents, but it still seems dense and difficult to read. Let's give it an airier look by increasing the space between the lines of text. Go to the Edit menu and choose the Select All option. Now choose the Paragraph option from the Format menu. In the Paragraph dialog box, locate the Line spacing text box, click on the down arrow to its right and select the Double option from the drop-down menu.

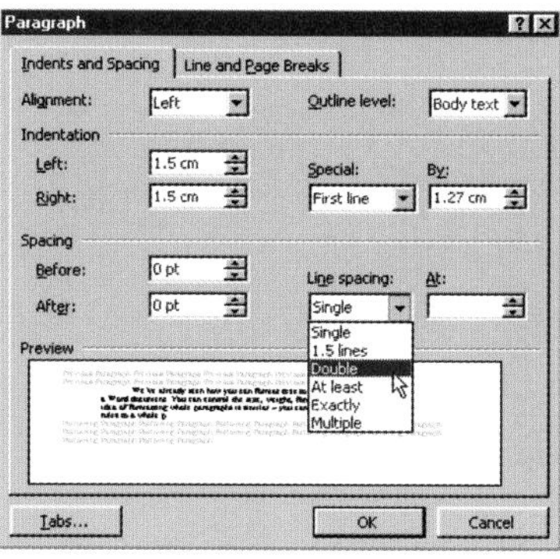

2 Click on OK and then click once on the document to see it with double line spacing. The text is much more legible. It's worth thinking about applying double line spacing to documents such as essays, where presentation is particularly important, and space may be needed for the teacher to make marks and comments.

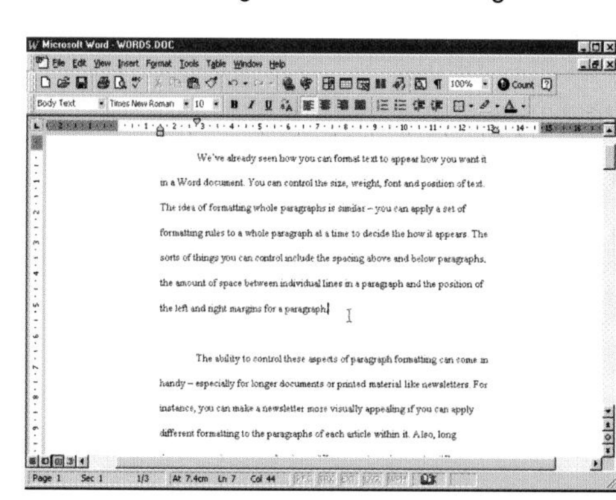

3 Word gives you a variety of line-spacing options, of which we chose Double in step 1. However, you can choose the line spacing to suit your own preferences. To do this, select all the text, go to the Format menu, select Paragraph and choose Exactly from the Line spacing drop-down menu. Type in the space you want (this is measured in points, which is shortened to 'pt') in the At text box. We have selected a depth of 14pt.

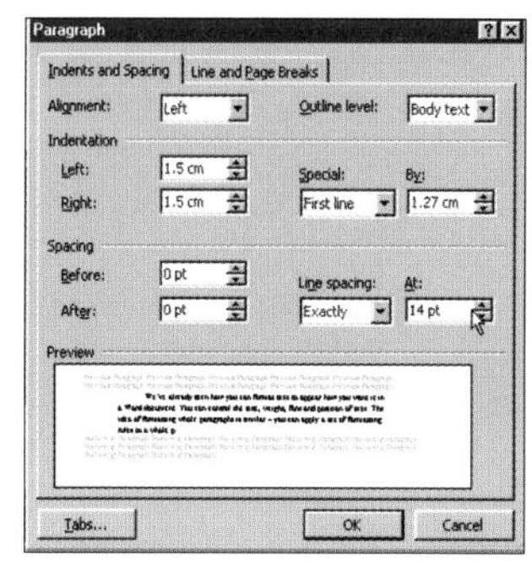

4 When you click OK and then click on the text, you will see that the lines have closed up a little but the text is still legible. This paragraph formatting feature gives you great flexibility when you're working with different typefaces and type sizes, so you can create exactly the type of document presentation you are looking for.

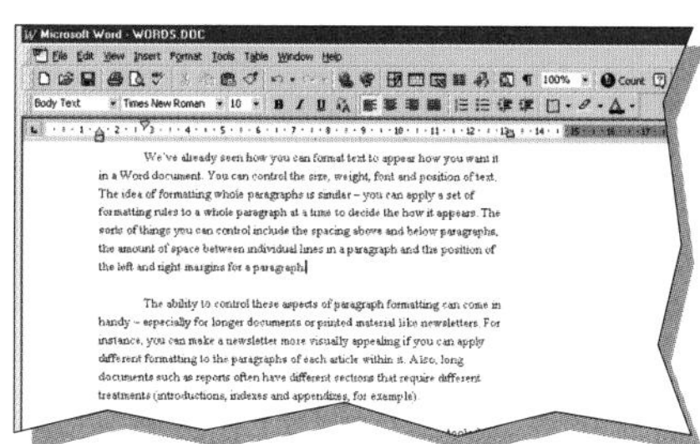

5 When you are writing Word documents, the usual way to create space between paragraphs is to press the [Enter] key twice. This creates an invisible character called a carriage return. You can make these characters visible by clicking on the Show/Hide button on Word's top toolbar (inset below).

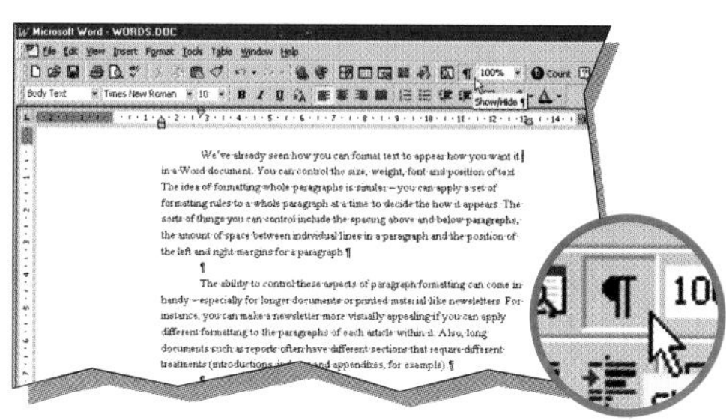

6 In the same way as you can change the spaces between lines, you can adjust the spacing between paragraphs. To do this, delete the extra carriage returns between the paragraphs of your document, then click on the Select All option from the Edit menu. Open the Paragraph dialog box. Click on the up arrow to the right of the Before text box in the Spacing section. Here we put a 6pt space (about half a line) above each of the paragraphs. The After box puts a 6pt space below each paragraph.

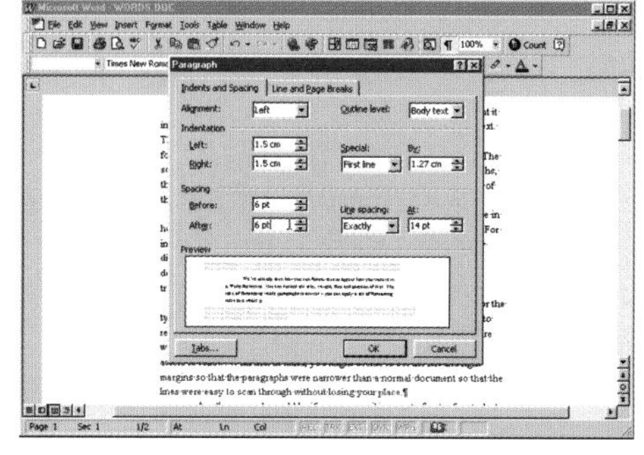

7 When you're happy with the changes you've made, click on the OK button to finish. Even on screen, the document shows that a lot of thought has been put into its presentation by the changes we've made to the paragraph formatting and line spacing.

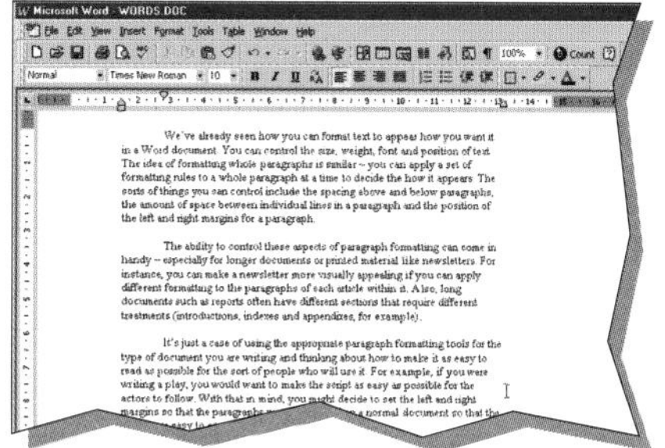

PC TIPS

At any time in the paragraph formatting process, it is possible to back-track by clicking on the Undo command on the Menu bar (inset). Even if you've made several changes, you'll have the option of undoing them all.

Microsoft® Word

Bullet point lists

Word's bullet points are a simple and effective way of giving clarity and an extra professional punch to ideas and lists. Here's how to use them.

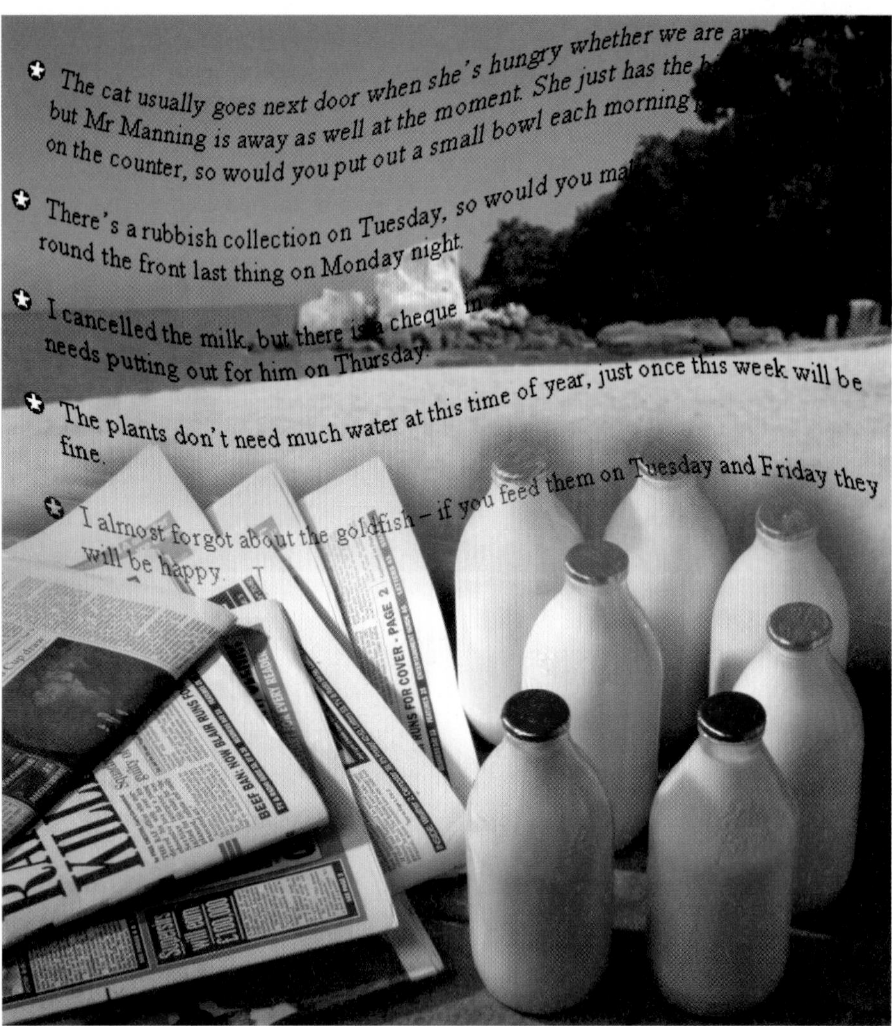

The cat usually goes next door when she's hungry whether we are
but Mr Manning is away as well at the moment. She just has the
on the counter, so would you put out a small bowl each morning
There's a rubbish collection on Tuesday, so would you
round the front last thing on Monday night.
I cancelled the milk, but there is a cheque
needs putting out for him on Thursday.
The plants don't need much water at this time of year, just once this week will be fine.
I almost forgot about the goldfish – if you feed them on Tuesday and Friday they will be happy.

A bullet point is simply a small shape – typically a dot like this ● – that you use to highlight items in a list. With a bullet indicating the beginning of each item, you can see at a glance how many points there are in the list and where each begins.

Bullets stand out much more clearly than standard keyboard characters, such as dashes, and look much more elegant than underlining. Bullet points are emphatic and help ensure that an important list doesn't get lost in a long letter or document. It is no coincidence that bullet point lists are frequently used in all types of important business documents. You can use them to give extra punch and emphasis when listing important factors in many and various kinds of home documents, from key points in school essays to lists of tasks you want someone looking after your house to do.

● Bullet styles

Bullets are usually just large black dots, but you can choose from a whole range of different sizes, shapes and colours (ours, for example, are red). If you want to make your letters and documents look truly unique, you can even make your very own style of bullet points. A standard feature of Word is that you can insert numbered lines instead of bullet points. These numbered points will help when you want to refer back to them later on in the document.

Although you can add bullets as you go along (see Automatic Bullets, left), they are easy to add to a list you have already created. In most cases, you need only press a single button. Even with numbering, one command can number the entire list. Word will then automatically move on to the next number every time you press the [Enter] key to add a new item. Even if you add a new item in the middle of the list, Word helps by automatically renumbering the rest of the list.

AUTOMATIC BULLETS

Word allows you to add bullet points to a list as you type it in. To do this, start a new line by typing an asterisk (*), a space and then the words for the first item in your list. As soon as you press the [Enter] key to start a new point, the asterisk will turn into a bullet.

Type the next item in your list and it will also be bulleted – you don't need to type the asterisk or the space. To stop the automatic bulleting – so you can start typing normal paragraphs of text – press the [Delete] key at the start of a new line.

Making a bullet point list

In this step-by-step example, we show you how to add various styles of bullet to a list of tasks for someone who's looking after the house while you're away on holiday.

1 First type in a sample document. We have created a letter that includes a list of pointers for a friend who is looking after someone's house. There's also a short introduction to the letter, which doesn't need bullets.

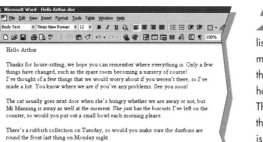

2 To add the bullets, first select the text of your list. Do this by moving your mouse pointer to the left of the first line and clicking and holding down the left button. Then move the cursor over the whole list until all the text is highlighted.

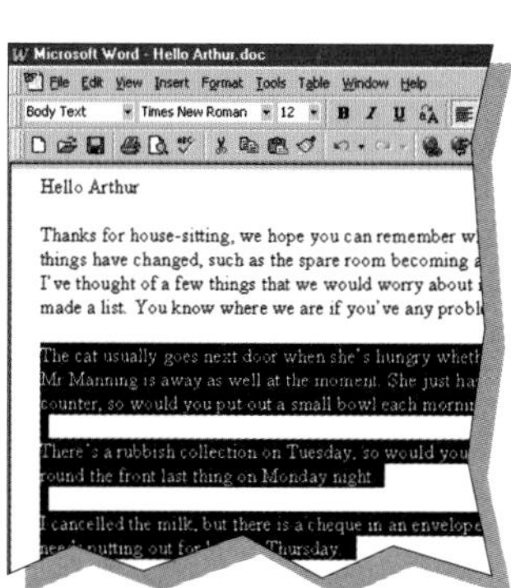

3 Press the Bullets button on the Formatting toolbar. A standard bullet appears at the start of each paragraph and the text moves over to fit it in.

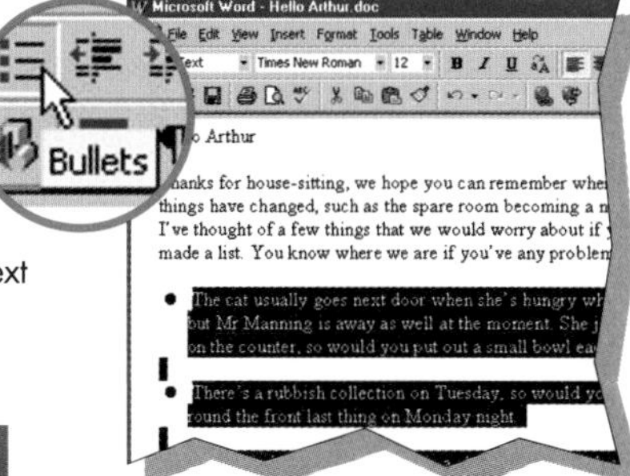

4 You can easily change the appearance of the bullet points. Click on the Format menu and select the Bullets and Numbering command from the drop-down list.

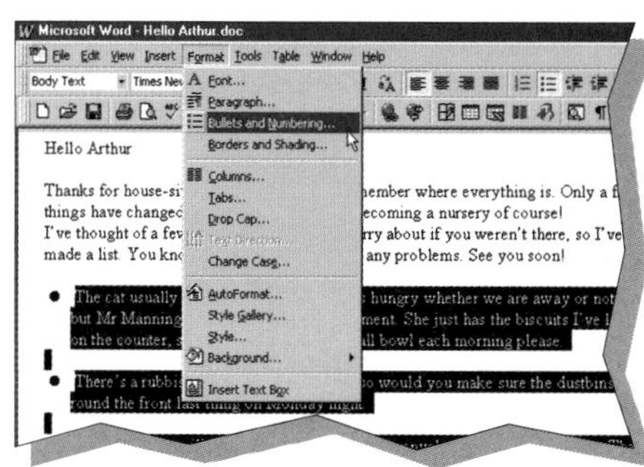

PC TIPS

Removing bullets from a list is as easy as adding them. First, select the bulleted text (as shown in step 2), then press the Bullets button on the toolbar once more. The bullets will disappear from the list of items and your text will look normal once again.

5 Click on the picture of the particular style of bullet you want to use and press OK. For this exercise, though, press the Customize button.

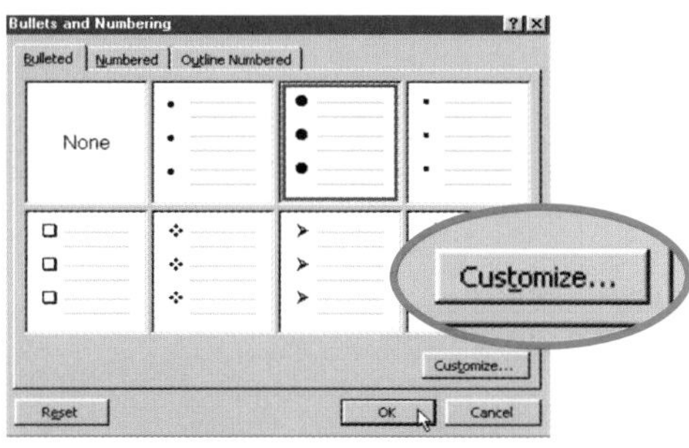

6 The Customize Bulleted List dialog box pops up. Click on the Font button on the left.

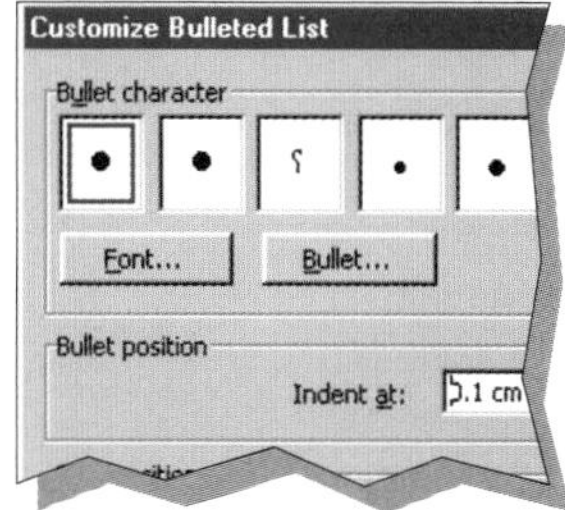

7 You can choose any character from any of the typefaces on your PC. Here, though, select Wingdings and press OK.

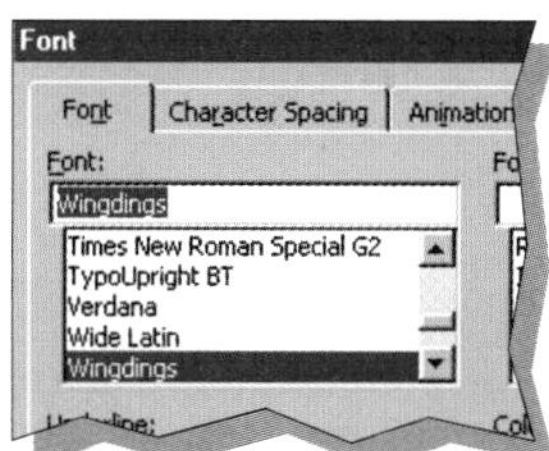

8 As you can see, there is a huge range of symbols in Wingdings. Click on any of the shapes that takes your fancy – we've chosen a circle with a star in it. Then click OK to make that shape into your standard bullet point.

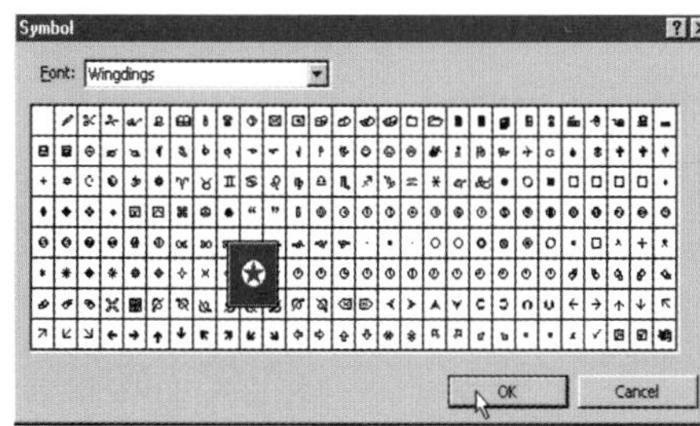

9 Before returning to your letter, you can also specify the amount of space used between the side of the page, the bullets and the text. To increase or decrease the space, use the two small arrow buttons next to the numbers at the bottom of the dialog box.

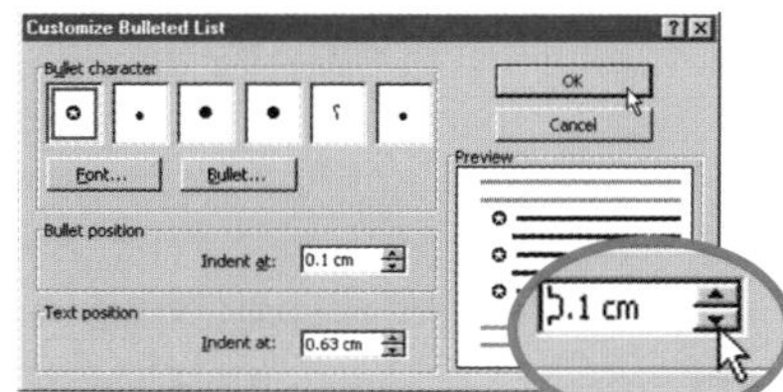

10 Press the OK button on each dialog box to see your custom bullet points in place in the text.

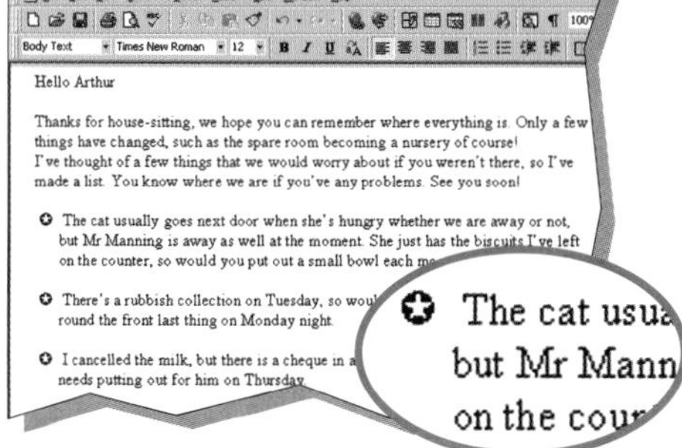

Styles made easy

Word's formatting tools are great, but changing typefaces, type sizes and adding bold and underlining can quickly become a chore – especially on a long document. Use Word's styles to make changes quickly and easily.

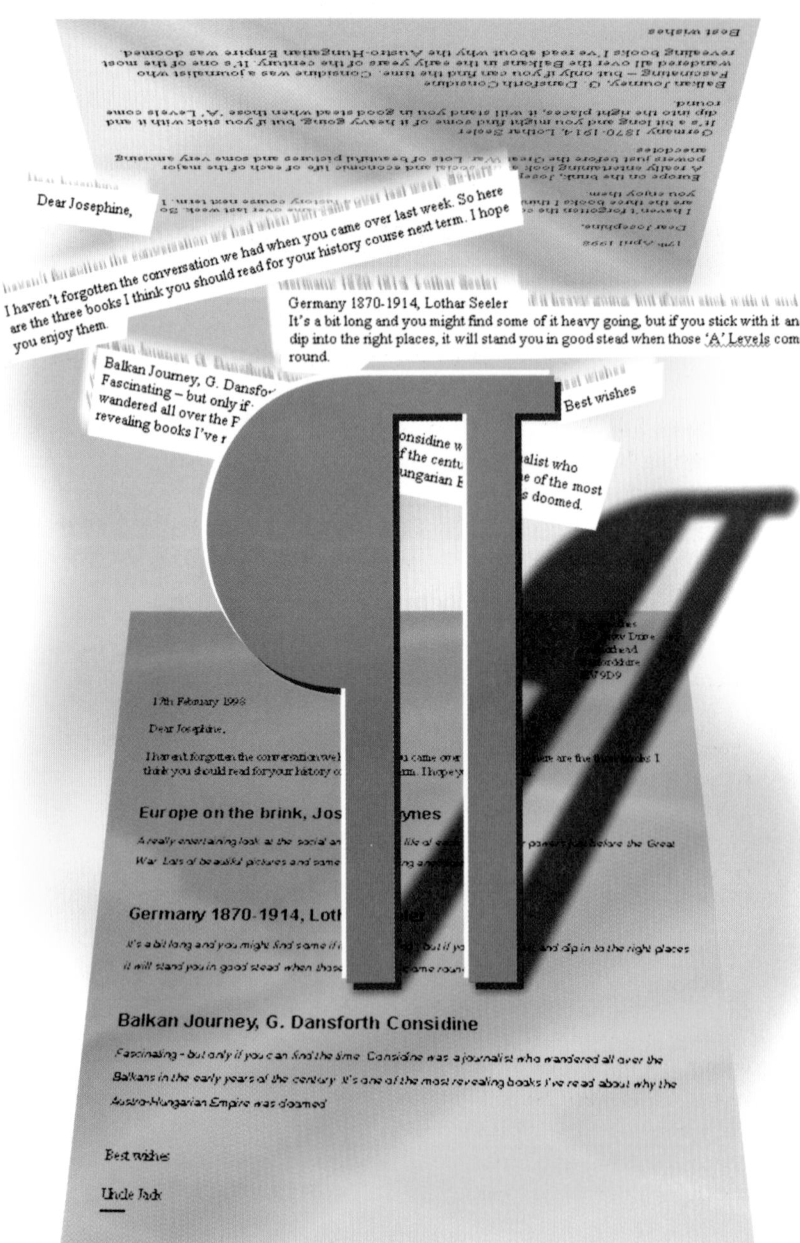

Styles determine the look of text, main headings and sub-heads, as well as other parts of your document, such as list elements. You can set them up to look the way you want.

One of Word's best features is its huge variety of formatting commands. In previous exercises we've seen how selecting words and paragraphs in your letters and then clicking on Word's buttons and menus allows you to personalize your documents, making them easier to read by changing the type styles and formats (see Stage 1, pages 34–35 and 38–39).

Over time, you will find that you develop your favourite combinations of formatting options. For example, you might like the main text of formal letters to use the Times New Roman typeface in 10 point, with one-and-a-half line spacing. You could use another typeface, size and spacing combination to make your name and address at the top of your letters look like a professional letterhead.

● The hard way

Although formatting text in Word is simple, applying these combinations quickly becomes repetitive, and the longer your document is, the more likely you are to make errors.

Imagine, for example, you wanted to change all the headings in your document. This could involve six different operations: you would have to select your text, convert it to your chosen typeface, change it to the required size, insert the desired space before each paragraph and then add bold and underlining. If you had to make each of these changes, it would take a lot of time and you might forget to make all the changes to all the headings.

● The easy way

Fortunately, Word provides a better way to make these frequent formatting changes. By using a feature called styles, you can make all these changes with one click of the mouse. At a stroke this feature cuts out the tedious, repetitive work, so you need never worry about inconsistency in your documents because you forgot, for example, to add bold to some of the headings.

Word has a range of ready-made styles that are easy to use. By default, all documents you create are in the Normal style: 10 point Times New Roman with no extra formatting. To change the text style in your document, select it with the mouse, click on the drop-down list of styles at the far left of the Formatting

PC TIPS

Although styles are usually applied to paragraphs, you can apply them to single words and phrases. For instance, if you highlight a word and a style, Word will apply it to that word only, instead of the whole paragraph. If you don't highlight any text, Word applies the style to the paragraph that contains the text insertion point.

toolbar and click on any of the options listed. Each style has a name, and the formatting commands it combines are shown in preview form so you can see what your text will look like before you make any changes. This takes the guesswork out of choosing styles.

● Your own style

Word's built-in styles are fine, but if you find them unappealing or too restrictive, you can make your own, give them a name and they will appear in the drop-down list of styles along with the other typefaces.

Word remembers the styles you created so the next time you start up your computer and open a document, your own styles will still be there, along with the others. This is useful if you create lots of similar letters. By using styles, you remove the risk of inconsistencies creeping into a series of letters or documents.

Using Word's ready-made styles

Word has a set of styles that you can apply to any of the documents you create. With just a few clicks, you can dramatically change the look of your letters in seconds.

1 Here's a simple one-page letter containing a short list of three books. To draw attention to them, we want to treat the titles and authors as headings. We'll format them so they stand out more. We could select each heading and then click on several of Word's individual formatting buttons, such as Bold. However, to make several changes at once, we'll use Word's styles. First, put the text insertion point anywhere in the first heading.

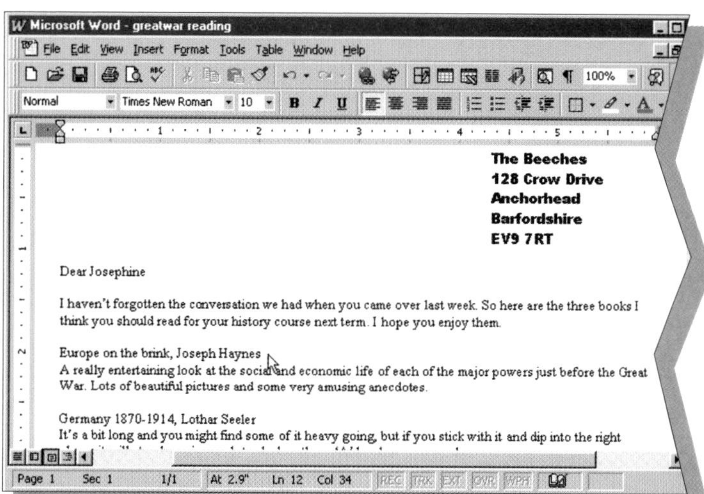

2 Locate the styles drop-down list on the left of the Formatting toolbar. Click once on the downward-pointing arrowhead to see the range of styles available.

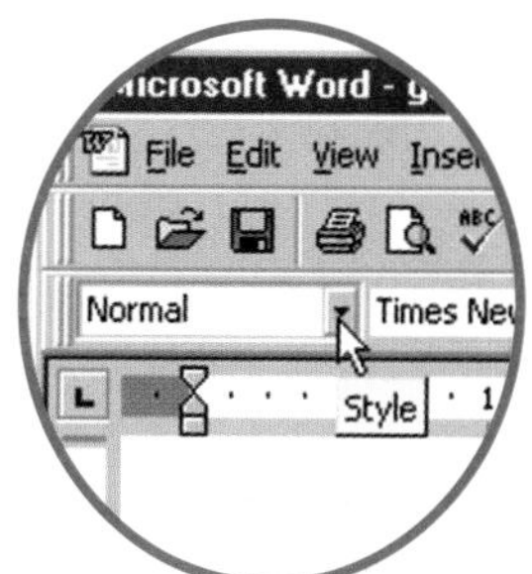

3 Word conveniently shows the styles in preview form, so choosing a new look for the heading in your document is as simple as choosing the most appropriate one from the list shown. The small box of information displayed next to the style name tells you useful information about the style, including how it is aligned (on the left in this case) and the size of the typeface (14 point in this example).

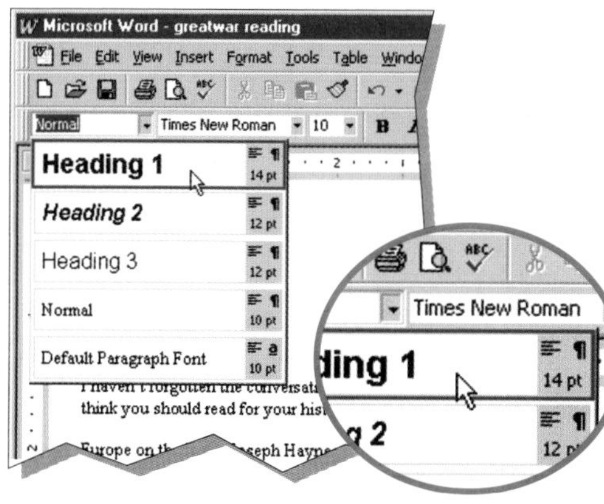

4 In this example, we'll use Heading 1 for the book title. This instantly improves the look and readability of the letter. It now becomes much more professional in its appearance.

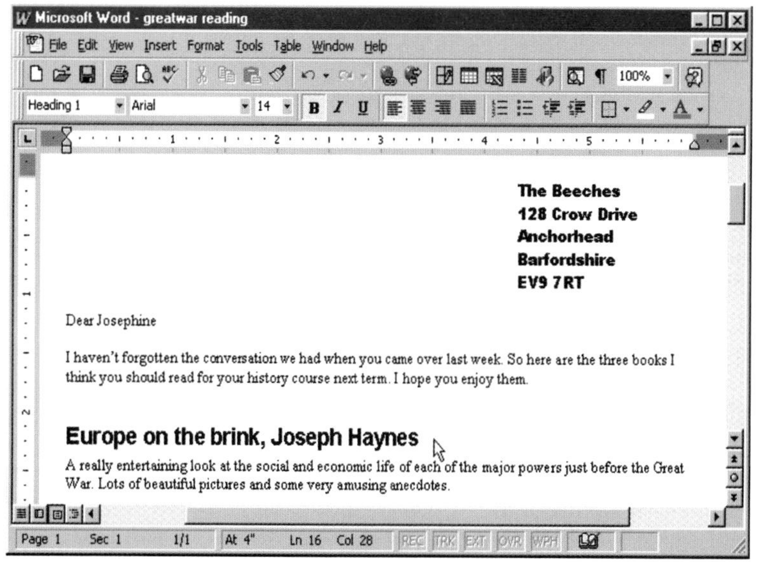

Creating your own styles

You might find Word's ready-made styles a little dull for some letters, but you can very easily create your own. Here's how to give your documents a personal look.

1 Creating your own style is as easy as telling Word what combination of formatting you want and giving it a name. Start by selecting Style from the Format menu.

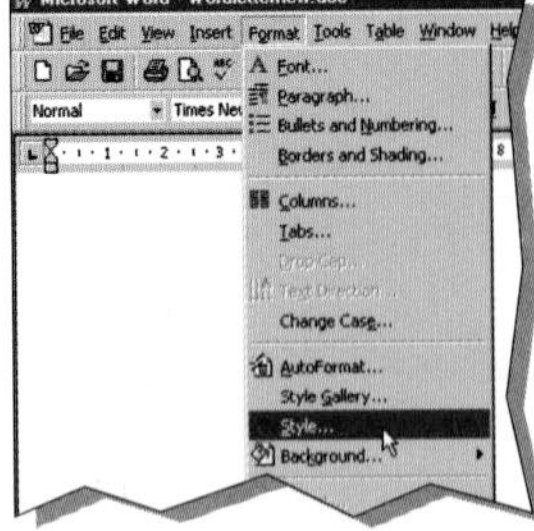

2 The Style dialog box appears. Initially, there are only a few styles listed. Click on the New button to access the New Style dialog box.

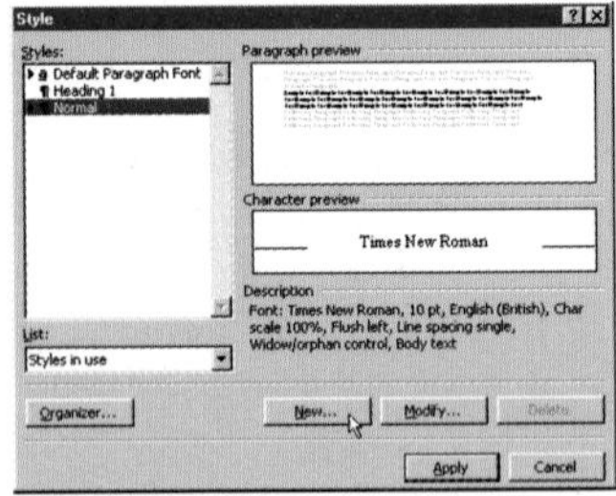

3 Type a name for your style. We've chosen 'My text style'. Leave the other options as they are and press the Format button. A list of options will appear: choose Font to start specifying the appearance of the text in your style.

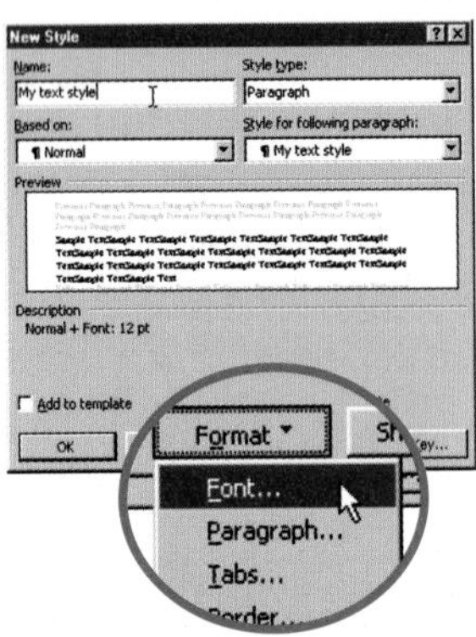

4 This is the usual Word Font dialog box. We've chosen Bookman Old Style in 10 point size for our text. Once you've made your choices, press the OK button to return to the New Style dialog box.

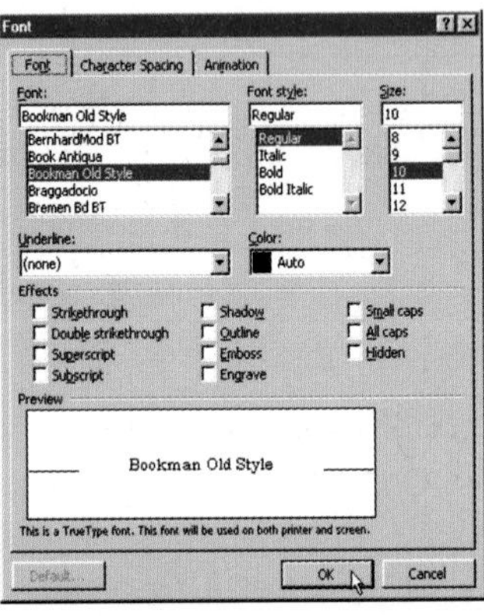

5 Click on the Format button again, but this time select the Paragraph option from the drop-down list.

6 This is the standard Paragraph dialog box (see pages 40–43). Here you can adjust the space between lines and the way text behaves when it reaches the end of a line. We've chosen a justified alignment, a 1.27cm (1/2 in) indentation for the first line of each paragraph, line spacing of 13 points and a space of 6 points before each paragraph. Choose your options and then press OK.

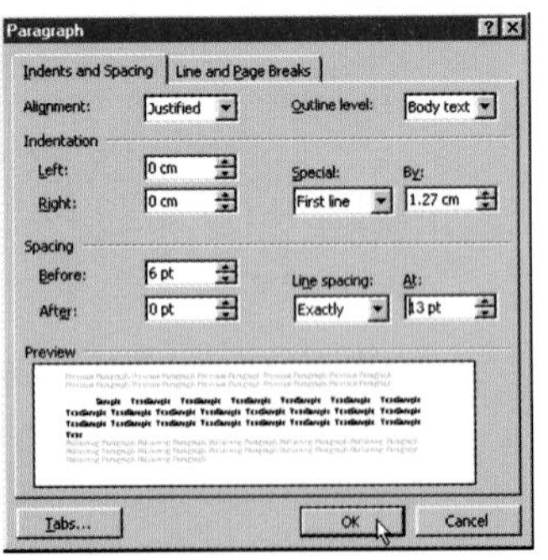

7 When you return to the New Style dialog box, you will see the elements of your style listed in the Description section; the combined effects are also shown in the Preview. Press the OK button.

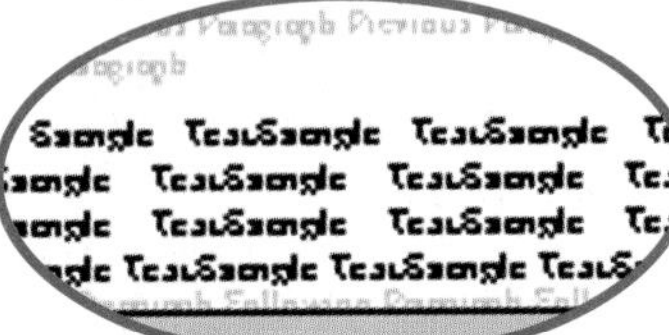

8 The Style dialog box now lists your new style in the list on the left. To start using the new style in your document, you only need to press the Close button.

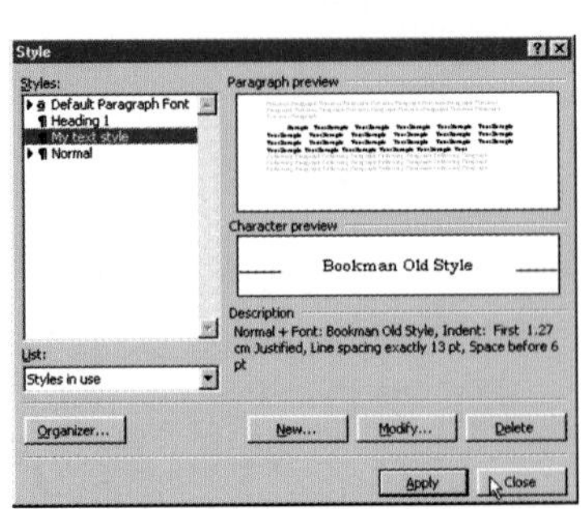

9 Applying the new style to text is as simple as using one of Word's built-in styles. Type in some text. Place the text insertion point in the paragraph and select My text style from the drop-down list of styles (inset). The instant result is shown far right.

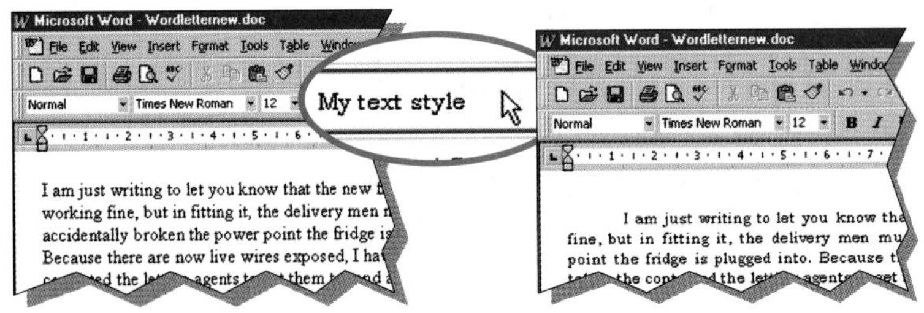

STYLES FROM TEXT

If you already have a document containing text that you have formatted by hand – using Word's individual format commands – you can quickly create styles straight from the text. Open the document and place the text insertion point in the text that has already been formatted. Select Style from the Format menu and then press the New button (as in step 2). You will see that Word has picked up all the details of your formatted text.

You need only give this combination a name and press the OK button. The new style will now appear in your list of styles.

Getting more from styles

Here are some useful techniques for getting the most out of your text styles.

PC TIPS

It's possible to add as many new styles as you like, but you might find that the drop-down list gets very long. You can avoid this problem by adding styles to a different template.

For example, you can create a 'funletter.dot' template which contains wild and jazzy styles, or a 'formalletter.dot' with more sober styles for business letters.

Choose the right template when you choose New from the File menu and you won't have to wade through lots of irrelevant styles.

WORD'S STYLES are powerful tools to help minimize the time and effort you spend making your documents look good, leaving you free to concentrate on the actual words of your document. To really get the most out of Word's styles, there are a few options that are worth trying. First, if you want your style to be available in all your documents, tick the Add to template option before you press the OK button on the New Style dialog box.

You might find that you want to change a style you've already created – perhaps because you've just added a new typeface that you want to use. Use the Modify button on the Style dialog box and you can then change any aspect you want.

You can also add special keyboard shortcuts (see below) to be able to format your documents even more quickly.

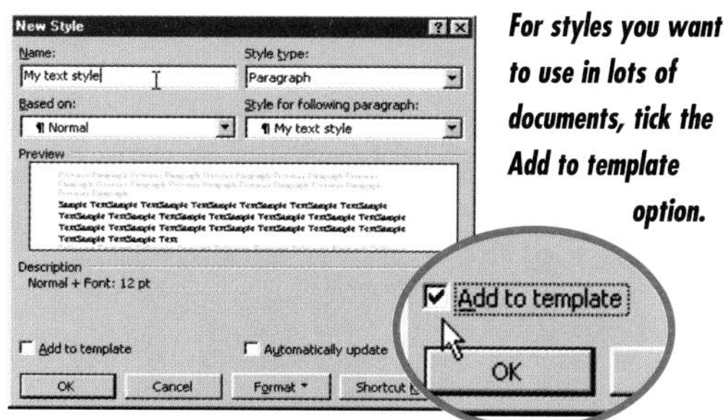

For styles you want to use in lots of documents, tick the Add to template option.

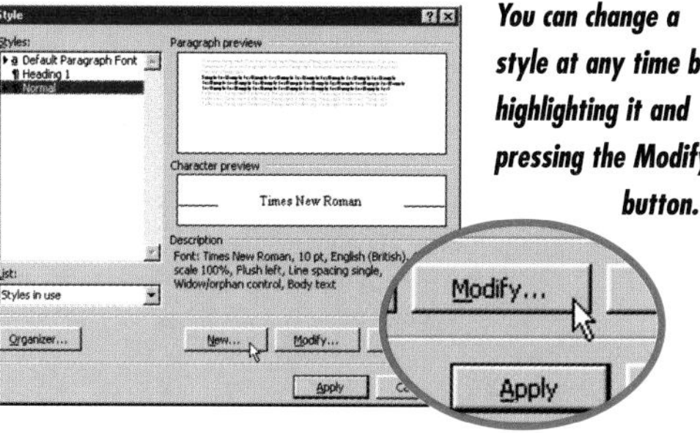

You can change a style at any time by highlighting it and pressing the Modify button.

Assigning styles from the keyboard

Once you have created your favourite styles, you can use them to greater effect by assigning them a keyboard shortcut of their own. Here's how to do it.

1 When creating a new style (or modifying an existing style), press the Shortcut Key button.

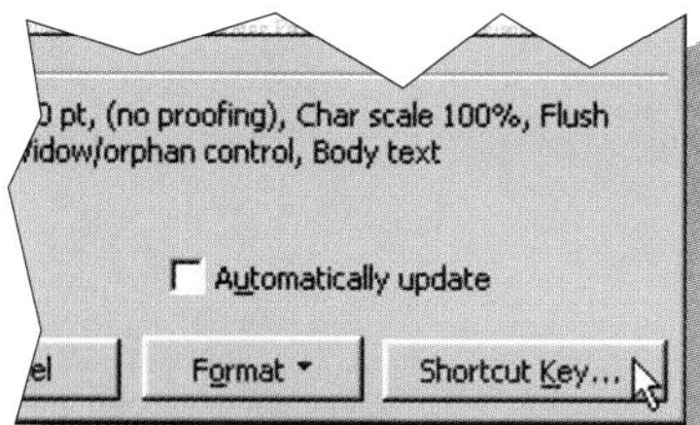

2 The Customize Keyboard dialog box pops up. You can see the style you are working on (here, it is the My text style we created on the opposite page). The cursor is flashing in the Press new shortcut key text box.

We need to find a keyboard shortcut that isn't already being used. For example, Word uses [Ctrl]+[C] as a shortcut for selecting the Copy option from the Edit menu.

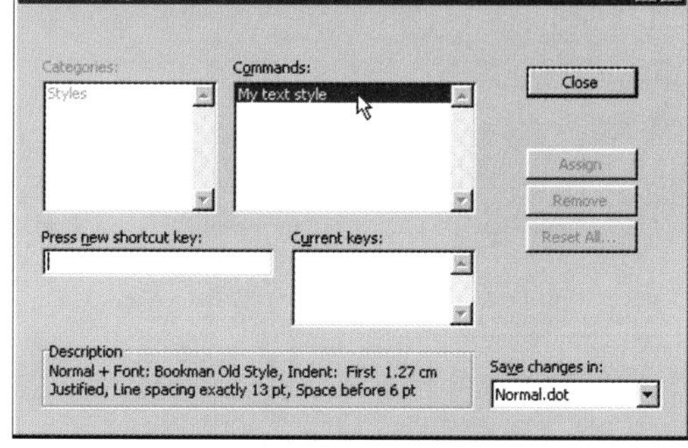

3 Try pressing [Ctrl]+[C]: the shortcut appears but Word tells you that this is already assigned. Press the [Backspace] key until the text box is empty again.

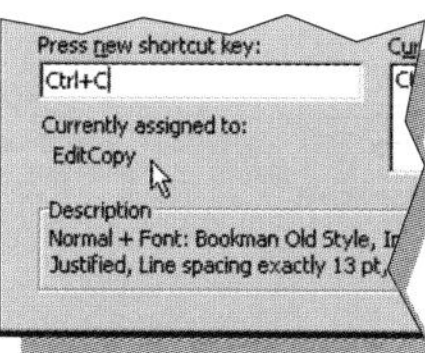

4 Try pressing [Ctrl]+[Shift]+[1]. Word interprets this as [Ctrl]+[!] and tells us that this keyboard shortcut is not taken, so you can press the Assign button.

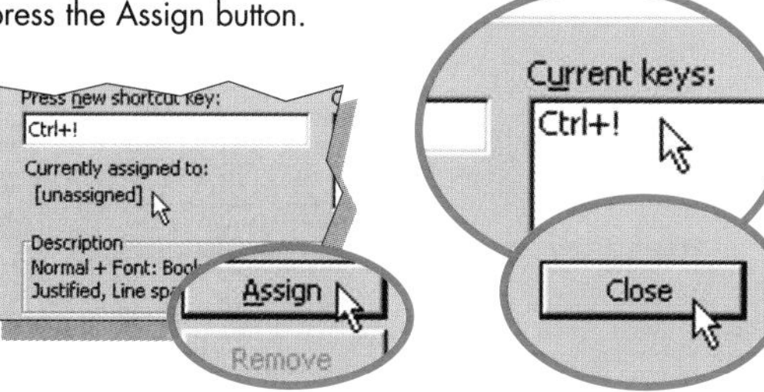

5 You will see your new keyboard shortcut listed in the Current keys text box. Press the Close button.

6 Press the OK button on the New Style dialog box and return to your document. Now, place the text insertion point in a paragraph of text and press the [Ctrl]+[Shift]+[1] keyboard shortcut. You will see the paragraph immediately change to the formatting contained in the My text style. If you're already typing, the new text that you key in will come out in the My text style until you select a new style.

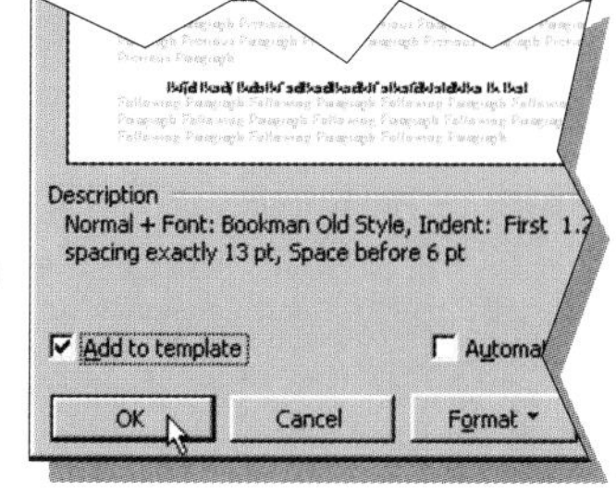

Basic typography

With so many fonts to choose from, a computer user can fall into the trap of making a page look confusing and difficult to read. However, you can avoid this by learning the basics of typography.

Typography – the art of choosing and using typefaces – has changed radically with the arrival of computers, modern word processors and desktop publishing. At least, its ease of use has changed. The laborious process of using individual metal blocks for each letter has been replaced by quick, clean and easy electronic processes. Today, you can change the size of all the text on your page with a keystroke. Previously, a small army of typesetters had to rebuild the whole page physically using thousands of letter blocks – a time-consuming and very expensive process.

● Swings and roundabouts

Such flexibility does have a slight downside as it's very easy to take typography for granted, ignoring (or being ignorant of) the principles that have been honed over generations. The result is often a page that would make a classically trained designer blush.

Not that design shouldn't be different and adventurous – far from it. However, a working knowledge of the occasions when it's appropriate to be different and adventurous and when it's not will help you to produce more effective and legible pages.

So what are the basics of typography? Well, for starters, the most obvious difference between fonts (typefaces) is that some are serif (which have tiny flourishes at the ends of each stroke of a letter) and some are sans serif (which don't have flourishes). You can see the flourishes very clearly on the big letter T in the first paragraph on this page; the heading is a sans serif font and has no flourishes at all.

● Serif or sans serif?

Serif fonts have an elegant, authoritative feel, partly because they have been around for so many years. Serif fonts are also easier to read, as the serifs create lines that hold the eye. They are thus well suited for smaller text, such as the main 'body' text in a letter, magazine or newspaper.

A sans serif font, however, imparts a sense of modernity and 'arty' fashionability. Sans serif fonts are harder to follow, so they are less commonly used for body text. When they are, the font tends to be a bit bigger and more widely spaced in order to make it easier to read. It will probably be part of a more 'airy' page, with lots of white space around other items on the page, too. As a result, the word count per page will be significantly lower than

Although it looks good for special effects, mixing and matching fonts is rarely a good idea – the page is unsettling to look at and words are not so easy to make out.

with a serif font. Again, sans serif fonts are well suited for arty publications, where the pictures and overall look matter most.

Headlines, logos and slogans, such as those found on advertisements, provide much greater freedom in font selection because they are larger and so legibility is less of an issue. However, the increased size of such 'display text' presents its own range of problems because small details become so much more obvious (see page 53). For very small amounts of text, such as in logos, designers may well create their own typeface, or customize an existing font, to create a unique look.

Read all about it

Owing to the varying suitability of fonts, many publications choose to mix and match, with sans serif display text and serif body text – the most obvious and influential example being *The Guardian* newspaper. Have a look at a front page and note the difference between the dense body copy and the spacious display text. Compare this with a more traditional newspaper, such as *The Daily Telegraph*, which is much 'busier' and tends to have a greater mixture of different items on each page. As a general rule, unless you have a specific reason to do otherwise, try not to include more than two fonts on a single page. Less, in this case, is definitely more.

Styles within styles

There seem to be countless different fonts, and their variety can be daunting at first. However, classic typefaces fall into only a handful of categories, which have developed in the 500 or so years since the invention of the printing press.

Each style can have several different examples and these may be further subdivided into different weights (bold, extra bold, or 'black'), or different widths (narrow or condensed and expanded), but the same general rules apply. There are also various specialist fonts, such as the script-style Embassy (used for wedding invitations, for example), typewriter-style fonts, such as Courier (which was particularly trendy at the end of the 1990s), plus a host of weird and wonderful one-offs. The box below will give you some pointers for effective font usage.

Know your fonts

Here we introduce you to some of the fonts that have become popular since the invention of the printing press.

BEING PRESENTED with a font list for the first time can be daunting as there are so many typefaces. However, most classic fonts fall into a handful of categories or are just variations on other fonts.

Fonts have developed over time, as improved printing techniques have allowed typefaces to become subtler and more precise. The oldest (actually called Old Style) tend not to have much difference between thick and thin strokes and have quite rounded serifs – Garamond is a good example. Such fonts gradually became more developed until they ended up with an appearance such as Bodoni, which is quite heavy and formal-looking and has major differences between the thick and thin strokes. It is also completely vertical with very straight serifs and no bracketing (i.e. curve) between the serif and the main part of the letter. You'd have to take a deep breath before you approached a page of Bodoni: it's more suited to formal publications and documents and only then, ideally, as display type.

Isabella

Garamond has rounded serifs and is a tasteful and classic font.

Sir John

Bodoni is a much more formal font, ideally suited to important official documents.

Bodoni was something of a natural typographical conclusion, after which type became more esoteric, deriving its influences from wider sources. This led to 'Egyptian-style' faces, with thick, slab-like serifs, less contrast between thick and thin strokes and generally a very simple appearance. A good example is Century. Its boldness makes it a good display type, and it is very popular for children's books because of its simplicity and legibility.

Harold

Century (Old Style) is great to use when clarity is needed.

Finally, there are the contemporary faces, such as Helvetica, the classic sans serif font, which only really came into its own in the 1960s. This is a very 'clean' design, that's readable in larger type sizes and has a very contemporary look and feel.

Mrs Smith

Helvetica is one of the simple sans serif fonts that seems to survive the vagaries of fashion.

The range of fonts supplied with Windows and Word is more than enough to get you started, but you might like to install others as you become more typographically aware.

Adding a drop capital

A 'drop cap' is a classic way of livening up text. Word automates the process, but you can tweak the effect manually for more satisfying results.

1 We'll start by adding a drop capital to the first paragraph in a newsletter. Type in some suitable text and turn the document into a multi-column format by using the Columns button on the Formatting toolbar (inset).

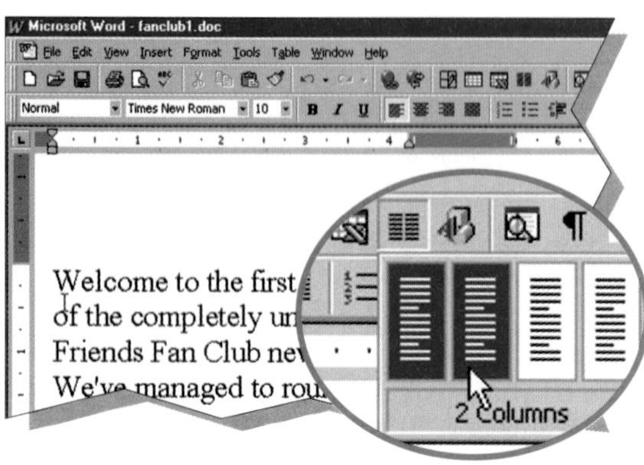

2 Click on the Format menu and select Drop Cap from the list of options.

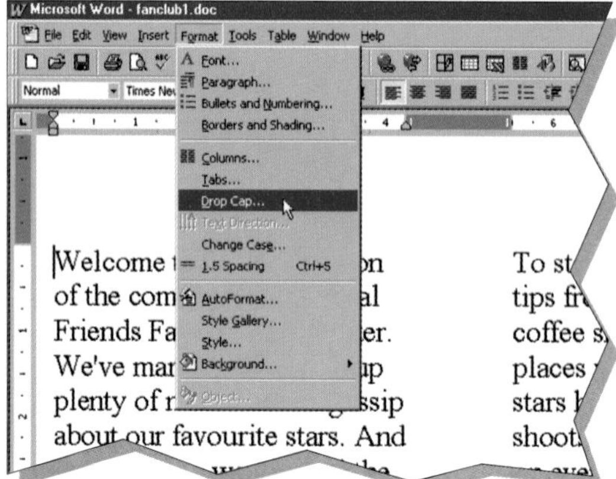

3 The Drop Cap dialog box will appear. The first of the small pictures will be selected, indicating normal text. Click on the middle picture (inset).

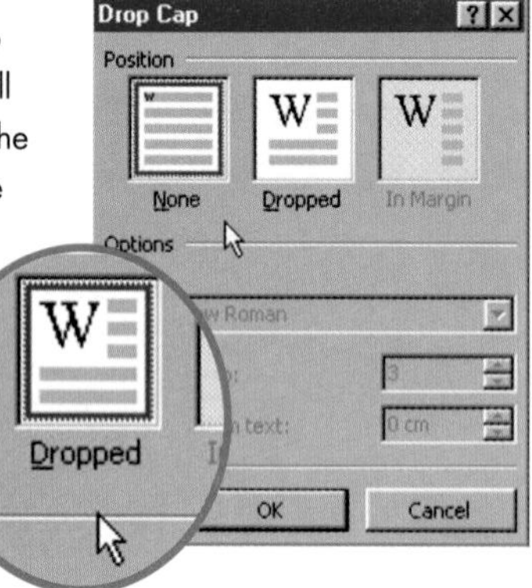

4 You'll see that the lower part of the dialog box, labelled Options, which was greyed out before, is now 'live'. Click on the drop-down list of fonts and select a different font. We've chosen Arial Black to provide a good contrast to the main text in the paragraph, which is still Times New Roman. Press the OK button.

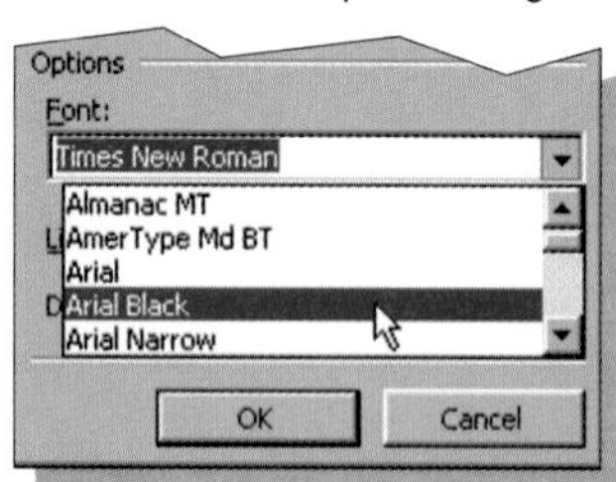

5 Word now inserts a ready-made text box that contains the first letter of the paragraph (which has also been automatically removed from the paragraph text itself). The rest of the paragraph text runs around the drop cap letter – just as in a newspaper or magazine story.

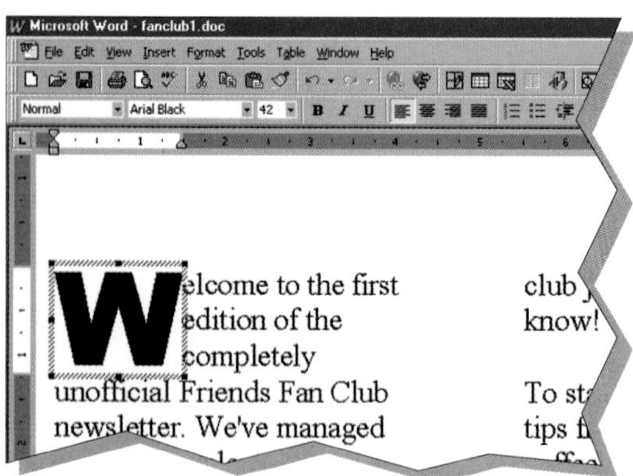

6 Now all you have to do is click anywhere else in the Word document to see what the paragraph looks like without the outline.

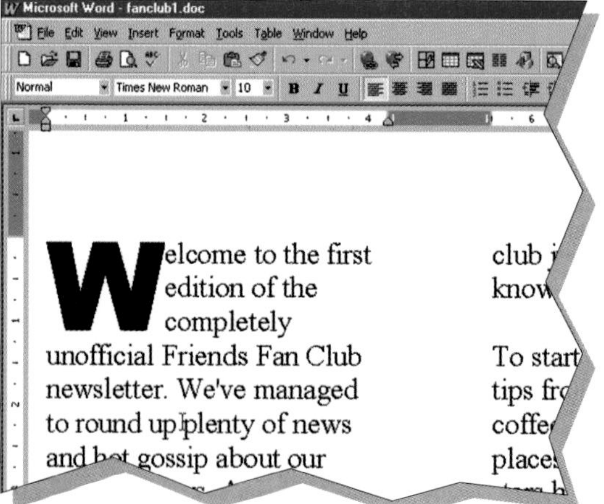

LEADING

This is the space between the lines of text. The term comes from the use of strips of lead used to make the space in old-style typesetting. It is more obviously called line spacing in Word.

The default used by Word specifies the gap in terms of lines but you can specify this in points to get more flexibility. Leading for body text is typically 15–20 per cent greater than the point size: 9 pt text would be leaded at 10.5–11 pt. In larger point sizes, this can look too gappy (as in the red example shown below), and you might want to set the leading in 'block' leading, which is the same value as the point size of the headline (as shown in the blue example).

Adjusting spacing on headline text

When you start to handle display type or headlines there are different things to consider than when you are using a smaller type size.

1 We've started with a single headline, changing the font size to 60 points so that it almost fills the page. We've also centred the headline and added some rules to make it stand out. However, there are some problems that appear when text is increased to such a size: there's a little too much space between most of the letters and there's far too much space between the 'W' and 'a', whereas the 'r' and 't' are almost touching.

2 Select all the text in the headline, using the mouse to highlight it, and then select the Font option from the Format menu.

3 The Font dialog box appears. Click on the Character Spacing tab to access the options that control the amount of space between the letters. You'll see your selected text at the bottom of the dialog box.

4 The second line of options in the dialog box is labelled Spacing. This lets you specify how much the text is squeezed together or pulled apart. Click on the small downward-pointing arrow head next to the By text box. The first time you click, you'll see the Spacing text box change to read Condensed, and the By text box will read 0.1 pt. Keep pressing the arrow head until it reads 1 pt. Then press the OK button.

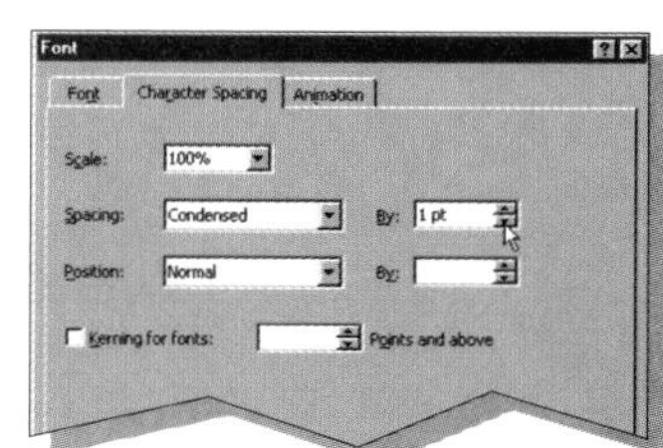

WHAT IT MEANS

KERNING

Sometimes the default values for the gaps between the characters of a font are too large or (more rarely) too small. When you tighten or loosen these gaps by the same value across a body of text it is called tracking.

However, there are some occasions when the problem exists only between a couple of letters: common examples include AT, AV, Te, Yo and LY, to name just a few. This can be adjusted when you alter the gap between just two letters. This is called kerning.

5 You'll see your headline is now a little tighter, although there's still too much space between the 'W' and the 'a'. Select the 'W' on its own.

6 Bring up the Character Spacing tab of the Font dialog box again. This time, type a larger figure directly into the By text box. Here we have put 8 pt. Then press the OK button.

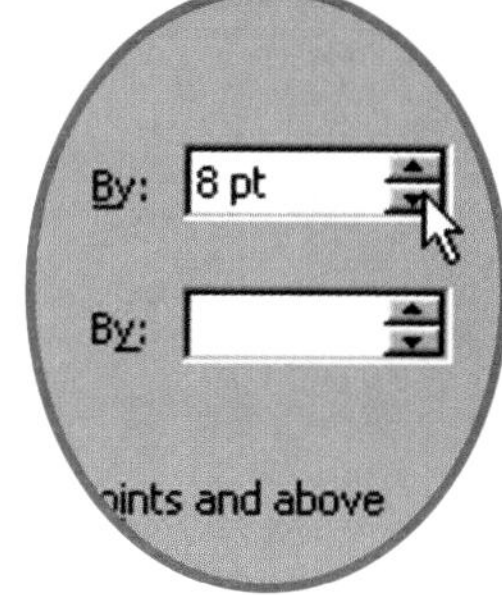

7 You'll now see that the first two letters of the headline look much better and the 'W' no longer appears to be a separate entity.

8 Look more closely at the rest of the letter spacing and repeat the exercise where necessary. For example, to make sure the 'r' and the 't' don't touch in our example, we expanded the spacing by 2 pt.

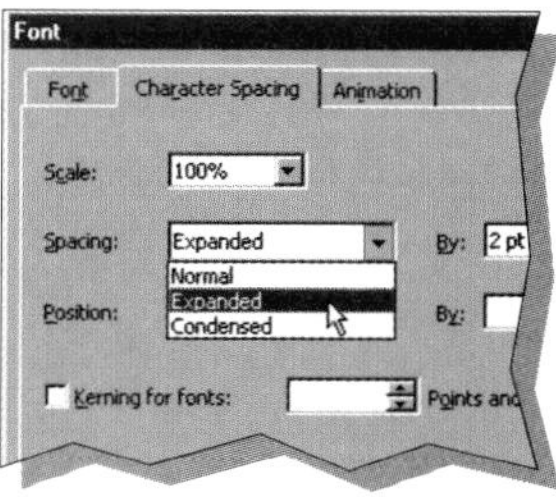

9 Once you've been through the headline, you'll have a design that looks a lot better than the original way Word displayed the text. You need only do this trial-and-error spacing for large text sizes and, with a little practice, you'll soon find it easy to get rid of unsightly gaps.

Copying and pasting cell contents

It's essential to be able to copy and paste information in Windows programs. Here we show you how easy it is to use this technique to transfer text and numbers between cells in Excel.

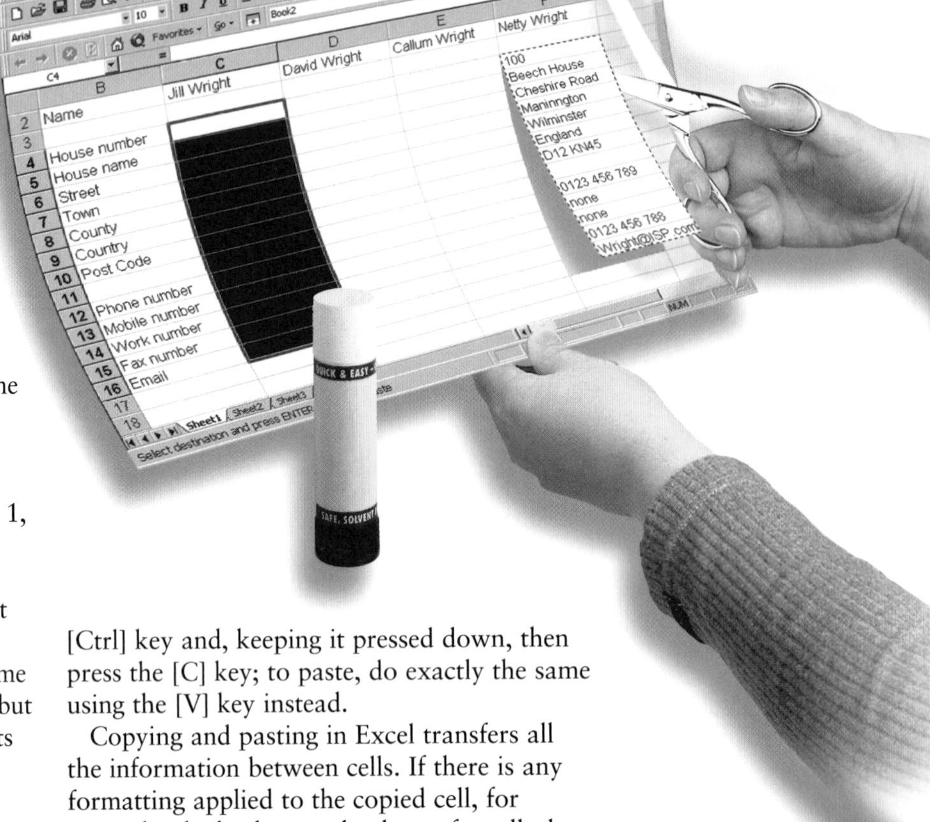

Techniques that allow you to cut and copy text or numbers from one place and paste them somewhere else are extremely useful. We've seen how you can save time by cutting, copying and pasting text in Word (see Stage 1, pages 16–17) and parts of pictures in Paint (see Stage 1, pages 72–73), and the same techniques can be used in Excel to paste text and numbers between spreadsheet cells.

Copying and pasting in Excel can be as time saving as it is in other Windows programs, but it also has the added bonus that spreadsheets often contain numerical data, which is essential to move accurately. You can't be certain of avoiding mistakes if you retype data in cells, but copying and pasting – when done correctly – is always accurate.

● Select the cell

The first step of a copy and paste operation is to select the cell whose contents you wish to copy. To do this, click on the cell and a thick black rectangle will appear around it. Next, copy the cell's contents by going to the Edit menu and choosing the Copy option.

Now you need to select the cell where you want to paste the information. You select this cell by using the same technique as you used to select the first cell – click on it. Finally, paste the information by going to the Edit menu and choosing the Paste option.

There are keyboard shortcuts for the copy and paste operations. To copy, press the [Ctrl] key and, keeping it pressed down, then press the [C] key; to paste, do exactly the same using the [V] key instead.

Copying and pasting in Excel transfers all the information between cells. If there is any formatting applied to the copied cell, for example, the background colour of a cell, the colour of text or numbers and their typeface and size, it will also be transferred to the cell where you paste.

PC TIPS

Filling adjacent cells

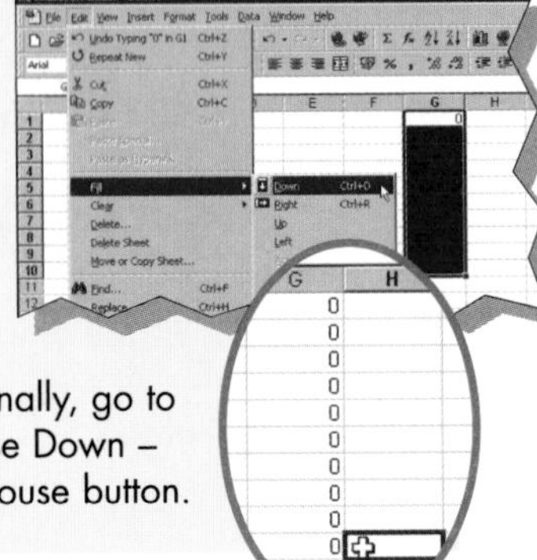

You may need a quick way of filling a row or column of cells with the same data. Here's how to do it using the Edit menu's Fill option. Imagine that you want to put zeroes in 10 adjacent cells in a column. First, select the top cell, type a zero into it and press [Enter]. Now click on this cell again to select it and drag the pointer down to select the nine cells below it. Finally, go to the Edit menu, click on the Fill option and choose Down – the cells fill with zeroes when you release the mouse button.

Copying and pasting addresses

The advantage of copying and pasting the contents of cells in Excel is that all the other information – formatting and formulae – are copied as well as words and numbers.

1 In this example, we've started work on a new Excel spreadsheet to use as an address book. We've already included Mr Bunn the baker and now we're adding Granny Bunn, who lives at the same address. To save the effort of typing the address again, we'll just copy and paste it.

2 We want to copy Mr Bunn's address, so select the cell that contains the address by clicking on it. Notice how a thick black border appears around this cell to remind you that it is the currently selected cell. You can also see that its contents are shown in the Formula bar.

3 The next step is to take a copy of Mr Bunn's address. To do this, you have to go to the Edit menu and select the Copy option. As with all other Windows programs, the keyboard shortcut in Excel for copying is to press the [Ctrl] key and, keeping it pressed down, press the [C] key.

4 As a reminder, Excel has now put a flashing dotted line around the cell that contains the address we've just copied. The next step is to select the cell into which we want to paste this address. Do this simply by clicking on the relevant cell (in this case, cell B10). The thick black border appears around this cell.

5 Now let's paste in the address. To do this, go to the Edit menu and select the Paste option. Don't forget that, as with other Windows programs, the keyboard shortcut in Excel for pasting is to press the [Ctrl] key and, with it pressed down, then the [V] key.

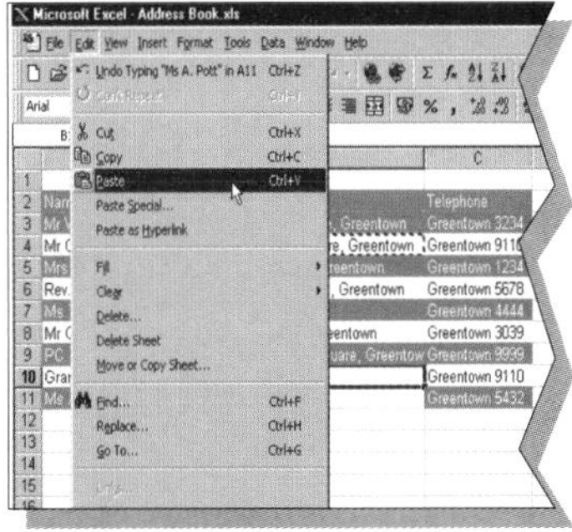

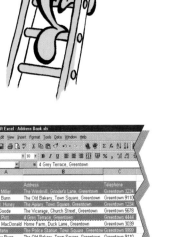

6 Now let's see what happens when we copy from a cell with a coloured background and different-coloured text. Click on the cell that contains Ms T. Pott's address (cell B7) and then press the [Ctrl] + [C] keys to copy this cell's contents.

7 Paste this address into cell B11 by selecting the cell and using the keyboard shortcut of pressing the [Ctrl] + [V] keys. Next, press the [Enter] key to dismiss the flashing dotted line from around cell B7. Notice how this has transferred the text and cell background colours as well as the actual words.

PC TIPS

Quick copy to adjacent cells

It's often the case that you want to copy some text or numbers to the next cell across or down. In Excel, there is a quicker way to do this than copying and pasting.

First, select the cell from which you want to copy. A thick black rectangle appears around it with a small black square at the bottom right corner. Position the mouse over this square, press and

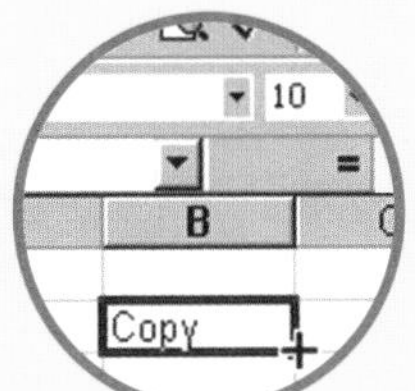

hold it down and you will notice that the cursor changes to a cross. Now, drag the cursor across until the next cell is selected and release the mouse button. The text or numeric contents of the cell will be copied onto the adjacent cell.

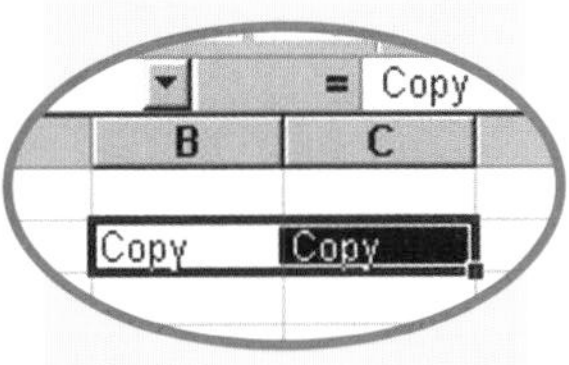

Printing spreadsheets

Once you've created a spreadsheet, you will usually want to print it out. But what if it has so many columns that it won't fit on the page? Don't worry, Excel has features that help you to produce printed spreadsheets – regardless of their width or length.

When it comes to printing, an Excel spreadsheet is a different kind of document to one created in a word processor, such as Microsoft Word. With Word, you can carry on typing as long as you wish. When you have filled up one page, the text carries on to the next, as in a book. The width of the text is usually set to fit on the printed page, although if you want to change the amount of text you can move the margins to make columns wider or narrower.

It's much the same when it comes to printing. Microsoft Word treats the document as a collection of pages, with left and right margins, and prints as many pages as are required for the length of the text. If you need to print wide columns of text, you can tell the word processor to print out in landscape format (sideways across the page), instead of the usual portrait format with the page upright.

Printing irregular documents

Spreadsheets in Excel are different, however, as an Excel worksheet can be both long and wide. It is easy to print a small worksheet that is only a few columns wide and not too many rows long, but it can quickly become too large to fit on a single page.

To overcome this, Excel divides the worksheet into sections that fit the paper in your printer and prints each section on a separate page. Alternatively, if you don't need the whole worksheet, you can print out the part you need on a single page.

To see how this works, let's look at a worksheet showing household expenditure (opposite), which you might want to print out to show to members of the family.

PC TIPS

Print Preview

Like Microsoft Word, Excel has a Print Preview option to let you see how your worksheet will print before you send it to the printer (see step 2, opposite). It's a particularly useful option in Excel, since sometimes you might want to print only a section of a larger worksheet.

Printing your chart

We saw how to enter data and create a pie chart in Stage 1 on pages 58-59. Here, we'll show you how to print out the chart so that it fits perfectly onto the page.

PC TIPS

Page breaks

When you have a large worksheet that won't fit onto one sheet of paper, Excel sets automatic page breaks so that it can be printed on several sheets. If you only need part of a worksheet to fit on one page, you can insert a manual page break to show Excel where you want to start printing.

Suppose you want to print from the part of the worksheet that

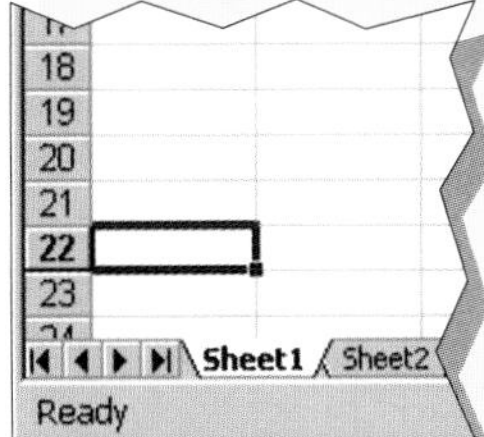

begins at cell A22. First, select cell A22 by clicking on it to highlight it, then click on the Insert menu. Select Page Break from the menu and a dotted line will appear above row 22 to indicate the start of the new page.

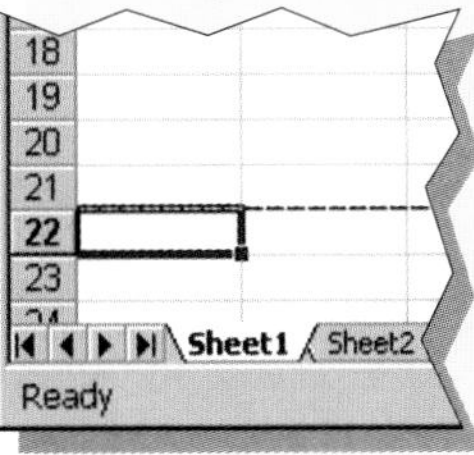

1 Type in some categories and numbers and use the Chart Wizard tool (see Stage 1, page 59) to create a 3D pie chart on the right of your worksheet. Drag the borders of the chart so that it's prominent on the right-hand side of the page.

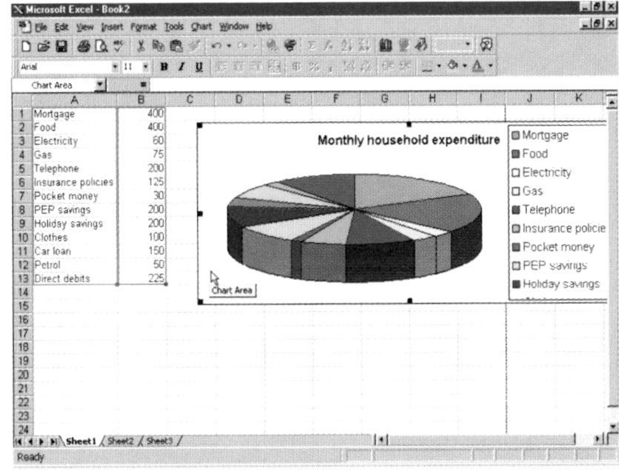

2 Click on the left-hand side of the page, where you have typed in the figures. Go to the File menu and select Print Preview. You will now see a view of how the worksheet would appear on an A4 page. Notice that the right-hand side of the chart is missing – it is too wide to fit across an A4 page in this upright (portrait) format. But it would fit if the paper was the other way round.

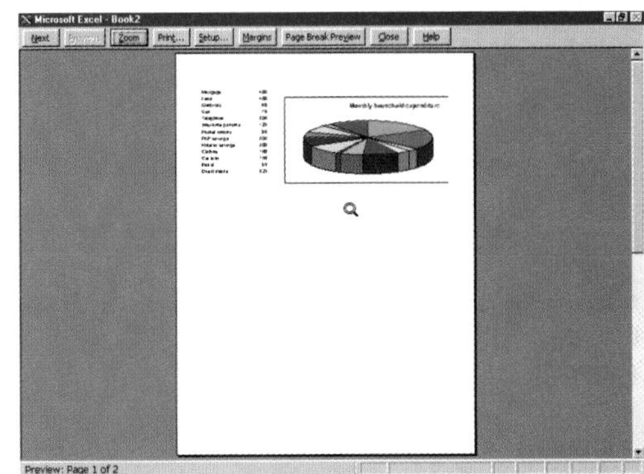

3 Click on the Close button on the toolbar above the page to close the Print Preview. Now click on Excel's File menu and select the Page Setup option. A dialog box will pop up to show you the settings that control how your Excel worksheet fits on the page.

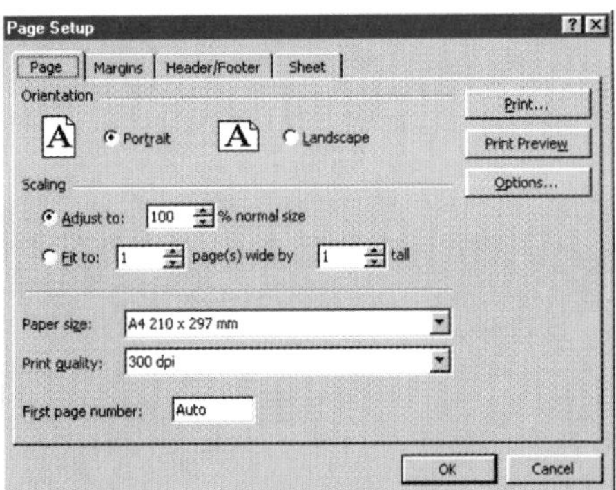

4 You will see that there are two options displayed at the top of the dialog box, under the heading Orientation. These control which way round the page will appear on the printed paper. The two small page icons (containing the letter A) on the left of each option show the difference between portrait and landscape orientation. Click on the Landscape option and press the OK button to return to the worksheet.

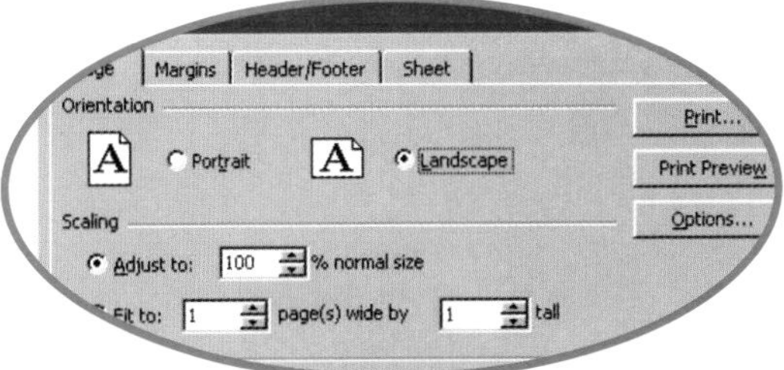

5 Now, when you select the Page Preview option from the File menu, you'll see how the worksheet fits on the page without being chopped off on the right-hand side. Of course, with landscape orientation, you get fewer lines on a page, but in this case that doesn't matter. If you can get into the habit of using Page Preview before you print your worksheets, you'll avoid wasting paper and time.

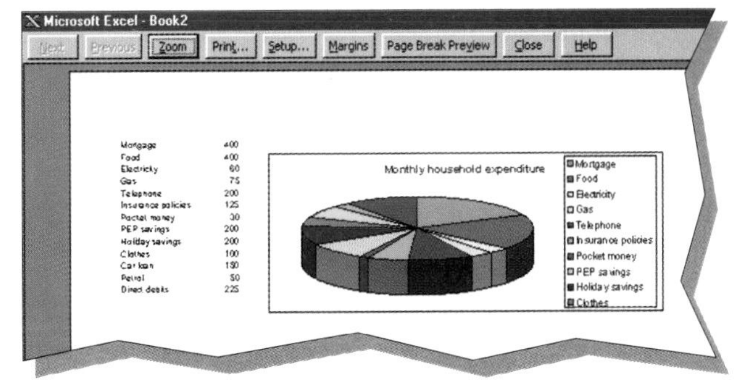

Adding or altering cells

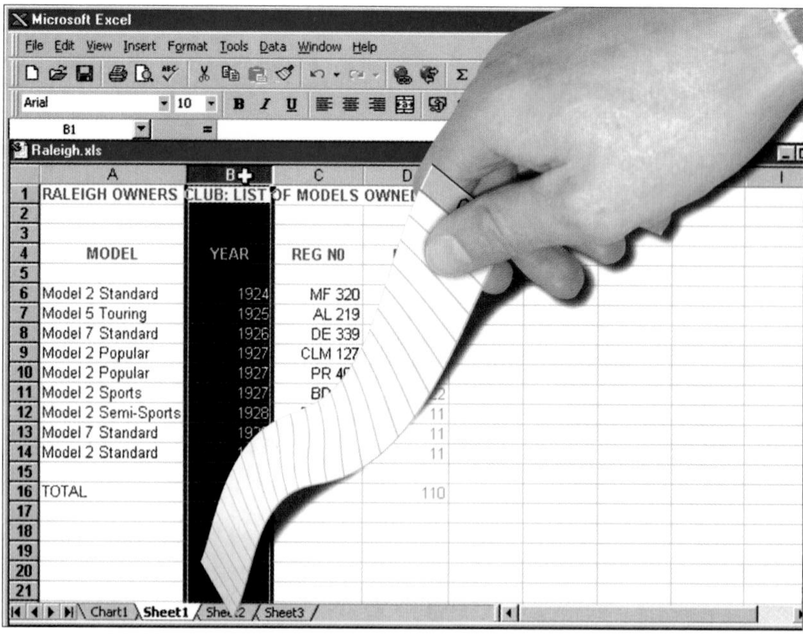

No matter how well you plan your spreadsheet before creating it, you will inevitably need to make alterations as you go along. Fortunately, Excel makes it easy to move data around or add information to the worksheet.

Once you have started to use your spreadsheet program, you might find that a better way of presenting the information comes to mind. Alternatively, you might come to realize that some of the information contained on the worksheet is unnecessary, while other figures or data need to be added.

When updating an existing worksheet, this will become even more apparent. For example, it is more than likely that the monthly household expenditure figures and categories needed for December will be very different to those required for April.

● Multiple changes

You can, of course, make changes to your worksheet at the level of individual cells. While this method is fine for small worksheets, it can be extremely laborious and time-consuming when you have a larger spreadsheet or when you want to make changes and improvements to a larger area. For example, if you are keeping lists of house contents and prices for insurance purposes, you will want to update the figures. However, for some uses you might also find that you need to incorporate additional elements in your worksheet in order to adapt to your changing needs. For example, if you are keeping a club list, you might discover that you need to add a completely new column to reflect an additional club activity, or a new row to cover a new member.

As we'll see in the step-by-step example opposite, Excel allows you to add to or delete from your spreadsheet quickly and effectively.

Drag and drop your cells

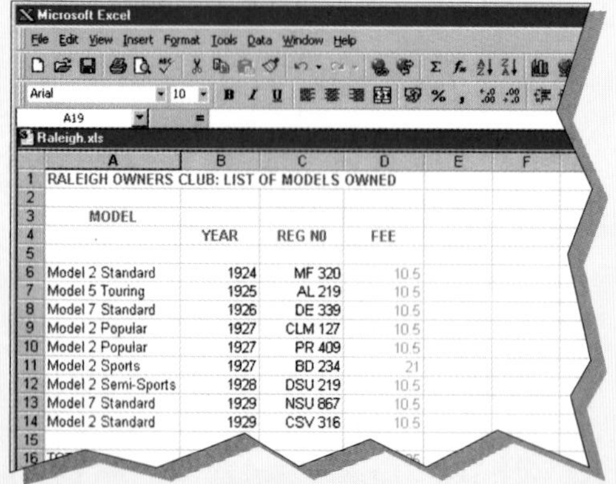

You can easily move an individual cell by using the mouse to drag and drop it. In the example above, the first category listed – 'Model' – is in the wrong row.

To move it to the correct position, click inside the cell to highlight it, then move the cursor to the edge of the cell. The normal cross-shaped cursor changes to an arrow pointer. Drag the cell down one position – you'll see the cell outline move – and drop the cell into place.

Updating your spreadsheet

In this step-by-step example, we use a cycle club membership spreadsheet to show how you can update information to accommodate changing circumstances.

IN THIS EXAMPLE, we have already given the worksheet some formatting by adding some different colours and centring the category headings in their various columns (see Stage 1, pages 56–57, for formatting details). Now we need to update some of the stored information. The first task is to record the receipts of an increased membership fee. After that, we need to add an entirely new column to the worksheet that will contain some additional information about the members. For this exercise, you can either type in the data shown in the example below, or use the same principles on a worksheet you've already created. They will apply equally well.

1 The club membership fees have increased, so we need to delete the old figures. Begin by moving the cursor over cell D6 and clicking inside it.

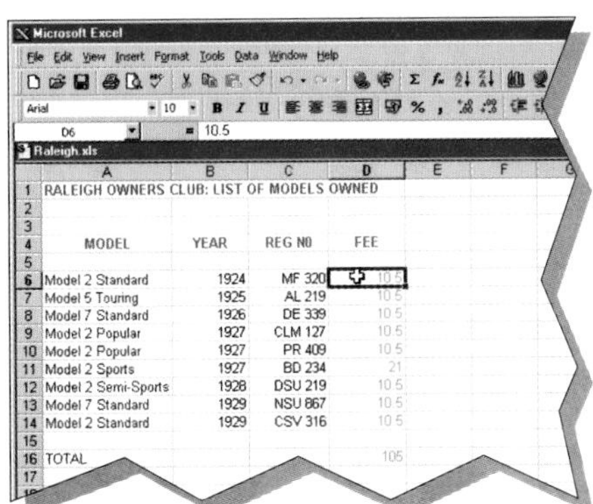

2 Holding down the left button, drag the mouse down to cell D14. The figures we want to delete will now be highlighted and appear as white on a black background.

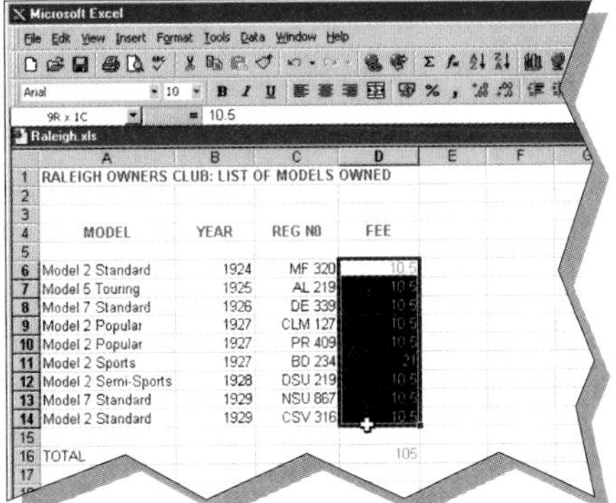

3 Press the [Delete] key (located on the keyboard to the right of [Enter]) to delete all the figures in the selected cells. The new membership figures can now be entered.

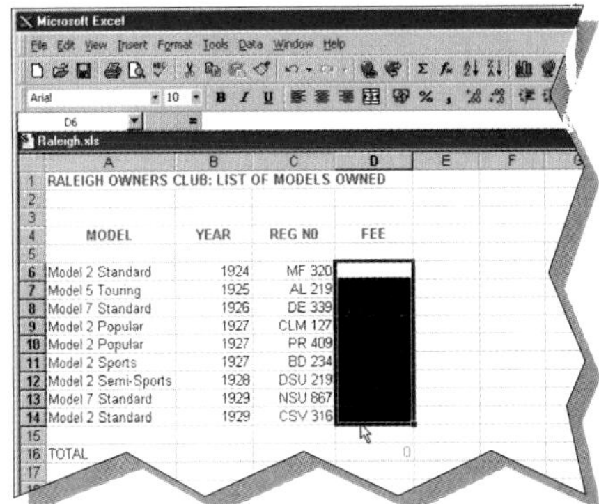

PC TIPS

Sometimes you will need to insert more than one column. For example, if you need two new columns between B and C, click on the column header to the right (C) and drag the mouse to highlight a second column (D). When you select Columns from the Insert menu, Excel will add the two new columns.

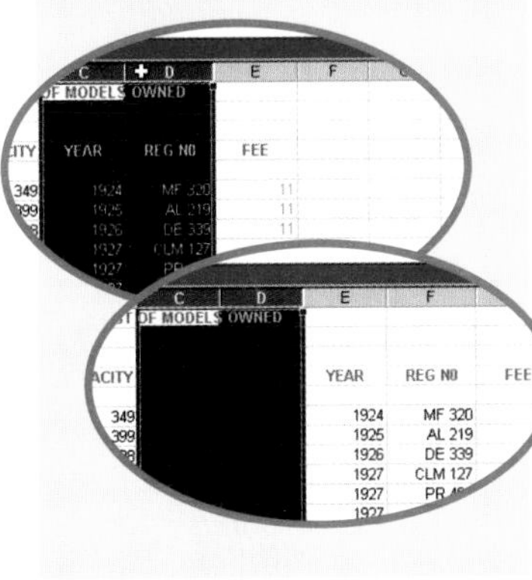

4 Now, imagine we want to include additional data, such as a column describing our members' bikes. To do this, we need to add a new column between existing columns A and B. Click on the header of the column that is to the right of where you want the new column (in this case, column B). The whole of column B is now highlighted. Click on the Insert menu and move the pointer down to highlight Columns.

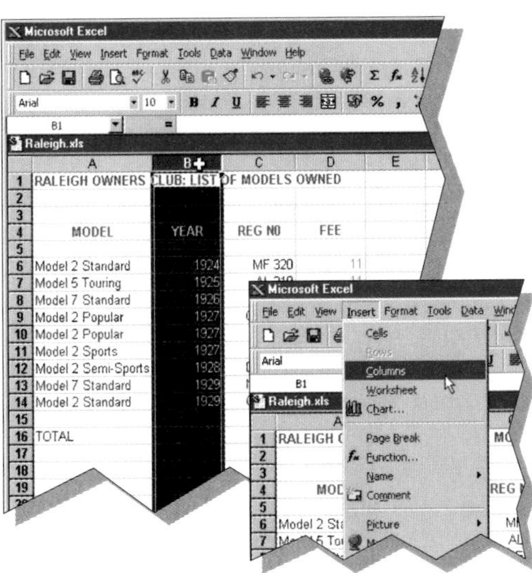

5 When you release the mouse button, Excel inserts a new blank column to the right of column A. The old column B moves to the right and is renamed column C. The new column B will be the same width as the column to its left (column A). We can make this narrower if we want (see Stage 1, pages 56–57) before typing in the new heading and data to complete the update.

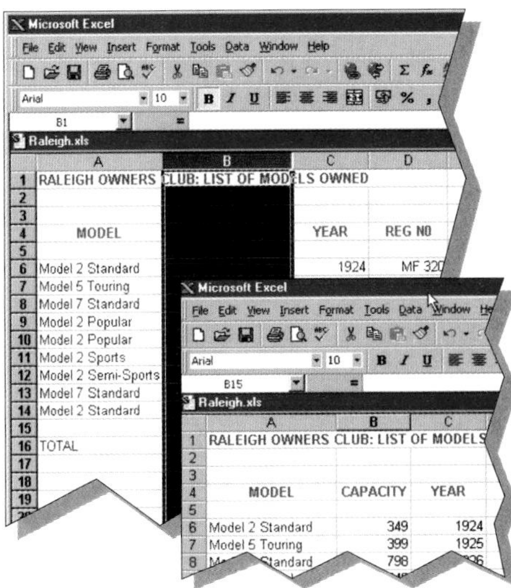

Quick calculations

Excel's formulae can be too time-consuming when you just want to work out a few figures. So here's the quick and easy way to get results with the AutoCalculate tool.

Back in Stage 1, we learnt to use Excel to type in data, perform calculations with that data and present the formulae and results in a spreadsheet. However, Excel is just as useful for those times when you want to make a quick, *ad hoc* calculation on a set of figures, such as working out an astronomy problem for homework. In fact, Excel's powerful features make it a much more flexible tool than using pen, paper and a calculator.

The secret of using Excel to do on-the-spot calculations is that it provides an easy-to-use built-in tool for working out common functions without even having to type in a formula. This tool is called AutoCalculate and its default (and most obvious) function is Sum, which adds up a set of numbers.

● Summing it up

Here's how to use it. Imagine that you have typed the numbers '45', '44', '2', '656' and '7878' into cells C2, C3, C4, C5 and C6 of your worksheet and that you want to know quickly what they add up to. To start, all you have to do is click and drag the mouse to highlight and select the cells. Then look in the Status bar at the bottom of your Excel window. In one of the grey boxes on the right-hand side, you will see text that reads Sum=8625 (see far right below). This is the result you were looking for and all you had to do was highlight the relevant cells.

It is just as quick to perform other functions with AutoCalculate. These include: Average (which calculates the average of the figures in the selected cells); Count (which counts the number of cells selected); Count Nums (which tells you how many of the selected cells contain valid numbers); Max (which tells you the highest value number in the cells selected); and Min (which tells you the lowest value number in the cells selected).

If you want to set up AutoCalculate to display the result of one of these functions instead of Sum, you have to change the setting manually. For example, let's imagine now that you wanted to calculate the average of the five numbers in cells C2 to C6

from our earlier example. The first step is to right-click on the Status bar to bring up the AutoCalculate options menu. Notice how Sum has a tick beside it. This indicates that it is the active function, but we want to change that, so click on Average to select it as the current function. Finally, go back and highlight cells C2 to C6 and you will see the text Average=1725 appear in a grey box in the Status bar.

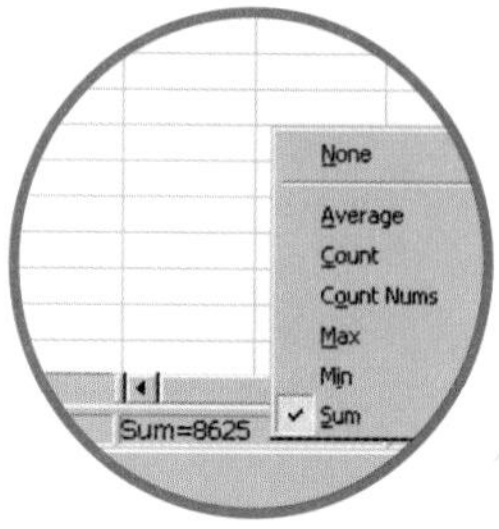

AutoCalculate's default setting is Sum, which adds up a highlighted column of numbers.

Making the most of AutoCalculate

AutoCalculate can be useful when you want to do several quick calculations on a set of figures without the bother of creating formulae. Here's an astronomical example.

1 Here is some data about Jupiter's moons that we're going to analyse as part of a homework project. Let's imagine that we wanted to find the total of all the radii of orbit of Jupiter's moons. One way to work it out would be to put a formula in cell C21. We've already seen how to use the AutoSum tool in Stage 1, pages 60–61, and the formula we would need to type in is '=SUM(C5:C20)'. When you press [Enter], the result appears in cell C21.

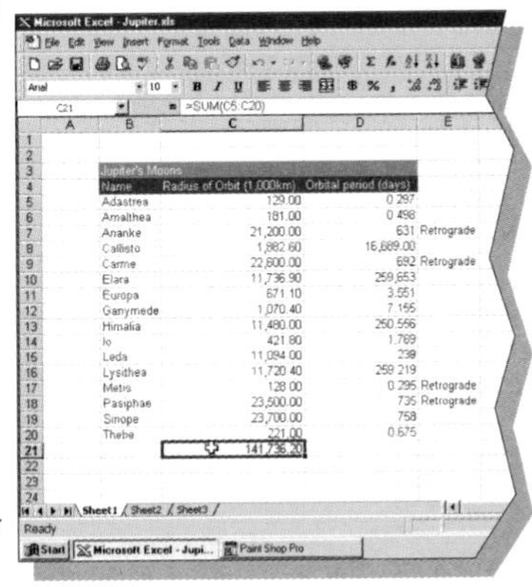

2 However, writing formulae can be tedious and we might want to work out several different things about the radii of orbit. Instead, we could use the AutoCalculate tool. First delete the contents of cell C21 and highlight all the radii of orbit (cells C5 to C20). Now if you look towards the bottom right of the screen, you'll see the result has appeared in the Status bar – Sum= 141,736.20. By default, AutoCalculate shows the sum of the numbers you have selected.

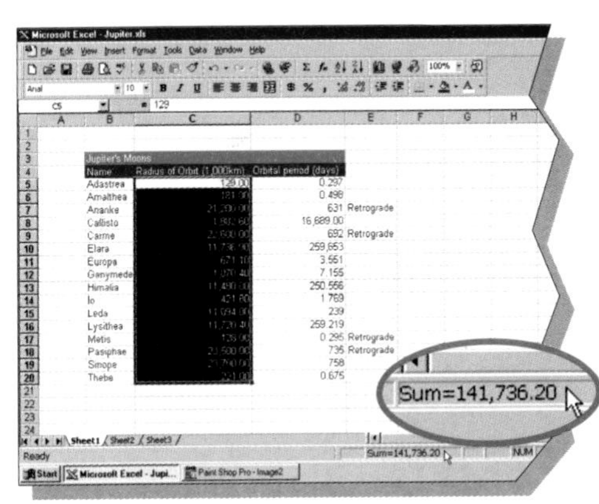

PENCIL AND PAPER

When you highlight a row or column of numbers, the AutoCalculate facility adds up the numbers and shows their sum in the Status bar. However, as soon as you click on another cell in your spreadsheet, the result will disappear from the Status bar. For this reason it's a good idea to keep a pencil and piece of paper handy when you're using AutoCalculate so that you can write down the results as you go.

Auto Calculate Record
Sum of radiuses of orbit of Jupiter's moons = 141,736,200

3 Now let's try to work out the average radius of orbit for Jupiter's moons. As above, we could place a formula in cell C21, but we have to use another function to calculate the average rather than the SUM function. So the formula we need to type in is '=AVERAGE(C5:C20)'. When you press the [Enter] key, the result appears in cell C21.

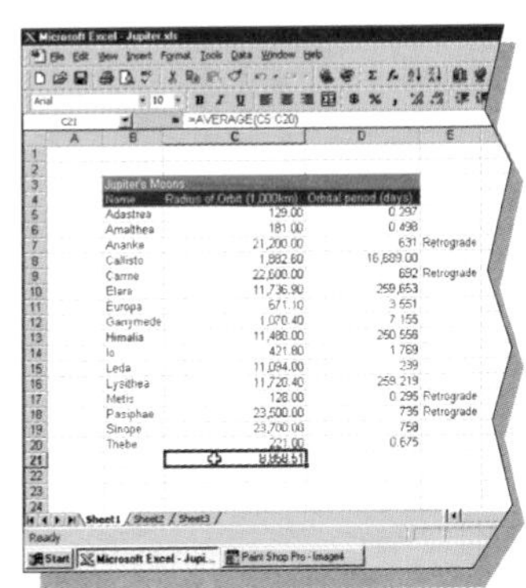

4 Luckily, average is one of the AutoCalculate functions. First delete the contents of C21. Next we have to tell the tool to switch from working out the sum to working out the average. To do this, simply right-click anywhere in the Status bar and select Average from the menu that appears.

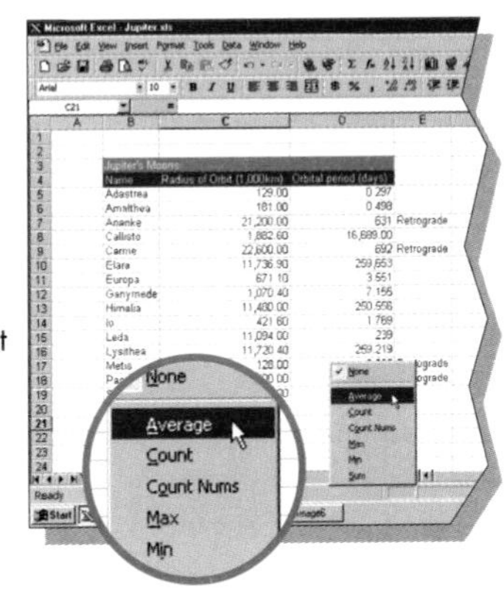

5 Now it's easy to see the average of the radii of orbit. Just use the drag-select technique with your mouse to highlight all the radius of orbit data and the result will appear in the Status bar where it says Average=8,858.51.

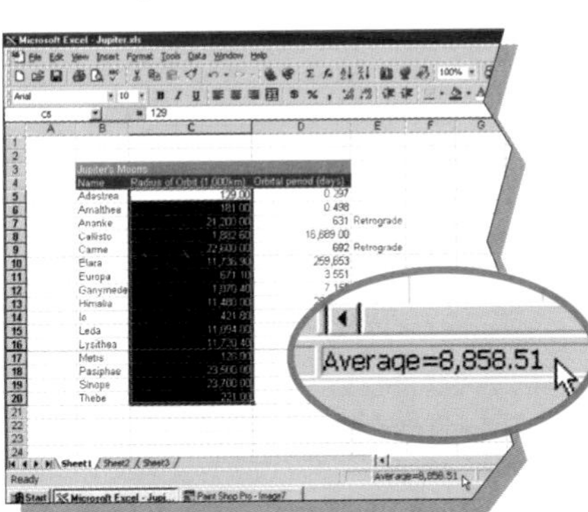

6 AutoCalculate also includes functions that calculate the highest and lowest figures from a selected set of cells. To use these functions, right-click on the Status bar and choose Max (for the highest figure) or Min (for the lowest figure). Then highlight the cells to which you want to apply it. The result appears in the Status bar.

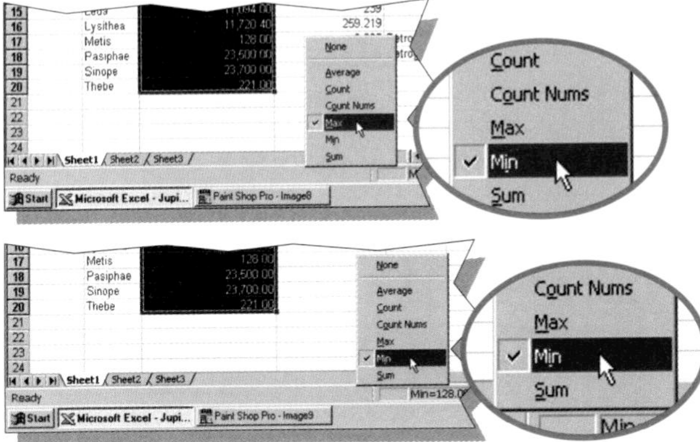

Keeping work secret

If you want to keep workbooks on your computer hidden from prying eyes – or if you want to stop anyone else inadvertently (or deliberately) making changes to an important Excel document – why not use your own secret passwords to protect them?

Excel can act as a sentry by not letting changes be made to a workbook unless the correct password is used.

If you share a PC at home, you might create documents you don't want others to see. It would be such a shame, for instance, if somebody accidentally opened your top secret list of Christmas presents. Similarly, you might not want other members of your family worrying over the intimate details of the family finances by discovering just how much you splashed out on that holiday for them.

● Personal files

You can cut down the chances of the wrong people accidentally seeing a document by setting up a systematic filing system on your PC. If everyone in the family has his or her own folder (such as Jane's Documents, Mum's Letters and so on), then the chances of them opening a file by mistake are considerably reduced. However, this doesn't make the documents secure. Anyone who wants to pry will know exactly which documents they need to open to find out secrets. Alternatively, you could keep sensitive documents only on floppy disks, which you could keep locked up in a safe place. This is certainly more secure, but it would be annoying to have to insert disks every time you want to work on your files – and the chances of losing or damaging a disk are high. It is also easy to forget to delete the copy from the hard disk after working on the document.

● The foolproof method

By far the simplest and most secure solution is to add a password to your Excel workbook. This is a simple procedure, which effectively makes it impossible for anyone who does not know the password to open up the workbook and view the contents.

PC TIPS

Password protection

A password is useful only as long as you can remember it yourself. Don't try to be too clever – you have to get it exactly right each time. Choose a short, simple word that you can recall instantly, but not one so obvious that somebody else might guess. This means that things like 'secret' or 'password' or the name of the family dog should not be used. If you cannot rely on your memory and have to write down your passwords, keep them in a place no one else is likely to look.

Using passwords

Protecting your Excel documents with a secret password is simple; the hardest part is choosing the password itself.

PC TIPS

Passwords not only prevent others from opening a protected file, but can also prevent files from being altered by unauthorized people. This is useful when the file holds information that others need to know but that you do not want changed – except by yourself.

Anyone who wants to make changes must supply the password. Those who don't know it can open the workbook but in Read-Only form. This means that they can view it but any alterations they make to it cannot be saved. You can create such a set-up by using the Password to modify option in the Save Options dialog box (above), rather than the Password to open text box. Now, when the file is opened, only those knowing the password can make changes to the workbook.

1 Open the Excel workbook that you want to password protect. Here, we've chosen to keep a list of Christmas presents secret. Choose Save As from the File menu.

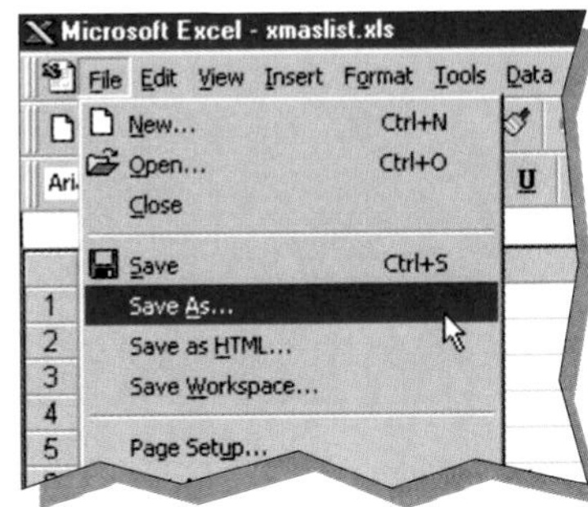

2 From the Save As dialog box, click on the Options button at the far right.

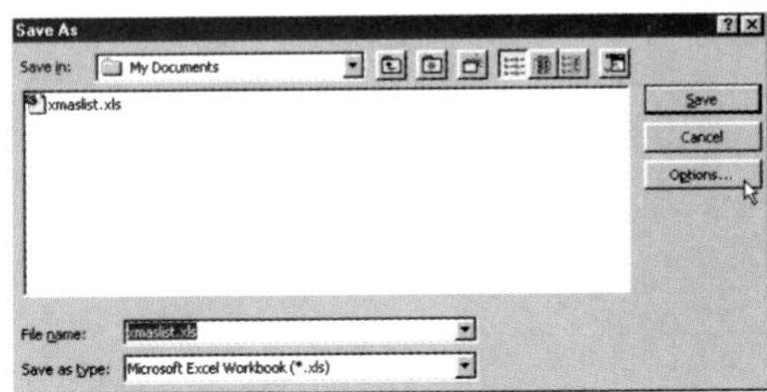

3 A Save Options dialog box appears. The cursor will be blinking in the Password to open text box ready for your password (ignore the other options for now).

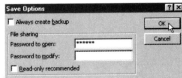

4 Type in the word you have chosen. You will see that asterisks appear instead of the letters; this ensures that anyone else looking at your screen can't see it as you type it for the first time. When finished, click on OK.

5 The Confirm Password dialog box will appear. Excel asks you to type in the password again. This is done to make sure you have chosen something you are likely to remember.

6 Type in the password again, exactly as you did before, and then click OK. The dialog box warns you that passwords are 'case-sensitive' – that is, it matters whether you use small or capital letters. If you get it wrong, Excel takes you back to step 5 to start again.

7 The Save As dialog box reappears. Click on Save to save the workbook together with the password.

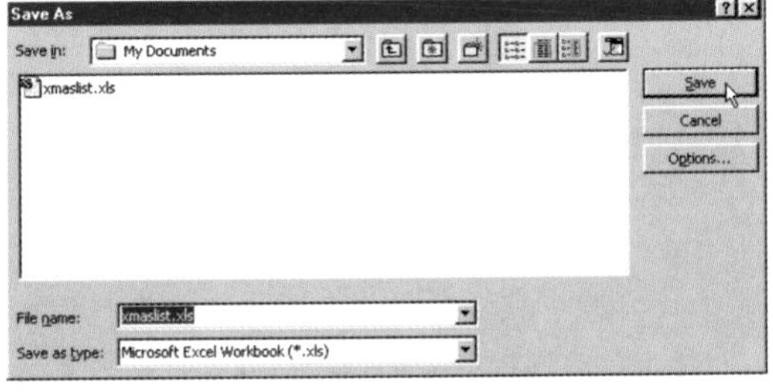

8 Since you're saving the workbook with the original name, a dialog box appears to ask if you want to replace the existing 'xmaslist.xls' file. Click on the Yes button to continue. Note: as soon as you click on the Yes button and save over the existing version of this file, there's no way to go back to the old, non-protected workbook, so you must choose memorable passwords.

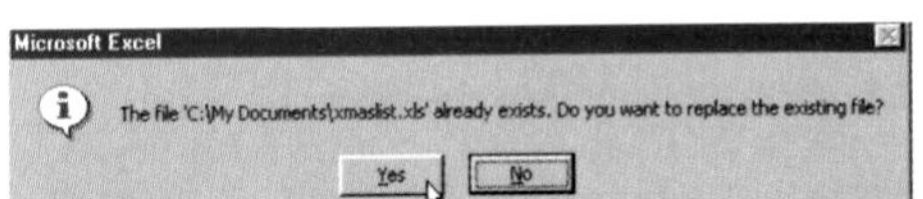

9 To see what effect password protection has, close the workbook and then try to open it again. You will find that instead of the file opening immediately, Excel will show you a Password dialog box. This reminds you that the workbook is protected and prompts you to enter the password. To open the workbook and work on the worksheet as normal, just type in the password and click on OK.

10 If you type in the password incorrectly – or if someone who shouldn't have access to the workbook tries to guess the password – a warning box appears (below). Without the password spelt exactly right and with the same capitalization as you typed in steps 4 and 6, no one will be able to open the worksheet.

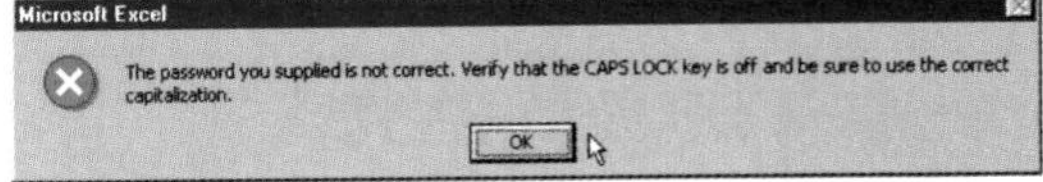

Monitoring your mortgage

With its powerful calculation capabilities, Excel can help you make informed financial decisions. Here we look at how it can assist when you want to buy a home.

We've already seen how Excel can help give you a very clear idea of where your household budget is being spent (see Stage 1, pages 58–59). Excel can also be a great help when it comes to making important financial decisions. You can use Excel to simplify tricky calculations and compare costs, payments and interest rates at a glance.

By creating a worksheet in Excel, you can play with alternative scenarios – the kind of 'what if?' questions you have to ask yourself when making big decisions. If you're taking out a mortgage, for instance, you might ask yourself: 'Should I opt for the lender who offers the upfront discounts – or forget the discounts and go for the lender who offers slightly lower monthly payments instead?'

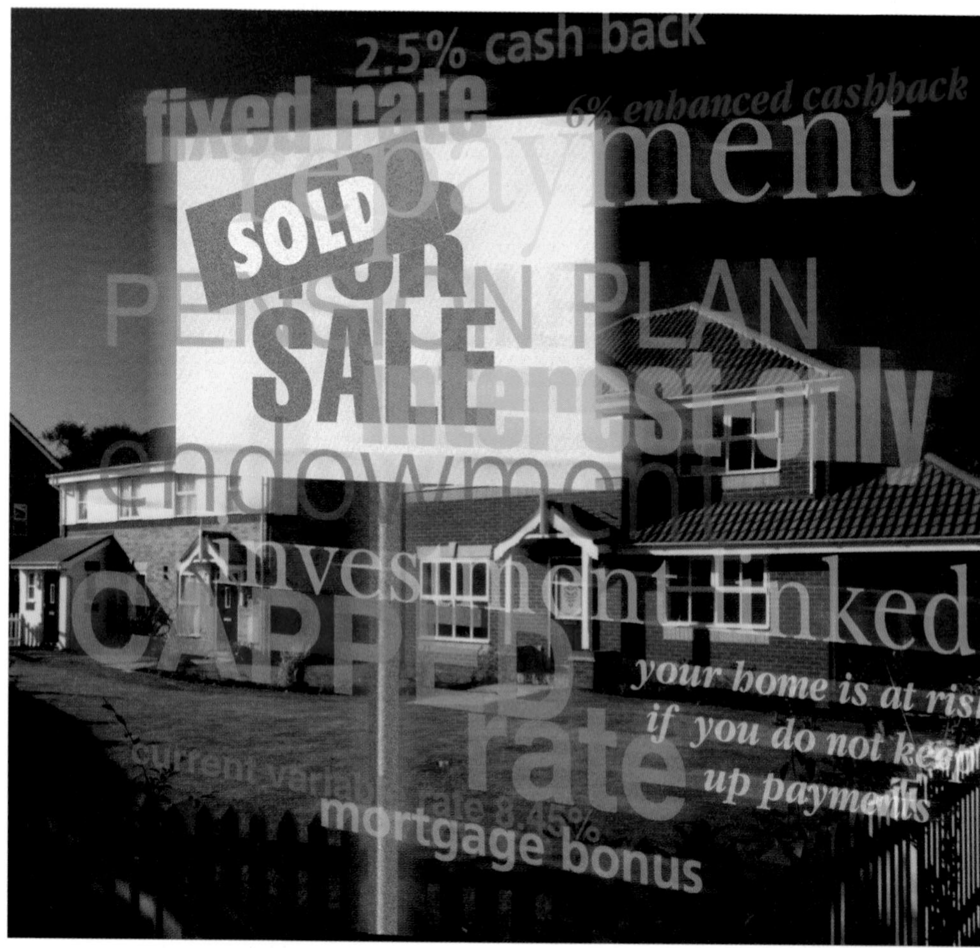

You can use Excel to help with your calculations before signing on the dotted line, but always get someone to double-check your sums before making any long-term decisions based on the results.

● How Excel rates

You can do this sort of exercise on the back of an envelope, with a pencil and a calculator, but it is messy and laborious and there is a high chance of getting your sums wrong. Also, to see the effect of small differences in the monthly payments between two loan offers, you have to work through the calculation by hand. By putting together some of the Excel features we have covered so far in *PCs made easy*, you can easily set up a spreadsheet that works out the overall costs automatically and enables you to see in an instant the effect of many different changes.

Opposite we have set up a worksheet that examines and compares two hypothetical mortgage offers. We don't delve into interest rates, but we do look at how other kinds of payments – survey, arrangement fee and so on – can affect the overall cost. In particular, we use Excel's number-crunching capabilities to help ensure that we see the full picture of the two finance deals that are on offer. We'll see how apparently massive savings in the upfront costs of one mortgage, for instance, might be wiped out in the long term by repayments of just a few pounds more.

By breaking a confusing range of costs down into simple, step-by-step calculations, Excel makes cost comparisons simple. Of course, you still have to check your sums – and take care to put the right figures in the right boxes. Excel does only what it is told.

Comparing mortgage costs

The great thing about Excel is that it lets you change individual parts of a calculation, showing you the effect each has on the other figures. Here we look at mortgage costs.

1 Start with a blank worksheet and add row headings as shown here. To make the calculations easier, we've divided our house-buying costs into one-off expenses (the arrangement fee and house survey) and monthly payments (insurance and repayments). Notice that the height of rows 7 and 13 has been reduced to bring the calculations closer: this is done in the same way as changing the width of a column (see Stage 1, pages 56–57)

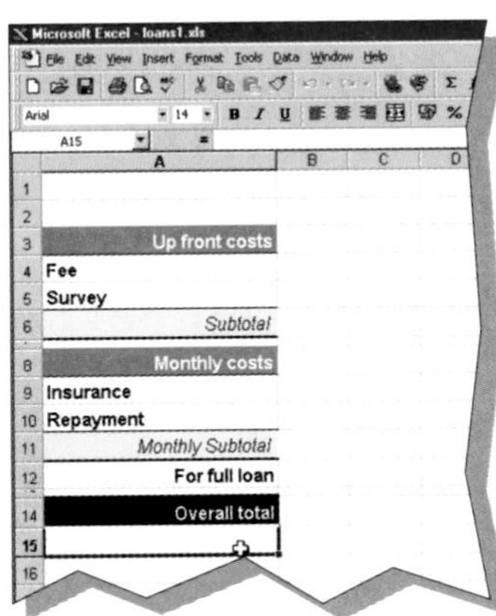

2 Now we can start adding the figures from the first of the lenders. Add a column heading (we've used 'ABC bank') and then type in the figures. (Note: we've used some cell formatting to help make our worksheet easy to read – see Stage 1, pages 56–57 for details of how to add formatting to cells in your worksheet.)

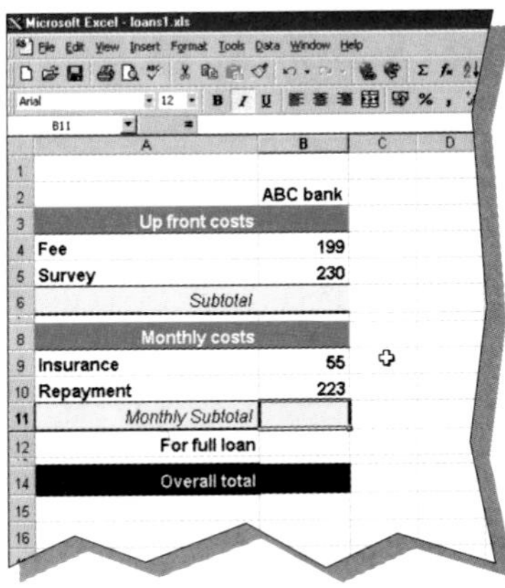

3 For each of the subtotals, select the relevant cells (B6 and B11 in our example) and click on Excel's AutoSum button. Excel will add the two figures above each cell to produce the subtotals.

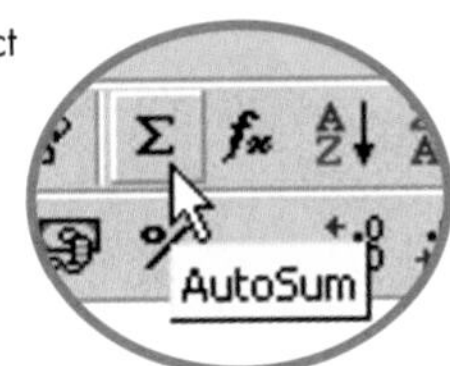

4 A simple formula will calculate the total of the repayments over the full term of the loan. Click on cell B12 and type '=B11*12*25'. This multiplies the monthly subtotal by 12 and then by the number of years (25 in our example). When you press the [Enter] key, Excel will calculate the figures for you.

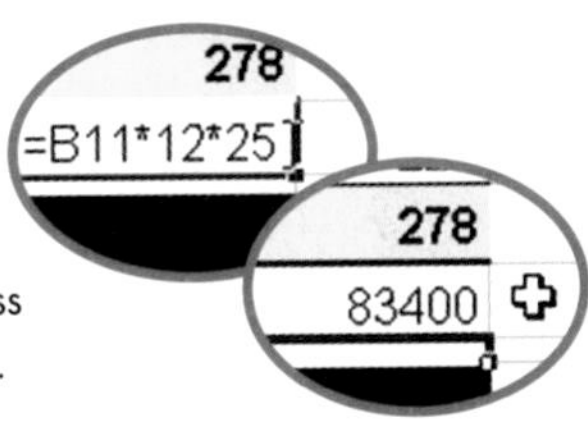

PC TIPS

Quick copies

On page 55, we showed a quick way to copy cells. You can also use this technique to copy a formula. For example, delete the calculation from cell C6 and click on cell B6. Click on the small square at the bottom right of the cell and drag it one cell to the right. Release the mouse and you'll find that Excel not only copies the formula but automatically makes the appropriate adjustments to it in the process.

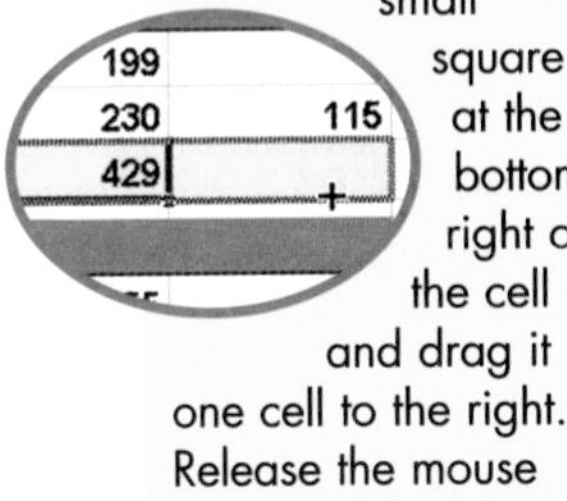

5 Now we'll add a formula to calculate the overall cost of the loan, including upfront costs and monthly repayments. In cell B14, type '=B6+B12' and press the [Enter] key.

=B6+B12

83829

6 Now we'll add some figures from another lender to see how they compare. In our example, this lender offers some special incentives: no loan arrangement fee and a half-price survey. Start by creating another column for the lender and add the initial figures as shown on the screen to the right.

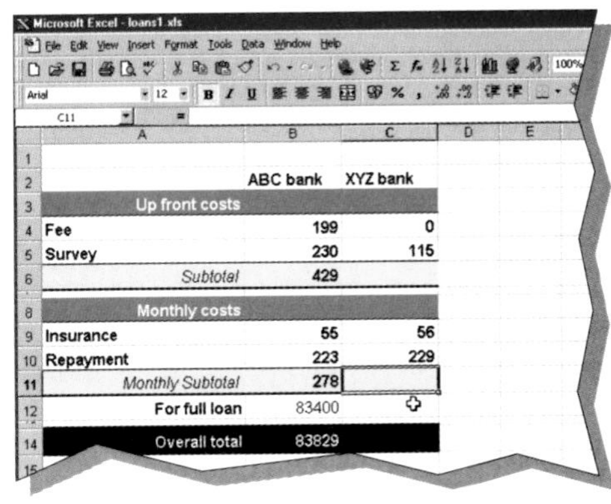

7 Now add similar calculations for the subtotals, multiplications and additions for our second lender. Each formula will look almost identical to those used in steps 3, 4 and 5; the only change is that you must replace each 'B' in each formula with a 'C'. For example, in C14 you should type '=C6+C12' instead of '=B6+B12'. It's good practice to get used to entering such calculations by hand, but once you're confident with Excel formulae, you can use Excel's built-in intelligence. For example, if you use the Quick copies tip (left) for formula copying – where only the column or row name changes – you'll find these worksheets easier to make.

8 Finally, we can add a simple subtraction calculation to show the differences between the two loan quotations. Pick a cell (we've chosen D14), type '=C14-B14' and press the [Enter] key. Excel will now show the overall difference between the two loans as a single figure. From our hypothetical example, it's clear that despite the lower upfront costs of the quotation from XYZ bank, the loan is actually substantially more expensive in the long run. Use Excel for the number crunching, and you can focus on the real decision.

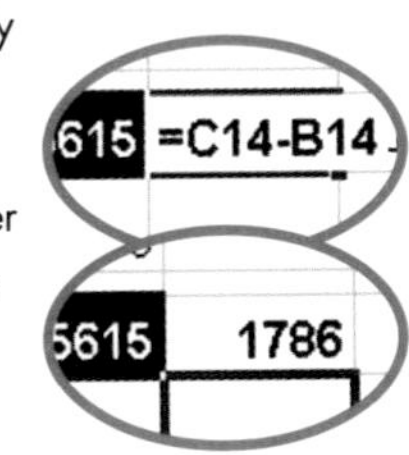

Calculating the effect of tax changes

Do you struggle with a calculator to work out how tax changes will affect you? Here's how to save trouble by setting up an Excel worksheet to do all the hard work for you.

Don't let tax problems get on top of you. Instead of getting submerged in paperwork, try using your computer to tidy things up for you.

In Stage 1 and on the previous two pages we have shown several examples of ways in which Excel can keep track of how you spend the money you earn. But what about the part of your salary that you never see: the money you pay in tax?

Whenever the government announces changes to tax rates or tax allowances in a budget, you will see people frantically tapping away at calculators, trying to work out how much better or worse off they'll be. However, you can make things a lot easier by setting up a simple Excel spreadsheet to do the number crunching for you. Once you have set up the basic headings, salary data and financial calculations, you need only type in the new details and let Excel work out automatically what the changes will mean for you.

● Modifying your worksheet

We'll see how you can do this using the Excel skills you've already learnt. In our example (opposite), we'll stick to a simple situation with just one change to the basic rate of tax and a straightforward tax-free allowance. Obviously, the way in which taxes are calculated varies from country to country and from one government to the next. You might also find that your tax situation changes when you get married. However, modifying the worksheet to reflect these different situations is easy. Save the worksheet each time you make changes, and you'll be able to see the effect of promotions and pay rises – and new rates of tax – in seconds.

SIMPLIFY YOUR CALCULATIONS

The idea of setting up a spreadsheet formula to do your tax calculations might seem daunting. However, like so many practical problems, the task becomes much simpler if you break it down into smaller steps. So, instead of attempting to do the whole calculation using a single complicated formula, we've split it into three steps and set up an easy-to-understand formula for each one. The first formula calculates your taxable salary, the second one works out how much tax you have to pay and the final one tells you how much salary you'll have left after paying tax.

Step-by-step tax calculations

Tax is a complicated area, but the basic calculations are usually simple. We've used an easy example to show you how to break the calculation down into steps.

FIRST YOU need to set up some cells to type in the figures needed to perform the calculations: you'll need to set aside one cell for your annual salary, another for the tax-free allowance and the last for the tax rate. One way of handling the calculation is to create a formula in the next cell to work out your salary after tax in a single calculation. However, this formula would be complicated and it would be all too easy to make a mistake when typing it in. Instead, we'll opt for a step-by-step approach that uses separate formulae to calculate your taxable salary, the amount of tax payable and finally your salary after tax (see Simplify Your Calculations, opposite).

The other advantage of this technique is that it's easier to modify the worksheet to reflect changes and differences in the way that your tax is calculated.

PC TIPS

Monthly wages

You can also work out the difference that tax changes would make to your monthly wages by adding one more formula to the worksheet. To do this you need to calculate the difference between your salary after tax under the old tax rate and your salary after tax under the new rate; divide the result by 12 to get the monthly difference. Use the worksheet created in the steps opposite and click on cell D6. Type '=(C6-B6)/12' and press the [Enter] key. Excel now displays the difference as a monthly figure. In our example, it's a negative, indicating that we will be worse off with the new rate.

1 We'll break the tax calculation down into simple steps with headings for 'Annual Salary', 'Tax-free Allowance', 'Taxable Salary', 'Tax Rate', 'Tax Payable' and 'Salary After Tax'. Type these into cells A1 through to A6.

2 The next step is to fill in the figures. Type your annual salary in cell B1, your tax-free allowance in B2 and type the percentage rate of tax in cell B4. In this example, the tax rate is 22 per cent, so we've typed in the number '22'.

3 Work out your taxable salary by subtracting your tax-free allowance from your annual salary: click on cell B3 and type '=B1-B2'. Press the [Enter] key and Excel will calculate the result.

4 Next, let's calculate how much tax you have to pay. To do this we'll multiply your taxable salary by the tax rate and, because the rate is a percentage, divide by 100. Click on cell B5, 'type =B3*B4/100' and press the [Enter] key. Excel will display the result instantly.

5 The final step is to work out your salary after tax. This is simply your annual salary minus the tax payable. Click on B6, type '=B1-B5' and press the [Enter] key once more.

6 Let's imagine the tax rate changes. To compare new and old salaries, we'll need a duplicate set of figures. We could type these – but it's better to get Excel to do the hard work. Use the mouse to highlight cells B1 to C6.

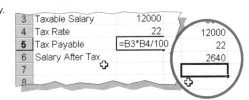

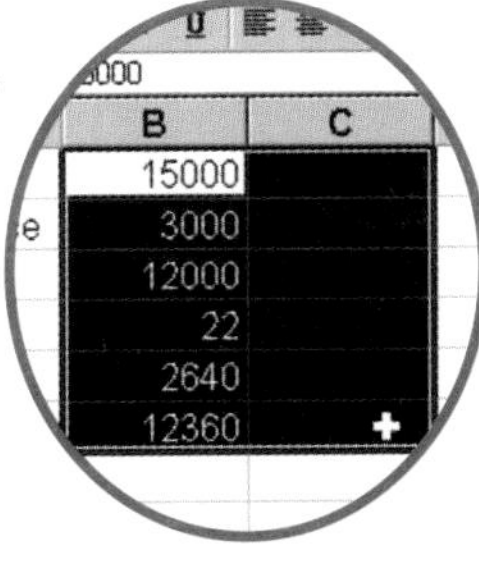

7 Click the Edit menu and choose the Right option from the Fill sub-menu. Excel copies the contents of the highlighted cells in column B into those in column C.

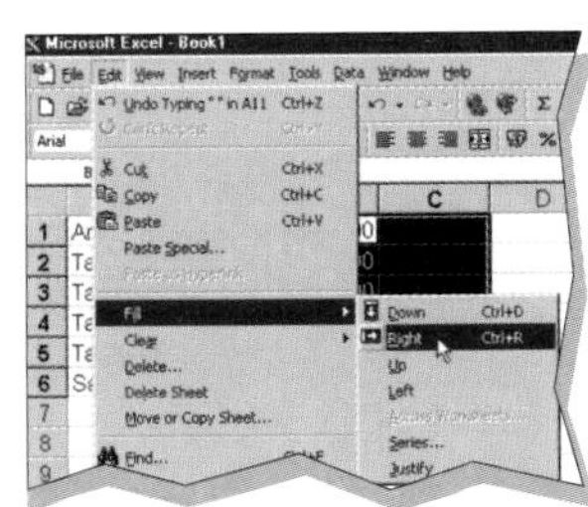

8 Type the new rate of tax into cell C4 and press [Enter]. Excel will instantly work out the calculations in cells C3, C5 and C6. The C6 cell shows the overall effect of the new rate of tax.

Introducing CorelDRAW

In Stage 1, you learnt how to master Microsoft Paint. Now let's take a look at a more versatile graphics program – CorelDRAW. This section outlines what CorelDRAW can do and how to do it.

CHECKPOINT

THE CORELDRAW SUITE

The CorelDRAW suite is a range of programs based around CorelDRAW, a sophisticated art program that you can use to create stunning pictures such as this stylish car (right). In addition to the main CorelDRAW program, there are several companion programs.

- Corel PHOTO-PAINT is a much more powerful bitmap-based program than Windows' Paint. It's great for touching up scanned photographs, for example. The smaller programs are as follows:
- Corel OCR-TRACE allows you to convert bitmap images (such as those from Paint) to create a vector image which you can edit in CorelDRAW.
- CorelTEXTURE helps you to create your own texture effects, such as marbling and textile finishes. You can use these textures in other programs – CorelDRAW, Paint, even Word and Excel.

In this section, we focus on the core program, CorelDRAW 9, but many of the functions are common to earlier versions of the program.

Microsoft Paint is fine for simple projects and basic graphics, but for anything more polished and creative, you need a more versatile graphics program. At present, the most popular art program is CorelDRAW.

● CorelDRAW advantages

The biggest difference between CorelDRAW and Paint is that CorelDRAW is vector-based, and Paint is bitmap-based. With Paint, you select an area of pixels (dots) and alter their colour. With CorelDRAW you build a picture by plotting lines and points to draw objects (shapes). The advantage is that an object can be moved and remodelled with no effect on the rest of the picture. In Paint, once you've drawn a picture, the only way to edit it is to erase bits and start again. In CorelDRAW, you can change the colour or shape of any part of the picture. It's easy to use, too: editing is a simple drag and drop affair.

Making a start with CorelDRAW

Here are just some of the clever things that you can do with the power of CorelDRAW, using the Christmas card design created in Stage 1, pages 78-79.

1 One of the good things about **objects** is that you can change their shape at any time. The Christmas tree in this example was difficult to draw in one go, so it was roughly sketched and then modified to the shape we needed. Any image can be altered in this way.

2 CorelDRAW comes with a range of clip art images. As you can see from the dialog box below, you get a preview of each object to help you choose. In our Christmas card design, the snowflakes, clouds and the snowman's carrot nose are all clip art objects.

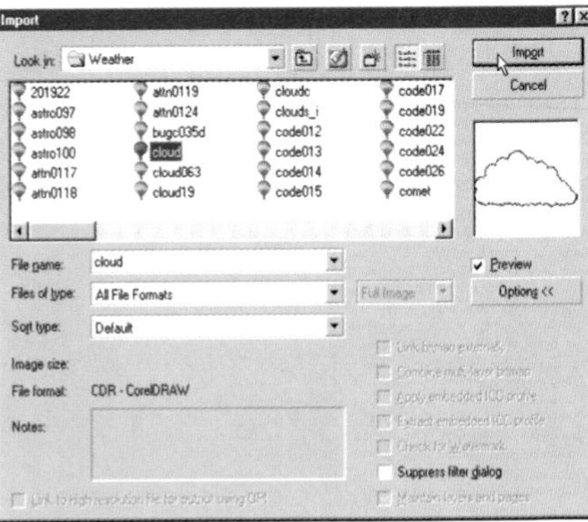

3 You can build up pictures by drawing or importing simple shapes and then moving them together. You can overlap all these shapes exactly as you want and then choose whether to bring an object to the front or send it to the back. In our example, we can have the snowman in front of the Christmas tree – or behind it.

WHAT IT MEANS

OBJECTS

In vector-based drawing packages, each item in a picture is referred to as an object. This is because every line, shape, graphic and piece of text is separate from the others and can be edited and moved independently. This means you have a lot more scope to change and evolve your picture as you work on it – unlike a bitmap editing program such as Microsoft Paint. CorelDRAW can create and edit many different types of images, using options that just aren't possible in Microsoft Paint.

Any complete shape is an object and can be moved independently of every other shape in the picture. You could, for instance, pick up the snowman's head – without his face.

Alternatively, you can pick up and move a group of objects, such as the whole snowman. This lets you rearrange the image quickly or copy bits of one picture into another.

4 With CorelDRAW you can move objects separately or you can select groups of objects and move them together. Here we have selected all the objects that make up the snowman and moved them as a single item – tilting the snowman on its side. We could do the same for the leaves and trunk of the tree.

5 CorelDRAW has a tool that lets you create any shape – by drawing it. Do this by defining the corners of an object (a little like you would with Paint's Polygon tool) and then turn the straight lines into curves. In our card, we've used curves to create an irregularly shaped mountain.

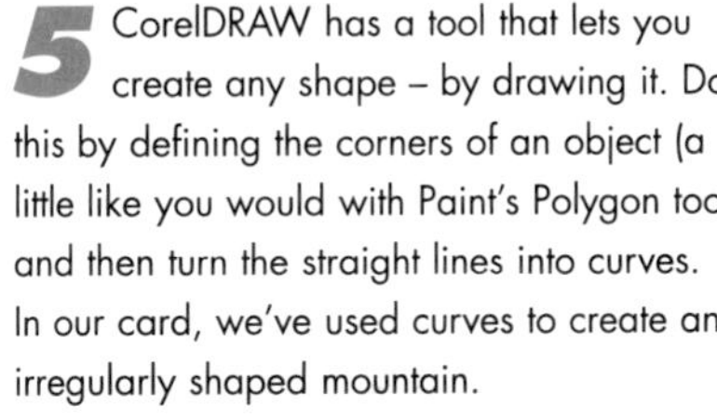

6 CorelDRAW gives all kinds of possibilities for texture and colour. There is a whole variety of textures on the clip art CD-ROM, for example. By adding some of these colours and textures into a picture – or customizing your own – you can transform it, as we have done with our mountain.

CorelDRAW basics

Although the opening screen of CorelDRAW presents you with a mass of toolbars and buttons, it works in a similar way to the familiar Microsoft Paint or Word.

Menu bar
CorelDRAW's Menu bar gives you access to all the CorelDRAW commands.

Standard toolbar
On the first toolbar, you'll find buttons for frequently used commands such as opening and saving files.

Property bar
The second toolbar is used to change the properties – size, position and so on – of objects in your image.

Toolbox
The toolbox contains the tools you will use most frequently when creating drawings and illustrations.

Ruler
The ruler around the edge of the drawing area is in inches by default, but you can easily change this to a variety of other measures, including millimetres, as shown.

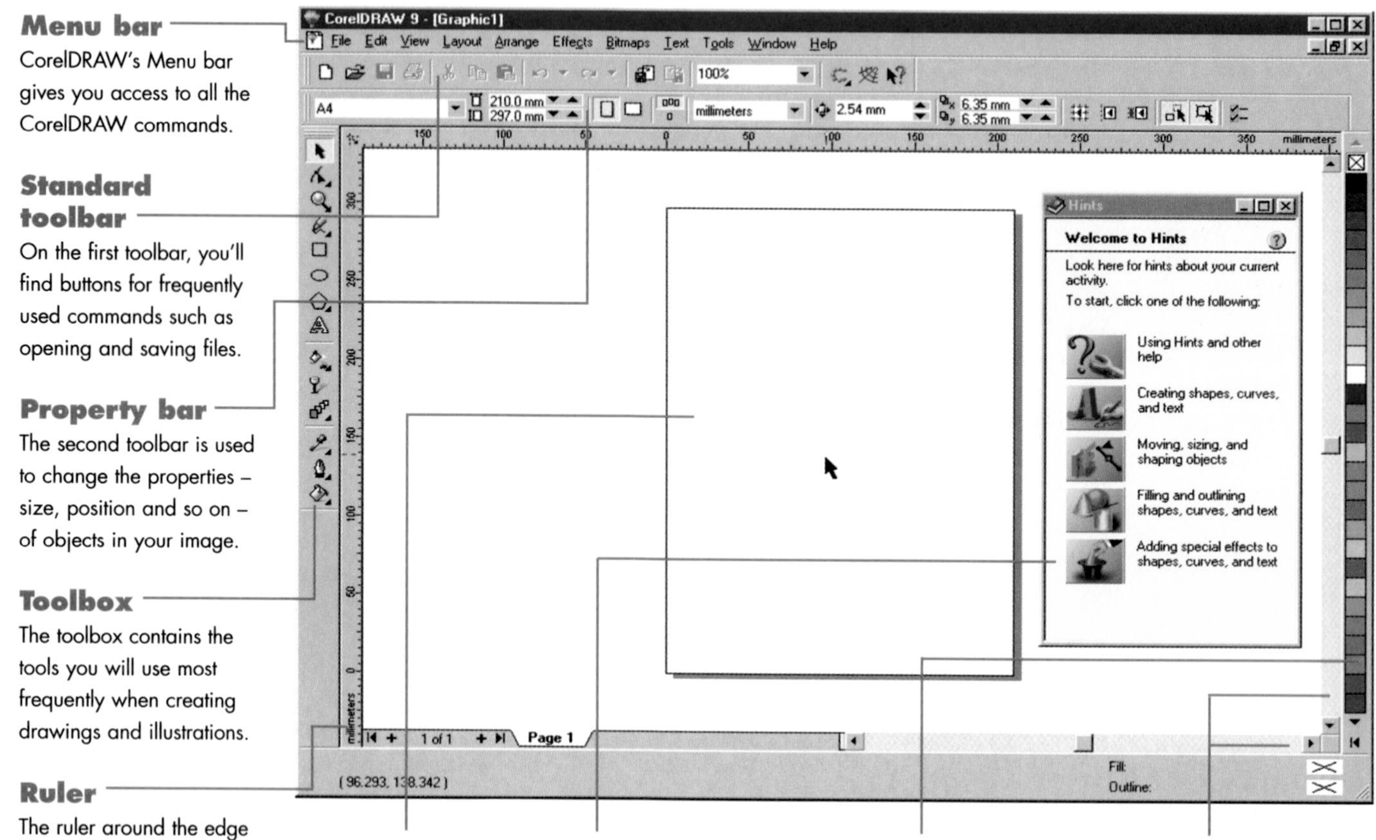

Drawing page
This is the area where you draw your pictures. It is initially set as an A4 page, but you can change to any size you need.

Hints
Select Hints from the Help menu and another window floats on top of the CorelDRAW window, offering lots of useful hints for the first-time user.

Palette
You get a standard palette of colours by default, but you can create and add your own colours to the colour palette.

Scroll bars
Like most Windows programs, CorelDRAW has vertical and horizontal scroll bars to let you move around the page.

To start CorelDRAW, press the Start button, select the Programs option and then the CorelDRAW folder. Within this folder, you'll see a number of items that were installed along with the main CorelDRAW program. Select the option labelled CorelDRAW.

When the program starts up, you will see a Welcome Screen window. This has several options: for now just click on the New Graphic icon. You will see the blank page screen shown above. Use the notes given to find your way around the major elements that are on this standard CorelDRAW screen.

The program window is very similar to most other Windows programs. If anything, with its two toolbars, toolbox and colour palette, it looks a little like a cross between Word and Paint. Many of the buttons are very similar to those of Paint. Some of the icons will look unfamiliar at first, but don't worry: we shall introduce them as we delve deeper into CorelDRAW. For our first step-by-step exercise, we'll get started by looking at CorelDRAW's basic shape-drawing features (opposite).

Getting started with shapes

CorelDRAW's ability to let you move and colour shapes helps you to make effective pictures and graphics very easily from the simplest outlines. Here's how to get started.

PC TIPS

Object ordering

Things can get a little confusing using just the To Front and To Back commands (see step 9), especially when you have multiple objects stacked on top of each other. You can move an object up or down one layer at a time by using the Order commands. Click on a shape with the right mouse button. You will see a pop-up menu: click on the Order item and select Forward One or Back One to move the object up or down in a stack of objects. (In the example below, we have moved a red circle behind a square and brought a green pentagon to the front of the stack.)

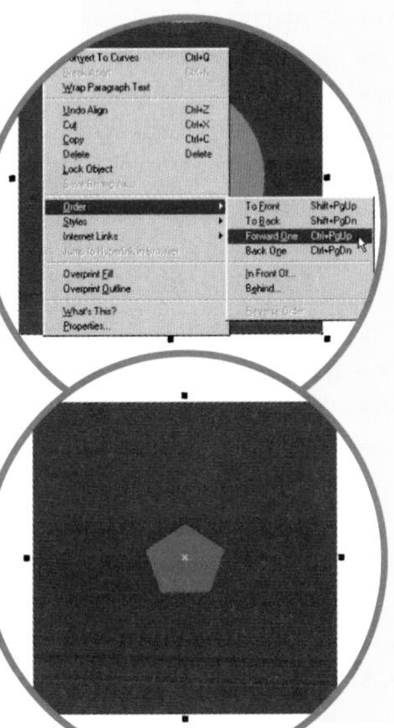

1 Let's start by drawing a few simple shapes. Look at the toolbox located on the far left of your screen. Find the Rectangle Tool; it's the fourth tool from the top. Click on it once.

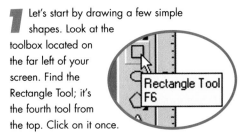

Rectangle Tool
F6

2 The Rectangle Tool works just like the one in Paint; click and hold the left mouse button where you'd like one corner of the rectangle and drag the mouse. You'll see an outline of the rectangle appear. Release the mouse button when the rectangle is the size you want.

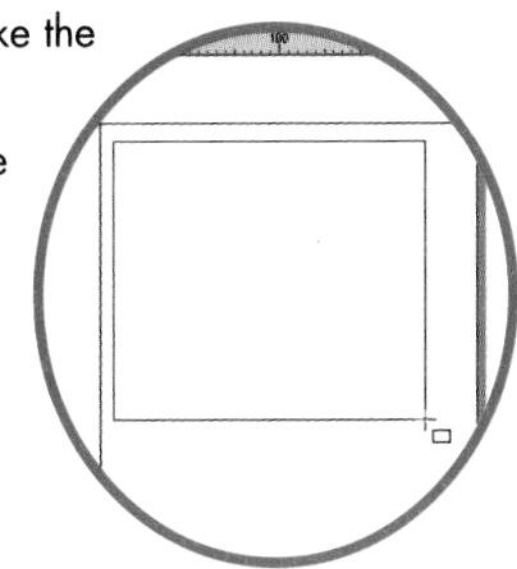

3 Now try an ellipse. Click on the Ellipse Tool, which is just beneath the Rectangle button on the toolbox.

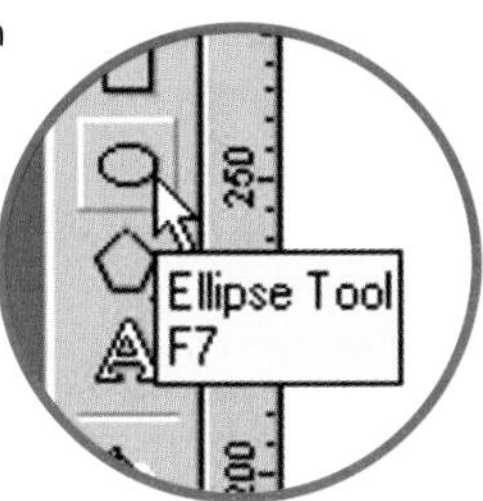

4 Again, the Ellipse Tool works just like the one in Paint. Click and drag from one corner of the ellipse to the other. Release the mouse button when you've got the shape you want. Don't worry if the ellipse isn't positioned exactly where you want it. You'll see how easy it is to move a shape around your drawing.

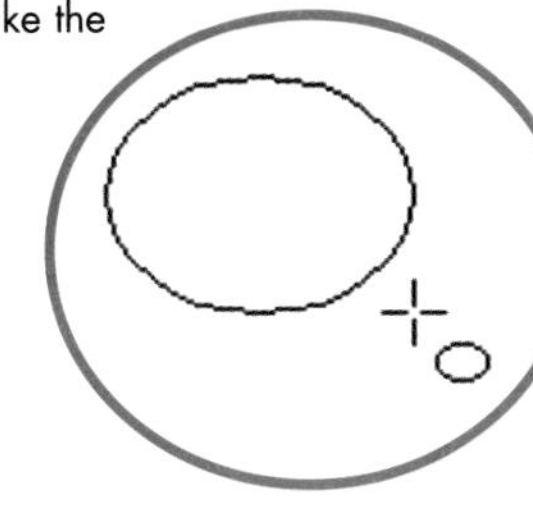

5 To change the colours of the two shapes you need to select each one in turn. Click on the Pick Tool at the top of the toolbox and your cursor will change into a black arrow.

6 Now click on the rectangle to select it (eight small squares appear on its edges). Fill it with colour by clicking on one of the colour squares in the colour palette on the right.

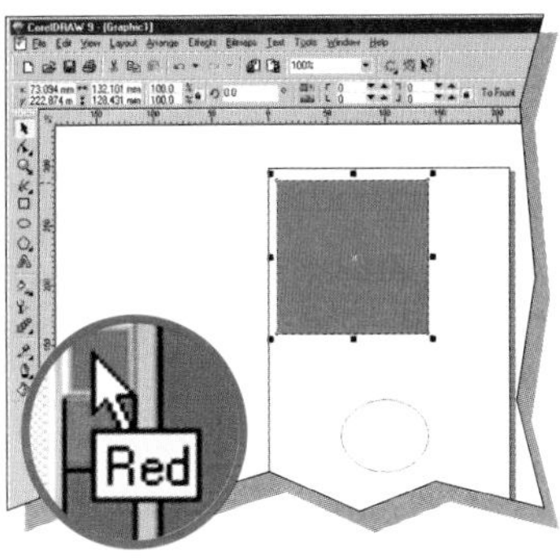

7 Select the ellipse you drew in step 4 and choose a different colour for it.

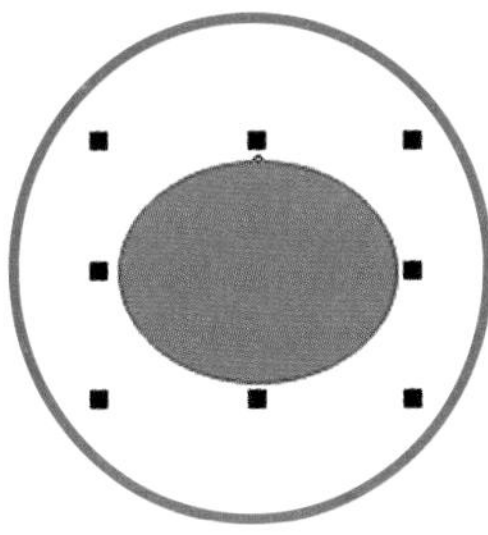

8 To illustrate the practical benefits of the way CorelDRAW works compared with bitmap-based programs, such as Microsoft Paint, we'll look at how to move and arrange these two simple shapes. Click on the ellipse with the left mouse button, and keep it pressed. Drag the ellipse so that it covers part of the rectangle. This action is very easy in CorelDRAW, but it's almost impossible with a bitmap program such as Paint.

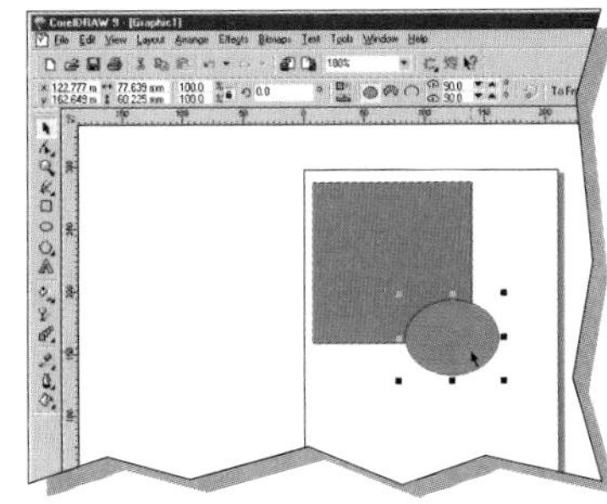

9 If you'd rather have the rectangle covering the ellipse, you can make it do just that with one click of the mouse. Select the rectangle and click the To Front button on the Property bar – the rectangle is now on top of the ellipse. Using these simple tools, you have the beginnings of a simple logo which might be used on a letterhead.

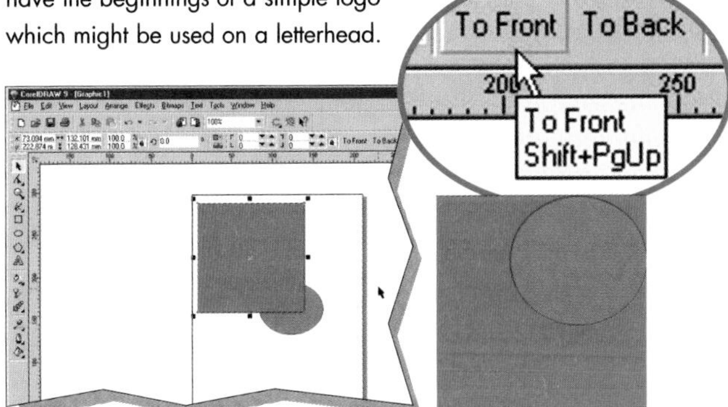

Making a poster

Creating attractive, eye-catching posters to advertise a local charity or artistic event – or simply to hang on your wall – couldn't be simpler with CorelDRAW.

CorelDRAW, with its ability to combine graphics and text, is perfect for creating posters. In CorelDRAW, you manipulate the component parts or objects of a picture. This lets you roughly sketch in the separate elements of your design, then work on them and move them around until you have the image exactly as you want it. The vast amount of clip art that comes with CorelDRAW is also a big help, as you'll find that it has at least a few images associated with most everyday items and activities.

The example we have used in this exercise is a poster for a performance of *The Mikado*. But you can, of course, equally well create lots of other designs, such as business cards, invitations, certificates and signs. Everything can be produced quickly and easily with the clip art and text options. The nature of CorelDRAW also means you can easily reuse parts of your design in other projects.

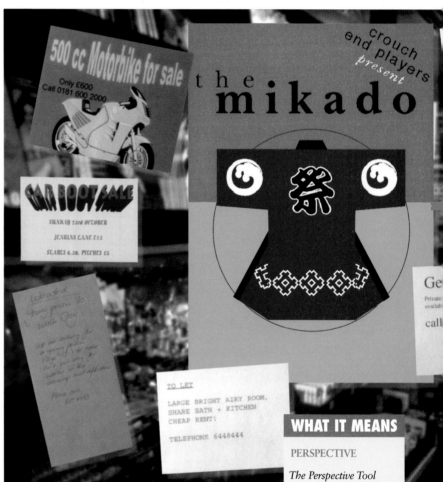

By using CorelDRAW, you can make many different styles and sizes of poster to suit your needs, whatever they happen to be.

● Graphic effects

There is a wide range of easy-to-use effects that you can try with both text and pictures. You can rotate text or images to any angle, for example, with a single mouse movement. You can also use tools that allow you, with very little work, to add greater depth to your images and make text look more appealing. Simply adding a few extra colours to a scene here and there can also make it look much more interesting, attractive and eye-catching.

Once you start using CorelDRAW, you'll quickly pick up the basics and begin to try more advanced options, such as the Perspective Tool. These allow you to create some impressive results, with professional-looking images such as those shown on the following pages. It's no surprise that many professional graphic artists use CorelDRAW for just this type of work.

By mixing clip art images and text effects, you can create anything from text illustrations to business cards.

WHAT IT MEANS

PERSPECTIVE

The Perspective Tool makes an object appear to recede into the distance. The parts of an object that are farther away from the viewer appear narrower than the parts that are closer.

Adding perspective using CorelDRAW is simple because it allows you to manipulate the shape of an object by dragging at its corners. Whatever is inside the object stretches to fill out the new outline.

Simple special effects – Rotation and Skew

In CorelDRAW, you can twist or turn pictures and words, making them any shape you want. This allows you to change them so that they fit into any space with just a few simple moves of your mouse.

THE KEY TO changing the shape of an object is the set of handles that appear on it when it is selected. These handles can be moved to make changes to your objects. At the simplest level, you can use the eight small black handles on the edges of an object to change its width and/or height. You do this in the same way as you would change an object's size in Word (see Stage 1, pages 46–47). CorelDRAW, however, has many more shape-changing options than Microsoft Word. Here we show you how to use two of the easiest but most useful: Rotation and Skew. With these you can turn objects about a central point, or make them appear slanted.

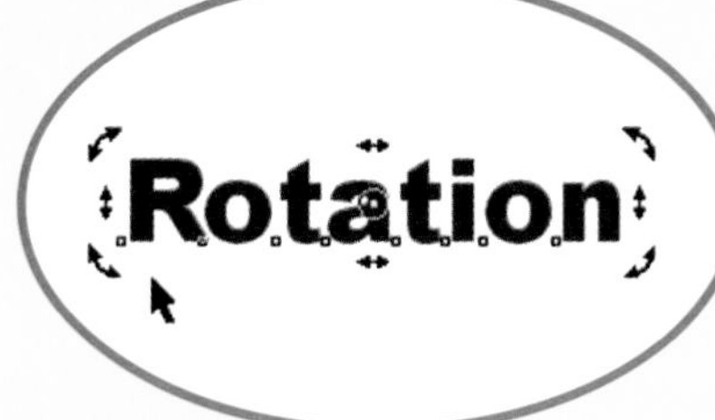

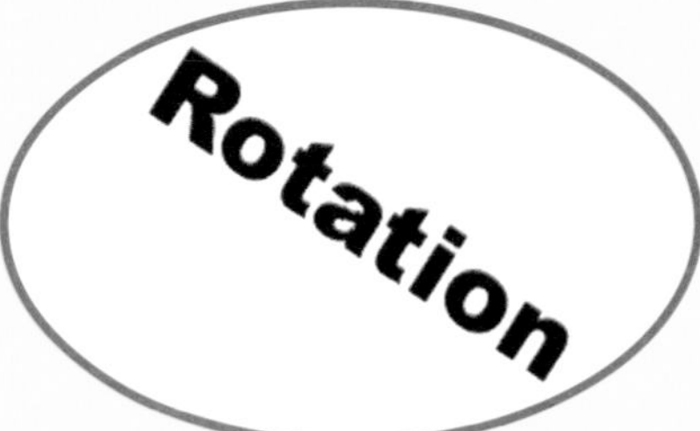

To use CorelDRAW's simple special effects, double-click on an object – we've selected a simple text object. You'll see a set of rotation and skew handles. Like the standard handles, there are eight of them positioned around the edge of the object and their appearance reflects their actions. There's also a dot inside a circle that represents the centre point, which will be used for the actions you carry out on the object.

The rotation arrows appear at the four corners of the object and allow you to rotate it around the centre point (the small bullseye in the object's middle). When you pick up one and drag it, you will see an outline of the object move to show the new position (above, centre). Release the mouse button and CorelDRAW redraws the object.

The skew handles are centred on the sides of the object and let you stretch it from side to side or from top to bottom. Drag the top centre handle to the right. As you drag it, a dotted outline shows its new position (below, centre). Release the mouse button and the object is redrawn.

PC TIPS

Object size

For some types of design, you might want to make sure that certain objects are of an exact size. CorelDRAW will show you the exact length and height dimensions of the objects at the bottom of the window as you draw them.

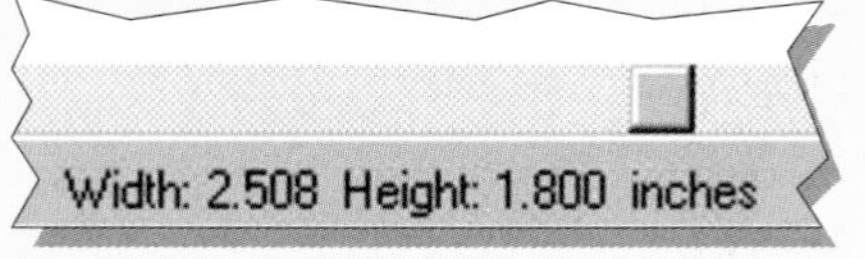

CorelDRAW's library of clip art covers a huge range of themes, with everything from motoring to plants to aircraft. There's a good chance that there'll be something in the library for whatever type of poster you want to create. You can see what's in the library by browsing through the CorelDRAW manual. In it we found a section on Japan, and in that was an image of a kimono which, as you'll see on page 75, came in very useful for our Mikado poster.

Playing with text

With CorelDRAW, you can create some exciting poster effects just by moving and reshaping the text.

BEFORE YOU START working on your poster, write down all the information you can think of that needs to go on it – title, dates, times, prices and so on. As the first stage of your design process, it's a good idea to work out roughly where each piece of text needs to go. You can then begin by typing each part into a text box, as shown in the example below.

1 Click the Text Tool, marked A on the toolbar (see inset), and then click the mouse at the top of the page to start typing the first piece of text. Click on a new position to start each new text box until you have all your text items in roughly the correct position (right).

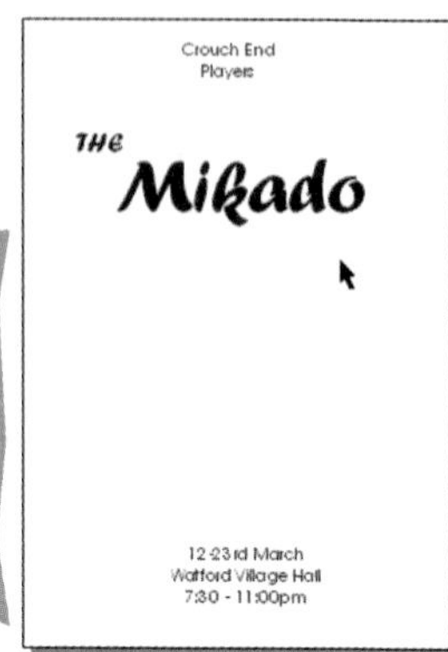

2 You can move any text object as easily as moving a shape (see page 71). First, we'll rotate one of the text elements: select the Pick Tool from the toolbox (far right) and click twice on the top line of text. This selects the particular part of the text you want to work with.

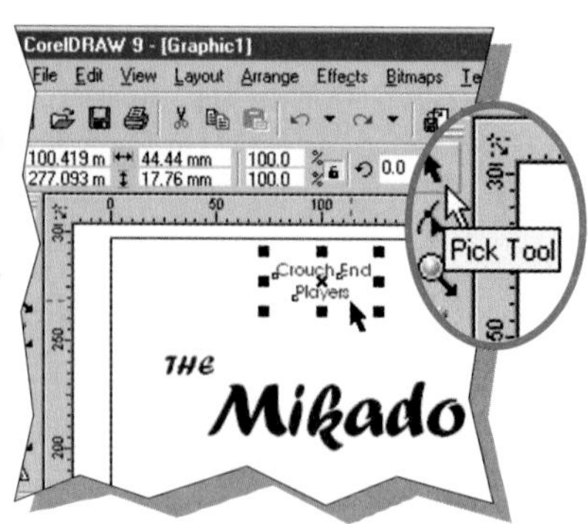

3 You will see the rotation and skew handles appear. Drag the bottom-right rotation arrow to the left with the mouse. Release the mouse to see the effect of your rotated text, then drag the text object up to the top right-hand corner of the page.

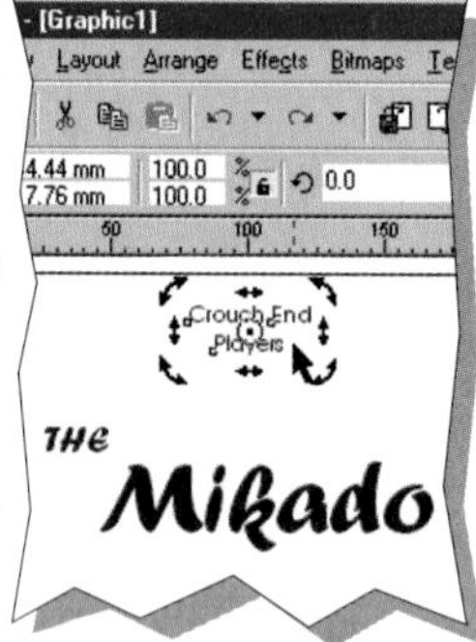

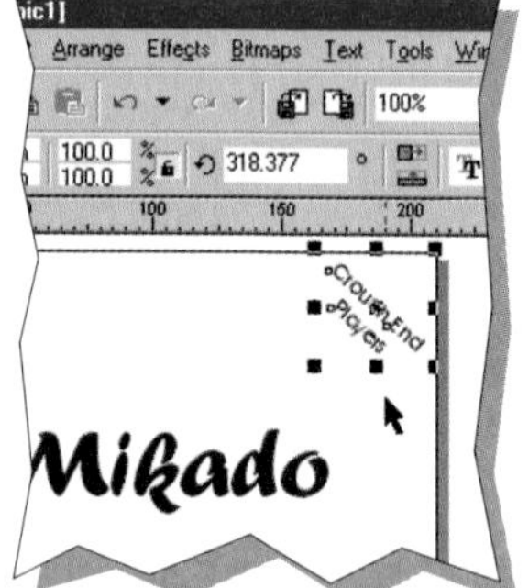

4 Another fun effect to try out is to add perspective to some of the text. This is a powerful tool that's very easy to use. Click on the Mikado text (or whatever the most important text part of your poster is), then click on the Effects menu and select Add Perspective.

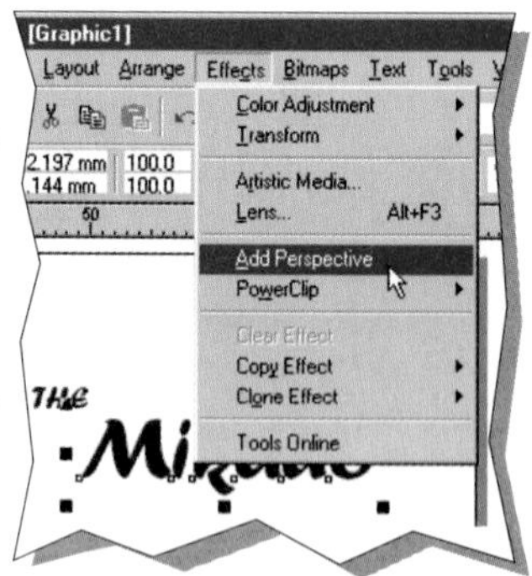

5 A red grid will appear over the text. At each corner are some small black handles. You can drag the handles to a new position and the shape of the text box will change: click on the handle at the bottom left corner of the grid and drag it downwards. As the outline shape of the object changes, you'll see the new shape of the letters in the text box.

6 Before we add the graphics (see opposite), we'll change the background colour from plain white. Click on the Layout menu and select Page Setup from the list of commands.

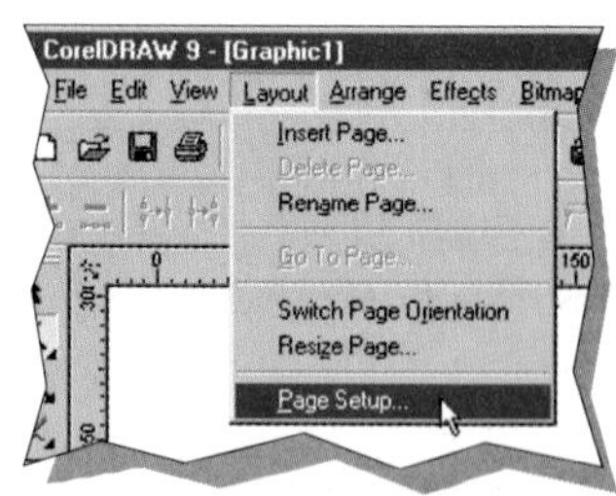

7 The Page Setup dialog box appears. Click Background in the panel on the right and select Solid. Then select a colour from the drop-down palette.

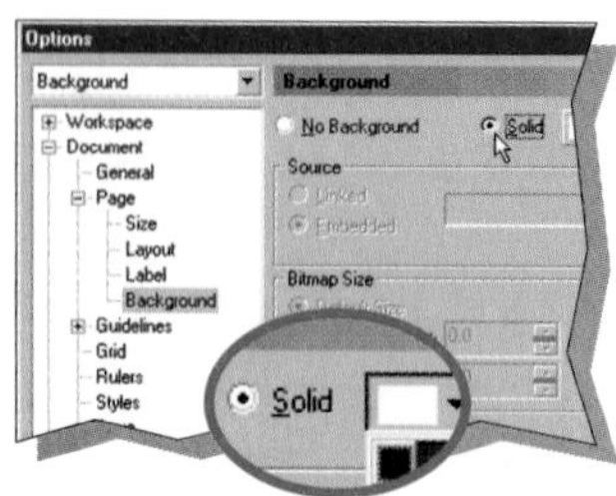

8 To give the poster more interest, we'll make the bottom half of the page a different colour. To do this, draw a rectangle over the bottom of the page, colour it using the palette at its right and then set it as the bottom layer (see page 71).

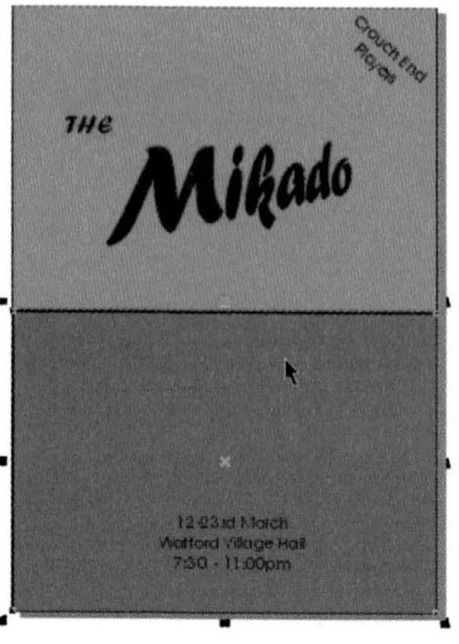

9 The rectangle has a black border, which is distracting. Change it to the same colour as the rectangle (green in our example) by clicking on the colour palette with the right mouse button.

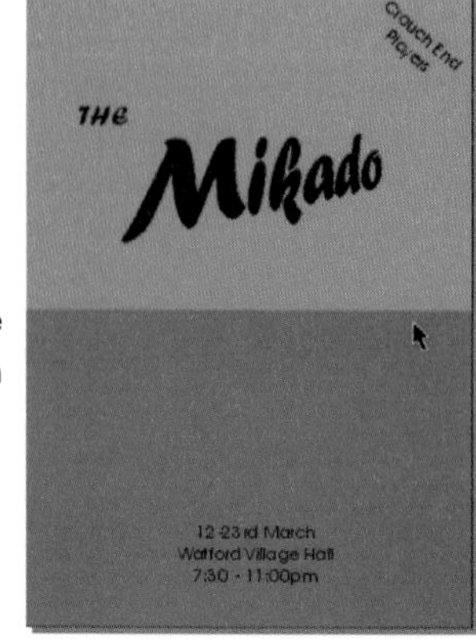

Playing with images

To make a really eye-catching poster, you can incorporate pictures from the CorelDRAW CD-ROM into your design. Here we show you how to start designing your own posters.

1 Insert the CorelDRAW clip art CD-ROM into your CD drive and select Import from the File menu.

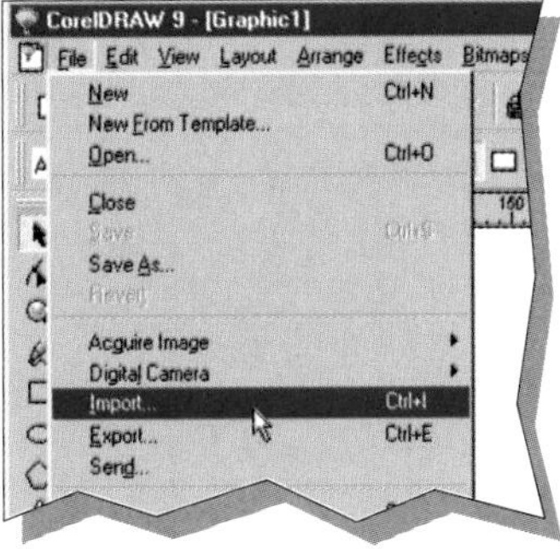

2 Use the Look in box of the Import dialog box to locate the picture ('happi_2.cdr') in the Custom folder (inside the Japan folder).

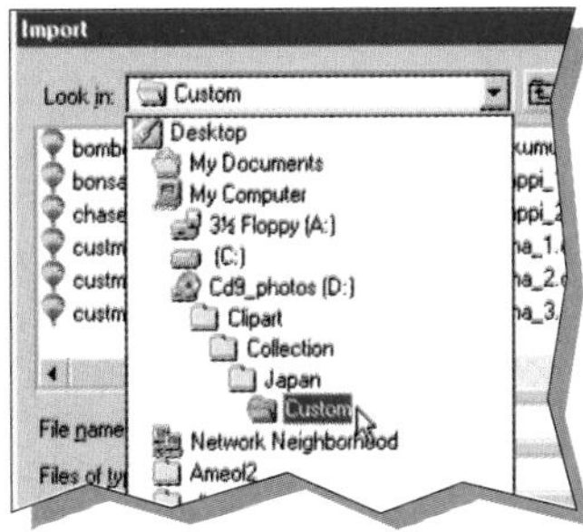

3 When you locate the file, click on its name. CorelDRAW will show you a preview of the file on the right side of the dialog box so that you can be sure it's the right one. Press the Import button while the file is selected.

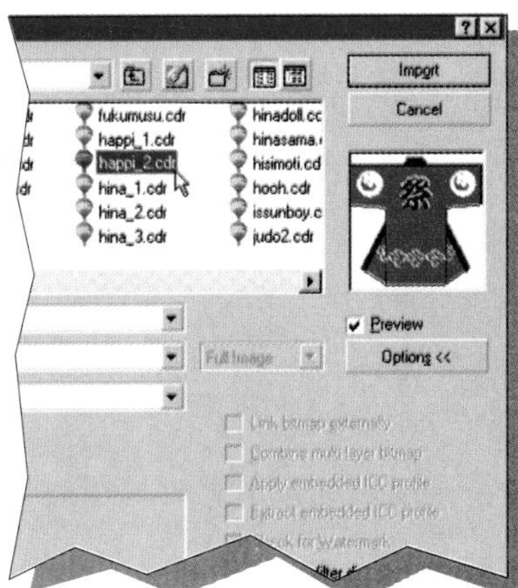

4 When the picture is imported, it might be the wrong size. However, changing it is easy: drag one of the corner handles, just as you would do to change the size of a rectangle or an ellipse. First, click the padlock icon on the Property bar so that it is closed. This 'locks' the proportions of the picture so that any changes of size affect both height and width equally.

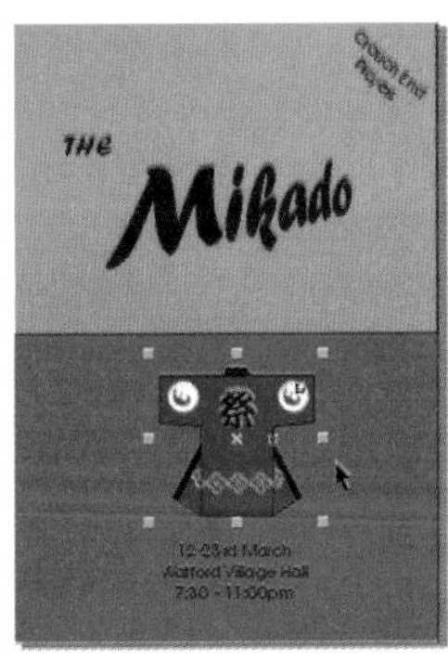

5 By moving one of the corner handles (below), you keep the same proportions. (Try moving the side handles and CorelDRAW changes the proportions, right.)

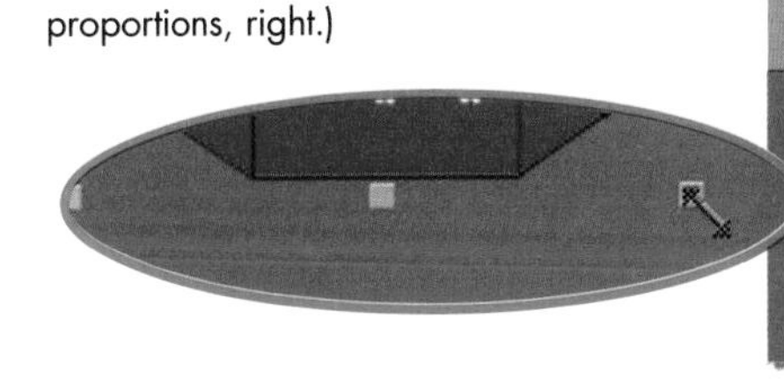

6 To round off the poster, we'll draw a circle around and behind it. Select the Ellipse Tool from the toolbar and draw a circle. Drawing a precise circle can be tricky, but by pressing the [Ctrl] key as you draw it, you will get a perfect circle every time.

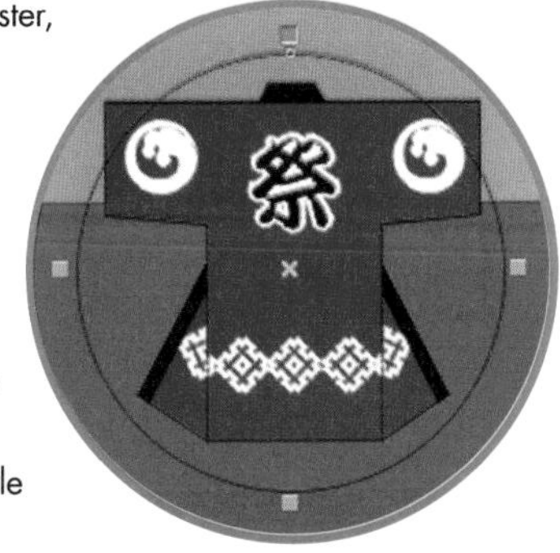

7 You might need to move the circle slightly after you have drawn it. Use the Pick Tool to centre it around the kimono. You'll also notice that CorelDRAW has placed the circle on top of the kimono. It would be better if the circle were behind the kimono. To do this, click once on the kimono to select it, click on the Arrange menu and select the To Front command from the Order menu.

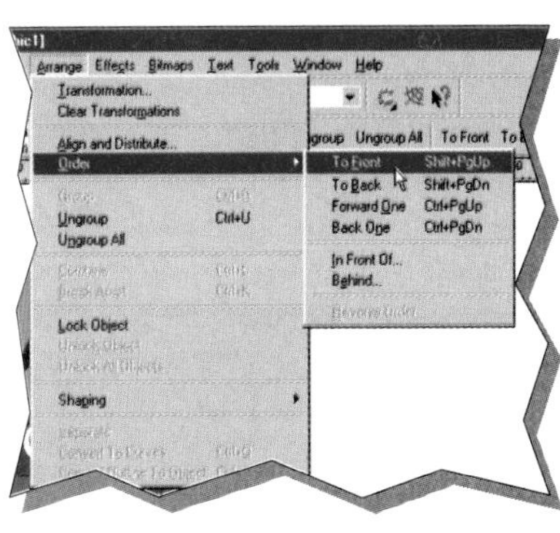

8 Now our poster is complete. Using these simple text and clip art techniques, you will be able to create many simple but effective posters. The only limitation is your imagination – just don't be afraid to experiment!

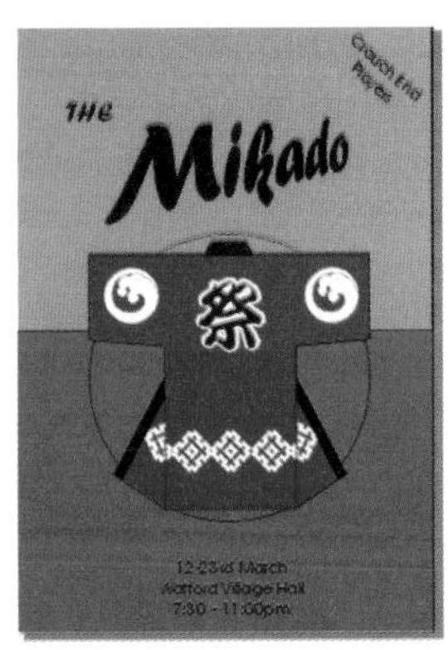

9 Don't forget to save your poster. CorelDRAW's save operations are much the same as those of Word and Excel. Use the Save in box to locate your *PCs made easy* or My Documents folder, type a name for your poster into the File name text box and press the Save button.

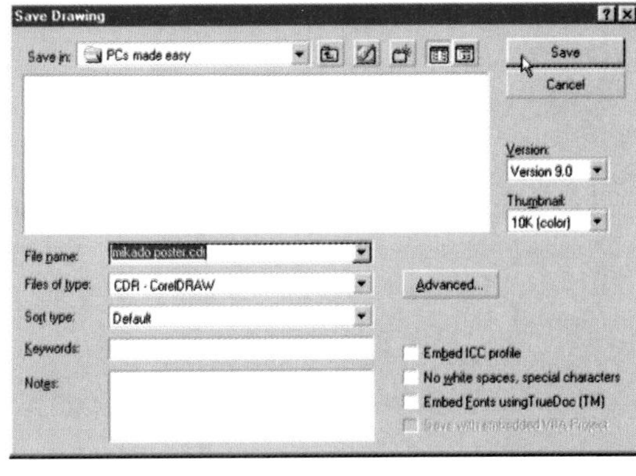

Working with curves

To get the most out of CorelDRAW you need to learn how to tweak its simple rectangle and ellipse forms into the exact shapes you need for your pictures. Convert the edges of a shape into curves and you can stretch it any way you want.

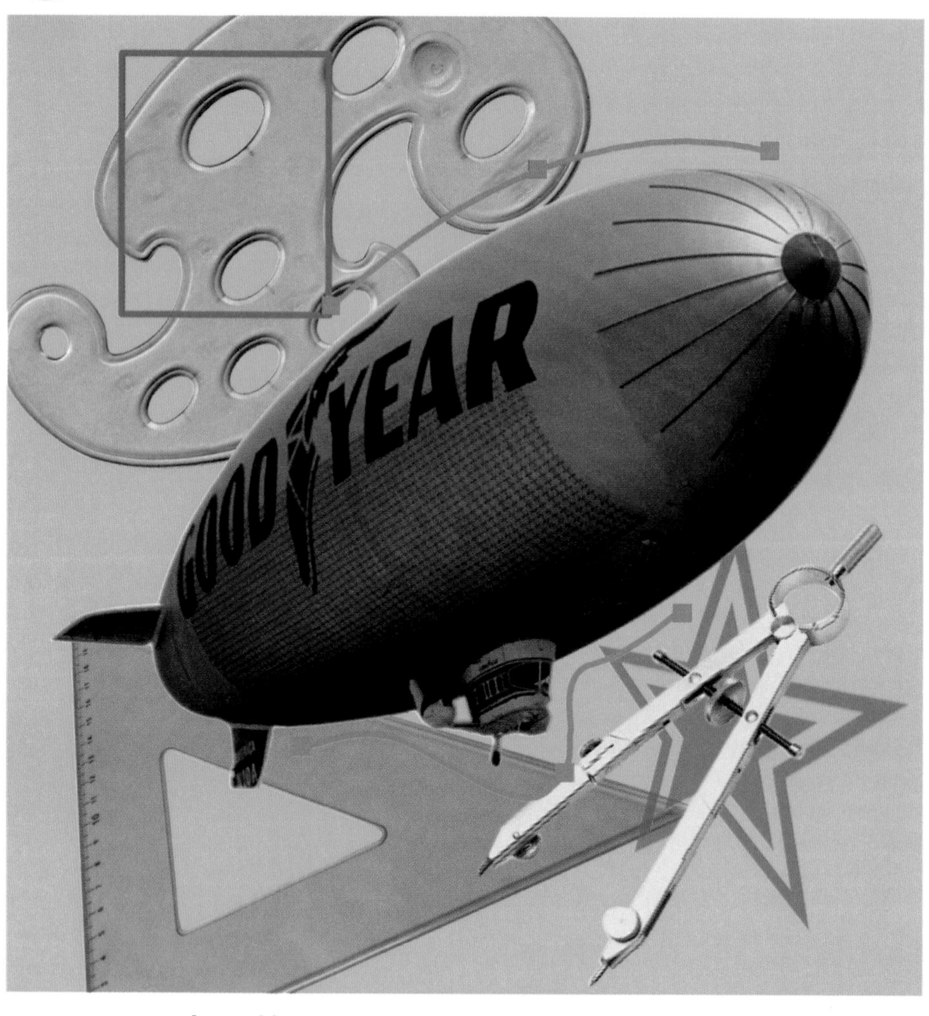

When using the standard Rectangle and Ellipse tools in CorelDRAW, you might have wondered how to create complex shapes. The answer is that rather than having a tool for every possible shape that you might want, you make a new shape by adapting a simple one to create something more complex.

As with most CorelDRAW drawing functions, the first step is to create a rough approximation of the desired shape and then gradually mould it into exactly the shape you need. Using and creating special curved lines is particularly important here, since most real-world objects contain curves, and computer images can look very false if they only contain straight edges, circles and ellipses. Fortunately, CorelDRAW is particularly adept at creating and manipulating curves.

New tools, new shapes

CorelDRAW has just three standard shapes – rectangle, ellipse and pentagon. Even drawing quite simple objects such as an egg, a kite or an archway would be impossible without using CorelDRAW's curve tools.

To create new shapes, you start with a standard rectangle or ellipse and change the lines or curves used for its edges. You can take a shape with straight edges and convert any or all of its edges to curves.

By moving special handles on the edges of an object you can reshape it at will.

Nodes and handles

In CorelDRAW, you can make complex shapes with nodes and bezier curves. For example, you can convert a rectangle with four corners into a rectangle with four nodes. Initially, the shape looks the same, but now you can drag each node into a new position to make new shapes. You can also add and delete nodes to change the shape further.

Most importantly, you can change the route taken by the line between nodes – this is very useful for creating shapes with smoothly curved edges.

Bezier curves are a little tricky to get the hang of initially, but with practice you will soon master them and be able to get far more impressive results than you could without them. Later in the course we'll show you how you can create bezier curves from scratch.

WHAT IT MEANS

BEZIER CURVES

A bezier curve allows you to draw smoothly shaped curves very simply. Each node on a bezier curve has special handles which you can move with the mouse to subtly alter the curve between nodes.

You can also convert a straight line – such as one of the sides on a square, for example – to a bezier curve and bend it to a new shape.

Turning shapes into curves

If you want unique and useful shapes in your drawings, you'll need to experiment with CorelDRAW's Shape Tool and bezier curves. Here's how.

THE POWER IN CorelDRAW lies in its ability to perform limitless changes to the shapes in your drawings. Even the simplest shape can be transformed into a more complex form that's almost impossible to create from scratch.

1 For this exercise, we'll show you how to transform an ordinary rectangle into a much more complicated curved shape. Start with a new, blank CorelDRAW page and select the Rectangle Tool from the toolbox. Create a fairly large square shape on the blank page with the mouse.

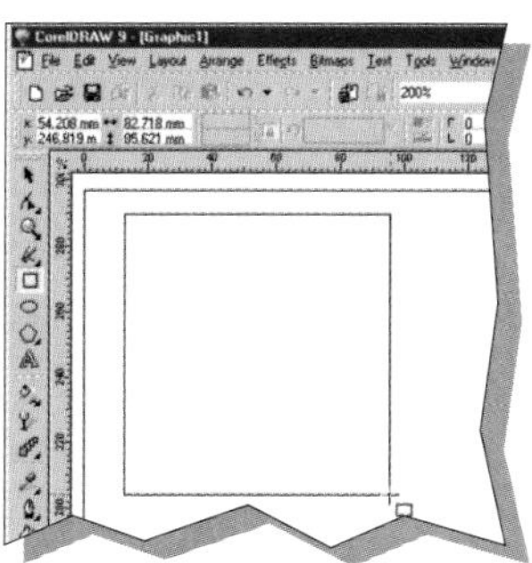

2 Colour it with a bright primary colour by clicking on the colour palette (but leave the outline untouched for this exercise). To alter the shape of the rectangle select the Shape Tool from the toolbar.

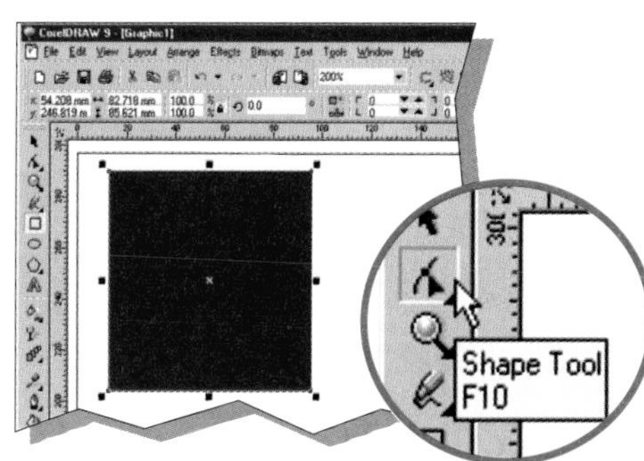

3 Now move the mouse pointer to one of the corners of the rectangle and click and hold the left mouse button. As you move the mouse up and down, and from side to side, you'll see a thin outline showing the rectangle gradually turning into a more circular shape.

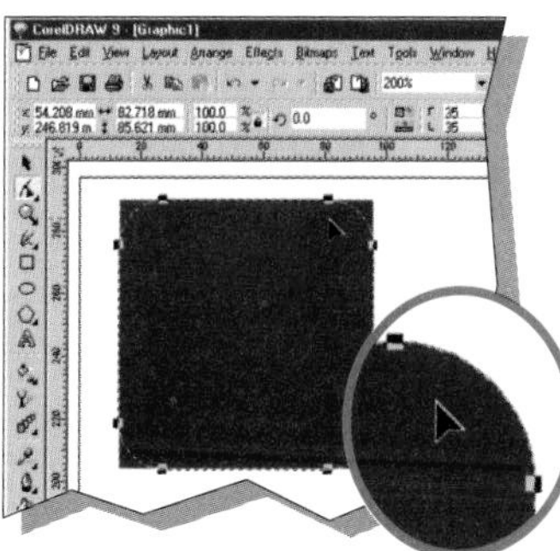

4 If you want to have greater control over the shape, and change it more radically, then you can convert it to a curved shape. There is a button on the far right of the Property bar called Convert To Curves. Press this to change the shape's edges into a sequence of curves.

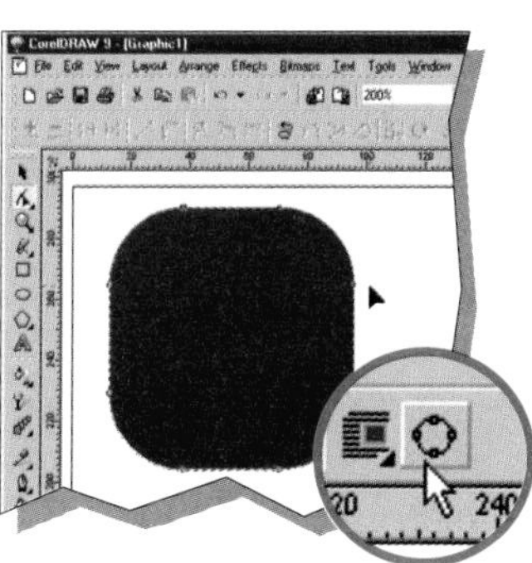

5 Now use the Shape Tool (see step 2) again to move a node. You will find that you can move the node anywhere you want, not just within the restrictions of the original rectangle shape. You will also see extra lines and handles appear on the curves (right).

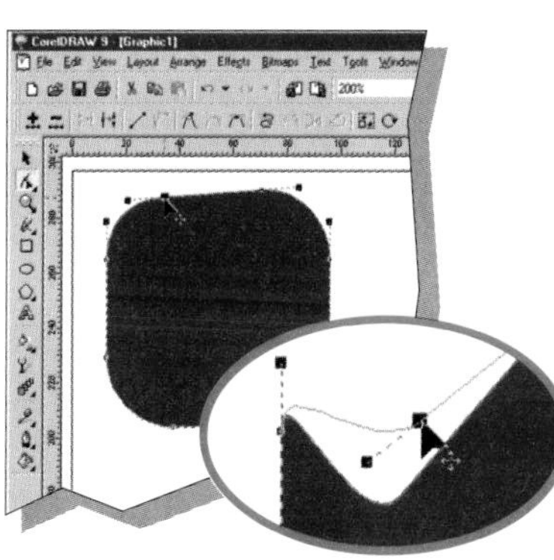

6 You will find that by altering the position of these handles in relation to the node they are attached to, you can make the curve steeper or shallower.

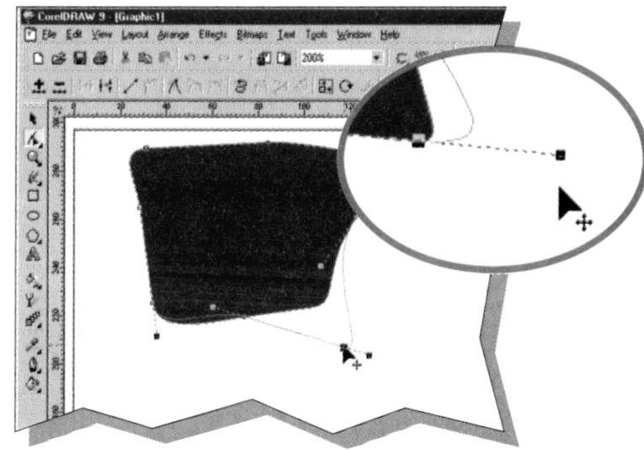

7 By adding new nodes to a simple shape, and by moving the control points of the nodes on your shape, you can create objects that are much more useful than the shape you originally started with. You will also find that because your new shape is created by manual means – rather than from a set of ready-made shapes plucked out of a toolbox – it is unique. This helps to add a more natural look to the shapes you create.

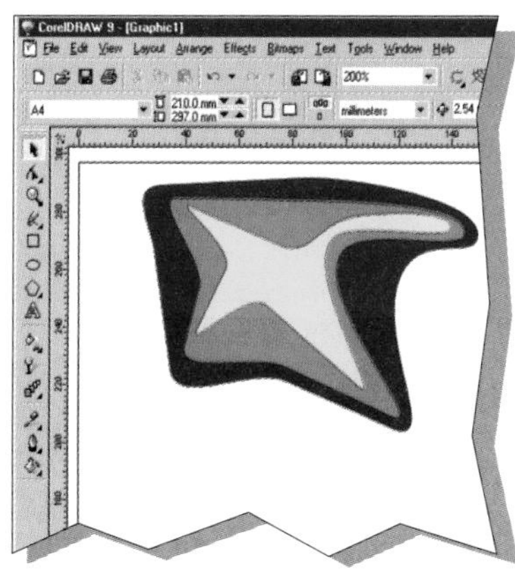

PC TIPS

Adding and deleting nodes

If you want more – or fewer – nodes in your shape, you can use the Add Node(s) and Delete Node(s) buttons on the Property bar (right). To delete a node, select it with the Shape Tool and press the Delete Node(s) button. To add a node, select two adjacent nodes and press the Add Node(s) button.

Using clip art pictures

Even if you don't fancy yourself as much of an artist, you can still produce professional-looking pictures in CorelDRAW. This is thanks to a CD-ROM included with the program, which is full of ready-made clip art images.

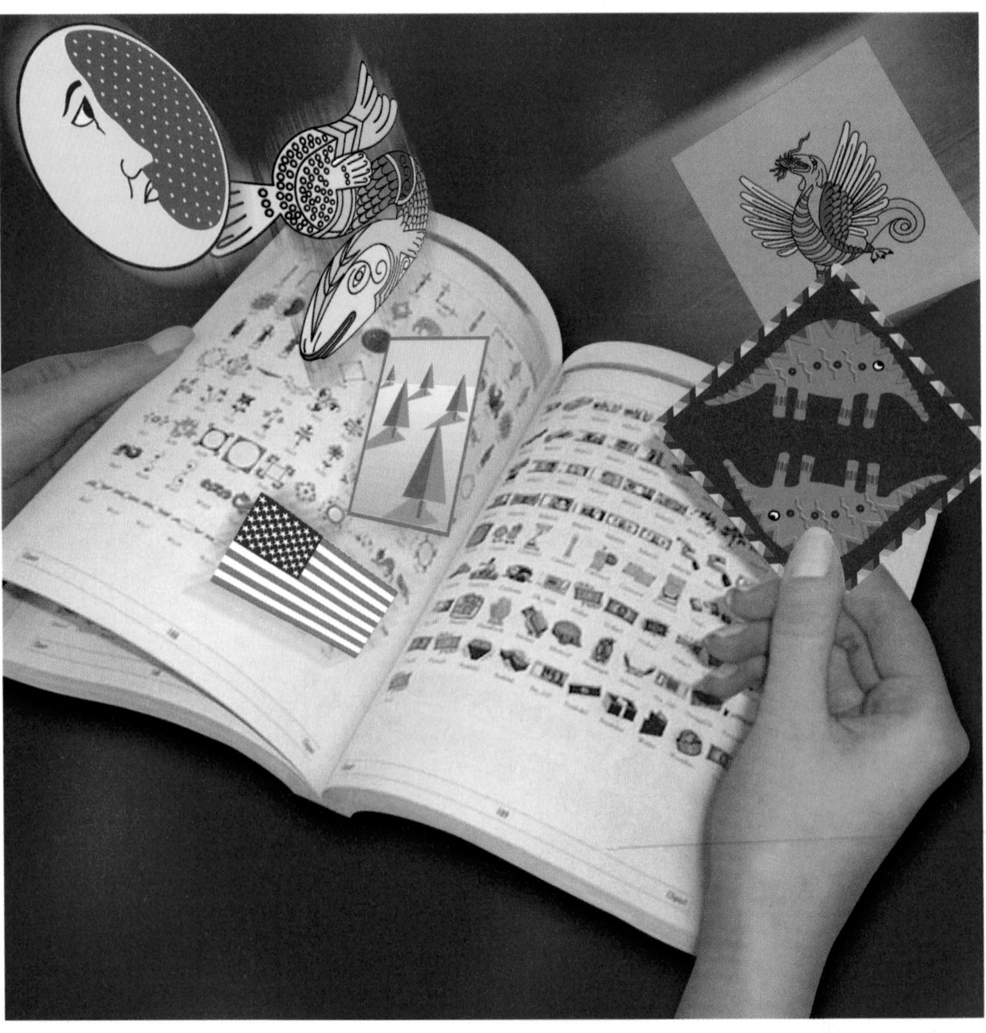

One secret to success in creating your very own high-quality images is to see how other such pictures are built up. CorelDRAW comes with a host of professionally created pictures – known as clip art – which you can copy, use wholesale or modify and adapt for your own artistic works. Most of the second CorelDRAW CD-ROM is packed full of these useful images – over 25,000 of them.

These pictures can be used in whatever way you want – either unmodified as they stand or as the basis for your own creations. If you are doing a simple document and want to add some interesting and colourful designs quickly, then you can easily import a clip art image without ever needing to worry about drawing complex shapes.

The clip art advantage

If you look back to our first CorelDRAW picture of a Christmas scene (see page 69), you will remember that we used a clip art image of a carrot for the snowman's nose. We could have drawn this, but the existing clip art was likely to be much better than our own hand-drawn image, unless we were to spend an inordinate amount of time on it.

You can also use clip art as the starting point for your own pictures. Imagine that you want to draw an aeroplane – a complex and time-consuming object to draw from scratch. It would be easier to import a clip art image that is roughly what you want, then alter it to suit your exact needs. There is so much clip art stored on the CorelDRAW CD-ROM that you can be sure that for most subjects there

CorelDRAW comes with a host of professional images ready for you to use in your pictures. There are so many that there's a special catalogue of them included with the software.

will be some sort of image associated with them. In fact, because there is so much it can take a long time to find the picture you want.

● Choosing a clip art image

When you're using CorelDRAW itself, you can browse through the images by opening the Clipart window (under the Scrapbook entry in the Tools menu) and then scroll through the thumbnail pictures (small versions of the full pictures). But the easiest way to find what you want is to use the CorelDRAW clip art manual. This large colour book contains pictures of all the clip art stored on the CD-ROM. It also gives you the name of the folder and file where the clip art is stored.

CorelDRAW's clip art is split up into two main sections: vector graphics and bitmap photos. We'll deal with photos later in the course (you'll find that they are actually stored on a different CD-ROM).

The vector graphics are also broken up into groups: first there are text fonts, borders and frames, and symbols; and then the main section of colour and black-and-white pictures. These are further divided into categories that cover almost every subject under the sun. Just flick through and you'll be astonished by the variety and detail of available images.

● Using clip art

We've already shown how to import clip art using the File menu (see page 75). This is the easiest method if you know which file you're looking for. If not, it is better to use the special Clipart window which shows how the folders on the CD-ROM are organized, together with previews of the clip art in each folder. To add the clip art to your picture, you simply drag and drop it from the window onto the page. Clip art often appears full screen, so the first thing you might have to do is shrink it to a more suitable size.

You can also alter and edit the clip art as if you'd created it yourself. Clip art is made up of lots of individual objects, just like any other CorelDRAW image. This means that you can change everything, from the colour of the smallest pane in a stained-glass window, to the number of figures in a crowd scene.

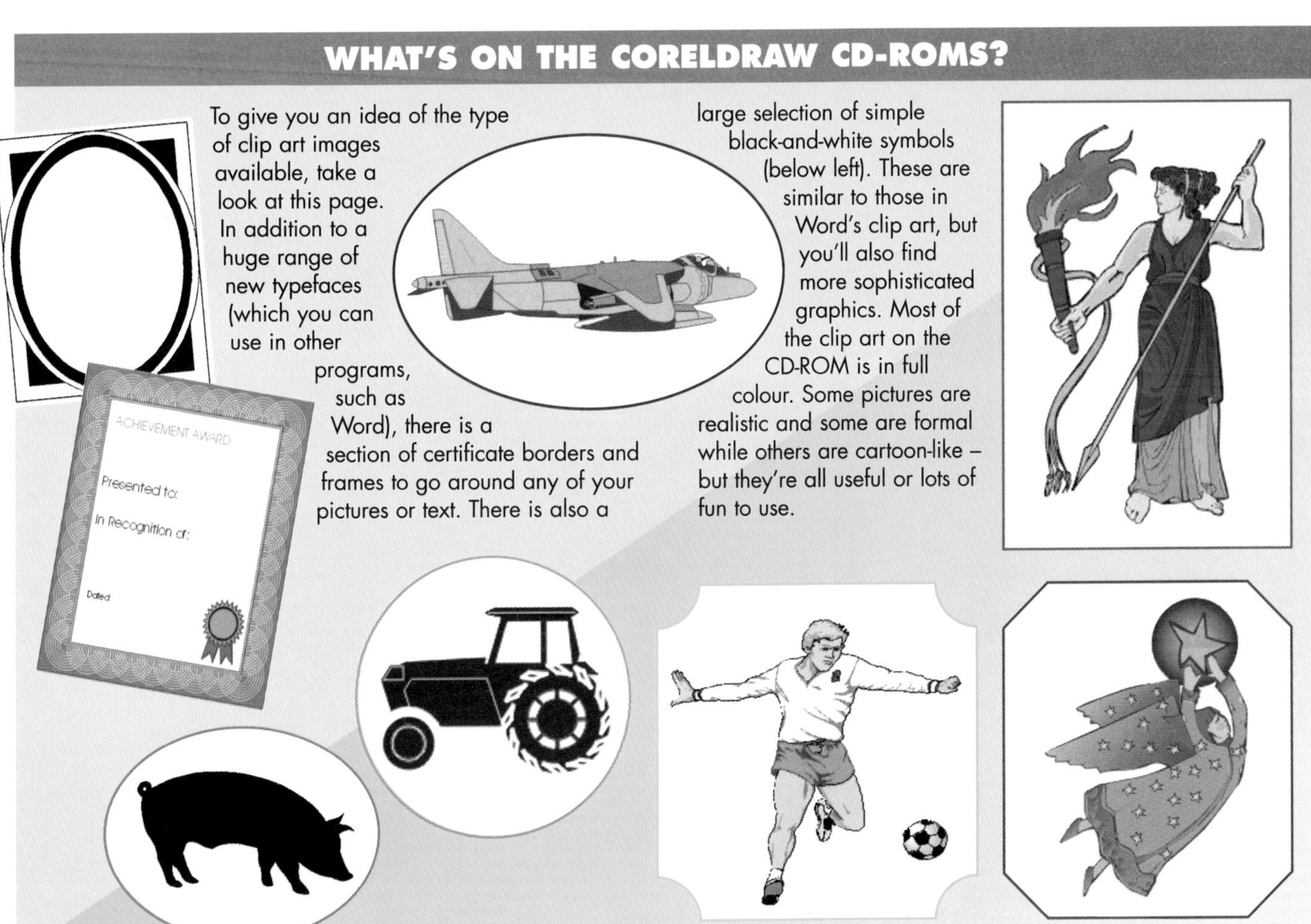

WHAT'S ON THE CORELDRAW CD-ROMS?

To give you an idea of the type of clip art images available, take a look at this page. In addition to a huge range of new typefaces (which you can use in other programs, such as Word), there is a section of certificate borders and frames to go around any of your pictures or text. There is also a large selection of simple black-and-white symbols (below left). These are similar to those in Word's clip art, but you'll also find more sophisticated graphics. Most of the clip art on the CD-ROM is in full colour. Some pictures are realistic and some are formal while others are cartoon-like – but they're all useful or lots of fun to use.

Working with ready-made clip art

Now you've imported the clip art you want to use to make a picture, let's take a look at just how much control you have over what the final image will look like.

1 You've already learned how to import clip art via the File menu, but you can also do it through a special dialog box. From the Tools menu, select Scrapbook and then click on the Clipart option.

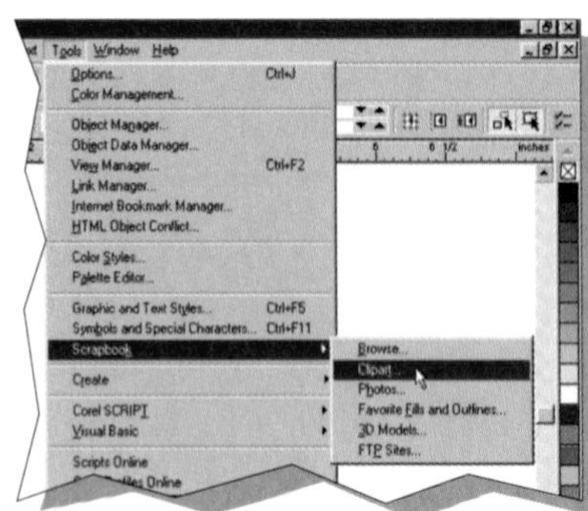

2 The Scrapbook window will appear, but first CorelDRAW will ask where to look for the clip art CD-ROM. Put the CorelDRAW CD-ROM number 2 in the drive, click on the drive in the list offered and press OK.

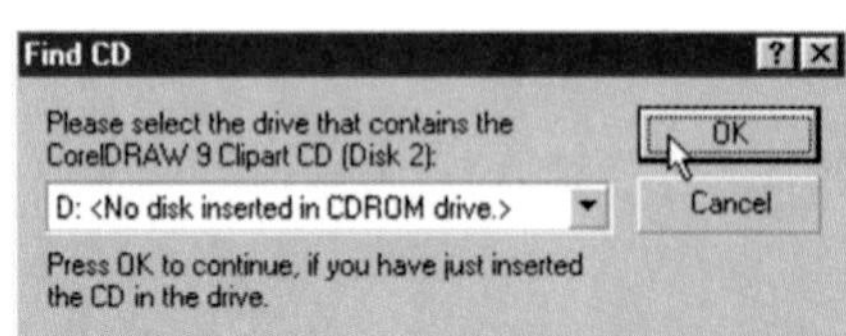

3 The Clipart window will normally show a thumbnail of all the pictures in the current folder. You won't see any pictures yet, as they are organized in folders. Double-click on the Collection folder.

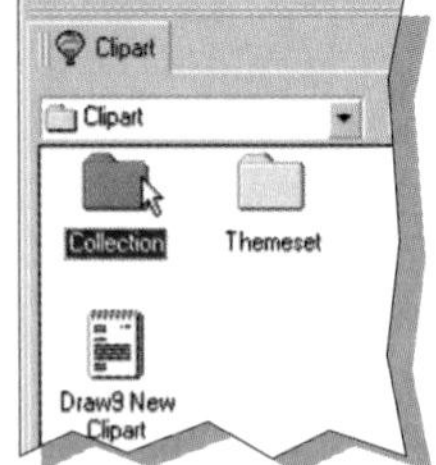

4 You'll see more folders, named according to the pictures in them. We want the Windmill picture, which the manual tells us is in the Residnl folder, within the Building folder. Double-click on each of these folders in turn.

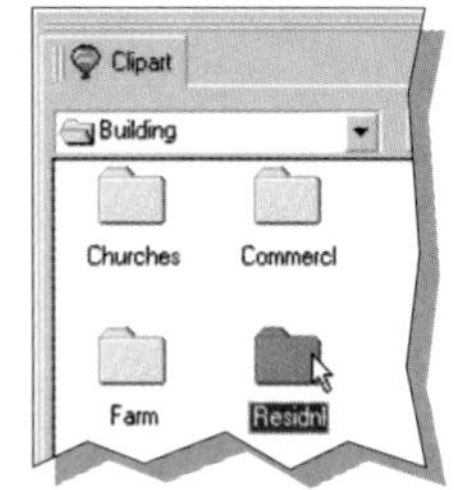

5 The window will now display thumbnails of all the pictures in the folder. Use the scroll bars to look through the folder until you see the 'Windmill' file. Drag and drop it from the Clipart window onto the blank CorelDRAW page.

6 Once you have dropped in the picture, it appears on your page. It's made of many individual objects **grouped** together. We want to move individual parts of the picture. Click once on the picture to select it and then press the Ungroup All button on the Property bar.

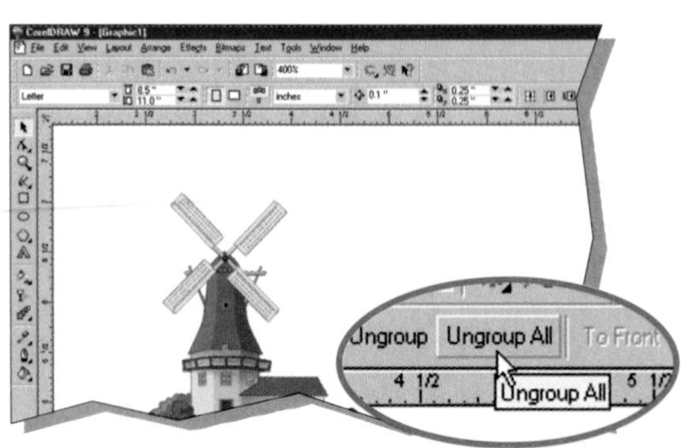

7 You'll now find that you can move the individual objects in the picture around on your page. Experiment a while and you'll see just how this complex-looking picture is built up of numerous simpler items.

8 With the objects ungrouped you can also change their colour properties. Right-click on one of the windmill blades and select Properties from the pop-up menu. Click on the Outline tab of the dialog box, then click on the No Outlines button (below, inset). Click the Apply button to return to the picture and you'll see that the blade no longer has a black outline.

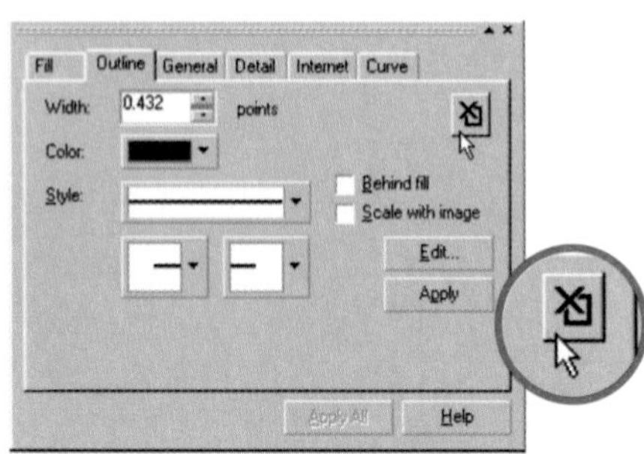

9 You can change each object in any way you like. In this fashion you can use the various clip art images as the basis for your own pictures, instead of having to start from scratch every time. Try changing the blade colour to red by clicking on red in the palette.

WHAT IT MEANS

GROUPED

Many objects in a picture are composed of lots of smaller items. To make it easy to move and position the whole object, you can join items together in a group. In our example, each windmill blade is made up of more than 20 objects, so moving one blade piece by piece would be very awkward. When grouped you can move the individual pieces as one. Ungrouping is useful for editing items within a group.

Using clip art in your own pictures

Clip art is often extremely useful as a basis for creating your own pictures and it's generally easier than starting from scratch. Let's see how this works by practising with the windmill image we looked at in the step-by-step exercise on the opposite page.

SHORT CUTS

If at any time you want to see a complete picture of your page, free of any obscuring toolbars, palettes or windows, then simply press the [F9] key on your keyboard. This will give you a full screen, uncluttered view of your work. To go back to the normal screen just press [F9] again.

1 Starting with the original clip art windmill, we'll change the colour of its wooden blades. We could select each individual part of the blades, but this would take much too long. We'll use CorelDRAW's grouping facility. Hold your finger down on the left mouse button and draw a rectangle around one of the four blades.

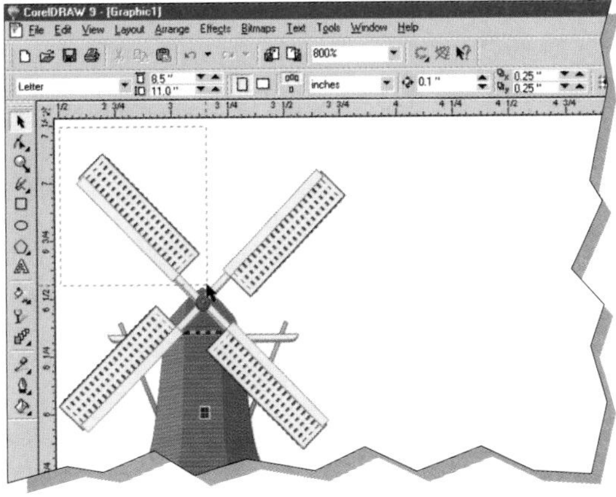

2 When you release the mouse button, you will see that all the objects within the rectangle are selected. Press the Group button on the toolbar to join them into a single object. Use the left and right mouse buttons to select both fill and outline colours from the palette. Then repeat the process for the other three blades.

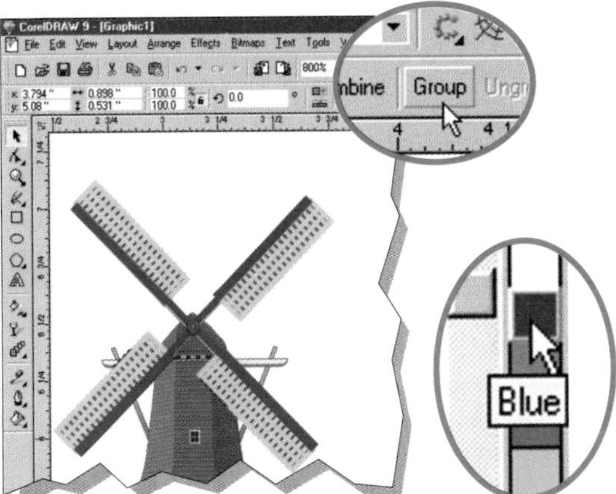

3 Removing the side building is just as easy. Select the building area by using the same method as in step 1. If you find you accidentally include other items in your rectangle, you can deselect them: click on each one you want to deselect while pressing the [Shift] key.

Now press the [Del] key on your keyboard and all the selected objects will disappear. You might find that a few parts are left, as shown here (far right). If there are only one or two, you can just click on each, deleting them one by one.

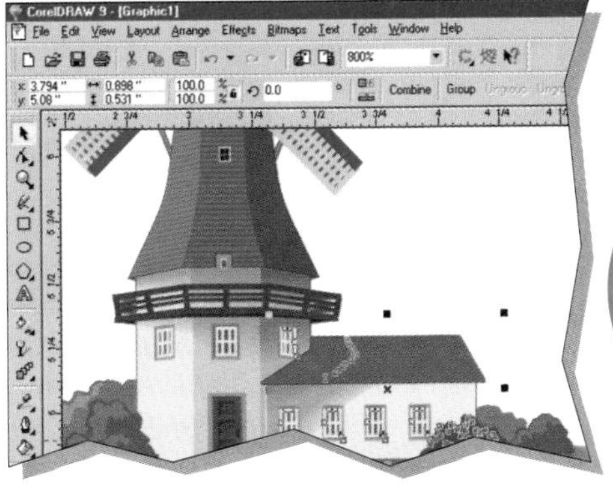

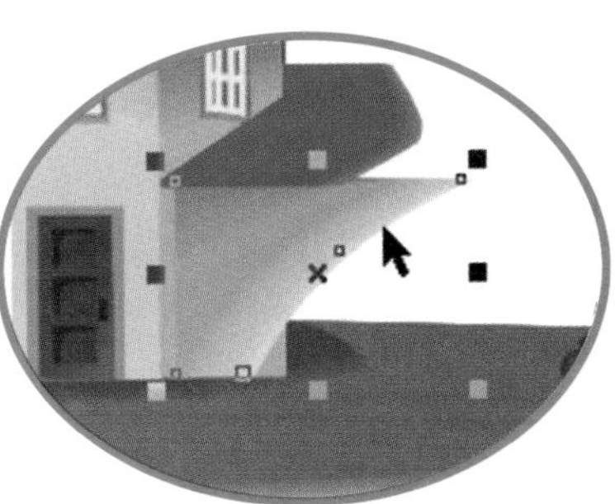

4 When you have finished, it will seem as if the building attached to the side of the windmill has never been there.

5 To finish off our scene we'll add a family. Look in the Family folder (which is in the People folder) and use a clip art image of your choice. You'll need to shrink the people so that they are in scale with the size of your windmill. You can also change the colour of their clothes.

CorelDRAW™

Using CorelDRAW's wide range of patterned and textured fills, you can create dozens of different effects as if by magic!

Special colour tricks

If you want to add subtlety and texture to your CorelDRAW pictures, the wide range of fill options are just the thing.

So far, our CorelDRAW pictures have ended up looking a little gaudy and unrefined. This is in large part due to the solid and uniform fill that CorelDRAW uses by default. With only a single, flat colour for the shape, this can look unnatural and cartoon-like. But there are many other fill effects you can use to help things look more exciting and realistic.

Different types of fill

There are six basic types of fill. The No Fill option is a type of fill that is actually more useful than it sounds, as it means you can wipe an object clean of any pattern or colour and start from scratch with it. Uniform Fill is the standard type and is the most similar to the fills in Microsoft Paint; it simply fills in an object with a solid colour.

More interesting is Fountain Fill, as it allows for a blend of colours within the object. It also lets you choose the way the colours blend together. Pattern Fill, as the name suggests, fills an object with repeating patterns, such as a chequerboard of black and white squares. Texture Fill is similar to Pattern Fill, except it uses complex patterns created by fractals. Textures are excellent for realistic fills because they look less repetitive than patterned fills.

The final type of fill is PostScript Fill. This is mainly aimed at professional graphics users who use special PostScript printers for very high-quality printing. Home computer users won't need to use PostScript Fill.

Experimenting with fills

As with many programs, it's well worth experimenting with these fill options. As you become familiar with them, you will find that by choosing the right fill you can quickly create drawings that would otherwise require a lot of effort. In the exercise opposite, we'll use both Fountain and Texture fills to colour in some simple objects. With a few clicks you can transform even the simplest of drawings into a much more realistic image with surprisingly subtle fill effects.

WHAT IT MEANS

FRACTALS

Fractals are very simple mathematical formulae that can be used to make complex-looking images. CorelDRAW uses the power of your computer to convert a fractal into a realistic texture. By changing CorelDRAW's settings, you can make many patterns, ranging from fluffy white clouds to green-clad landscapes.

Using shades and textures

You're not limited to cartoon-like solid fills with CorelDRAW. Many of the best-looking pictures use shaded and textured fills to create realistic and attractive graphics. Here's how even the simplest of drawings can benefit.

1 Start by drawing a simple picture. Here, we've created an Easter chick from a few very simple shapes.

2 We'll start by colouring the chick's body. We could use a solid yellow, but a more subtly shaded fill would look better. First, select the body, click on the Fill Tool at the bottom of the toolbar and then select Fountain Fill from the extra buttons that pop out.

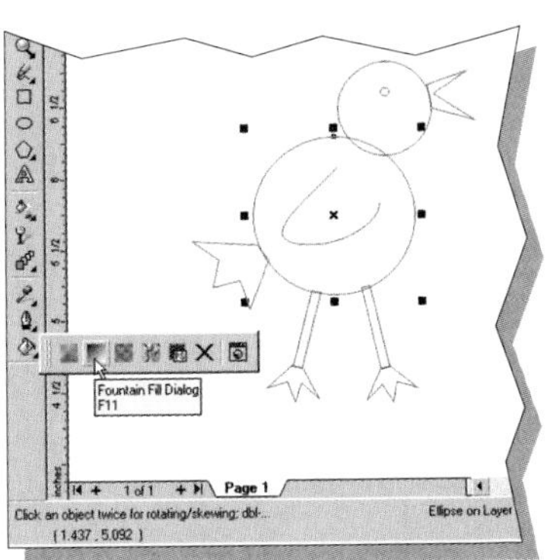

3 The Fountain Fill dialog box appears; click on the Type drop-down list at the top left and change it from Linear to Radial.

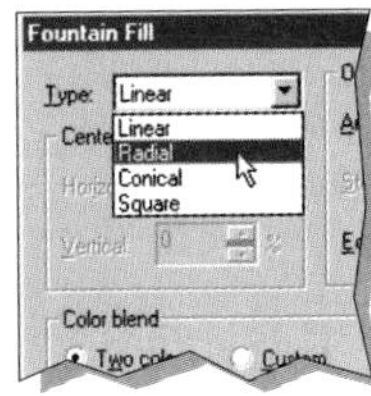

4 The small preview at the top right will change from its original, horizontally shaded square to show the Radial (circular shaded) fill.

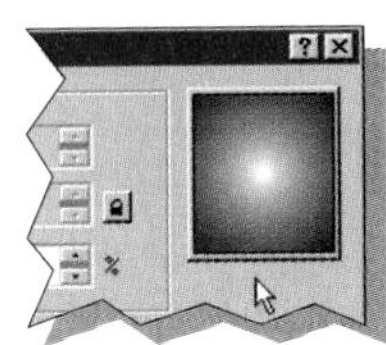

5 The preview is shown in black and white, but you can tell CorelDRAW which two colours to use for the fill. For our chick we'll choose two shades of yellow. In the Color Blend section, click on the From button. You will see a drop-down panel of colours. Scroll down until you find a suitable colour and then click on it. Choose another colour for the To button in the same way.

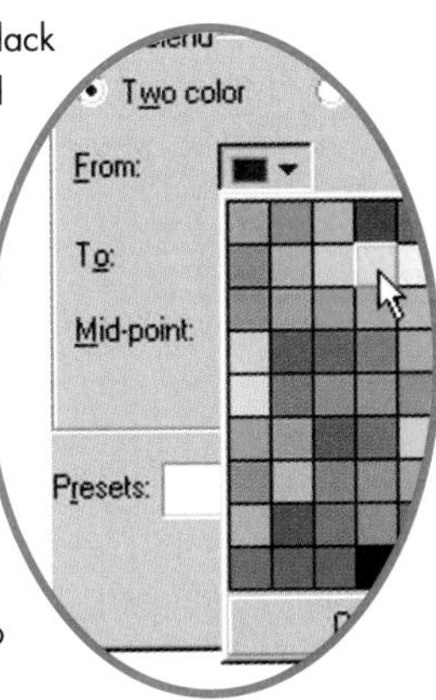

6 You'll see that the square preview of the fill at the top right changes to show your new colours. If they don't look right, go back and change the colours. When you're happy, press the OK button and the fill will be applied to the chick's body.

7 You can repeat the process with similar colours on the head and tail feathers, but right now we'll try a textured fill. Select one of the legs and click the Texture Fill Dialog.

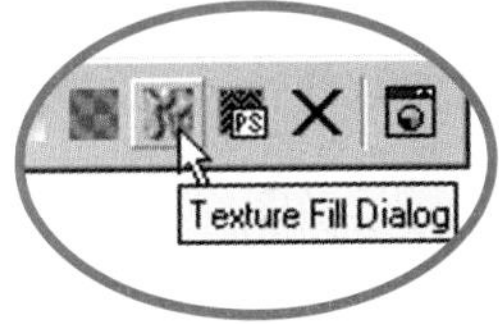

SHORT CUTS

When creating pictures, you'll often find that you use the same objects again and again.

CorelDRAW lets you duplicate an object or a group of objects. Select the object and press [Ctrl]+[D]. A copy will appear next to the original. This shortcut is quicker than using Copy and Paste commands.

8 CorelDRAW has plenty of ready-made textures to use in your pictures. The Texture Fill dialog box shows previews of the textures and allows you to customize them. Select Samples 7 from the Texture library drop-down box, scroll down the list of textures and select Wool.

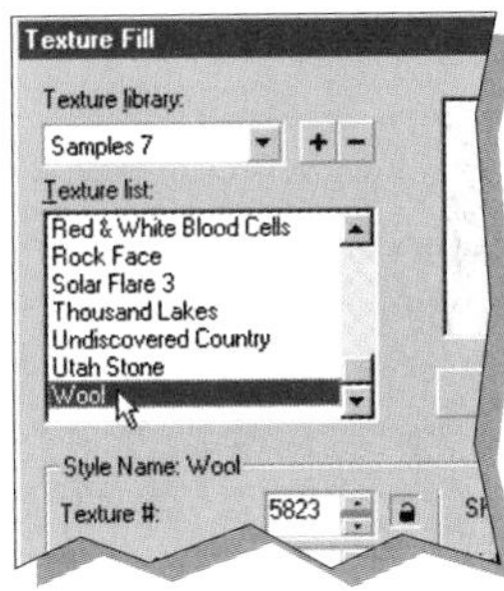

9 We want the texture to use colours appropriate for the chick's legs. Use the Shade and Light buttons on the right of the dialog box to select new colours. Also, change the Softness scale to around 75%, so that the pattern stands out more.

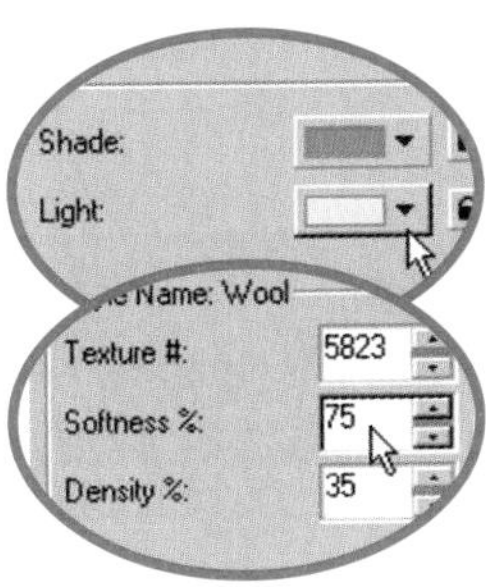

10 Use the same techniques to colour in the rest of the picture. Try out some of the other textures. Many are useful for different types of pictures, such as clouds and building materials.

PC TIPS

When creating a picture comprised of objects with solid, shaded or textured fills, you'll often find object outlines tend to spoil subtle fill effects. To remove them, click on the object with the right mouse button, select Properties from the pop-up menu and then click the Remove Outlines button on the Outline tab of the Object Properties dialog box.

Simple special effects

The computer-generated artwork that you see in magazines might look dauntingly complex, but many of the special effects employed can be accomplished with very little effort using CorelDRAW.

CorelDRAW's special effects usually work by altering or distorting an object you already have in your drawing. With the subtlety they add, you can create an impressive range of graphic images, some of which would not disgrace a professional designer.

The special effects are all available from the Effects menu and a few even have their own icon in the CorelDRAW toolbox. Most are simple to add and will operate automatically, so you don't need to be a graphics expert to give your drawings a special sparkle.

When using CorelDRAW special effects, the only limitation to what you can achieve is your own imagination.

Experiment with effects

In the following pages, we'll look at some of the most useful effects. You'll see how to: blend two objects together; simulate the view through special camera lenses; make a two-dimensional object look three-dimensional; and make an object appear transparent.

Flexible drawing tools

Special effects are flexible tools that can be edited when you apply them, or later, to change the effect they have on an object. Although effects alter the appearance of an existing object, the underlying object remains in the picture and can itself be edited at any time after the effect is applied.

The only exception is that objects which have already had one complex effect applied to them cannot then be modified by another. For example, you can't blend two objects together and then make them transparent. Otherwise, you can experiment as you wish: copy effects between objects or 'freeze' the effect and then copy and move that as a separate object of its own.

It is important not to use too many effects in a single picture or they will seem intrusive and gimmicky. But used in moderation, they can turn a routine image into an impressive one. The difference is 'taste' – something your PC can't provide. It has to come from you, which is what makes computer art just as creative as any other form of visual expression.

WHAT IT MEANS

SPECIAL EFFECTS

Although it brings to mind the wizardry used in Hollywood blockbusters, the phrase 'special effects' in the context of CorelDRAW refers to tools and menu options that are used to modify an existing object in the drawing.

The four main special effects

Here we look at four of CorelDRAW's most useful and versatile effects. They are all easy to use and give impressive results very quickly.

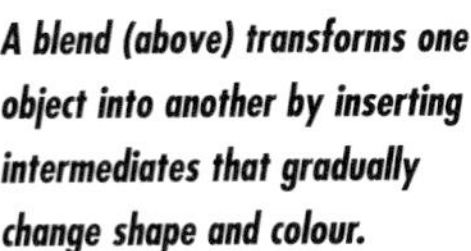

A blend (above) transforms one object into another by inserting intermediates that gradually change shape and colour.

Applying a blend

Blending is one of the most versatile special effects and can be applied to any objects you create using CorelDRAW. When you blend two objects, the program automatically creates a progression of intermediate shapes that gradually transform from one object into the other.

You can still edit and move the original two objects (as well as the entire blended object), but not the intermediates. The line along which the blend occurs can be straight or curved and you can alter the number of steps. With a lot of steps, the end result is an elongated shape showing a smooth transition between the two original objects. You can also create a compound blend so that the effect works between more than two objects.

Lenses can turn simple shapes and colours into attractive patterns. The circle below is acting like a 'rose-tinted filter' on top of the hexagons.

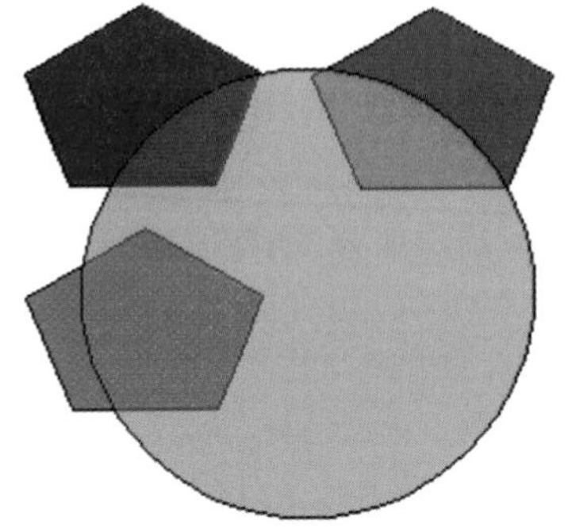

Lens effects

CorelDRAW offers numerous lens effects that allow you to simulate the use of certain types of camera lens on your picture. Just like the real thing, the lenses in CorelDRAW change the appearance of objects viewed through them. The type of change produced depends on the shape of the object and the type of lens chosen.

In our example on page 86, we will be using a fish-eye lens, but there are lots of other lens effects you can try out, such as magnify, brighten and tinted greyscale.

Extruding an object

When you extrude an object, you extend it backwards or forwards to give it the illusion of depth. In creating this effect, CorelDRAW adds extra surfaces to give an object a three-dimensional appearance. This can be a very

Extrusion makes a two-dimensional shape look three-dimensional. In this example, the word 'Success' is extended backwards, and enlarged during the process, creating a dramatic appearance.

effective way to create complex shapes without having to draw them. For example, extruding a rectangle can create a box shape, while extruding a circle can create a cylinder.

You can have lots of fun with this effect. Extrusion works with more complex shapes, as well, and you can even apply it to text.

Transparency effects

You can set a transparency level through the Effects menu or through the Interactive Transparency Tool. Both let you control the colours, patterns and textures displayed to create very subtle shading.

Here, transparency effects have been used to create a subtle, graduated colour on the 'sun' behind the flying bird.

OTHER SPECIAL EFFECTS

Add Perspective

This gives extra depth to a drawing by distorting objects to make them look as though they are disappearing into the distance.

Envelope

Envelopes enclose an object in an imaginary 'stretchy frame' which can then be reshaped and distorted. They work particularly well with text.

PowerClip

This command allows you to put one object inside another object. Any changes made to the 'container' will then have the same effect on the object inside.

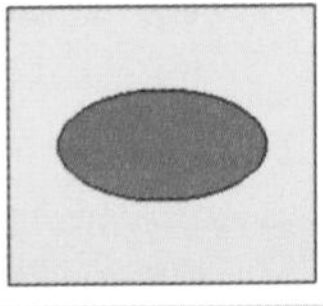

Contour

Applying contours creates an effect similar to the colours used to show height on a map. This works well on drawn shapes and also on text.

Using CorelDRAW's blend effect

Here we illustrate how blending works on two simple shapes. The Interactive Blend Tool is powerful and versatile, with settings that can be altered to create more subtle effects.

1 To show the basic principles of blending, create two simple shapes a short distance away from one another and fill them with different colours, as we have done here (see pages 70–71).

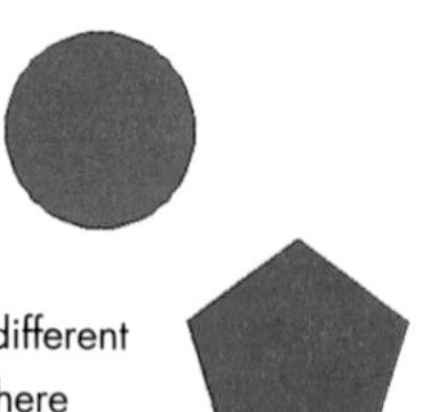

2 Click on the Interactive Blend Tool in the toolbox.

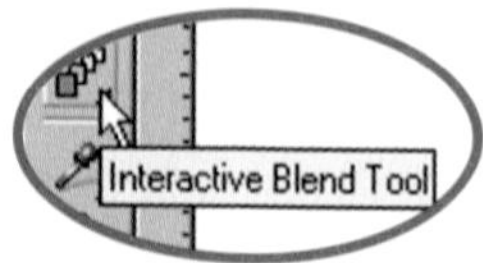

3 Click on one object and drag the mouse cursor on to the second. The direction you go determines which object ends up 'in front'.

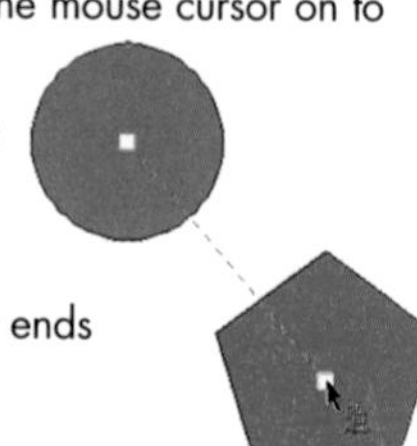

4 Release the mouse button and CorelDRAW will create a series of intermediate shapes in a straight line from the first object to the second. You can still edit the original objects to create further interesting effects. Select the red pentagon and move it around. As you do so, you'll see the blend move to follow the shape (right).

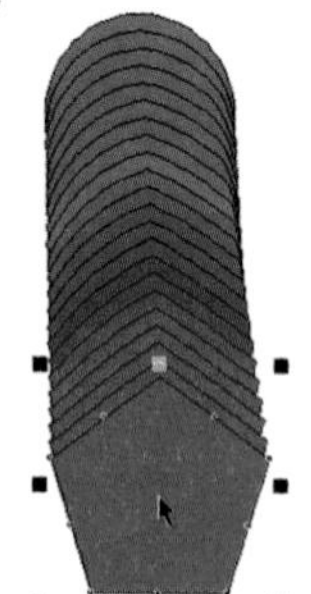

5 You can achieve more subtle effects by editing the end objects. Use the Rotation box (inset right) to turn the red pentagon. When you release the mouse, you will see the pentagon change to reflect its new orientation, together with all the intermediate shapes in the blend.

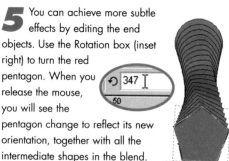

PC TIPS

One point to consider when blending multiple objects is that the original shapes can easily become unrecognizable if they are being blended with too many different-looking ones.

The intermediate colours can also become muddy and unclear if too many are blended at the same time.

Lens effects

These effects make an object behave like a camera lens. There are several different lens options, but they all work in a similar manner.

1 To begin, create four simple filled shapes. Make sure the objects are quite close to each other, as in this simple example, to ensure that the effect of the lens is obvious. Select one of the objects to be your 'lens'.

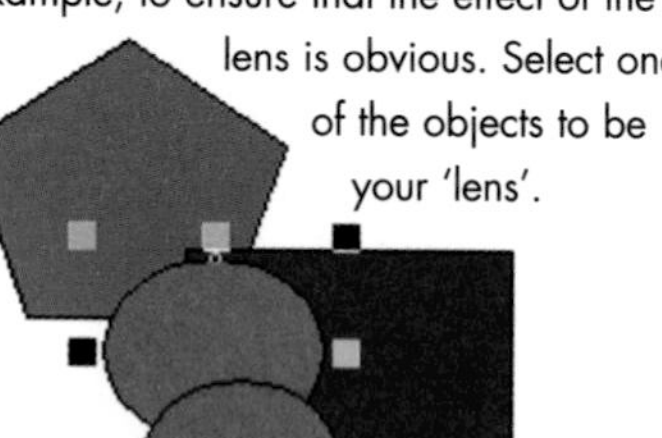

2 Click on the Effects menu and select the Lens command from the drop-down menu.

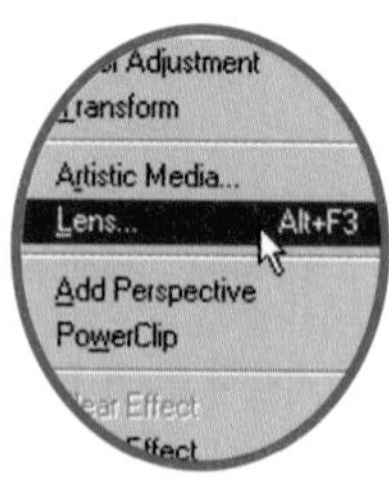

3 The Lens window appears. Select the Fish Eye option from the drop-down menu, then press the Apply button. The object selected becomes transparent because it has become your lens. Here you can see the subtle fish-eye distortion on the edge of the blue and red shapes. The green shape is unaffected because it is in front of the lens.

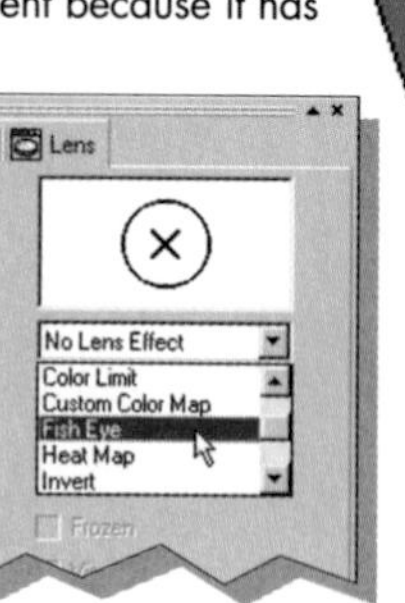

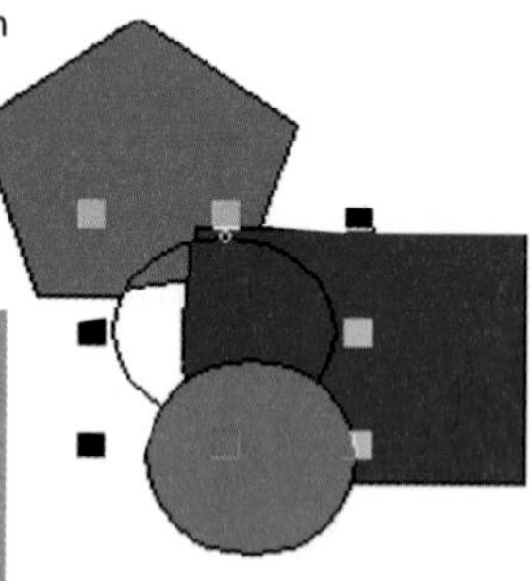

4 By default, the lens is pointing at the centre of the object. To move the viewpoint of the lens, tick the Viewpoint box in the Lens window, then click the Edit button.

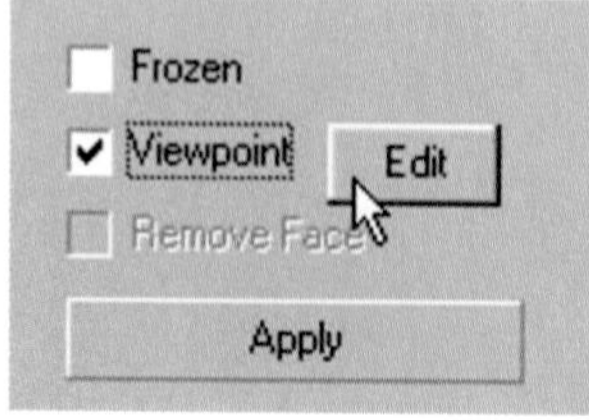

5 You can move the lens viewpoint wherever you like (it's indicated by a small cross), then press Apply in the Lens window to see the change (right). Experiment with moving the viewpoint and seeing how it affects your picture.

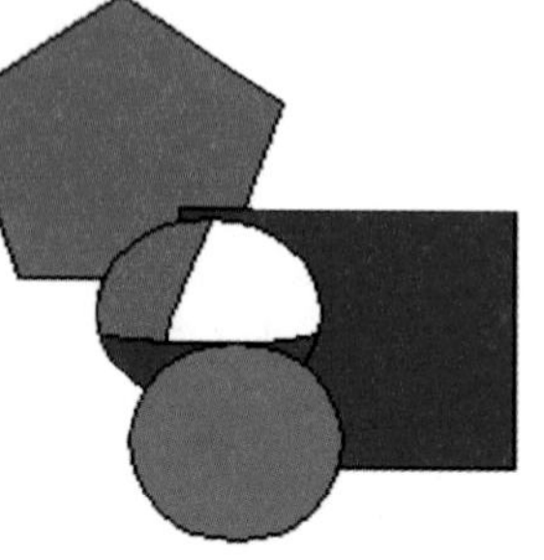

How to extrude an object

Extrusion is a great effect to use on text and simple pictures, giving them depth and dimension.

1 Start by creating a simple shape, using bezier curves or one of the ready-made shapes from the toolbox.

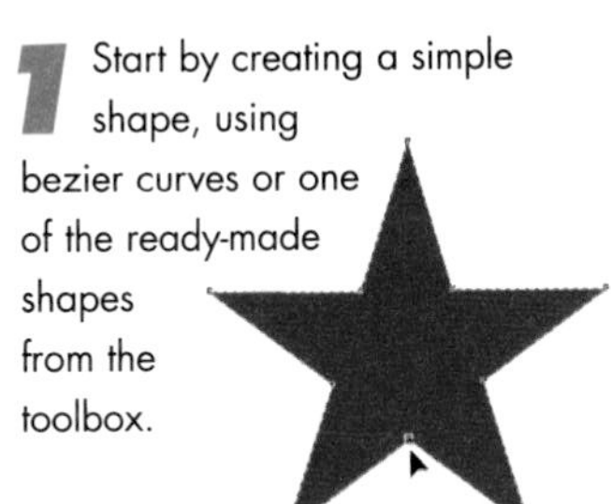

2 Now click on the small arrowhead on the fourth button from the bottom of the CorelDRAW toolbox to select the Interactive Extrude Tool from the set of tools that appears.

3 Click on your shape and drag the mouse in the direction you want the extrusion to appear. A wireframe outline shows the thickness of your extrusion.

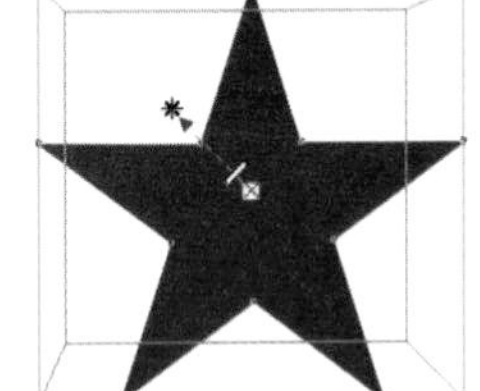

4 The extruded sides of your shape have the same colour as its front. To make the 3D effect more obvious, click on the toolbar's Lighting button and click on Light 1.

5 This casts some light and shade on to the object. The sides are now easier to see.

6 There's a small white marker on the extrusion line that is shown on your shape. Drag it back and forth to vary the depth of the extrusion.

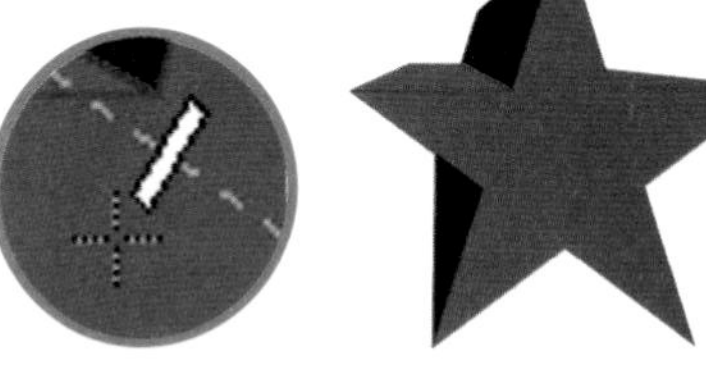

Using the transparency effect

The main use of the Interactive Transparency Tool is to apply subtle shades, instead of solid blocks of colour, by letting you mask out part of the original colour.

1 To try some simple transparency effects, create a drawing with several different coloured circles on top of one another. Then Select All using the Edit menu.

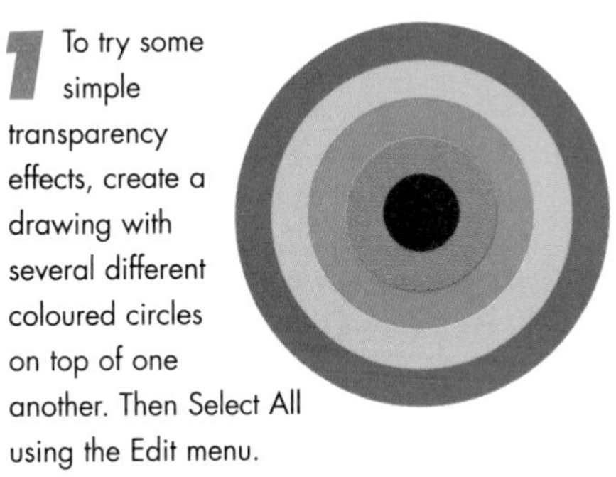

2 Click on the Interactive Transparency Tool in the toolbox.

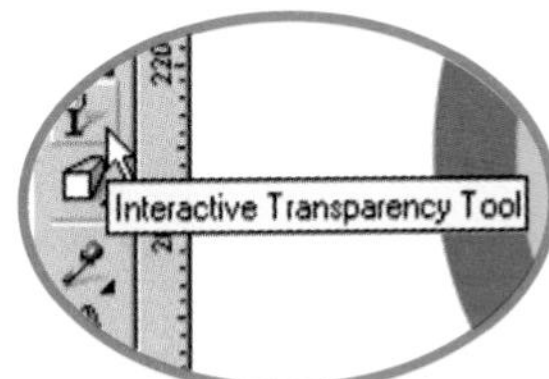

3 Go to the Property bar and select Uniform from the drop-down menu. Ensure that the slider to its right is at the midway point. This creates a 50 per cent solid colour transparency, so 50 per cent of the original colour shows through. This has the effect of softening the colours in the drawing (right).

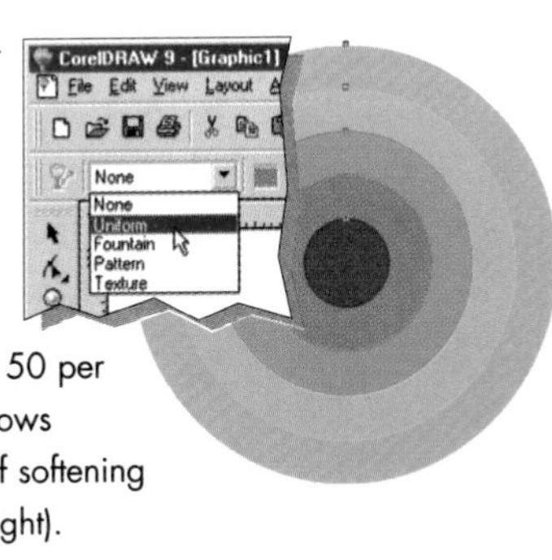

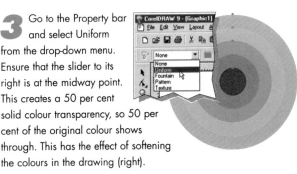

4 Transparency effects don't have to be solid or uniform. With the Interactive Transparency Tool still selected, click once to create a starting point for the transparency effect and hold down the button. An arrow appears. If you move the mouse, the arrow will follow the pointer. Drag it across the drawing and release it to indicate a finishing point for the effect.

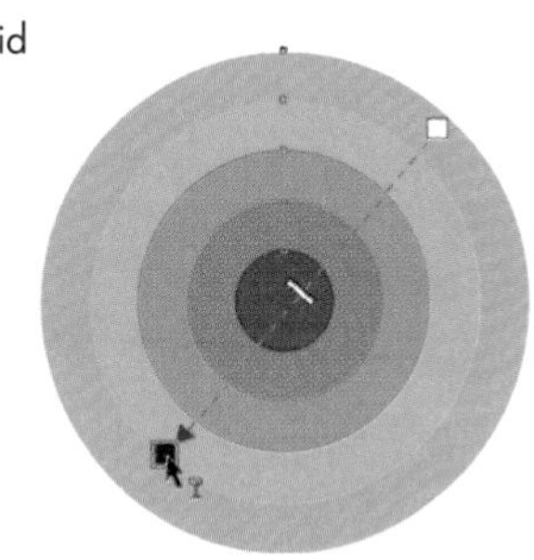

5 Click again and CorelDRAW uses the direction of the arrow as the basis for a smoothly graduated shading. Try experimenting – the degree to which the colour changes is affected by the length of the arrow. You can even take the point out beyond the drawing to produce subtle graduations.

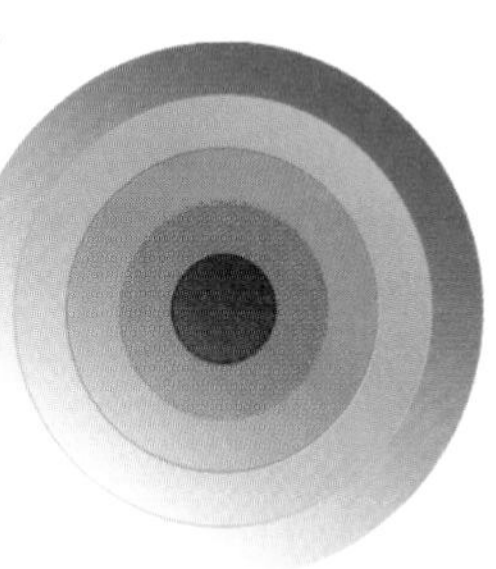

Combining objects

We've already seen how grouping objects together can help us move a composite image to a new position (see pages 80–81). Here we see how combining objects can make our creative drawing both easier and quicker.

Creating even a simple illustration in CorelDRAW involves bringing together a number of different objects. (The primitive snowman we drew in the exercise on page 69 involved a dozen or so items and even a simple piece of clip art can involve many more than that.)

Controlling all these different objects can be a fiddly business, but we have already looked at how you can group objects so that you can move them all together in one go.

However, on some occasions you'll find it more flexible, practical and efficient to combine the separate elements instead.

● Group differences

The Combine tool converts all selected objects into a single, curved object – automatically creating nodes you can edit – with uniform fill and outline characteristics. (This is different to grouping, which still treats each object as separate and distinct, even though you can move them around together.)

If any of the combined objects overlap, CorelDRAW creates 'clipping holes', allowing you to reveal what's underneath, also making it easier to get at the node of an object that's sitting behind another.

As well as allowing you to create complex shapes, combining objects dramatically reduces the file size and the amount of time it takes to redraw the screen. It's far smoother to move around a complex arrangement of combined objects than round a stack of grouped objects, each one of which has to be individually drawn by the computer.

It's easy to combine and then break apart objects. For example, in a complex creation you might find it easier to combine a number of elements and then work on them as a simple line drawing. To add colour you simply break them apart first (see PC Tips, opposite).

● Combining text

Just as objects can be combined, the same principles can be used effectively with text.

When you use the Combine Tool with text, the letters behave just like any other object that has been combined, and they become outlined shapes. When you move the combined text over other items, these show through (see PC Tips, right). Using Combine is the easiest way to achieve this effect.

PC TIPS

If you combine some text with a coloured rectangle to create a banner heading, you can then overlay the combination on top of a picture (see inset). The picture will show through the text to interesting effect.

Making a picture frame

Picture frames don't necessarily have to be rectangular. By combining two objects, one inside the other, you can create any number of interesting alternatives.

THERE ARE MANY reasons why you might want to combine objects. To see how useful combining is, we will create an interesting-looking picture frame and then place an image inside it.

For the image in our example below, we have used a CorelDRAW photo ('866048.wi' in the Travel folder of the third CD-ROM). You can, of course, use any image that you wish for this example.

1 First create a circle and fill it in with a colour. Make sure the circle takes up most of the page. Remember that you can create a perfect circle (instead of an ellipse) by pressing [Ctrl] as you draw.

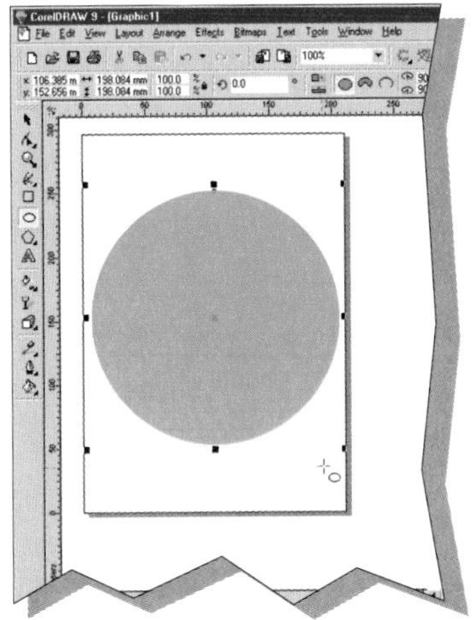

2 Next, create a pentagon shape in the middle of the circle with the polygon tool. Once again, you can make sure all its sides are even by holding [Ctrl] as you draw it. To illustrate how Combine works, fill in the polygon in a different colour, even though its shape will soon become a clipping hole.

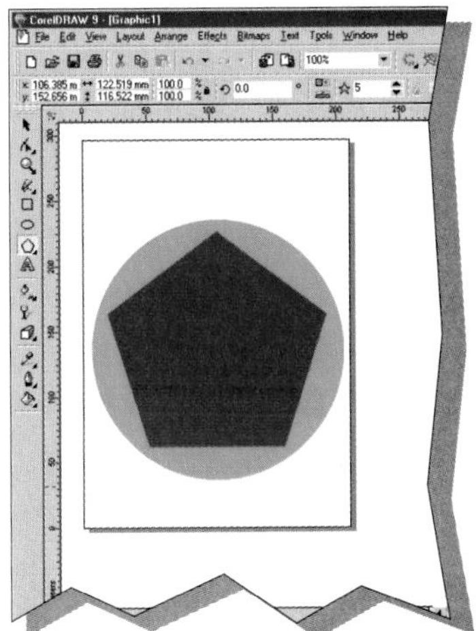

3 With the two shapes drawn, select them both with the Pick Tool. You'll notice that when you do so, the Property bar will automatically display the Combine button (if it's not there already). Press Combine and watch as the two shapes combine. The area of overlap (the whole of the polygon shape) will become a clipping hole.

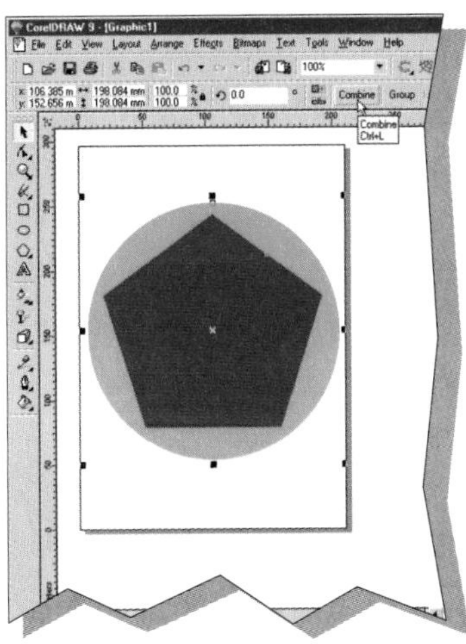

4 Even though the two shapes have been combined, you'll find that, thanks to the clipping hole, you can still edit the nodes of the original polygon object. Try this out with the Shape Tool and see if you can change the pentagon into a star shape, as we have done here.

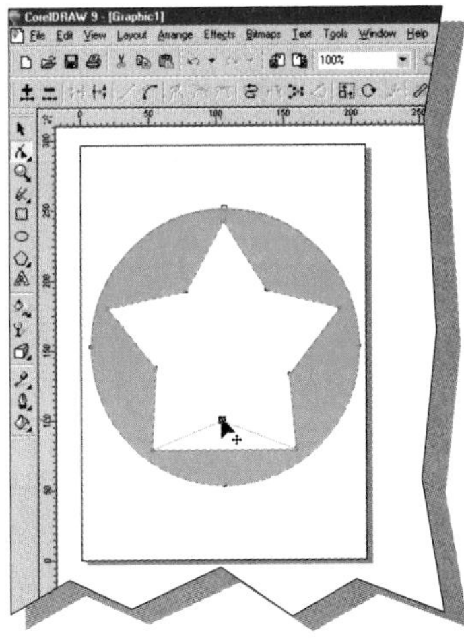

5 Now load in your image (see page 75). To see how the clipping hole allows other objects to appear through it, simply send the clip art to the back of the page. We've also cropped the clip art so that it doesn't poke out from the side of the circle.

PC TIPS

You can un-combine objects just as easily as combining them. Select a combined object and then select Break Apart from the Arrange menu. This will divide the combined object into its original parts.

Hardware

Sound advice

Your computer has great noise-making potential, from simply playing a compact disc to recording a song. Here's how to wire your PC for sound.

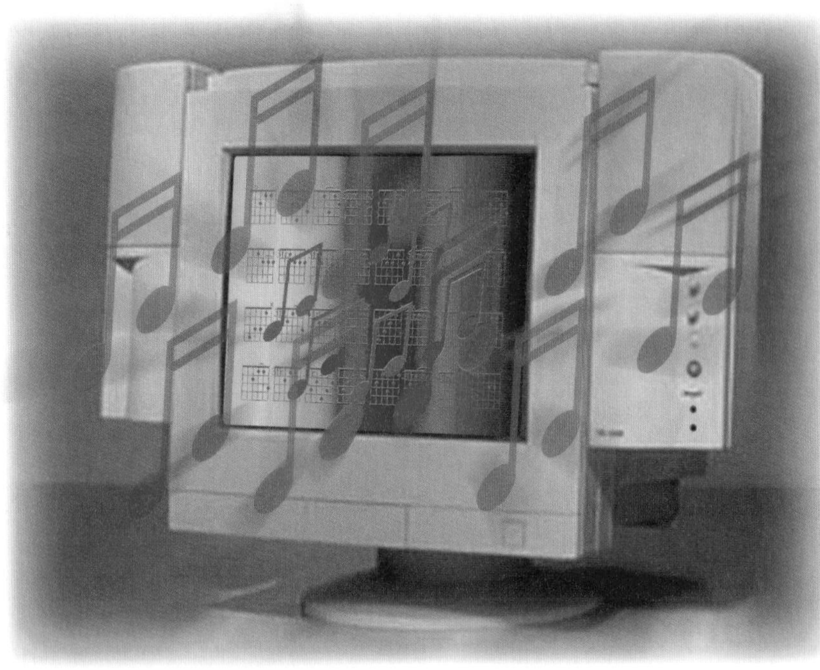

Computers can record and play back sounds and music to the same high quality used on audio compact discs. You can use your PC to help you compose and write music and link it to computer-compatible musical instruments. Then you can create any sound you like – from a rock band to a full orchestra.

If you only want to listen to music while you work at your computer, you can use it to play your favourite audio CDs or MP3 files from the Internet. Your PC can even program the order in which it plays each track on a normal music CD, just like any top-of-the-range compact disc player (see pages 26–27).

Check the rear of your PC to see if it has an output for headphones. If it does, you can use ordinary personal stereo headphones, which will make your game-playing and music-making more tolerable for others.

Sound and music are also very important in most computer games and your PC can produce stunning sounds and effects, even in stereo, that will enhance any game you play. It is likely that your computer is already capable of making all the noise you want it to. Have a look through the manuals that came with it to discover its noise potential. Refer to the guide opposite to find out what all the various music sockets on a typical computer are for.

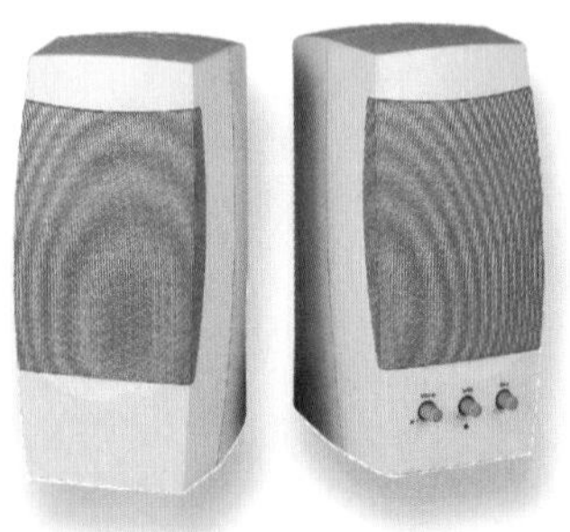

Special computer speakers are important if you want top-quality sound from your PC. The good news is that they are not expensive and don't take up much room.

● Sounding good

The quality of the sound that you hear will depend a lot on the quality and type of loudspeaker that you connect to your computer. If you aren't happy with the sound of your current speakers, it may be possible to improve them, either by replacing them or adding a sub-woofer.

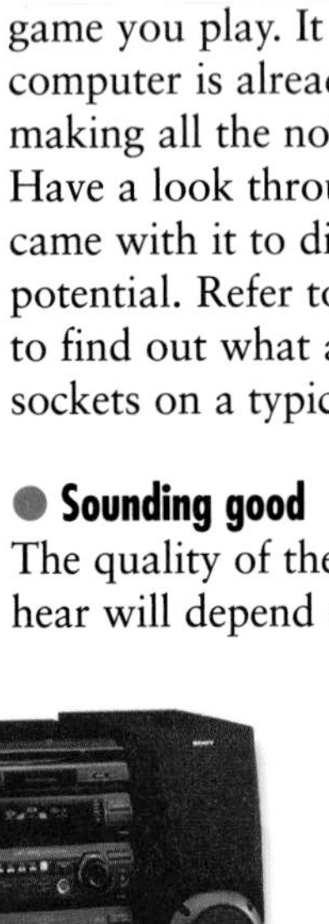

Plug your PC into your hi-fi system if you don't want the expense of buying speakers. You'll still hear good quality sound.

Many multimedia PCs come with stereo speakers to enhance the learning and entertainment experience. If your PC doesn't have speakers, they can be added.

If you have a hi-fi, there's a cheaper way of improving your computer's sound output. If your hi-fi is near your computer, you can use this to play the music and sounds from your PC. You will have to buy a cable to connect the sound card (see Stage 1, page 90) to the Line-in socket on your hi-fi amplifier.

A microphone can provide a link between your voice and the PC. If you have a powerful enough PC you can use speech recognition software or even make telephone calls.

WHAT IT MEANS

SUB-WOOFER

The loudspeakers that are used with computers are usually rather small. This means that they are not always good at producing deep bass musical notes. For bass notes, you need a larger speaker or a special device called a sub-woofer. A sub-woofer works with your normal speakers and makes sure that the deep, low bass sounds are played properly. Although adding sub-woofers will improve the sound from your computer, they can be quite expensive.

A look at the sockets for sound

Just like the rear of a hi-fi system, your PC has an array of sockets into which you can plug your musical accessories. Here's your guide to the sound sockets you'll find on a typical PC and what they do.

MIDI port

Although the icon indicates this is the joystick port, it can also be used to link your computer to an electronic musical instrument that can be controlled using signals called MIDI codes (MIDI stands for Musical Instrument Digital Interface). You can connect a MIDI synthesizer, drum machine or keyboard to your PC and input signals to the computer's sound card.

Loudspeaker socket

To hear sound and music, you need to connect speakers to the sound card. The music from compact discs (and many games) is in stereo, so you will need two loudspeakers. Computer speakers are all fitted with the same small jack plug – push it into the socket indicated on the back of your computer. Depending on the type of loudspeakers you choose, you might need to plug them into the mains as well as your PC.

Headphone socket

Many sound cards have a separate headphone socket that lets you plug a pair of standard personal stereo headphones into the sound card to listen to music or game sounds.

Volume control

Some PCs have a knob on the sound card (or speakers) to set the volume of the sound sent to the loudspeakers or headphones.

Microphone socket

If you want to record your voice or other sounds, you will need to plug a microphone into the sound card. Many multimedia PCs are supplied with a microphone, or you can buy one from an electrical retailer.

Line-in/Aux-in

This socket is used when you want to record sound from your hi-fi. Some computers need an adaptor for this purpose. Only one socket is shown here – your PC might have two that match the two phono outputs on your hi-fi. Check your computer's manual for details.

Line-out/Aux-out

Some PCs have an extra socket that lets you play sound from your computer through your hi-fi's speakers. Connect the Line-out/Aux-out to a spare input on your hi-fi to play sounds through your hi-fi.

1 The parallel port
Attach your printer to this port.

2 The monitor socket
Your monitor is plugged in here.

3 The serial port
For a device such as a mouse or modem.

4 The USB (Universal Serial Bus)
This is standard for adding extra devices.

5 The PS/2 mouse port
This is a specially designed socket for the mouse.

6 The keyboard socket
Looks the same as the six-pin mouse socket.

Advanced printing

Your printer can do so much more than produce formal letters. Even a basic printer can handle many paper shapes and sizes, allowing you to create all kinds of fun documents.

Even a basic printer is versatile. With the minimum amount of effort, you can make your own greetings cards and business cards, as well as print out envelopes of different shapes and sizes.

A printer is one of the most useful accessories you can buy for your computer, and the range now available includes many flexible and powerful machines. If you've only used your printer for letters, you've missed out on features that can turn it into a home print shop. For example, you can change the direction in which you print from portrait to landscape format, which is ideal for wide tables, photographs or text (see Portrait And Landscape, right).

● Paper types

The usual way of working with a printer is to fill it with standard paper and print out letters. However, your printer can work with a variety of different paper types, including thicker writing paper, index cards and even business cards. You can change from the normal A4 size of paper and print on small sheets for your diary or personal organizer.

The printer isn't limited to sheets of paper – you can print an address directly onto an envelope or even print onto transparent plastic for presentations. If you want to send a letter to several friends or contacts, you can print their addresses onto a sheet of peel-off labels.

Your printer can help you keep your computer area organized more effectively: there are sheets of special labels that you can use to print labels for floppy disks or CD-ROMs. All you have to do is type the details into your PC (where you can store the details) and then follow a few on-screen instructions before you press the Print button.

● Special features

Many of your printer's special features are set up either from Windows or from a word processing program such as Word – you do not have to learn how to program your printer. This means that you can change the way you print via a few mouse clicks – and without even altering the settings of your printer.

It's easy to see from where the portrait (above) and landscape (right) formats get their names from when you see them together.

PORTRAIT AND LANDSCAPE

The usual way of creating a letter or document is to write or print on a sheet of paper with the longest sides running downwards. This is known as portrait format, because portrait painters have always traditionally painted this way (you are reading this page in portrait format). Turn the paper on its side, and this is called landscape format, because this is the most suitable format for a panoramic landscape painting.

Great ways to get more from your printer

Your printer is capable of providing a lot more than just simple letters. Here we show you how to put power into your printing.

Almost every printer allows you to print a document either in portrait or landscape format. Portrait is the usual way of printing a letter, but landscape (where the paper is on its side) can be useful if you want to print wide spreadsheets, a sign or a banner. Although the paper always travels through your printer in the same direction, you can tell the printer to turn the text or image sideways so the finished printout is in the format that you want.

● Print a For Sale sign

Let's use the landscape format to print a For Sale sign for a car. Using Word, type in a few words suitable for a sign (below) and vary the size

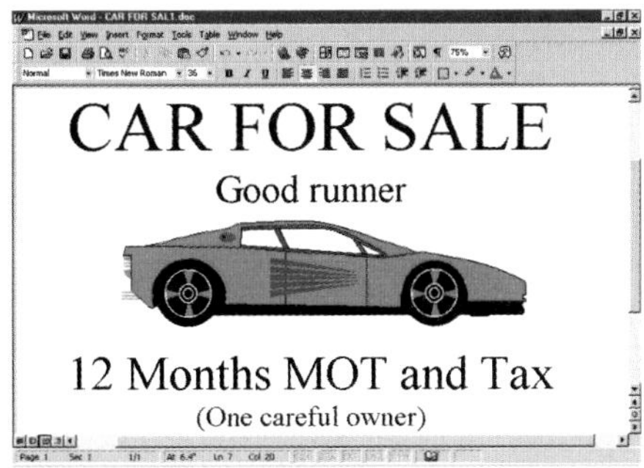

of the text for legibility and impact (see Stage 1, pages 34–35). You might also want to centre the text on the page and insert a car graphic using clip art (see Stage 1, pages 44–47).

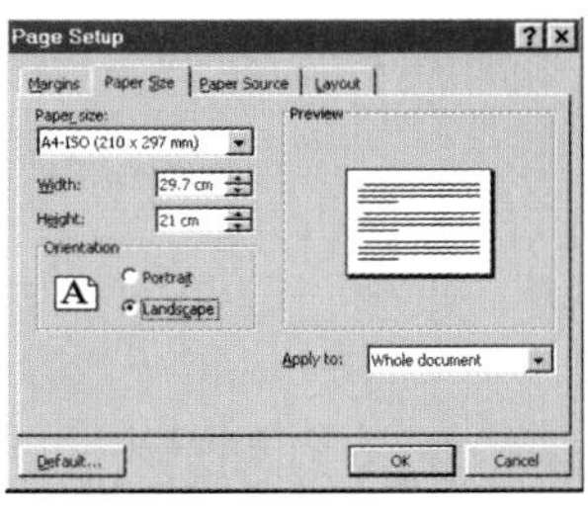

Next, from the File menu, choose Page Setup and then select the Paper Size tab (above). You'll see a choice for paper orientation – choose Landscape (see how the Preview format on the right changes) and then click on OK to save this change. Finally, click on Print as normal. There is no need to make any changes to the printer itself.

● Printing on both sides

There may be occasions when you want to print on both sides of a piece of paper. This isn't very useful for letters but for leaflets, newsletters and booklets it is really great.

Printing on both sides of paper requires some forethought. You need to plan how you want your document to look when it is printed, because you have to print the odd-numbered pages first and then turn the paper over and print the even-numbered pages last.

When you have entered all the information into your document,

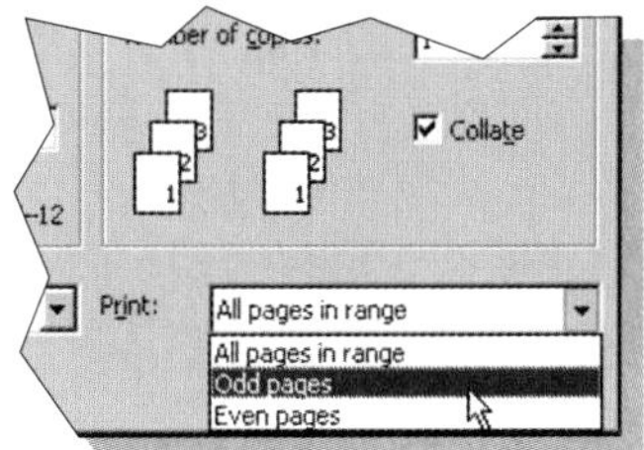

make sure that all the pages are numbered (see pages 34–35). Place the paper in the printer, click on the File menu and select Print. In the bottom right corner of the Print window, select Odd pages from the Print drop-down menu. Click on OK to print.

When the pages have printed, turn them over and place them in the printer tray again (see right, PC Tips, for a way of reminding yourself on which side of a sheet of paper your printer prints). Now select Even pages from the Print drop-down menu in the Print window and click OK. You'll soon have your document printed on both sides of your paper.

● Different weights of paper

Paper comes in many different weights and qualities (the greater the weight and the higher the quality of the paper, the more expensive it is), but most printers can handle a wide range of paper weights.

The weight of paper is measured in grams per square metre, or gsm. Standard printer paper is 80 gsm (the weight of this page of *PCs made easy* is 120 gsm). Paper weight is an important factor when printing at home. Paper that is too thick may jam the printer, so be sure to check your printer manual for the maximum paper weight your printer can handle. Most modern printers can use card, which has a weight of about 200 gsm, so you can print greetings, index and business cards.

PC TIPS

Check the print position

Working out which way to put paper or envelopes into a printer can be confusing, particularly if you are working with a strange printer. A simple way of working this out is to mark an 'X' on one side of the paper and place it in the printer paper feeder with the 'X' facing you. Now type a few words into your word processor and print the page. If the words print on the same side of the paper as the 'X', you now know which way to place the paper when you print your real documents.

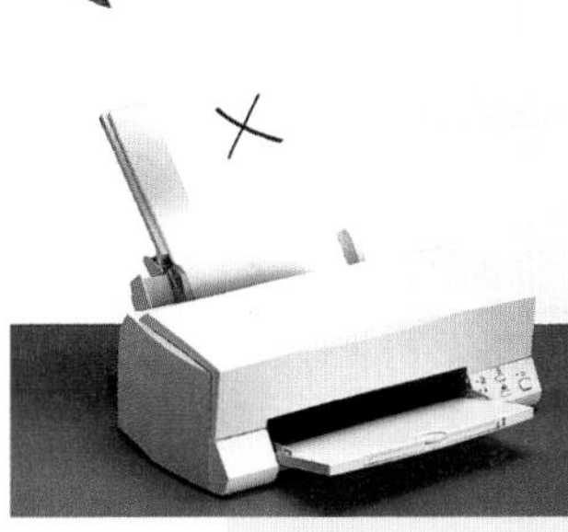

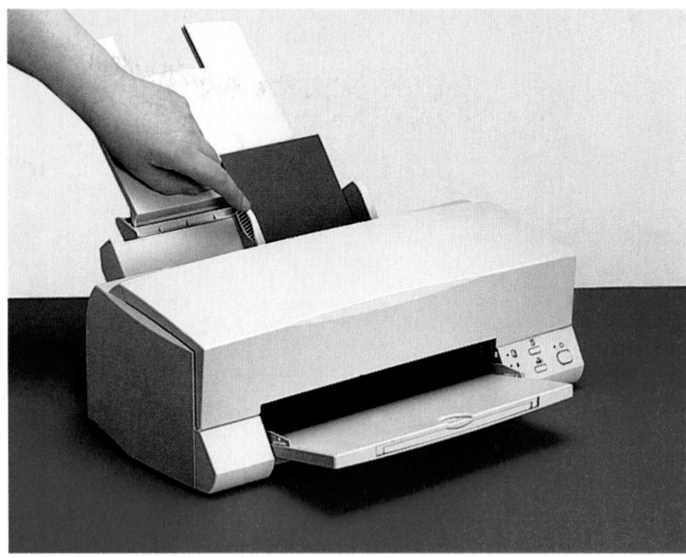

Whatever paper size or shape you print on, the only change to make on the printer will be moving the small guides which keep the paper straight as it feeds into the printer.

● Printing on different paper sizes

Most people use standard A4 sheets of paper for their printer, but there are other sizes. Almost all commonly available printers will accept a range of paper sizes from postcards up to A4. If the paper is too small, however, the printer will not be able to feed it through its internal mechanism correctly, so check the printer manual for the minimum paper size usable.

If you are using a colour inkjet printer (see Stage 1, pages 98–99), you can use special paper in a variety of sizes that provides the best paper for printing photographs.

To print on really small paper sizes (the type on which you might print business cards), you will find it easier to use special business card sheets. These comprise a number of cards together on a larger backing sheet that can be fed into a printer.

To print on a different size or shape of paper, you need to change the printing settings. You can do this while you are using a software program, such as Word. For example, if you want to print a collection of your friends' names and addresses on to separate small index cards, all you have to do is tell Word to expect a different paper size. You do this by clicking on the File menu and selecting the Page Setup option. Choose the Paper Size tab. In the left of the window, choose from the list of pre-defined paper sizes in the Paper size pull-down menu (below). You can also enter your own choice of paper size using the Width and Height boxes (right, inset).

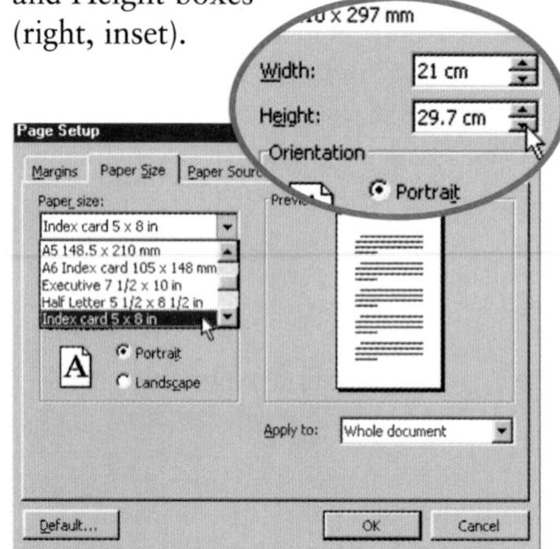

If you are printing on a non-A4 paper size, you should go to the Page Setup window to select the correct size option for your needs.

● Maximum printable area

One important feature in all printers is that you cannot print over the entire sheet of paper. Unprintable margins protect the printer from printing on to itself and causing damage to the internal components.

On a laser printer, the margins could be 5 mm all the way around the sheet, leaving the printable area within these margins. This margin is set inside your printer and every printer has different margins.

A good way of finding out the maximum printable area of your printer is to ask a program such as Word to tell you. Choose the File menu, then click on Page Setup. Click on the Margins tab. In the four margins boxes, type in '0' (zero) as a margin and click on OK. Word will display an error message that warns you that these are not correct margin settings. Click on the Fix button and you will see that Word fills in the minimum margin measurements that can be used with your printer.

It is possible to achieve superb colour results, even with a glossy finish, using photo-quality inkjet paper.

STRAIGHT-THROUGH PAPER PATH

When you print, your printer automatically takes a sheet of paper from the printer tray. On most printers, there is also a manual feed option that lets you feed in sheets of paper, one by one. Why would you use this option? Laser printers and some inkjet printers feed paper through a complex path of rollers inside the printer. The paper is sent on a twisting and turning route until the image being printed is formed. Ordinary paper is fine for this, but with envelopes and thicker paper, there's a strong chance that the printer could get jammed. To avoid this, go to the File menu and select Page Setup, then select the Paper Source tab. If your printer has a manual feed option, it will say Manual in the two lists on the left, so highlight them.

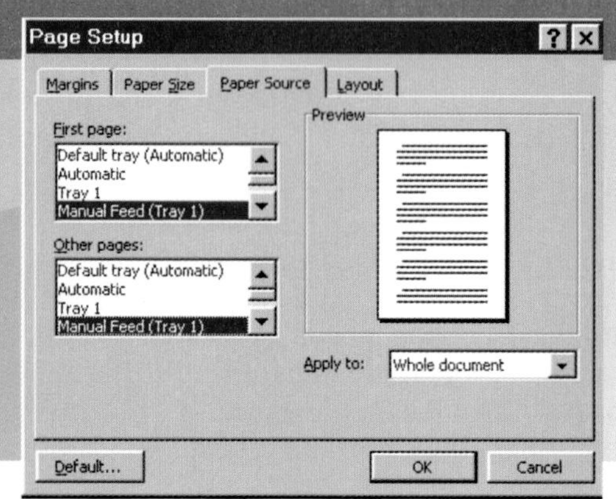

Printing an envelope

To give your correspondence a professional-looking appearance, here's how to achieve the perfect end-result.

1 As envelopes are generally thicker than normal printing paper, the first point you must address is the risk of the printer jamming. Before you print the envelope, make sure that you adjust the rollers for the thicker paper. This is often achieved simply by using a manually operated lever.

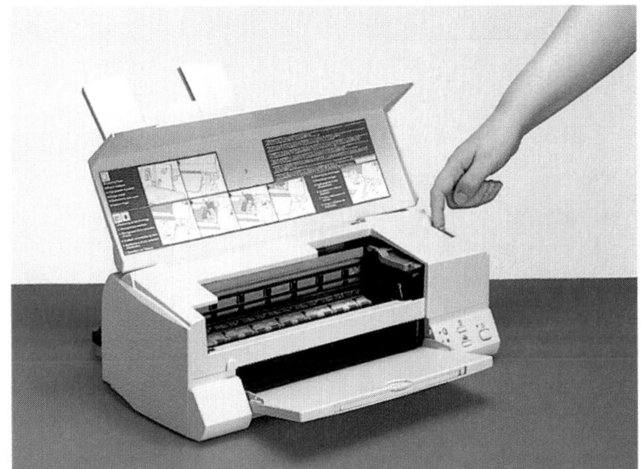

2 Make sure that you place the envelope in the printer the right way up. There may be a sticker or picture on the printer to help you, or you can turn to Word for assistance. Click on the Tools menu and select the Envelopes and Labels option. In the bottom right of this window there is a picture showing how you should place the envelope in the printer (inset). You might have to remove any paper before you place the envelope on the feeder (refer to your printer manual for advice).

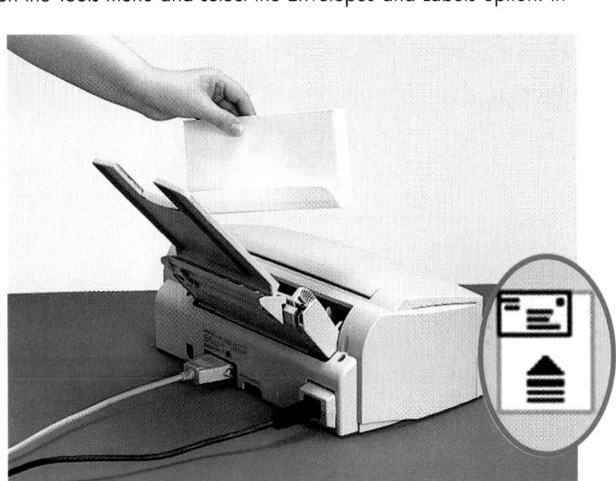

3 The envelopes might be larger or smaller than the paper you were previously using. Either way, you can move one of the guides to accommodate them. Don't make the guides grip the envelopes too tightly, though, or the envelopes won't feed into the printer. With most inkjet printers, the paper or envelopes just rest in the sheet feeder – there is no need to try and make the leading edge of the paper 'engage' in the rollers.

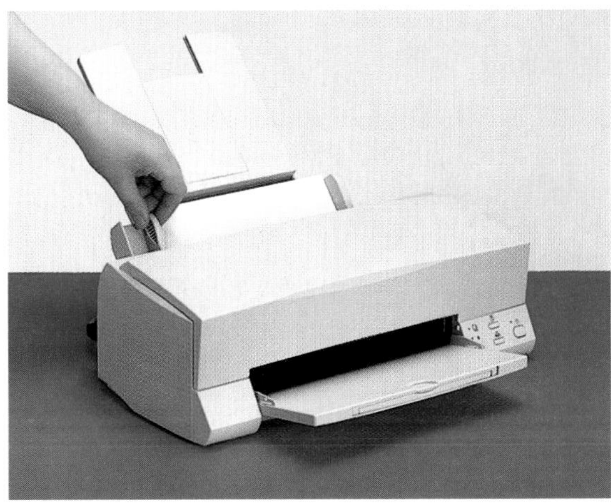

4 Here we can see an envelope coming out of the printer with the address face up. You can change the way you feed an envelope into your printer by clicking on the picture shown in step 2 (above) and selecting either the Face up or Face down options.

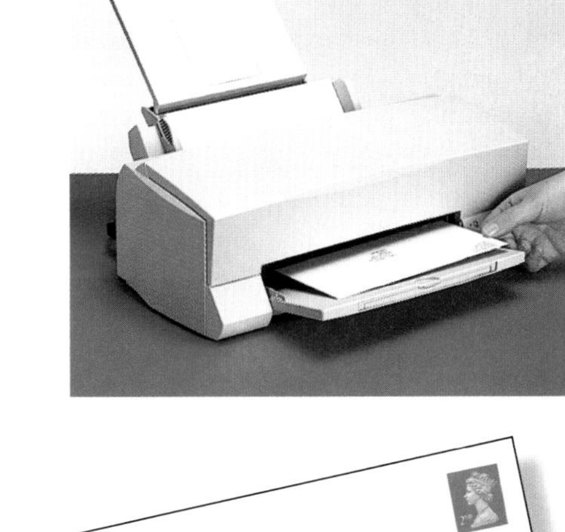

5 The envelope is now ready, with the recipient's address clearly displayed and the sender's address in the top left corner. Depending on your printer, you might be able to place a stack of envelopes on the printer's feeder tray or just one, as needed.

PC TIPS

Window envelopes

If your printer can't handle envelopes or it's too time consuming to change from sheets of paper to envelopes when you want to send a letter, an alternative is to use envelopes with transparent windows. With these you just have to position the recipient's address on the body of the letter so that it shows through the window when the letter is folded and put into the envelope.

Cutting inkjet costs

Inkjet printers can produce amazing results – and amazing bills for replacement cartridges! But there are ways of keeping costs down while still getting the most out of your printer.

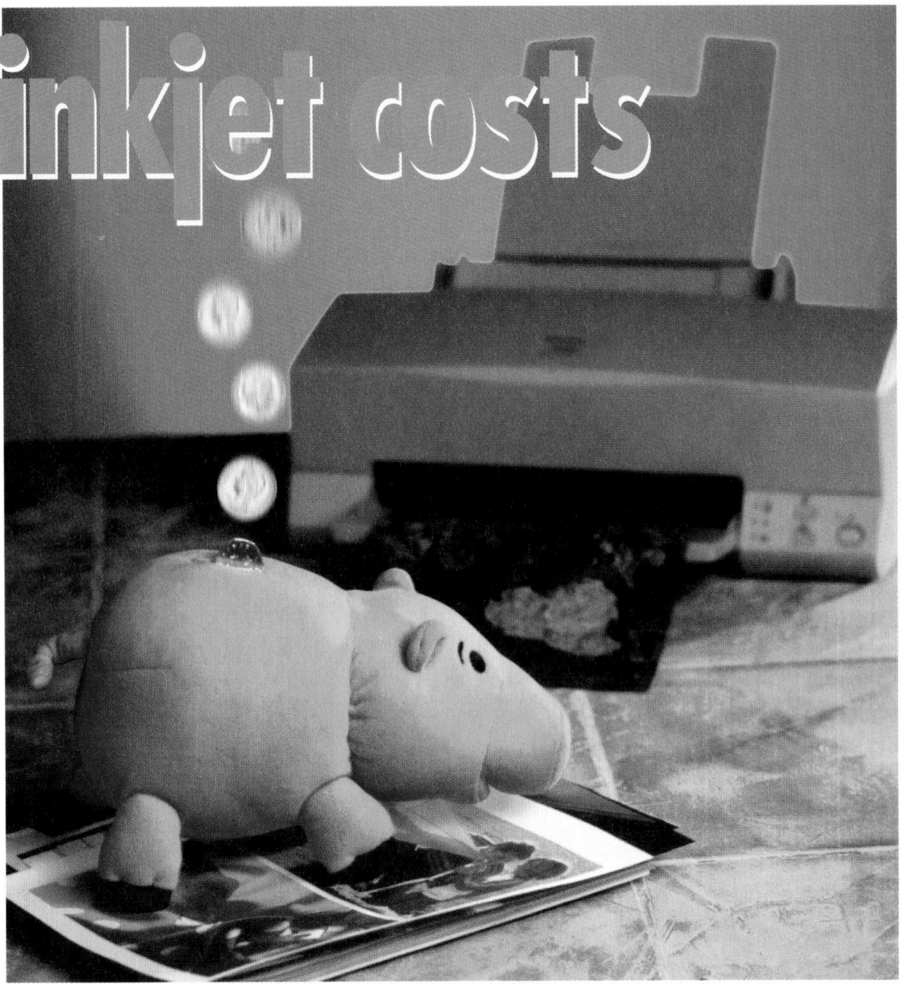

There are many ways to cut the cost of inkjet printing so you won't feel constrained about outputting your work.

Inkjet printers are inexpensive to buy, but can be horrendously expensive to run, churning their way through paper and ink at an alarming rate. But there are a number of ways in which you can dramatically cut your printing costs.

First of all, you can cut down on paper costs by using the right paper for the job. The price of paper varies enormously, with the most expensive costing perhaps a hundred times as much as the cheapest. The specially coated paper made by the printer manufacturers, for instance, produces great results but can cost a fortune – typically £30 for 50 sheets, which works out at an amazing 60p per sheet of paper! General inkjet paper costs around a tenth as much. So it makes sense to use the coated paper only when it is absolutely essential for top quality results and to use cheaper paper for all your rough drafts and less important printouts.

● Using copier paper

You can make even greater savings by using general-purpose copier paper, rather than inkjet paper, for drafts. It works perfectly well in most inkjet printers – yet usually costs less than 1p a sheet.

An additional advantage of using copier paper is that you can get it in different colours, or preprinted in a range of varied designs. If you can find the colour or design to suit your taste, this is a much more cost effective option than printing solid colour backgrounds.

● Monitoring ink consumption

You should take the makers' claims about ink consumption with a pinch of salt; the rate at which your printer uses ink depends to a large extent on the kind of pages you print. The makers' figures for ink consumption are often based on just 15 per cent ink coverage per page. If you print lots of pages with solid colour, or full-page photos, you get through ink cartridges much quicker.

One way to cut ink costs is to work out what kind of printing you are doing. Next time you start a new cartridge, make a list with five columns: draft black text, top-quality black text, a little colour, 50 per cent colour and full-page colour. Place a tick in the appropriate column for each page printed. Use a special mark for pages that are reprints with minor changes. You could be reprinting many ink-greedy top quality black text pages if you're only spotting mistakes on the printout. If so, you could print in draft mode first, switching to top quality for the final printout.

CHECKPOINT ✔

SIX TOP TIPS TO KEEP YOUR PRINTING COSTS DOWN

- ☑ Check the document on screen before you print. Use the Print Preview to check for layout errors.
- ☑ Recycle draft pages. Keep wasted printouts for other drafts, notes or drawing paper.
- ☑ Keep a record of your total expenditure for your printer.
- ☑ Use draft mode on your printer. This uses a lot less ink. Save it for those important documents.
- ☑ Shop around for new cartridges. Not only do prices vary from shop to shop, but also you might find a multipack that saves even more.
- ☑ If you use your printer a lot, consider refilling your cartridges.

Refilling an inkjet cartridge

We show you why you don't necessarily have to buy an expensive new cartridge every time the black or coloured inks run out.

IF YOU USE a lot of ink – two or more cartridges a month – think about using cartridge refill kits. These allow you to replace the ink without throwing the cartridge away.

Printer manufacturers frown on this practice – partly because they make lots of money from the high price of new cartridges. They argue that you might accidentally damage your printer through ink leakage.

However, if you are organized and careful, you can safely refill cartridges several times before replacing them with new ones. Do check that you are not invalidating your printer's warranty before doing so, however.

The refilling process should never be rushed. Take care, because spilt ink can irritate eyes and skin and wreck computer desks and printers. Clear an area where you can work comfortably and have absorbent paper towels ready for any spills.

You must refill cartridges as soon as they are empty, or else ink can dry and block the cartridge. Finally, if you are refilling a three-chamber colour cartridge, take extra care to ensure the ink doesn't mix, even in the filler syringe; make sure you wash out the syringe between each colour.

PC TIPS

Inkjet refill kits are widely available, although you might need to shop around to find a supplier who doesn't insist on trying to sell you more expensive, brand-new cartridges. Before buying a refill kit, make a note of the exact make and model name of your printer (with all letters and numbers), and the code number of the standard replacement cartridge (your manual will tell you this). Armed with this knowledge you should be able to get a refill kit to work with your printer.

1 Read the maker's instructions carefully and look for any variations specific to your printer. You might have to carefully tape over the holes for the ink cartridge reservoirs with masking tape to stop ink leaking.

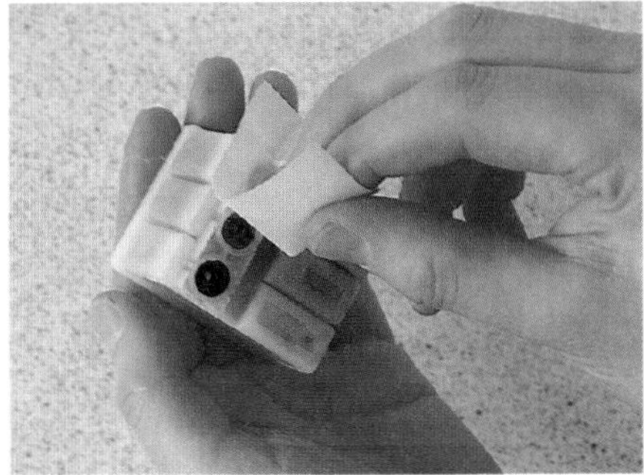

2 Turn the cartridge over and, if possible, lever off the first plastic cap with a penknife. If it does not come off easily, locate the ink fillers and bore through the plastic to enlarge them with a small drill or a penknife.

3 Load the syringe with ink and insert the needle halfway into the correct coloured reservoir. You might feel some resistance as many cartridges contain sponge. Then slowly press the syringe plunger to fill the reservoir.

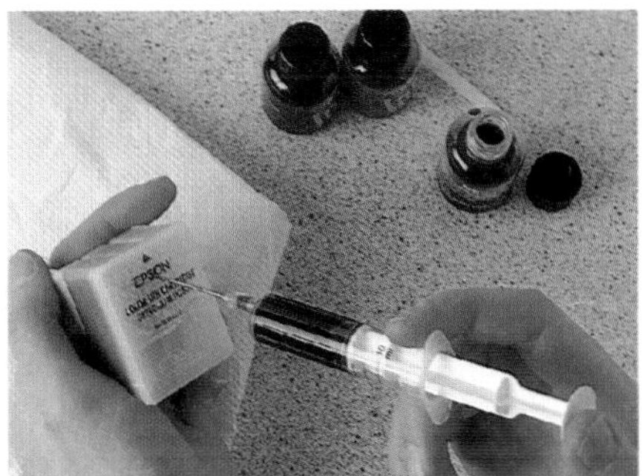

4 Take care not to overfill the reservoir – the maker's instructions should tell you how much to use. Wash out the syringe thoroughly with water between each colour, drawing water in with the plunger and squirting it out into a disposable dish until it runs clear.

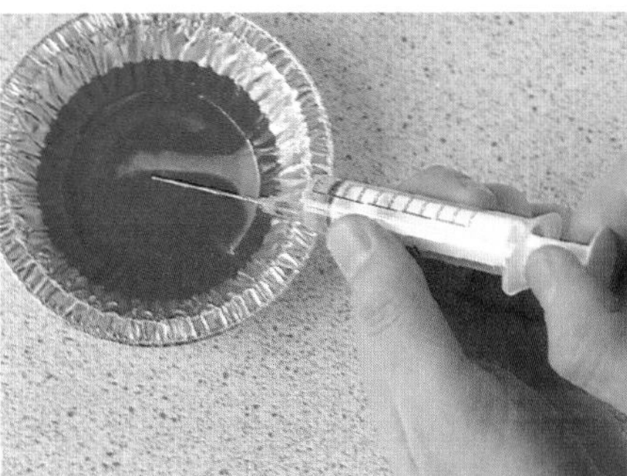

5 When the ink is in the cartridge, seal the reservoirs by inserting the rubber bungs supplied with the refill kit into each of the filler holes. Make sure you push these home firmly so that there is no chance of a leak around the sides.

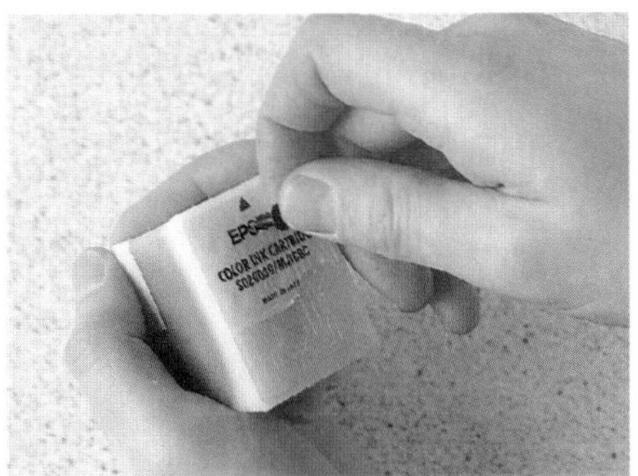

6 Stand the cartridge head down on blotting paper for two minutes to draw out excess ink and equalize cartridge pressure. Check carefully for any leaks. You must never put a leaky cartridge back into your printer. If you can't stop leaks, replace the cartridge.

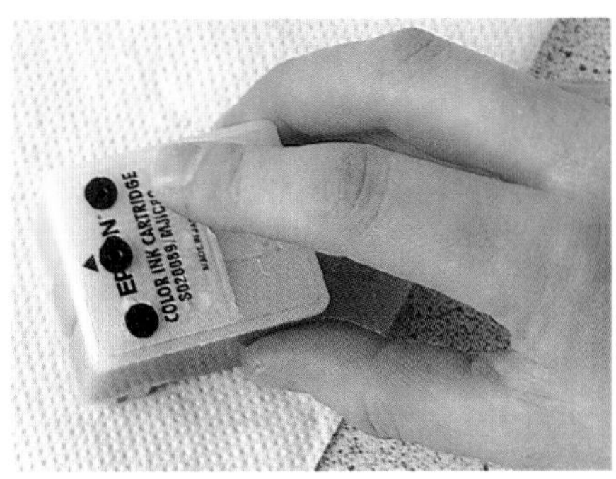

Recordable CDs

The CD has revolutionized both hi-fi and computer markets, offering huge storage capacity at a low price. But wouldn't it be better if you could write your own CDs? Now you can!

The Compact Disc is an incredible storage medium. A single CD-ROM can store up to 650MB of data – the equivalent of over 450 floppy disks. To achieve this amazing storage feat, the CD production process stores the 1s and 0s of binary data as tiny pits on the surface of the silver disc inside the CD. When you put the disc into your CD-ROM drive, the sensor in the drive uses laser light to detect the tiny pits and read the information.

However, the name CD-ROM stands for Compact Disc Read Only Memory, which means that the information stored on it cannot be changed: you can read it, but not write to it. Once a pit is pressed into the disc surface during manufacture, it is permanent.

With a special CD-R (Recordable CD) drive and disks, massive amounts of computer data can be stored in the form of a code made up of 1s and 0s.

Ideal CDs

The ideal would be a CD that you could write yourself. It would make backing up important information much easier. For example, making a back-up copy of a 6MB picture with floppy disks is very difficult (and time-consuming). However, a CD that is also able to record information could store over 100 such pictures before you even had to reach for a second disc.

In fact, recordable CD systems are now available, and they're known as CD-R (CD-Recordable). They comprise two parts: a special CD drive and a special CD that can then be read by any CD drive.

There are few restrictions on what can be written to such a CD – it could be data, programs or even music. The simple rule is that if the information

CLOSE-UP ON CD DISCS

Look at a CD-ROM disc and a CD-R disc side by side, and you'll spot some immediate differences.

The CD-ROM looks silver. One side has a label to indicate what's on the CD. On the flip side, if you look very closely, you should be able to make out the part that contains information (the area closest to the centre should appear slightly darker). Under a microscope, this would look like grooves composed of pits or indentations. The CD-R disc, by contrast, is silver or gold on one side and green on the other. The surface of the silver or gold side has a label on which you can write the CD contents. The green side shows the recording surface through the clear plastic. Once again, the areas that contain information will appear darker than the other areas. Under a microscope, the surface appears to be flat, but some parts will be shaded by the writing process.

can be stored on your computer's hard disk, then it can be stored on a CD-R.

CD-R drives

Information has to be stored on CD-R discs using a dedicated CD-R drive, as only these have the special lasers that can 'write' to the disc. Normal CD-ROM drives were designed only for reading information, so they lack this writing laser.

The write laser makes changes in a layer of photosensitive dye that the special CD-R discs contain. To write a bit of information, the laser heats up a tiny spot of the dye, which becomes less reflective. If you put the CD-R disc into a normal CD-ROM drive, the bits of information can be read from these spots just as if they were tiny pits in the surface of a normal CD-ROM disc.

The costs of CD-R

CD-R drives range in price from £150 to £250. Blank CD-R discs cost around £1 each. This is quite a bargain: £1 for 650MB of data.

However, the cost is not the main issue: writing to a CD-R can be a complicated process and is not for the faint-hearted. Due to the way information is stored on a CD, it's very easy to make a CD-R disc unreadable by accident. For example, a computer that hiccups in sending information to the CD-R drive – perhaps because another program interrupts the process – can ruin a CD-R disc.

ReWritable CDs

One of the limitations of CD-R is that it is a strictly 'write once' method. As soon as the write laser has heated a spot on the disc surface, it cannot be changed back to its previous state, so unlike your old hard disk, you cannot simply record over old files.

To tackle this limitation, many CD-R drives also work as CD-RW (or CD ReWritable) drives that allow the user to write and rewrite data to special CD-RW discs. Like the CD-R, these discs have a recording layer that can be altered by a write laser. The difference is that CD-RW discs can go through a special reheating process. This process returns the recording layer to its original state so that it can be written to again.

The future

The very latest storage medium to use lasers and optical discs is even more impressive. A Digital Video Disc (DVD) can store between 4.7 and 17GB (that's 4,700–17,000MB) on a disc the same size as a CD. This is up to 26 times more data than a conventional CD-ROM or CD-R disc.

DVD discs can also store complete movies with better-than-VHS quality and 'surround sound'. You can buy DVD players to connect to your TV, and thousands of movies have been released in DVD format. DVD drives are now fitted as standard on some home PCs. Already available as stand-alone devices are DVD-RAM drives. These are recordable disks that allow you to store massive amounts of data.

Inside a writable CD-R

Layers of a CD-R disc

Label and protective layer – to tell you what's on the CD.
Reflective layer – to reflect the reading laser back.
Writing layer – the layer of photosensitive dye.
Disc substrate – a clear plastic coating to protect the writing layer.

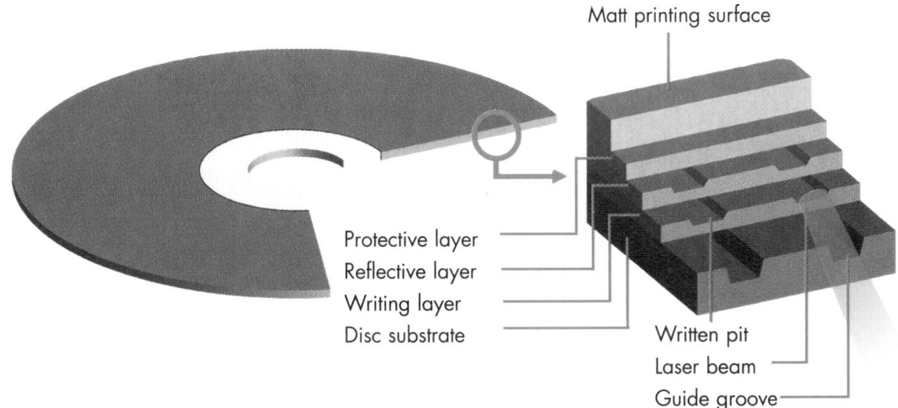

When the CD-R is written

Information is written to a CD-R as a series of 0s and 1s. When a 1 is required, the laser alters the photosensitive dye for that bit of data, creating a darker or less reflective part of the CD-R. When a 0 is required, the laser leaves the dye, and its reflectivity, unaltered.

When the CD-R is read

When the laser moves across part of the CD-R, it reads the less reflective or darker areas as pits or 1s and the reflective, unaltered areas as flats or 0s. In this way, it can read the information that you write to the CD-R as it would any CD.

ADDING A CD-R DRIVE

If you're interested in adding a recordable CD drive to your computer, make sure you find a local dealer who will install it for you. CD-R drives can be tricky to set up and use, and buying some expertise at the start will save you lots of trouble.

Make sure you also get some training; writing files to a CD-R is not as simple as copying files from your hard disk to a floppy disk. Ideally, get the dealer to go through the process step by step with your first CD. Pay attention to advice on shutting down programs that could interrupt the CD writing process and make discs unusable.

3D graphics cards

If you're a computer games fan, it's worth considering the boost in graphics quality that can be achieved by fitting one of these inexpensive add-ons.

With a 3D graphics card, some of your favourite games will look and play better and have added texture and realism.

The quality of graphics in computer games has taken a big leap in the past few years, largely thanks to a new breed of graphics card, often called a 3D accelerator.

These graphics cards have chips dedicated to the task of drawing realistic and absorbing 3D scenes. The main purpose of the 3D accelerator is to calculate and display polygons. Since the vast majority of modern PC games take place in 3D polygonal worlds, their graphics get a huge boost from the 3D accelerator.

The benefits

The improvement is twofold. First, a 3D graphics card increases the polygon power of your PC to such an extent that even a relatively slow computer (such as a 300 MHz PC) becomes fast and smooth when running 3D games. Second, it enables the PC to display special effects such as translucent water, lens flare and more detailed textures – all of which add extra realism to the game.

Without a 3D accelerator, a PC's main processor must do much of this complex graphics work itself. With a 3D accelerator, the main processor is free to dedicate itself to tasks such as working out the positions of the players and objects. The result is smooth action in a realistic, absorbing 3D world.

In recent years, 3D graphics cards have become cheaper and more readily available. Many can now be bought for little more than the cost of a couple of games. And if you shop around, you might also find attractive offers, such as a 3D card boxed together with one or more games.

Games power

This renewed interest in 3D graphics power is largely due to the success of dedicated games consoles, such as the Nintendo 64, Sony PlayStation and

WHAT IT MEANS

POLYGONS

The 3D world of the modern computer game is made up of many objects created from thousands of much smaller three- or four-sided shapes called polygons. The 3D accelerator card can draw and fill millions of polygons per second – fast enough to create the effect of smooth and realistic animation.

This fuzzy screen in the standard version of Jedi Knight (above), while not making this exciting game unplayable, lacks detail and is less 'realistic' than it could be. The same game, when played with a 3D accelerator card, is instantly improved (above). The texture of the surroundings looks better and the figures gain in realism.

Sega Dreamcast. These are able to produce games graphics that are often far superior to those of a standard PC.

The only way for a PC to compete as a games machine is to give it the extra circuitry of a 3D graphics card – similar to the electronics of the consoles – and combine this with the computer's existing processing power.

The reason why a PC needs an add-on to create console quality graphics is quite simple. The PC is, and always has been, a business computer at heart. This means that it's great at calculating tax returns and dealing with thousands of words of text, but has little built-in capacity for displaying moving three-dimensional images.

What you get

The easiest way to get an idea of what 3D cards do is to go to a computer store, play a 3D game and compare its visual effects with and without the enhanced 3D graphics. The pictures of popular games on this page demonstrate how the 3D-enhanced image is much smoother in texture and colouring.

Notice how the background objects and characters appear blocky in the standard version of *Jedi Knight*, while the walls and floor look washed out. In the enhanced version, the walls and floor appear as a single, smooth surface and the objects and characters are much more detailed. The improvements are even more striking when you actually play the game and can see the graphics move smoothly.

Costs

The popular Matrox Millennium G400 costs around £100. The slightly less powerful 2D/3D ATi Rage Fury Pro costs around £80. Cards with the latest chips (see Card Choice), such as the Creative GeForce 256 Annihilator, can be up to £200.

Such cards replace your PC's standard graphics card. Installing a 3D accelerator is relatively easy, but as you have to open up your PC to do it, you should get an expert to help you out, or find a dealer who will fit it for you. After the card is fitted, installing the card's software should take only a few minutes.

CARD CHOICE

These days, all 3D cards combine standard 2D functions plus 3D acceleration capabilities on one card, so they offer good value to most gamers. The most important factor to look out for is the type of graphics and associated chips – the 'chipset' – the card uses. Manufacturers develop and market new chipsets with increasing frequency, so make sure you buy the latest and best ones available if and when you decide to go for a 3D card.

One of the latest and fastest such chipsets is the nVIDIA GeForce 256, as used in cards such as the Guillemot 3D Prophet. Such chipsets are aimed not just at providing super-fast gaming, but at enhancing the crucial area of games graphics known as T&L – transform and lighting – the means by which one scene changes to another and is realistically lit. Other respected chipsets are the Voodoo3 series, used in cards from 3DFX, and the ATi Rage 128 Pro. Because of rapid development in the technology, it's well worth quizzing the sales people before you buy a 3D card to ensure that you're not getting one that will quickly be superseded by something better and cheaper. Similarly, bear in mind that games have to be written specifically to take advantage of the improvements in 3D cards, so be sure to ask searching questions about whether a new card actually has many games that show all its features.

The improvement is obvious in the game Quake II. On a basic PC (above left) the image is jagged and blocky. With a 3D accelerator (above right) it looks smooth.

Alternative input devices

The keyboard and mouse are not the only ways of controlling what happens on your screen. If you want to make your computing more fun – or more accurate – there are plenty of other options.

The most powerful and expensive PC components are inside your computer, but they wouldn't be much use to you without the simple and generally cheap components on the outside – the mouse and keyboard. Most people are happy with the mouse and keyboard supplied with their computer at the time of purchase, but you're not stuck with them. If you find the normal keyboard makes typing tedious, or perhaps your young children find it hard to get to grips with the standard mouse, there are alternatives to explore.

Your options include ergonomically shaped keyboards (see below, Ergonomics), a mouse that doesn't need a cable and special pen-based drawing tools.

Even just updating your mouse or keyboard can make work on your computer more efficient and enjoyable.

● Try the alternatives

You might find that the keyboard supplied with your PC becomes uncomfortable with prolonged use. You can easily change it for a better quality one. Some have a specially contoured layout which helps ease fatigue, while others have different key actions. Ask at your local computer shop to see if they'll let you try out the alternatives: you might prefer keyboards with firmer, more positive springing under the keys, while others favour softer keys. You might also like to use an in-built wrist rest.

The Logitech Marble Mouse combines elements from a mouse and a trackball to form a very precise, yet hand-sized, input device.

● Easier mouse-work

The earliest computer users had to make do with only a keyboard for entering information into their computers, but now the mouse has become a standard PC accessory. A mouse is often the easiest way to access menus, buttons and objects on the screen, but, like the keyboard, some of the mice supplied with home computers can prove difficult or

ERGONOMICS

The buzzword that has transformed the way you use and interact with a computer is ergonomics. This is the study of the way in which people use machines. It covers everything from the way that you sit at your desk and hold your mouse to the layout of the keyboard and the picture on the monitor. If you get these factors wrong, you'll find a computer is tiring and even painful (headaches, neck-ache or wrist problems are serious concerns for computer users). Ergonomically designed computer accessories are intended to minimize the chances of such problems.

uncomfortable to use. Don't worry, however, you're not restricted to a single, unloved mouse. As you'll see on this page and the next, there are plenty of alternatives that can make mouse-work easier, more fun and much more accurate to use for drawing and painting programs, such as Microsoft Paint and CorelDRAW.

Trackballs reduce the need for lots of space, cordless mice reduce cable clutter and there are mice specially tailored for young hands. An optical mouse uses a light-sensitive tracking device to plot its position. It is more precise than an ordinary mouse and needs cleaning less often. Artists frustrated by the tricky practice of painting with the mouse can add a special pen and pad to supplement the mouse for more natural artwork.

● The price is right

Many of these alternative accessories are not expensive, so if you're finding your existing components fatiguing, it's worth thinking about changing them. A good-quality keyboard should cost no more than £30–40: in fact the Microsoft ergonomic model is at the bottom end of that price range. Keyboards for children start from £15–25.

Surprisingly, a mouse is often more expensive than a keyboard: a high-quality replacement mouse is around £30 and a cordless mouse can cost around £40. For budding designers and artists, a drawing pad and pen starts at £50, and professionals can pay anything up to £800 for a top-of-the-range pad.

PLUG AND PLAY

Windows tries to make it easy for you to install new devices on your computer. When it starts up, Windows looks for new devices that you have added while the PC was switched off. This is called plug and play.

Many keyboards and mice replace existing components without any extra intervention, but you should always check with your computer supplier that any new device you buy is Windows plug-and-play compatible.

Gallery of devices

If you're looking to replace or supplement your keyboard or mouse, here's a round-up of the types of device available. Some are fun, others have more serious uses, but what they all have in common is that they take only around five minutes to add to your computer.

Ergonomic mouse

Unlike an ordinary mouse, the ergonomic version is carefully shaped to fit more precisely into your hand and provide extra comfort and support. The aim is to help mouse users avoid any of the twinges and aches that can afflict people who spend long hours at the computer. The ergonomic mouse is available in different sizes.

Internet-friendly mice

This breed of mouse can help anyone who spends lots of time on the Internet. Shaped like an ordinary mouse, it also has a tiny roller wheel between the two buttons (below). Instead of moving the mouse pointer to the scroll bars when you want to scroll down a Web page, you just roll the wheel. The page moves as if the wheel is rolling on the page itself. The wheel also lets you scroll around other documents, such as letters and spreadsheets.

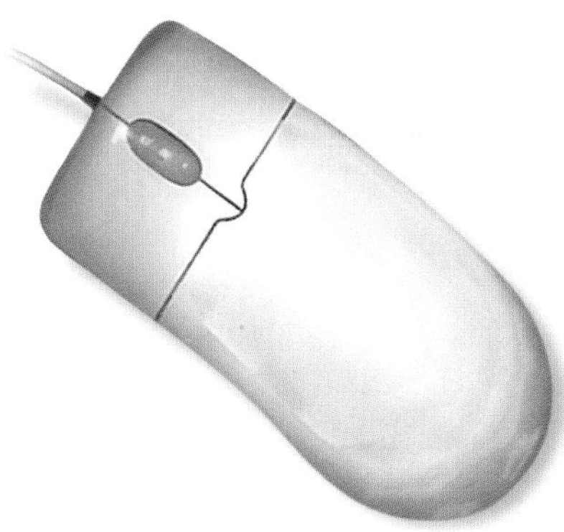

Art pad and pen

If you've been following the Paint and CorelDRAW exercises in *PCs made easy* you might have found that painting with the mouse can be tricky. The best option to improve your artwork is a drawing pad that works with a special pen. As you move the pen over the pad, its position is detected by sensors in the pad and translated into signals that control the pointer on the screen. The great benefit of a drawing pad is that it feels and works just like a pen and paper. Some pads even detect pressure for special effects, such as controlling the amount of paint put down on the picture.

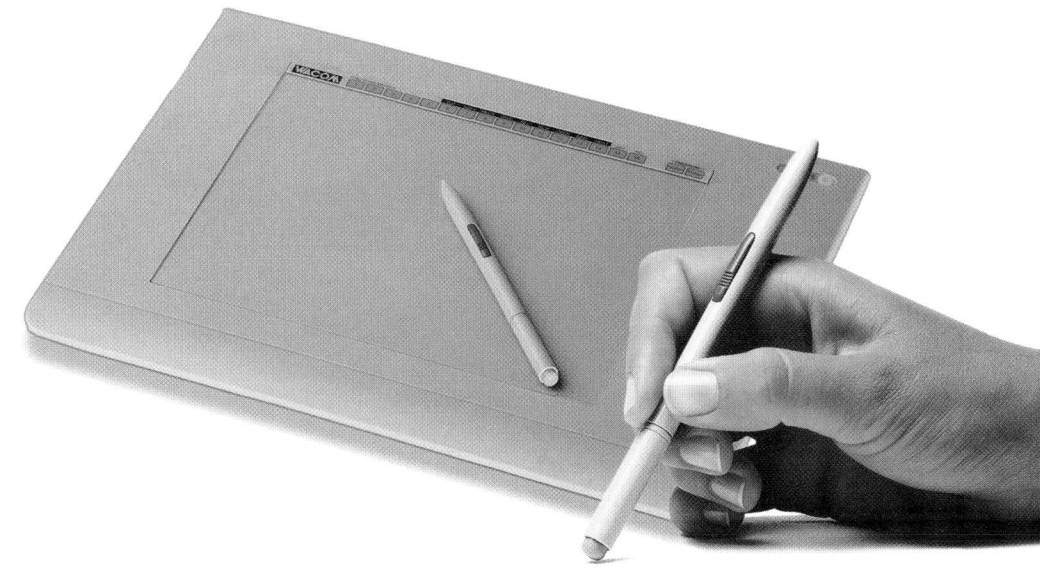

USB mouse

Traditionally, a mouse was connected to your PC's serial port or PS/2 socket, but the widespread adoption of the USB (Universal Serial Bus) interface gives you an additional and welcome connection option if your PC has USB sockets. The USB standard supports 'hot plugging', meaning that you do not have to turn the computer on or off if you swap the device, as it is immediately recognized and ready for work. Using a USB mouse also means that you do not run the risk of tying up your only serial port, which might be more usefully employed for a modem or other device.

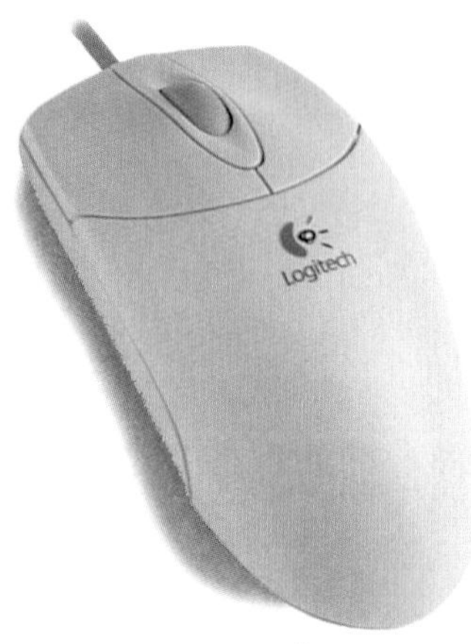

Cordless mouse

One of the problems with a standard mouse is that its tail keeps getting tangled up! One solution is to use a cordless mouse, which has a small base unit that plugs into your computer. As you move the mouse, it sends a signal to the base station to move the pointer. Some cordless mice use an infra-red light beam (like a TV remote control); these require a clear, unobstructed path to the base unit. Mice that use radio signals are not so fussy and can work on a cluttered table.

HANDWRITING RECOGNITION

Understandably, many new computer users would rather use handwriting to put words into a computer than learn to type. Despite this demand, however, handwriting recognition has failed to make its mark in mainstream desktop computing.

While handwriting recognition sounds useful, most of the handwriting recognition software requires you to learn a slightly newer way of writing words. It's also not 100 per cent accurate – which rather works against the benefits of handwriting recognition.

Gyroscopic mouse

This kind of mouse doesn't even have to be used on a flat surface. The gyroscopic mouse works by sending a radio signal to a base unit that can measure the distance of the mouse away from the computer – even when it's in the air and not on a desk. The gyroscopic mouse can also be used in a more conventional way by rolling it on the desk, or using a built-in trackball.

Novelty mice

Some mice are simple redesigns of standard mice, with bright colours and bigger buttons. If you are ever stuck for a present, this type of mouse certainly makes a great novelty gift.

Marble Mouse

This looks like a mouse with a big ball in it. Rotate the ball with your index finger to move the cursor on screen. It saves space and is more precise than an ordinary mouse.

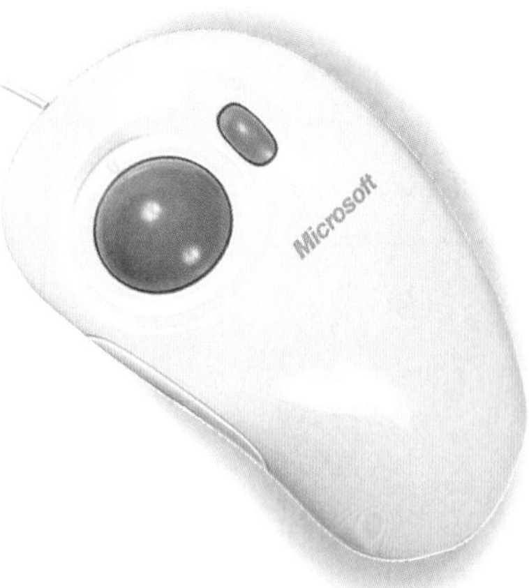

SPEECH RECOGNITION

It may sound like science fiction, but you can also control your computer by talking to it. A modern home PC is capable of listening to your voice (picked up by the microphone) and converting your words into commands. Speech recognition is still in its infancy, but today's programs give you a good idea of what computers in a few years time will be able to do. Already, voice-recognition programs let you choose menu commands and dictate text into word processors and other documents. These programs need a fast PC with plenty of memory to keep up with your speech.

As this technology progresses, the potential for physically impaired computer users will also develop.

Plugging in and playing with the Marble Mouse

It's easy to add a new input device to your computer. Here's your step-by-step guide to installing one of these new devices – the space-saving Logitech Marble Mouse.

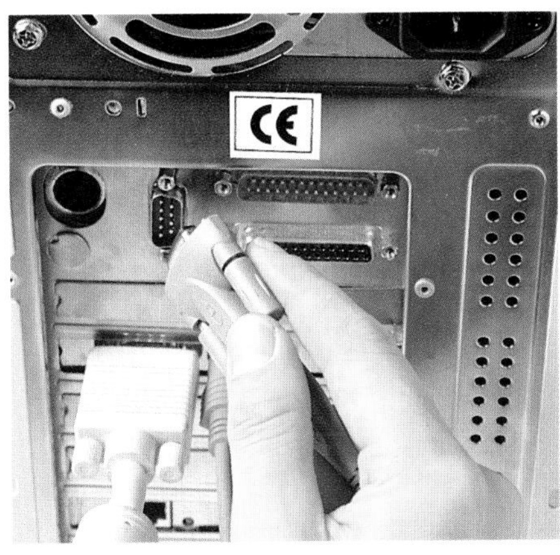

1 Switch off your computer. Although you do not need to open your computer to add a mouse, this is always a good first safety step before fitting any new accessory. Trace the keyboard and mouse cables to the back of your computer. Each of the cables ends in a plug that fits into a socket on the back panel of your computer. Often, the sockets on the back panel are not labelled clearly, so check carefully along the cable to see which is which.

2 Most input devices replace an existing device and plug straight into the socket used by that device (see Sockets, below right). The input device we chose – the Logitech Marble Mouse – plugs into a nine-pin serial port on our desktop PC via an adaptor, or into the six-pin PS/2 port (see page 93).

If using the adaptor (as we did), remember to tighten the thumb screws to keep the mouse firmly attached to the PC.

3 When you plug in the Marble Mouse and restart your PC, Windows starts working with the Marble Mouse straight away. Its left and right buttons work in the same way as those on an ordinary mouse.

Several other input devices, a replacement keyboard, for example, don't need new software to be installed – they work perfectl, well with your existing set-up.

4 With a mouse replacement such as this, you can alternate between a standard mouse and a Marble Mouse. Let your children use the standard mouse and save the Marble Mouse for the time when you need the precision it offers or if your desk space is very limited.

SOCKETS

Whatever type of input device you decide on, you must check the sockets available on your PC. Mice usually have a PS/2 or a serial plug, and most keyboards use a PS/2 or a 5-pin plug. It's easiest to replace like with like, so if you are replacing a PS/2 keyboard, make sure the new one also has a PS/2 connector.

A few devices, such as low-cost art pads, work alongside your mouse and keyboard. If you are not replacing an existing device, look to see if there is a spare socket for it on your PC's back panel.

Taking control of your games

If you want to play games to win, you need the right control tool for the job. Add a joystick or steering wheel to your PC for fine control over flying and racing games.

The sheer versatility of your PC's keyboard and mouse makes them perfect for some games, especially those that are strategy based. But, for hands-on games, joysticks, steering wheels and gamepads give you greater control and greater involvement too.

● Keyboard and mouse

The keyboard has over 100 keys, which is good for complex games. It is a digital device, which means that the switches are either on or off. This works well if you just want to fire a missile, but not when you need finer control over some aspect of your game – when you're playing a flight simulator and you want to angle the plane slightly left, for example. Keyboards often work best with simpler strategy games.

● Joystick

There are two types of gaming joysticks: digital and analog. Digital joysticks move in one of eight directions like the eight main points on a compass. This kind of joystick is rare with PCs and is generally used only on arcade machines. With PCs, the norm is analog joysticks, shaped like those used to control real fighter aircraft. Not surprisingly, they are mostly used for flight simulators, but can also work with racing or 3D adventure games. With analog control, the movements on the screen more accurately mirror the movements you put into the joystick. For example, moving the joystick a little way gives a correspondingly small movement on screen; moving it a long way gives a large movement on screen.

Joysticks like Microsoft's Sidewinder are the last word in game control, giving realistic 'feel' with force feedback.

● Types and prices

Joystick prices vary considerably. A simple two-button model can cost up to £20, but a state-of-the-art, multi-buttoned force feedback joystick can cost up to £80.

Less common are the throttle sticks used as add-ons by some flight simulator fans to help accentuate the feeling of flying. They look like aeroplane throttles studded with buttons, but they are expensive at around £60 or so.

Serious gamers can opt for two-handed flight sticks, known as yokes. These work in the same way as joysticks, but they are expensive (at around £100), due to their more complex construction. They are more true-to-life for non-combat flight simulators, however, and provide a realistic steering wheel.

Gamepads do the same job for PCs as those that are used on television game consoles, from Nintendo to Sega. They are ideal for simple action games, such as beat-'em-up games. Some people don't like the feel of the directional pad, so with most you can fix a small joystick instead. These are inexpensive devices, and you can usually buy one for £10–20.

● Steering wheel

Just as there are joysticks for flight simulators, so there are steering wheels to heighten the realism of motor-racing games.

For the ultimate in racing game control, you can also get a steering wheel with an additional brake and accelerator pedal to go on the floor under your desk. Simple steering wheels are available for around £40 – but you should expect to pay a much higher price for the more sophisticated versions.

WHAT IT MEANS

FORCE FEEDBACK

A new technology for many types of joystick is called force feedback. This is an attempt to bring the realism of the bigger 'sit down' arcade machines to the home computer user. For example, in a flight simulator, the joystick could actually push back to represent the physical stresses a pilot feels. It might be more difficult to turn in a tight corner, or become almost uncontrollable during a crash. CH Products and Microsoft make joysticks using this technology, and steering wheels are also available.

Setting up a joystick in Windows

Even with a basic joystick, action-packed games can be easier to play and more fun. Once you've plugged in a new joystick you have to set it up to work properly by running a simple calibration process.

ADDING A JOYSTICK is easy. Just plug it into the game port (labelled as the MIDI port on page 93) in the back panel of your PC. This port is the only socket that matches your joystick's plug. To do this, first turn off your PC, then plug the joystick into the port and tighten the screws that fix it into place (not all joysticks have these screws, so don't worry if you can't find them). When the plug is securely in the port, you can turn the PC back on again.

1 Select Control Panel from the Settings section of the Start menu. The Control Panel window appears.

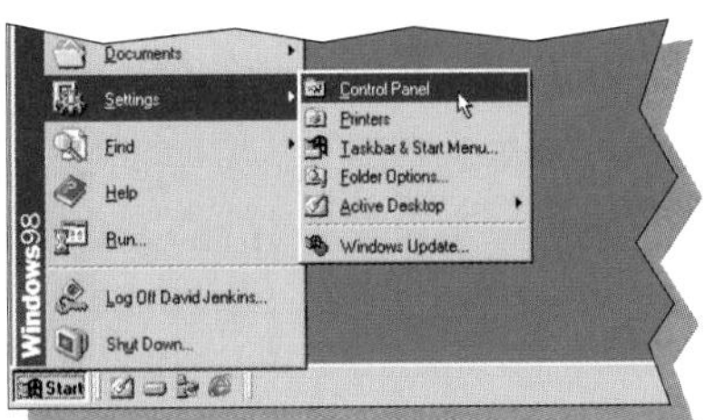

2 Double-click the icon labelled Game Controllers and the special Game Controllers dialog box will appear.

3 Unless you already have a joystick installed, the front page of the dialog box will be blank. Click the Add button to begin setting up your joystick.

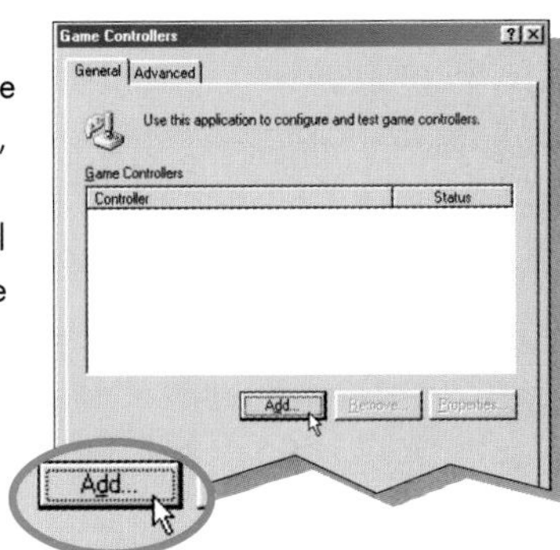

4 A new dialog box will appear with a long list of joysticks (and other types of game controllers) on it. If the name of your joystick appears on this list, select it and click the OK button. If your joystick does not appear in the list, click the Add Other button and insert the floppy disk or CD-ROM that contains the drivers for your joystick. If you do not have such a disk, you can create a customized joystick profile by indicating how many axes, buttons and special devices your joystick has.

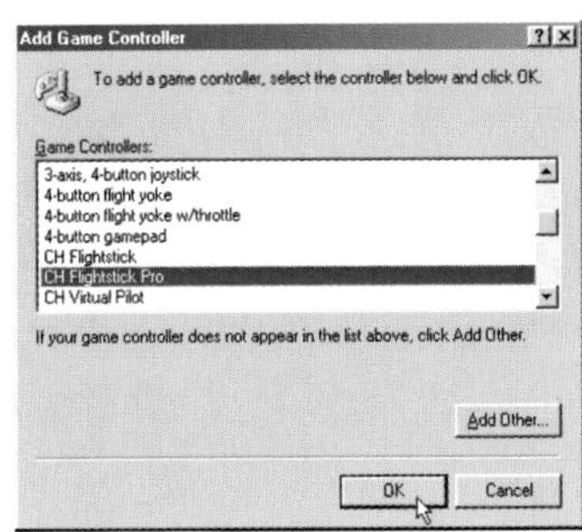

5 The name of your joystick will now appear in the main window of the Game Controllers dialog box. At this point, Windows will be able to recognize that your joystick is installed, but in order to make the most of it, you will have to **calibrate** it. Click the Properties button to begin this process.

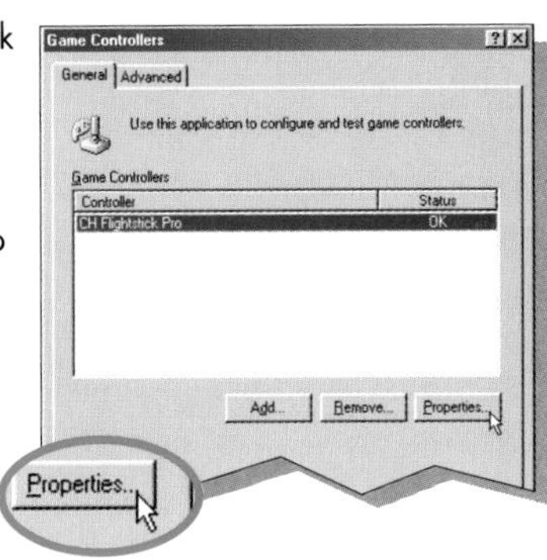

6 When the Game Controller Properties dialog box appears, tick the checkbox if you have a separate rudder or pedals controller. Then press the Calibrate button to begin the calibration of your joystick.

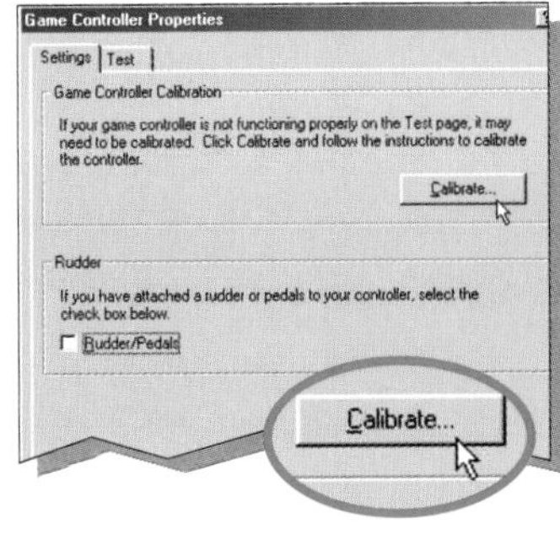

7 Follow the onscreen instructions exactly. To begin, you will have to centre the joystick and then move it in circles so Windows can work out the limits of its movement. Depending on the make of your joystick, you will also need to press the various buttons, hats or the throttle on your joystick so that Windows can identify them. Click the Finish button when you have worked through all the necessary steps.

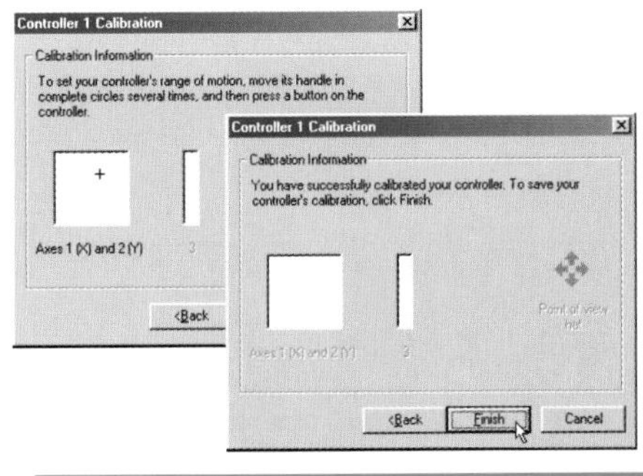

8 Before you close the Game Controller Properties dialog box you should test all the buttons and directions on your joystick to ensure they work; it's much easier to tell from the onscreen display than by just running a game and hoping for the best. To run the test, select the Test tab, move your joystick and press all its buttons. If something doesn't seem to be working, you must calibrate the joystick again, this time ensuring that the joystick is moved through all its possible positions.

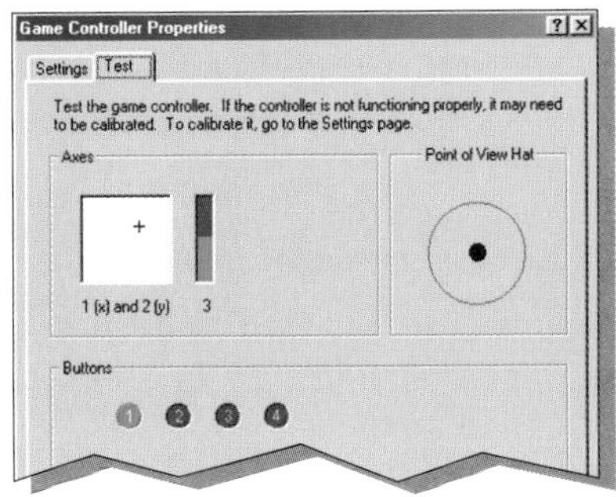

WHAT IT MEANS

CALIBRATE

When you calibrate your joystick, Windows is measuring its capabilities. The signal emitted by joysticks varies between models so measuring ensures that the programs on your PC can use the full range of movement of the stick.

Upgrading your PC

Your PC is built from components that you can replace to make it go faster. Often, upgrading doesn't even require you to open up the PC.

Is your software running slowly? Is your hard disk groaning under the weight of your files or do you long for a bigger and better monitor so you can see more of the image shown on screen? If so, you should upgrade your PC to take advantage of the latest developments in hardware technology.

This is especially important as your PC gets older: if you want to use the latest software, you might find that it runs slowly on a two-year-old computer, for example. Upgrading for extra performance is one of the most common reasons to spend more on your computer.

● Extra capabilities

Upgrading to add new capabilities to your PC is also important. Have you ever made a back-up copy of your documents? If not – perhaps it's because you just can't squeeze copies of your documents on to a floppy disk – think what might happen if your PC went wrong and you lost all your files.

When you need to keep back-up copies of larger files, such as photographs and sound files, you should consider getting a more capable back-up device, such as a tape drive or a Zip drive (see opposite). These devices plug into the back of your PC and let you copy huge amounts of information for safe-keeping.

If you have been using your PC for graphics, then you are likely to have found that working within the confines of a standard 14- or 15-inch monitor is awkward. This size of display might be fine for word processing, but with many other types of program, you'll find it easier to work with a bigger monitor. If you opt for a bigger monitor, you'll find it just plugs into the same socket as the old one, so it's easy to add.

● Built for change

One of the best features of your computer is that it is designed for a life of upgrades. Just about every component can be upgraded to keep up with new technology. You can raise the capacity of your hard disk, add a sound card, increase the main memory, plug in new speakers, a bigger monitor or a back-up drive. And because the PC uses standard connections, most upgrade accessories use the same type of cable, making them easier to install.

There are two types of upgrade you can carry out on your PC. The first is to add a new accessory that simply plugs into the back of your computer and covers upgrades such as, for example, a new mouse, modem or speakers. You don't need to be a technical wizard to install this type of upgrade and, fortunately, you don't even have to open up your computer!

The second type of upgrade fits inside your computer and needs more work and time to install; you will need to open up your computer and follow the installation instructions and procedures carefully. When you take the case off and look inside your computer, it might look intimidating, but if you're careful you can quite easily install a new sound card or memory, for example.

● Help at hand

If you have Windows 98 on your computer, it helps you when you have installed an upgrade. When you have fitted a new upgraded component, Windows will automatically try to detect it and attempt to set it up for you, making it much easier to get the new upgrade working.

Some upgrade components need special software –

called driver or controller software – to allow them to function properly, but this will be supplied in the box on either a floppy disk or CD-ROM. To minimize the chance of finding that a new piece of hardware doesn't work with your computer, look for an upgrade that is clearly labelled as 'Windows compatible'. Nearly all the hardware you can buy will be, but don't take it for granted.

Several years ago, upgrading was a minefield, but now PC manufacturers make it as easy as possible to fit, install and set up your new upgrade. One of the best developments is a feature called plug and play (see page 105). If your PC has this (and all new PCs do) and you are running Windows 98, then you will find upgrading a breeze. Simply plug in the new adapter card, modem or back-up drive and Windows will do the rest for you.

Popular upgrades for your computer

Here's a brief introduction to the main types of upgrade you can add to your home computer. Later in the course, we'll show you how to carry out these upgrades with simple step-by-step instructions.

Memory

One of the best ways to improve the performance of your computer is to fit more main memory (normally called RAM). If your PC has only 16MB of RAM, you will find a dramatic improvement in speed if you upgrade to 32MB. If you can afford to upgrade to 64 or 128MB, you'll get even more speed – especially for graphics programs. You might need some help in choosing the right memory chip (ask the original supplier of your PC for help), but fitting it is straightforward, even though it requires you to open your computer.

Sound card and speakers

To play sound, your PC needs to have a sound card fitted and loudspeakers plugged into the sound card. If you already have a sound card, you can easily upgrade the loudspeakers that plug into a socket on the back of your PC. Upgrading to speakers that include a sub-woofer will improve the quality of the sound your computer pumps out – especially for games and music. Installing a sound card requires you to open your computer, fit a new card into a slot and then set up Windows to use the new card.

Zip drive

One of the most boring computing jobs is making back-up copies of your files. It's so boring that many home computer users don't bother. However, if you don't make regular back-ups, you might lose all your files if your PC develops a fault. The Iomega Zip drive stores over 250MB of data. That's as much as 170 ordinary floppy disks. A Zip drive simply plugs into the back of your PC. You need only install the driver software.

HOW DIFFICULT IS UPGRADING?

Upgrading your computer can be easy, but for some upgrades it is more complex and you'll need to follow any supplied instructions carefully. As a general rule of thumb, if you do not need to open your computer to fit the upgrade, it should be easy to add.

If you do need to open the PC case, then it is likely to be trickier. If you're at all worried about performing the upgrade yourself, consider getting a local computer shop to do it for you. It will cost more, but the peace of mind is well worth it.

Bigger monitor

Many home PCs are supplied with a 14- or 15-inch monitor. If you want to use desktop publishing or graphics software, a bigger monitor is better, as you're able to see more of the image. The monitor plugs into the socket at the back of the PC. Once fitted, a simple adjustment to the display settings (see pages 12–13) will make the most of it.

Modem

A modem lets you link to the Internet and send and receive faxes and electronic mail. There are two types of modem. An internal modem fits inside your PC so you will need to open your computer to fit it; an external modem is the most popular and plugs into the serial port on the back of your computer, so you don't have to open your PC. Once fitted, Windows 98 should detect the modem and then ask you for the disk supplied with it to install the driver.

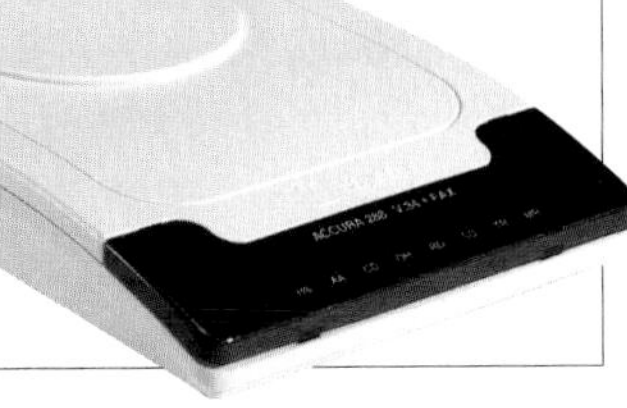

Home Learning & Leisure

Super science

An understanding of science is a key part of everybody's education, but many people find the whole subject uninspiring and difficult. However, with the help of your computer, learning about science has never been so much fun – and such little hard work.

For many people the very word 'science' conjures up images of dull chemistry lessons and impenetrable physics equations. But science is a vast subject covering many areas of study and so most people should find a topic to interest them, provided it is presented in an inspiring and entertaining way.

This is where that wonder of modern science – your computer – comes in! It can take advantage of the most basic of scientific principles – light and sound – to turn your home into a science wonderland.

There is a great selection of science CD-ROMs available, all of which aim to explore the subject in a new and exciting way. These cover almost every aspect of science and cater for all age groups and abilities, from the absolute beginner to the dedicated professional.

Children in particular will benefit from science-based CD-ROMs. There are programs available to teach young children about the world around them; programs to teach older children the basics of science; and programs to encourage both children and adults to explore the applications of scientific knowledge.

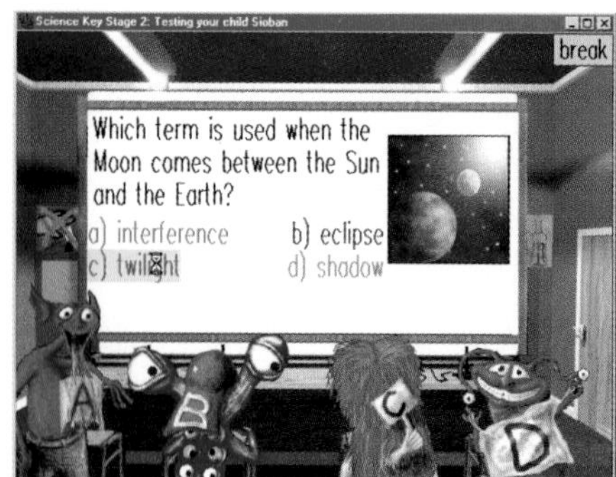

Information is presented clearly and entertainingly in the* Mad About Science *series. You can play a game when your guide decides you've done enough studying.

Junior scientists

Junior Science is aimed at children as young as four years of age. It teaches them about distance, light and direction through a story about a cat and a rooster. The cat does not want to wake up in the morning, but the sunlight shining into his bedroom keeps him awake, so he sets out to catch the sun. The adventures this leads to are fun and exciting, and along the way children are introduced to the sun, sky, clouds, colours, distance, light sources, directions, shadows and much, much more. This CD-ROM has high-quality animated pictures and good narration, as well as games and stories to make the adventures even more entertaining.

The adventures of the cat and the rooster in* Junior Science *will appeal to the youngest of scientific minds, explaining basic principles in an amusing way.

Science and games

Mad About Science is aimed at the 7–11 age group. It consists of two separate CD-ROMs, each dealing with a different subject area. The first, Energy, works like an interactive physics lab, while the second, Matter, deals with materials and how they change and interact.

Each CD follows a similar format, with bright cartoon graphics and a jaunty guide to take you through the 30-odd topics. There are question and answer sessions, experiments and plenty of interesting extra facts to keep the kids hooked. In addition, there are games – but only as a reward after at least three topics

SITES TO @ VISIT

Our scientific knowledge is changing all the time, so it's useful to keep up to date using the World Wide Web. You'll find everything from academic texts to popular museums.

Nature
The international weekly journal of science has its site at:
www.nature.com

Science Museum
The exhibits of the internationally renowned Science Museum in South Kensington, London, can be enjoyed at:
www.nmsi.ac.uk

Science à Go Go
The Science à Go Go site provides fun and up-to-date science stories:
www.scienceagogo.com

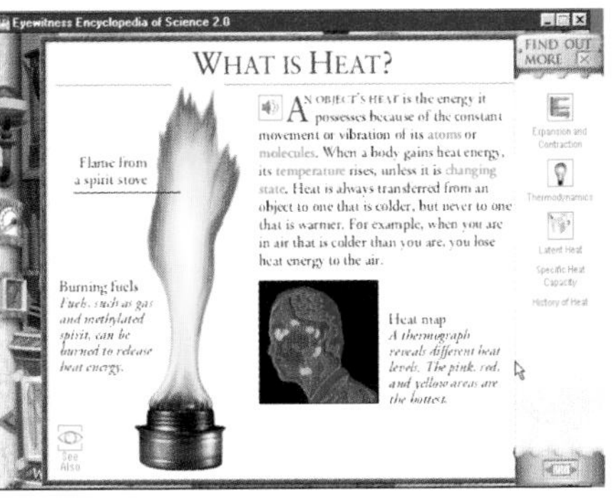

***The Eyewitness Encyclopedia of Science 2.0* is dedicated to bringing science to life using sound, video, animation and powerful cross-referencing facilities. It also imparts knowledge using combinations of text, sound and video. Hot links and a Find Out More panel make enquiries easy to pursue.**

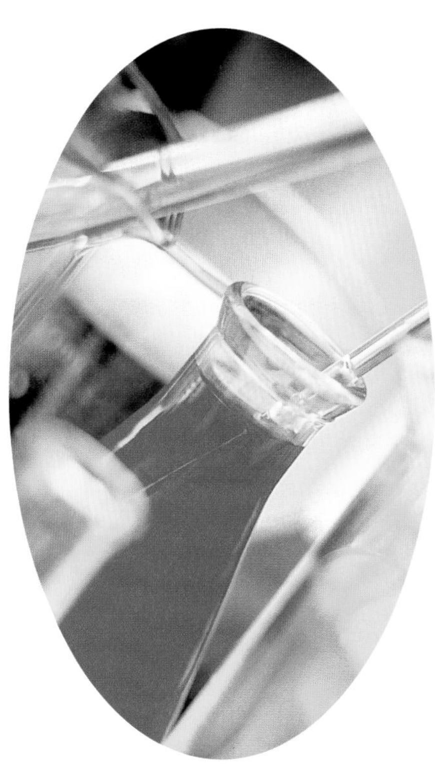

have been covered. The CD-ROMs work extremely well – and many adults could do worse than refresh their memory with a look at either or both of these discs.

● Eyewitness science

For older children there is the *Eyewitness Encyclopedia of Science 2.0*, a full multimedia program combining video with pictures, animation and sound. The information on this disc is grouped under four main subjects: Mathematics, Physics, Chemistry and Life Sciences. Each of the four subjects divides into a number of topics. Physics, for example, breaks down into Time, Atoms, Matter, Sound, Magnetism, Force and Motion, Light, Electricity, Machines, Energy and Heat. Each of these, in turn, contains a wide variety of informative articles.

In addition to the broad topic areas, there are four other sections: Earth and the Universe, the Periodic Table, a Who's Who and a Quiz. The Who's Who offers short biographies of famous scientists from all periods of history. There are explanations of scientific terms and links to additional related material. The biography of Darwin, for example, has a link to his round-the-world voyage aboard *HMS Beagle*, which inspired him to write *The Origin of Species*. If you have an Internet connection, you can also visit the encyclopedia's online science site.

Did the universe begin with a 'Big Bang' and will it end in a 'Big Crunch'? These are only two of the fundamental questions that Professor Stephen Hawking seeks to answer in his *A Brief History of Time*, which also includes an appreciation of the work of past astronomers, such as Ptolemy and Edwin Hubble.

● Origins of the universe

Other science titles explore the work of individual scientists. For example, there is a multimedia version of Stephen Hawking's best-selling book *A Brief History of Time*. In this book, Hawking explores some of the most difficult areas of modern physics, suggesting answers to some of the most often asked questions about the universe: where did it come from and where is it going? Did the universe have a beginning and, if so, what happened before then? What is the nature of time? Will it ever come to an end? His book isn't the easiest of reading and some of Hawking's 'simplified' explanations are far from simple, but his subject is fascinating and this CD-ROM uses diagrams and illustrations to expand on the text of the book to clarify his theories.

Hawking is thought to possess one of the greatest minds in physics since Albert Einstein, who is also the subject of a CD-ROM – *Ultimate Einstein* – which explores the great man's life, times and ground-breaking work.

CONTACT POINTS

Junior Science
Focus Multimedia
Tel: 01889 570156
Price: £9.99*

Eyewitness Encyclopedia of Science 2.0
Price: £19.99*
Mad About Science
Price: £9.99*
Dorling Kindersley Multimedia
Tel: 0870 0100 350

A Brief History of Time
Price: £9.99*
Ultimate Einstein
Price: £9.99*
Marshall Media
Tel: 020 7291 8318

*UK prices

Science on your computer

Physics and chemistry can be tricky subjects, and with exams approaching, they often seem positively daunting. It's at times like these that science CD-ROMs can help students of all ages.

In **GCSE Physics** *from Europress, there are even mini-assignments to complete after-hours, such as trying to spot the Titan moon with binoculars.*

Back in Stage 1 we saw how maths exams can be conquered with the help of your PC (see Stage 1, pages 114–117). In just the same way, unravelling the mysteries of science can be made easier with the advantages of computer-based study.

The way that multimedia can be used to enhance a previously dull subject is just one of the many reasons why the computer can be an inspiring learning tool – even for the most reluctant student.

● Time for science

Ideally, an educational CD-ROM should be structured around the modern GCSE curriculum, so that it follows the same modular structure taught in schools. In this way, while students can use a CD-ROM in parallel with their lessons – which can be a refreshingly different style of learning – they can also easily concentrate on any areas where they might be having difficulty when they are revising for exams.

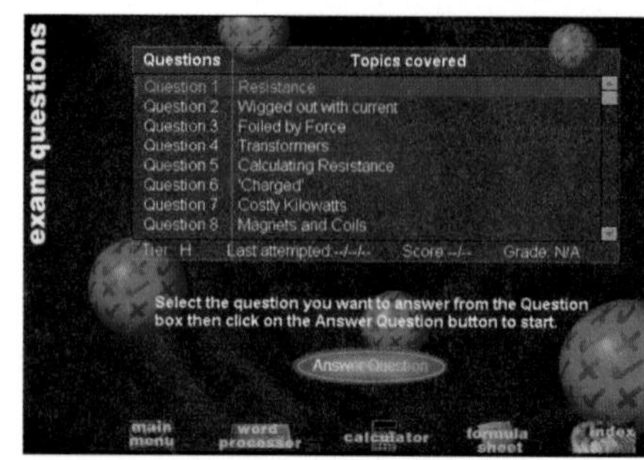

Even though multimedia educational CD-ROMs have lots of special effects to draw upon, their main aim is to make those real-life exam questions less daunting.

● Studying for physics GCSE

GCSE Physics from Europress covers the complete syllabus. Physics is a subject that can be, potentially, very dry, so the publishers have tried to make the contents of the CD-ROM as lively and interactive as possible.

The major subject categories are broken down into easily accessible sub-groups and then broken down further again. With a total of more than 150 topics, the confused student is able to get right to the heart of any problem area.

● Taught by history

Each of the distinct topics in this guide is taught by a famous historical scientific figure: for example, Electricity and Magnetism is taught by Benjamin Franklin; Energy by

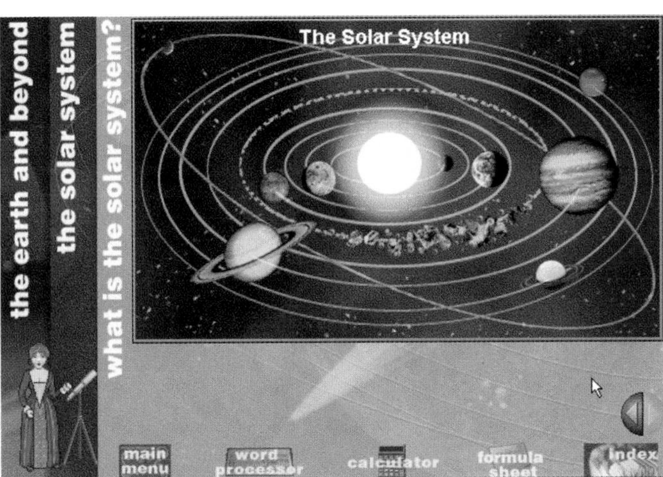

The astronomer Caroline Herschel worked with her famous brother, Sir William Herschel, and, on her own, detected eight comets in the years 1786 to 1797. Now, she will guide you round the universe in The Earth and Beyond section of the GCSE Physics CD-ROM.

the earth and beyond
exam questions

A typical star begins as a large, cool cloud of gas called a nebula. The cloud collapses, getting hotter until it reaches a steady size and state.

1. What force causes the cloud to collapse in the first place?
gravity [1]

2. Why does the cloud get hotter as it collapses?
Gravitational potential energy is converted [1]
into internal energy (heat). [1]

3. What process keeps the star shining (emitting energy) in the main sequence phase?
Nuclear fusion [1]

4. Explain what happens in the red giant phase of a star.
When hydrogen in core is used up, other reactions begin; helium is 'burned' to produce carbon etc. [1]
This occurs in outer layers of stars and they expand. [1]
Less energy is produced, so star surface is cooler (red) and larger (giant). [1]

5. Explain what happens when a supernova occurs.
Happens with stars of greater mass, so core temperature is higher. [1]
It goes through the red giant phase, [1]
but sudden collapse mixes remaining fuel at a very high temperature, and massive explosion occurs. [1]

Click on the answers you have written for each section of this question.

main menu | word processor | calculator | formula sheet | index

When the student has had fun and studied with the historical figure in each section, it's time to find out how much has been remembered. The results of each test can be stored and the student's (hopefully positive) progress monitored.

James Prescott Joule; The Earth and Beyond by Caroline Herschel; Waves by Zhang Heng; and Radioactivity by Sir Ernest Rutherford. Each has his or her own mini-biography – in case you need to be reminded who they are! As you work through a particular module, interactive diagrams pop up to explain things, such as how an electric motor works, for example.

A menu at the bottom of the screen offers convenient functions as you study: an impressive scientific calculator; a word processor that links to Windows WordPad; and a formula sheet with a categorized summary of every formula you could possibly need, from electric currents to thermal energy transfer. There's also an on-screen crib-sheet, which makes an excellent revision resource.

Finally, there are the exams. Each section has a selection of questions that you can look at on-screen. You can complete them as many times as you wish and the software remembers your score, grading you accordingly.

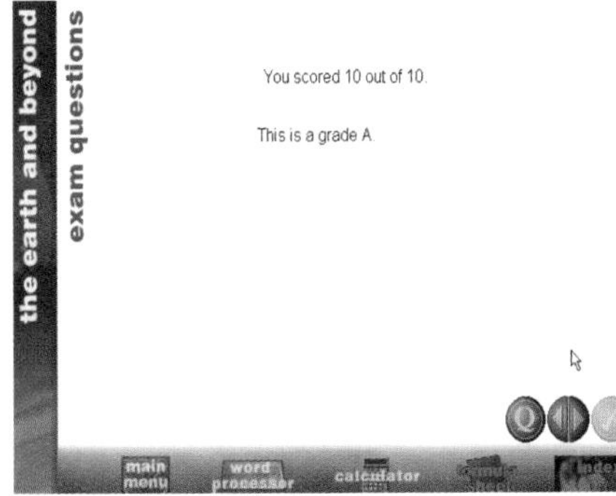

An important feature offered by most tutorial CD-ROMs is the ability to see how you are doing and collate your results over a period of time to track your progress.

Serious chemistry

Moving on to chemistry, *Letts Revise for GCSE Chemistry*, from GSP, contrasts with Europress' friendly guide by focusing directly on the knowledge needed to pass the GCSE exam. Covering the real nitty-gritty of the chemistry syllabus, there are few effects to distract students from the topics. Written by GCSE examiners, it's a text-packed revision aid with basic illustrations and a few animations to illustrate key points.

When starting the program for the first time, the student must set up a revision plan, based on the start date, the date of the exam, the number of subjects being taking and the number of hours of revision planned in each week. The program uses these figures to suggest dates for progress reviews and practice exam papers. Should students slip up in the test, the program gives a list of topics that need to be brushed up on.

The emphasis is clearly on helping motivated students pass the exam, rather than presenting chemistry in a lively and fun way to students who are having difficulty with the subject. Reinforcing the results-oriented nature of the CD-ROM, GSP offers an A*ABC Guarantee with the software. If your child doesn't get a C or higher GCSE grade at the examination, GSP gives you a £50 voucher you can exchange against other GSP titles. The CD-ROM also includes mock examination papers you can print out for more realistic exam practice.

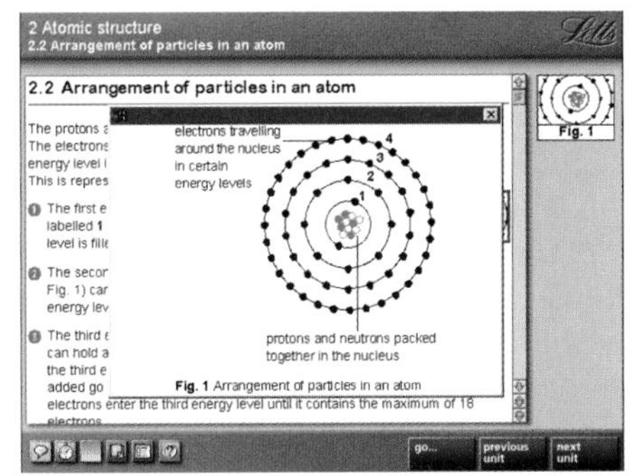

Letts Revise for GCSE Chemistry *is a results-driven and text-heavy approach to exam revision for motivated students, with few multimedia thrills.*

SITES TO @ VISIT
Europress
GCSE Physics
www.europress.co.uk
GSP
Letts Revise for GCSE Chemistry
www.gspltd.co.uk

Amazing space

Astronomy is a subject that has fascinated people for thousands of years. Although anyone with a pair of binoculars can enjoy the wonders of the night skies, if you use your computer, you can see even further into the mysteries of the sky.

With the help of your PC, the universe is within your grasp. You can simulate the night sky as it is now and discover what those tiny pinheads of light are called and how far away they are. You can travel into the past or the future to view the sky as a Roman legionary did or as it will be seen by your great grandchildren.

You can journey across the surface of Mars or travel to the furthest reaches of the universe. You can learn about gravity and black holes or explore some of the most fascinating questions ever asked, such as: what is at the end of the universe and can time flow backwards? Multimedia lets you do all this in ways impossible in a book or on television or video.

● Be an eyewitness

Astronomy software titles range from those designed for enquiring young minds to near-professional standard astronomers. For example, the *Eyewitness Encyclopedia of Space and the Universe* is designed for children

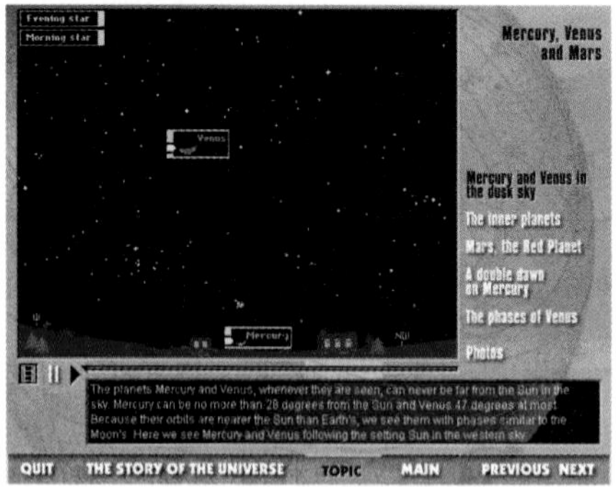

aged 10 and up. It provides a good knowledge base of the history of astronomy, space itself and even the story of humankind's battle to conquer it.

● A star is born

The *Eyewitness Encyclopedia* is packed with information about astronomers and astronauts, stars and planets, meteors and asteroids, and all the other remarkable phenomena in the universe. You can watch animations of a star being born and the formation of a black hole. You can even find out what it's like to live on a space station.

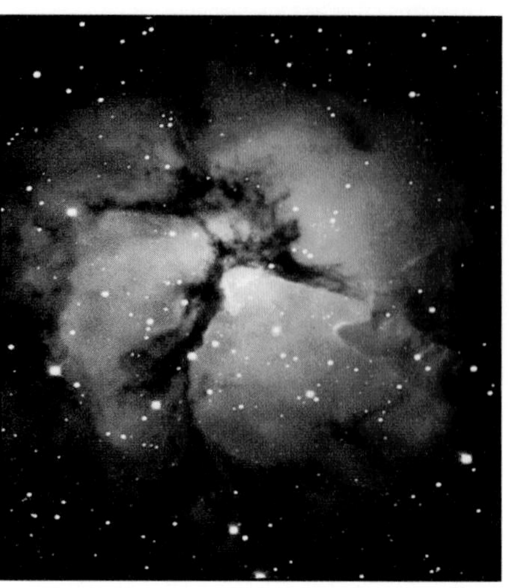

The wonders of the solar system and the universe beyond (above) are only clearly visible in photographs taken by the most advanced astronomical equipment.

No matter where you live, you can find out when and where to look for the planets and stars with the help of the Discover Astronomy *CD-ROM (left).*

There is a virtual observatory where you can view the night sky from anywhere on Earth and see how the sky changes as you move location. You can even travel through time to see how the sky would have looked 5,000 years ago, or how it will appear to observers 5,000 years in the future.

The wonderful thing about astronomy CD-ROMs is that

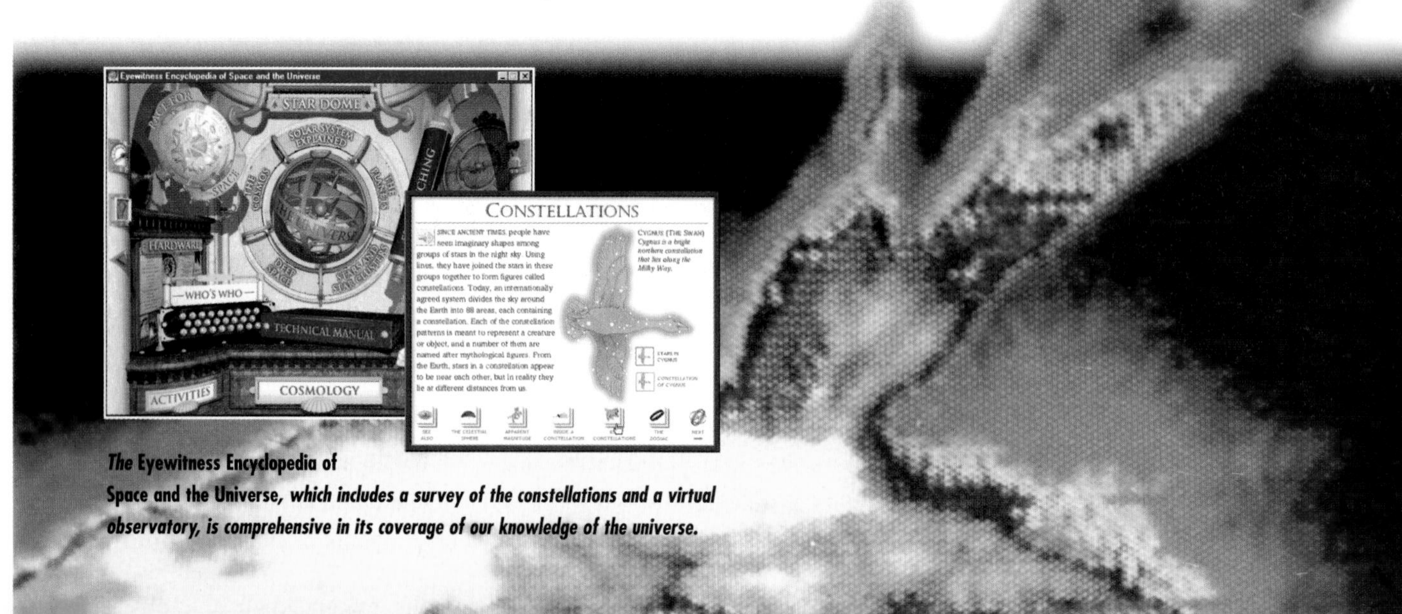

The Eyewitness Encyclopedia of Space and the Universe, *which includes a survey of the constellations and a virtual observatory, is comprehensive in its coverage of our knowledge of the universe.*

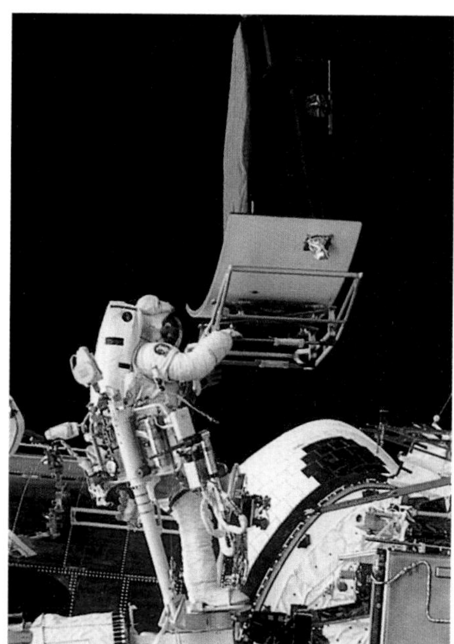

Freed of the optical interference of the Earth's atmosphere, the Hubble space telescope has given astronomers their clearest views yet of the universe. Here, an astronaut carries out repairs on the telescope.

they are available for different age groups, yet there is also a cross-over so that they can be enjoyed by all the family. This is most true when looking at general astronomy guides and at CD-ROMs that seek to explain the mysteries of the universe.

Russian help

An excellent beginner's guide to astronomy is *Discover Astronomy*, developed by former Russian space programme scientists. Hosted by Dr Jacqueline Mitton, the author of the *Penguin Dictionary of Astronomy*, you are taken on nine narrated and animated 3D tours that cover everything from the universe being born to the evolution of life on Earth. Simulations take you on a virtual tour through the solar system, visiting the planets and their moons and the stars and galaxies. The major astronomical concepts are explained and there's a gallery of 60 stunning astro-photographs.

Discover Astronomy comes from the people who made a sophisticated virtual observatory called *Redshift*. There are two versions available at different prices: *Redshift 2* and the enhanced *Redshift 3*. The latter plots the positions of a million stars and celestial bodies and, as with the *Eyewitness Encyclopedia*, you can view the night sky from anywhere on Earth, way back in the past or far ahead in the future. You can even see the night sky as it would have looked through the eyes of a soldier on the eve of the Battle of Hastings.

Redshift 3 contains plenty of video footage, 700 astro-photographs, 30 minutes of quality animation, as well as 3D animated tours. In addition, there's the complete 2,000-entry *Penguin Dictionary of Astronomy*.

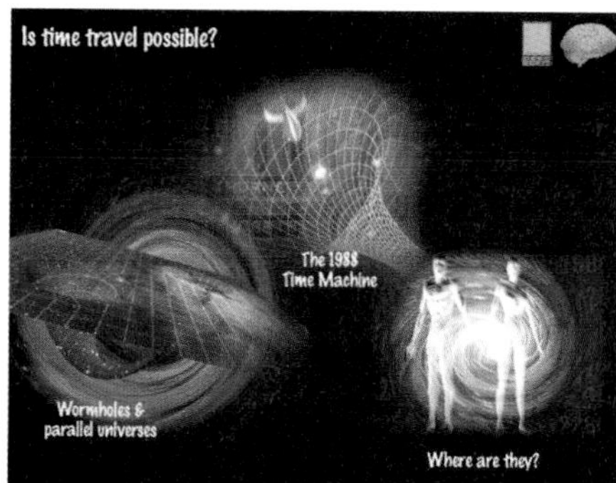

The History of the Universe *looks forward and tries to answer questions about the future of space travel.*

The solar system and beyond

Focusing more closely on our solar system is *The Planets*. It is based on a best-selling book by David Morrison, who worked for the Ames Research Center run by NASA. It also includes Fred Scaef's *Seeing the Solar System*, which contains an abundance of detailed information about the planets. It is probably one of the most comprehensive guides to our solar system, but a highlight is a feature called the Planetary Traveller. This is a computer-simulated trip across the planets' surfaces, from the sun-scorched terrain of tiny Mercury to the frozen wastes of distant Pluto.

The History of the Universe delves far beyond the solar system to the very edges of the universe, from the beginnings of time to the end of existence. It is an extremely colourful program that uses captivating animations and presentations to pose and try to answer some of the most complex questions about existence. It explores topics such as black holes, the Big Bang – and even such 'science fiction' ideas as parallel universes. There is a look at the ancient civilizations that studied the heavens and an introduction to the great names of astronomy, from Aristotle, Kepler, Galileo and Newton to the scientists of today. The CD-ROM also examines ground-breaking astronomical achievements, providing clear explanations of topics such as gravity and relativity. There is, in addition, a glossary containing an explanation of 280 technical terms.

Travel through space with **Redshift 3** *and see spectacular images of the planets, such as this view of Mercury.*

In all, *The History of the Universe* has 50 animations, 75 interactive presentations, two timelines and 70,000 words of text. There are also puzzles and a general knowledge quiz. For those with access to the Net, there is a Web site providing updates and further information.

CONTACT POINTS

Eyewitness Encyclopedia of Space and the Universe
Price: £19.99*
Redshift 3
Price: £19.99*
Dorling Kindersley Multimedia
Tel: 0870 0100 350
www.dk.com

Discover Astronomy
Focus Multimedia
Tel: 01889 570156
Price: £9.99*
www.focusmm.co.uk

The Planets
Marshall Media
Tel: 020 7291 8318
Price: £9.99*
www.mip.marshallmedia.com

The History of the Universe
Ransom Publishing
Tel: 01491 613 711
Price: £19.99*
www.ransom.co.uk

*UK prices

Learn French the multimedia way

French is a language that many of us study but few of us master. However, the range of helpful CDs available makes learning effective and fun.

Nearly all of us spend some years at school learning French, and the majority of us forget almost all of it once we have left. Trying to recover what you once learnt by using a book is hard work. The addition of cassettes so that you can listen to dialogues and copy pronunciation is a step forward, but is still not ideal. The multimedia CD, however, seems to provide the perfect medium for language-learning on your own; it can store huge amounts of data in the form of text, still or animated images and, crucially, sound.

Multimedia CD-ROMs can offer interactive practice sessions, with hints, tips and exercises to measure your progress. The CDs available for learning French show that software designers are well aware of the possibilities and are exploiting them with a high degree of success.

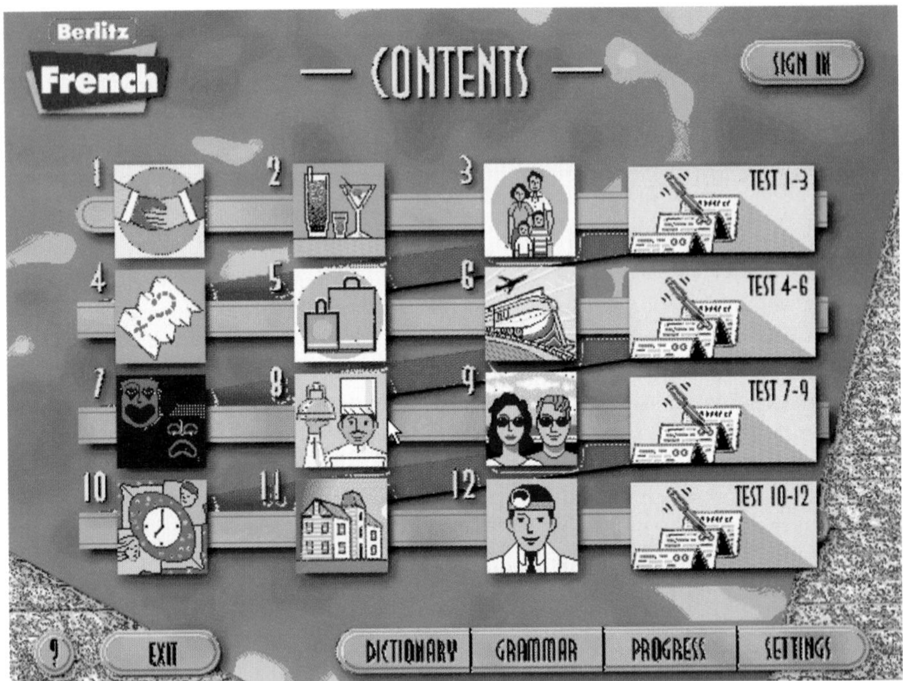

The contents screen of Berlitz French shows the variety of situations covered, from simple greetings and introductions to a visit to the doctor. This is an evolution of the classic courses on cassette.

National Curriculum

Start to Learn French, from Focus, is a single CD designed to take you from knowing no French through to GCSE level. Its target market is obviously the school student (it supports the National Curriculum), but there is no reason why students of all ages should not find it a useful way of starting or brushing up their French.

The core of the program consists of a variety of straightforward, but nevertheless demanding, interactive learning and testing modules. There are exercises where you must add the missing word to a story or sentence; dictation passages to write down; blocks of words to rearrange; and word puzzle games where you must find the French words in a square of letters. Regular practice drills reinforce the grammar and vocabulary you are learning and there is a 5,000-word dictionary if you find yourself stuck for the *mot juste*. *Start to Learn French* is a relatively simple CD-ROM with few frills, but for that very reason it is extremely easy to get started and to make significant and measurable progress.

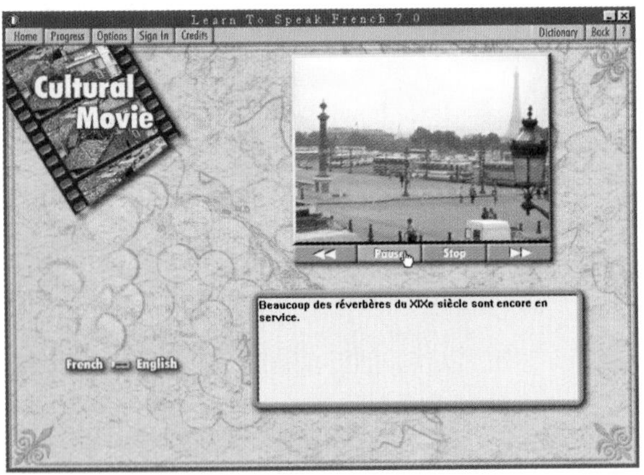

A view from one of the Cultural Movies in Learn To Speak French. The range of topics gives you a very good feel for what French life and culture are like and is a welcome change to wordy modules.

Three CD set

Learn to Speak French, from Mattel Interactive, describes itself as 'the complete interactive learning solution' and is an altogether more lavish production. The program consists of no less than three CDs, with a hefty accompanying workbook

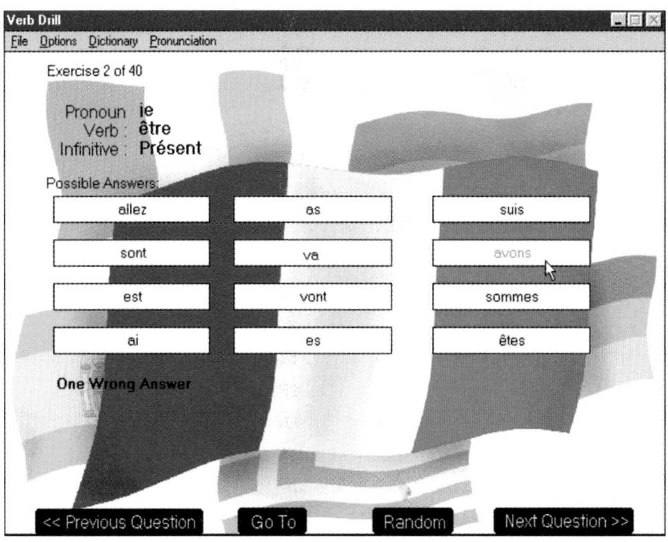

The grammar guide in* Learn to Speak French *is extremely thorough and clear, taking you to a pretty advanced level.

Included in the* Learn to Speak French *CD-ROM are a range of word puzzles to put some fun into learning the language.

full of exercises, grammar and vocabulary reference. The program also contains a speech recognition engine so that you can use a microphone to speak phrases and have your pronunciation played back and checked. There are also some excellent QuickTime film sequences in the Cultural Movie section.

All the French spoken on the CD is by native speakers who are very often shown in a window on screen. This is not just entertaining but genuinely useful, as watching the speaker's mouth can be a great help in improving your pronunciation.

Real life

The exercises are geared to real-life situations: ordering food and drink, organizing a rail journey, giving and receiving directions and so on. You can consult the program's extensive grammar guide and vocabulary for further help at any time.

The 10 learning units in the program take you from the very simple beginnings to complicated situations, such as moving house or having a hair-do. The program is so well designed and presented that there's a good chance you'll want to stick with it.

Language school

Berlitz French, also from Mattel Interactive, is a two-CD set produced in conjunction with the Berlitz language school. Berlitz itself might be a 120-year-old institution, but this program is bang up to date. Like the method used in the Berlitz schools, it relies heavily on listening and repeating words and phrases, so without a microphone to record your own speech you won't get the most out of the program. But there are plenty of activities and exercises to reinforce the practice.

Each of the separate modules consists of seven different learning activities. With the Word Bank you listen and repeat words and phrases – a simple but effective way of burning them into your memory.

Closer Look takes you through the finer points of the grammar and vocabulary used in the module, while Learning Tips gives background information on French life and culture. In Drag and Match you must match up a picture of a speaker with the correct dialogue, while in Empty Passages you have to fill in the blank spaces, either by speaking or by typing in the words. In Listen and Click you have to listen to a dialogue and then click on the appropriate picture.
All of these exercises are backed up by a full grammar reference and a 12,500-word dictionary. Overall, the program can take you from complete ignorance to somewhere just short of A level standard.

Whichever of these CDs you choose to try out, you'll find you can work on your accent much more effectively, while at the same time learning the basic grammar and vocabulary you need to get the most out of the French language.

Here is a typical start to a module in* Learn to Speak French*. You listen to the dialogue and watch the QuickTime movie as Mme Bertrand speaks.

CONTACT POINTS

Start to Learn French
Focus Multimedia
Tel: 01889 570156
Price: £9.99*

Learn to Speak French
Price: £50.00*
Berlitz French
Price: £40.00*
Mattel Interactive
Tel: 01664 481 563

*UK prices

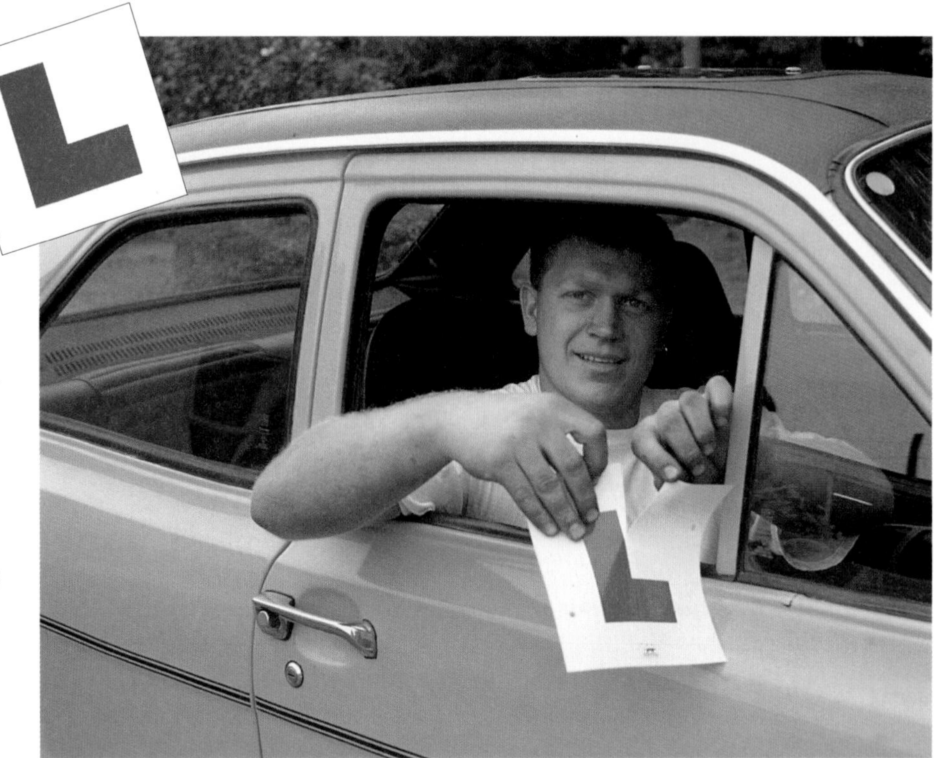

Driving school

If you're learning to drive or simply want to brush up your driving skills, why not get behind the wheel of a driving tutorial program?

In the same way as pilots often learn to fly new aeroplanes in computer-operated flight simulators before they ever get in the real aircraft, so you can use the power of the PC to learn driving skills in the safety of your own home.

While CD-ROM driving tutorial programs are nowhere near as sophisticated as flight simulators, they can improve the skills of more experienced drivers and provide invaluable help for the student driver who is preparing for a driving test. Now that driving tests include a written element, the only way to learn the answers to all the questions is by serious study, followed by repeated testing. Driving tutorial programs help you do this in an interesting and effective way.

● Official packages

Among the best-known driving tutorials are *Official Driving Instructor* from Europress and *Driving Test Success* from Focus. Both set out to give you a thorough grounding in the essential skills and rules of the road. With the help of animations and videos of real driving situations, these discs are intended to help the beginner pass the driving test and the experienced driver to become a better driver. You'll also find a good deal of general information and questions to test your knowledge.

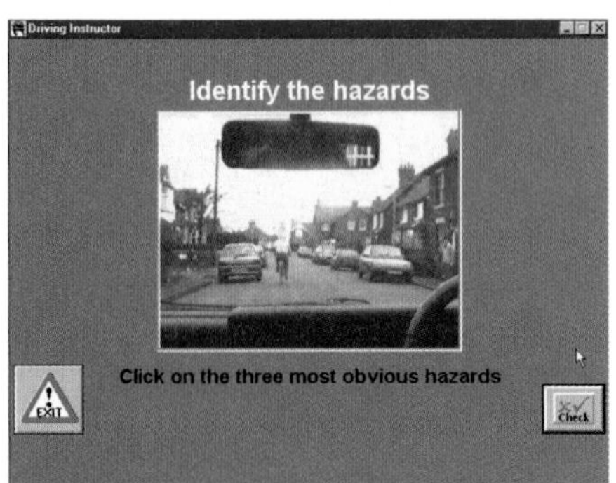

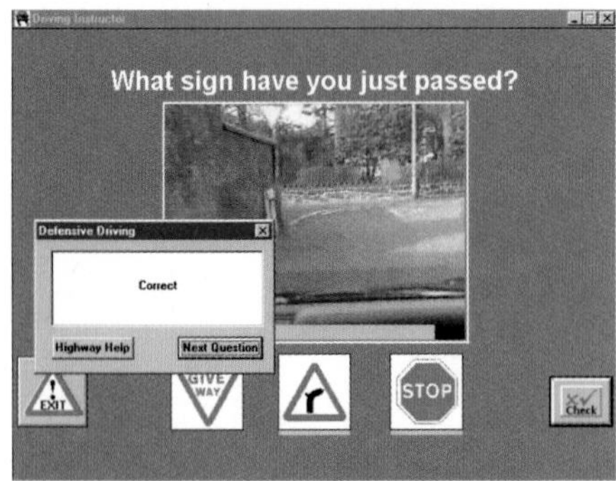

The Road Skills section of* Official Driving Instructor *includes a range of live driving sequences in which you encounter many driving situations, testing skills such as your awareness of road signs and potential hazards.

● Driving Instructor

Official Driving Instructor is divided into eight main sections, covering topics such as Signs, Pedestrians and Children, and Motorways. The main sections most people will use are likely to be The Car and Driving, and Self-Test.

The Car and Driving contains five sub-sections covering the main skills a learner driver must acquire, as well as a section on Defensive Driving that all drivers, however experienced, would benefit from studying. The CD-ROM presents information about the correct driving methods to employ and often uses video footage to back this up, either demonstrating a point or by asking the user to say what is going right or wrong.

This is perhaps seen at its best in the Defensive Driving section. A video of a driving situation is played and you are asked, for example, to click on the hazards in the picture or to say which road signs have been passed. It's simple but extremely effective, and it quickly reminds

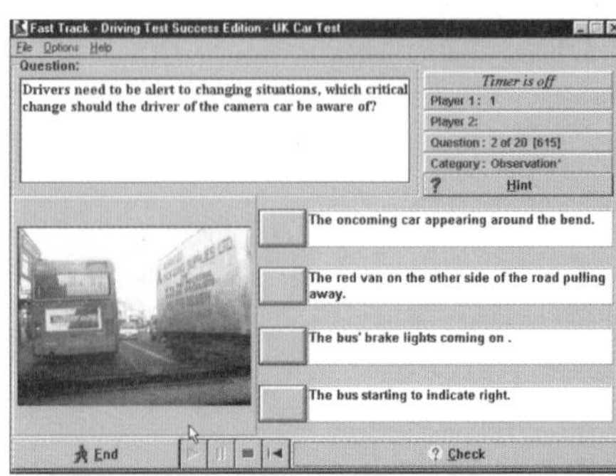

The video clips in the Observation section of* Driving Test Success *pose tricky questions to alert new drivers to hazards they won't be aware of.

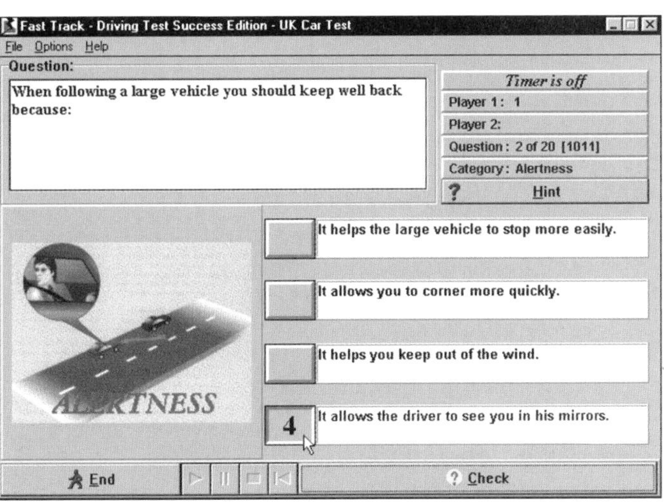

The questions in* Driving Test Success *are presented in multiple-choice format.

experienced drivers how easy – and dangerous – it is to lose concentration when driving.

Once you have learned all these lessons, you might want to test your new-found knowledge. *Driving Instructor*'s Self-Test section contains 397 questions in all, presented in a multiple-choice format. You can test yourself on particular areas of knowledge, ask the computer to select areas for you or take on everything. At the end of your test, you get a percentage result, giving you a clear idea of how close you've come to passing – or failing – the driving test.

● Driving to success

Focus' *Driving Test Success* CD-ROM aims to be a completely comprehensive guide to the questions you will encounter in the driving theory exam. It contains absolutely every question in the 'question bank' that the Driving Standards Agency uses to generate the real exams. It also covers both car and motorbike driving tests.

You can read questions from the screen, and you can also have them read out to you. In Learning Mode, you get instant feedback on whether you've got the answer right, and there's a Hints button to help you if you're stumped.

If you want some practice for the theory exam itself, you can switch to the program's Virtual Examination Mode. Based on the answers you give to the questions asked, the software identifies strengths and weaknesses so that you can brush up in key areas later.

There are also extra questions that take you beyond what is strictly required in the driving theory exam: the Extra Signs section includes more than 80 questions on road signs, and the Observation and Common Mistakes sections provide another 80 safe driving practice questions. The latter are based on the 80 video clips built into the software.

● What you learn

There's no doubt that these CD-ROMs will help learners as they approach the driving test. They're no substitute, of course, for time spent driving a car, nor do they mean to replace proper study of the full Highway Code. But what they do excel at is supplying a fresh and interactive way of improving and testing your driving knowledge.

Given the written element of the driving exam, taking lots of randomly generated tests is an effective way of making road sense stick in the mind. The video footage gives a feeling of the real world and sharpens drivers' observation skills. While these CD-ROMs are aimed at the learner driver, experienced motorists might well be surprised at how these videos can help brush up their skills.

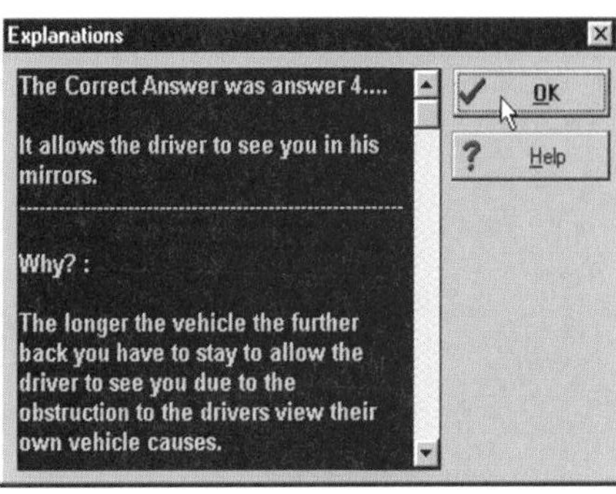

Explanations
The Correct Answer was answer 4....
It allows the driver to see you in his mirrors.
Why? :
The longer the vehicle the further back you have to stay to allow the driver to see you due to the obstruction to the drivers view their own vehicle causes.
OK
Help

If you're not sure you understand the reasons for an answer, click the Explain button to get an explanation.

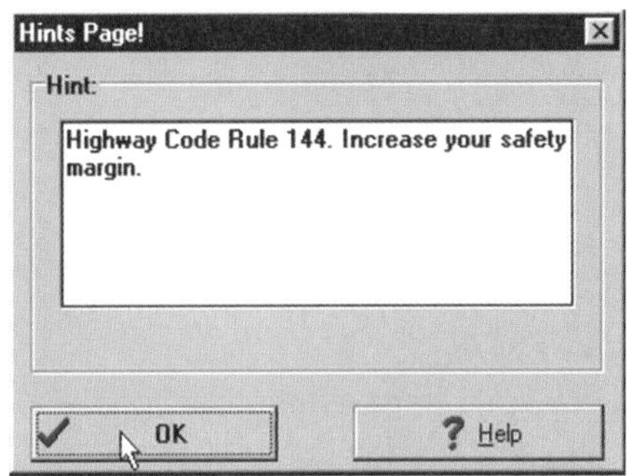

If you're stumped by one of the* Driving Test Success *questions, click the Hint button to get a clue that should help you choose the right answer.

CONTACT POINTS

Official Driving Instructor
Europress
Tel: 0800 328 7007
Price: £9.99*
www.europress.co.uk/

Driving Test Success
Focus Multimedia
Tel: 01889 570156
Price: £9.99*
www.focusmm.co.uk

*UK prices

Family health encyclopedias

Help yourself and your family to better health by using your computer and its multimedia capabilities.

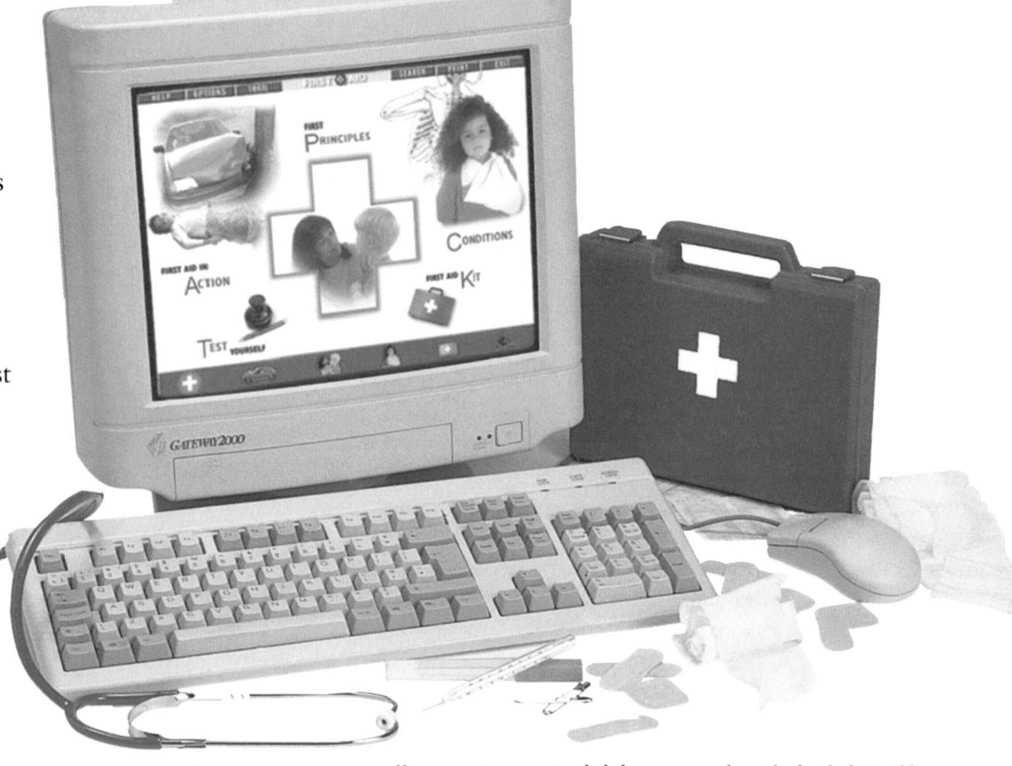

Your computer can not only help ensure you keep the family first aid box stocked, it will even show you what to do in the event of an emergency.

Modern-day pressures and emotional stresses conspire with the pollution of the cities in which many of us live to make it difficult for us to stay healthy. It could also be said that many of the foods we eat are bad for us and most of our favourite drinks do us little good either. But, with a little application and help, you can learn how to stay healthy and get fit by understanding how your body works and knowing what you can do to keep it working properly, or what to do if you fall ill.

● Fully booked

There are many medical reference books available, but these are often full of difficult medical terms and provide little practical, day-to-day information. A better alternative is to use the multimedia power of your computer in the form of an electronic medical encyclopedia. As with books, these discs are not a substitute for expert advice – if in doubt, always contact your doctor.

A CD-ROM-based medical reference work will enable you to find the information you need instantly and efficiently cross-reference all the information relevant to your query. Video demonstrations, animation and illustrations are used to show how to exercise correctly or perform life-saving first aid. On some of the discs, animation demonstrates how parts of your body work. The choice of which to go for is up to you.

You don't have to wait until you're ill before you use your computer health advisor. There's also lots of comprehensive information about medicines, keeping fit and looking after your family.

● A wealth of choice

One of the programs available is *BodyWorks*, a 3D tour round the human body. It might sound gruesome, but it's actually fascinating to see beneath the skin, view the bones of your skeleton or journey through all the internal organs to discover how they work.

A LITTLE REASSURANCE

If you're the type of person who prefers not to know what your medical treatment might possibly involve, you are probably not the ideal purchaser of a medical encyclopedia program. However, the clear and concise explanations, narration and video footage of straightforward surgical procedures could reassure a worried patient that this is now a relatively minor and commonplace procedure that offers a chance to return to good health.

Consult the BMA

To help empty your shelves of your existing medical reference works, there is Dorling Kindersley's *The BMA Family Health Encyclopedia*. It is full of authoritative, easy-to-understand information, with more than 750 illustrations, 200 photographs and 60 animations and videos – all that information on one CD-ROM certainly saves a lot of shelf space. It has full British Medical Association approval and manages to remain completely free of jargon and complex medical terminology.

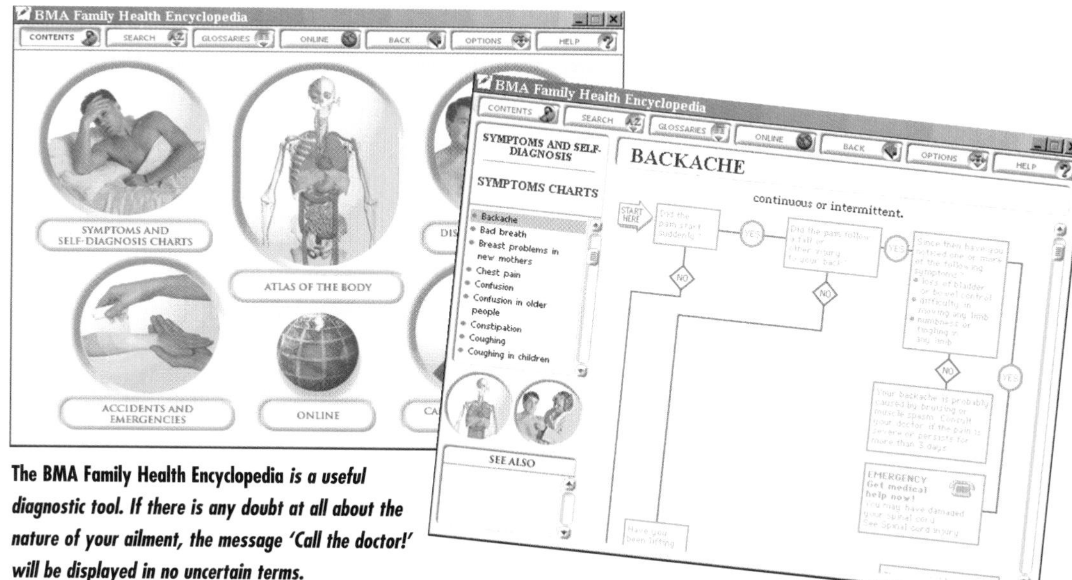

The BMA Family Health Encyclopedia ***is a useful diagnostic tool. If there is any doubt at all about the nature of your ailment, the message 'Call the doctor!' will be displayed in no uncertain terms.***

Five sections

The encyclopedia itself is divided into five sections, comprising: Symptoms and Self-Diagnosis Charts; Atlas of the Body; Diseases, Disorders and General Health; Accidents and Emergencies; and Caring for Yourself and Others.

You can also access Dorling Kindersley's Health Club Web site from within the encyclopedia, where there are articles about health-related topics, from whether you have the right kind of training shoes to diet and healthy recipes. Symptoms and Diagnosis contains 99 easy-to-follow charts setting out a series of questions to which you answer Yes or No. The diagnosis depends on these answers, and the program will then alert you if you should make an appointment to see the doctor.

Diseases, Disorders and General Health contains 650 straightforward articles, all cross-referenced and thematically presented to assist diagnosis, accompanied by explanations of common medical tests (the kind you may expect if you visit the doctor) and treatments.

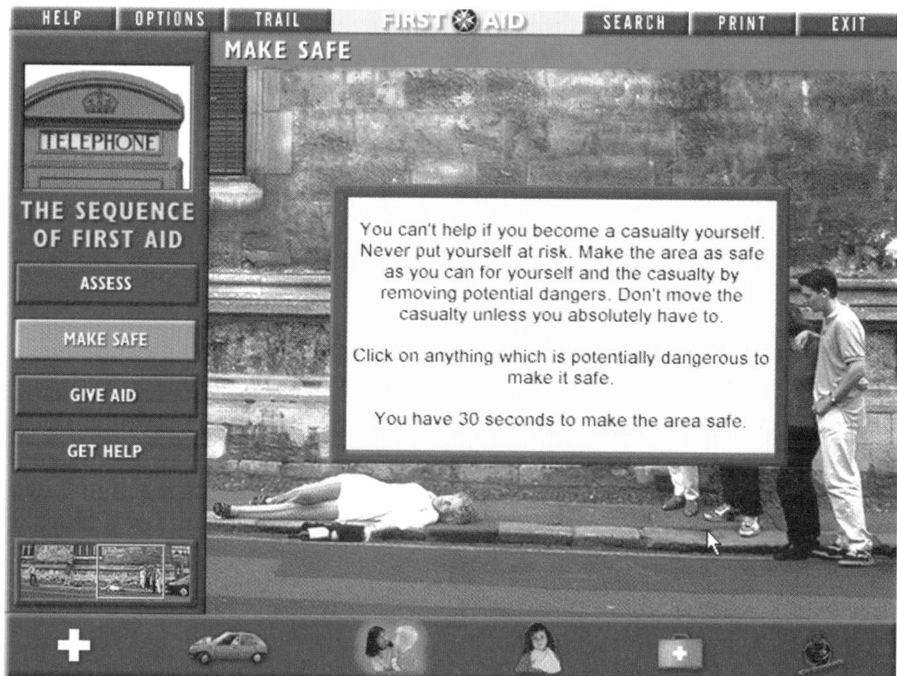

This isn't a real incident, but part of the **Interactive First Aid** ***CD-ROM published in collaboration with St John's Ambulance. Shown here is a section that allows you to see how much you have learned in the other parts of the program. This is the type of knowledge that could result in you making a life or death difference in the real world.***

FIRST AID

St John's Ambulance

If you want more specialist first aid advice, *Interactive First Aid* is published in collaboration with St John's Ambulance. This could be the most important CD-ROM you ever buy, because not only is it an excellent reference tool, it is also an invaluable teacher, helping you to acquire the knowledge and skills to practise first aid in the real world.

The CD-ROM has four chapters: First Principles; Conditions; First Aid in Action; and the First Aid Kit. It takes you through all the steps of assessing an accident scene, making it safe, getting help, giving aid to casualties, recognizing symptoms, knowing what treatment to give and recognizing danger signs. You can then test yourself with one of the five accident scenes.

CONTACT POINTS

BodyWorks 6.0
Guildsoft
Tel: 01752 895100
Price: £39.95*

The BMA Family Health Encyclopedia
Dorling Kindersley Multimedia
Tel: 0870 0100 350
Price: £19.99*

Interactive First Aid
Focus Multimedia
Tel: 01889 570156
Price: £9.99*

*UK prices

Food and wine

You have been feeding your computer a healthy diet of text documents, spreadsheets and graphics. Now let your computer give you a good helping of the world's best food and wine.

In many respects, your computer can be a useful aid when you are planning a meal. But, when the cooking actually starts, can a computer really help?

We all have our own techniques and habits when it comes to preparing food. There are different methods that can make life easier, but it can be difficult sometimes to learn effectively from a cookbook, and trial and error can be expensive – both on your pocket and on the patience of your family. This is where your PC rides to the rescue, giving you access to a wealth of culinary information on both CD-ROM disk and the Internet.

Your PC can't assist you with the washing up, but in the planning and preparation stages of a meal it can help not only by printing your shopping lists, but also by showing you the right way to do things in the kitchen.

● Recipe for success

No matter how experienced you are in the kitchen, the *Schwartz World Cuisine Recipe Book* will expand the range of dishes you can prepare. It includes more than 200 recipes that feature hints and tips, ingredient lists for each recipe that you can print out to make shopping easier and many full-colour photographs of the finished meal, to illustrate the presentation and serving suggestions.

Each of the CD-ROM's recipes can be adjusted to suit the number of people you are cooking for: for example, if the recipe says it serves five people and you have eight hungry mouths to feed, the program increases the quantities that are required. It will also adjust the amounts that will be required on your shopping list.

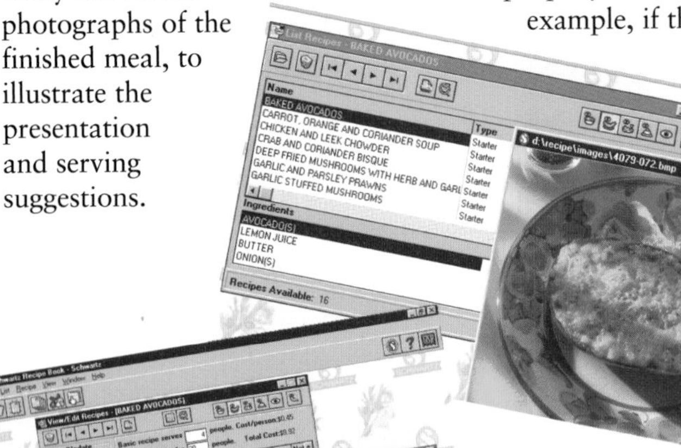

There is a world of exciting new recipes at your fingertips with the Schwartz World Cuisine Recipe Book. You can use it to plan a meal according to how much time you have or how much money you wish to spend. A useful feature is the facility to enter your own favourite recipes so the program will grow and grow.

● Interactive food and wine

Having a huge range of recipes at your fingertips is welcome, but many of us might feel we need a little more of a helping hand with some of the basics of cookery and kitchen techniques. *The Interactive Food Guide*, from Focus, aims to supply this confidence-boosting knowledge, as well as a substantial number of recipes from around the world for you to practise your new skills on – 23 of which are accompanied by video sequences with voice-over to take you through each step. There are also reference sections and tips on specific techniques.

The companion CD on wine, *The Interactive Wine Cellar*, has similar aims, optimistically offering to make you 'a wine expert in five minutes'. It provides a gentle introduction to the often bewildering world of wine and its terminology, with video sequences and voice-overs to make things fun. On the way you'll find out about the main factors in the experience of wine-drinking, the major wine regions of the world and the major wines themselves. There's also an extensive glossary of wine terms.

Oz Clarke's Wine Guide offers a more in-depth examination of the world of wine, but is far from being too highbrow for the beginner. TV wine guru Oz Clarke guides you through an encyclopedia of more than 7,000 wines. It also includes 54 video sequences and a colourful and educational tour of the world's wine-producing areas. The sequences aim to improve your tasting techniques – the sniffing and sipping – to enhance your appreciation of all wines.

You can also take a tour of the 57 wine regions of the world, scroll through maps and discover each region's geography, climate, vintages and main wine producers.

Now you will be well equipped to enjoy experimenting with food and wine combinations. Don't worry if you get it wrong – it's another good reason to have a food and wine experience.

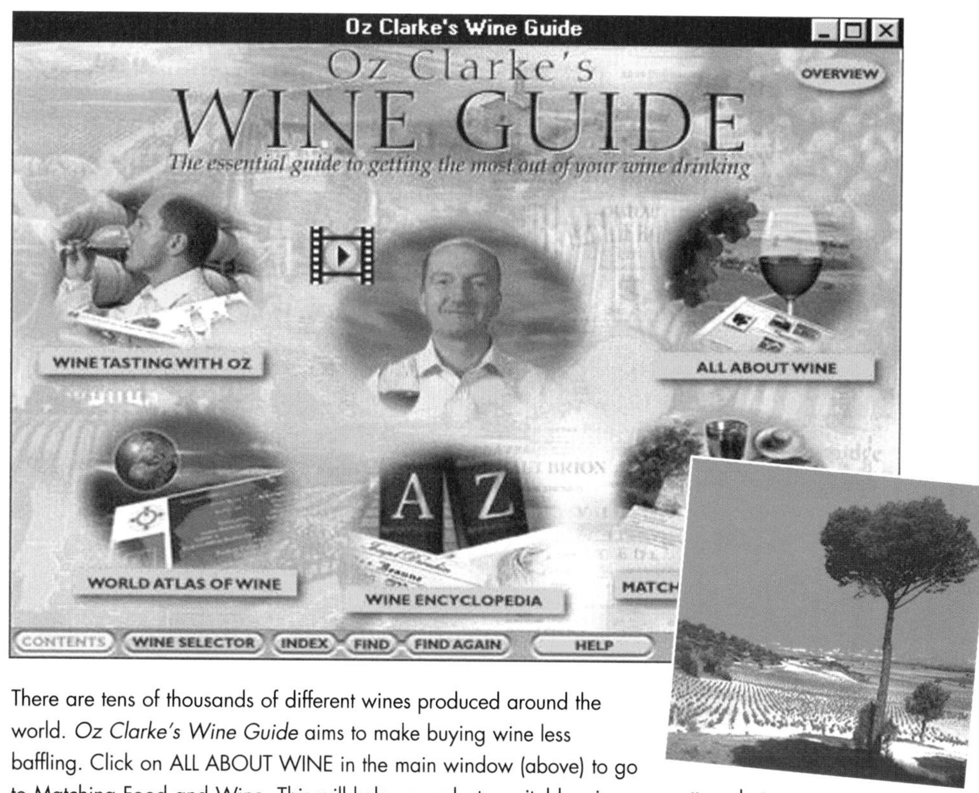

There are tens of thousands of different wines produced around the world. *Oz Clarke's Wine Guide* aims to make buying wine less baffling. Click on ALL ABOUT WINE in the main window (above) to go to Matching Food and Wine. This will help you select a suitable wine, no matter what you are eating. Then you can look at the WINE ENCYCLOPEDIA section, learn about the origins of your chosen wine and even see a picture of the area it came from, like this one (above right) of the Spanish uplands of Rioja, where the wine of the same name begins its life.

SITES TO VISIT @

Enter 'food' or 'drink' into your Internet search engine and you'll be offered a wide variety of appetizing sites.

Visit an electronic magazine on all things to do with food and drink. At this address you'll find articles on selecting wines, recipes and hundreds of restaurant reviews: www.winedine.co.uk

Find thousands of recipes and lots of cooking tips and tricks, courtesy of the Compucook site: www.my-meals.com

Looking for a restaurant in a certain area? Then let your computer do the searching. Just enter 'restaurant' and your preferred location to view a list of possibilities: www.eyp.co.uk

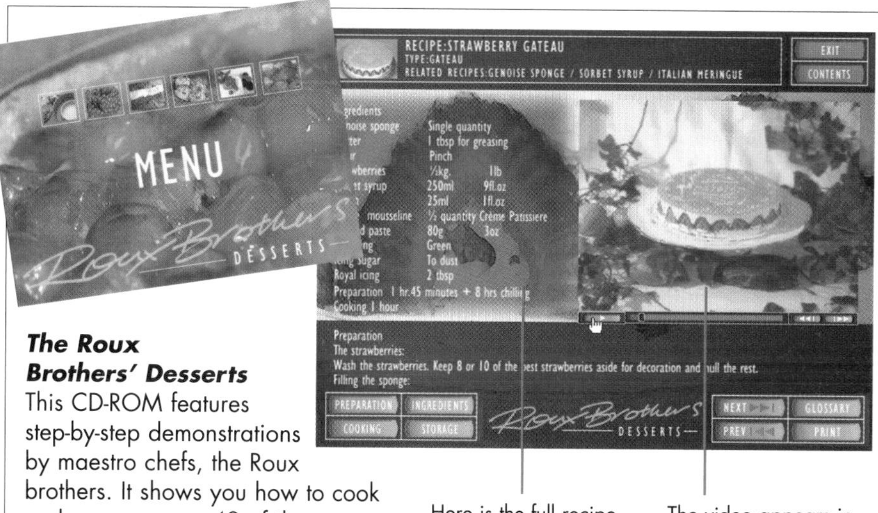

The Roux Brothers' Desserts
This CD-ROM features step-by-step demonstrations by maestro chefs, the Roux brothers. It shows you how to cook and prepare over 40 of the delicious desserts they are famous for and demystifies many of the difficult aspects of preparation. Tricky sequences can be viewed over and over again until you grasp the technique (right). Clicking Print will produce a list of ingredients and all the preparation and storage information you need.

Here is the full recipe. The preparation instructions appear in the window below.

The video appears in this window. Here, it shows the finished gateau.

To boldly go...

The voyages of the Starship Enterprise have spanned over 30 years. Your computer can help you learn more about the cult series Star Trek.

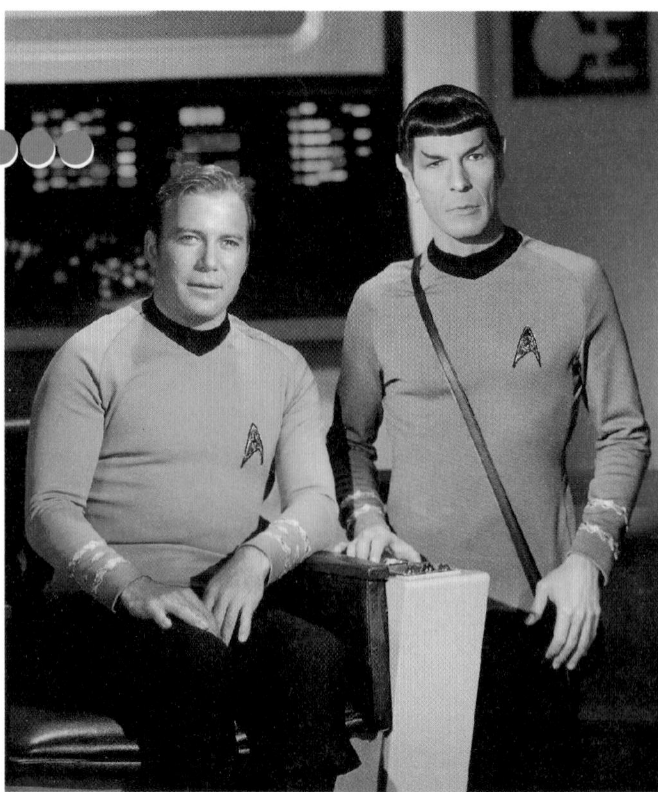

Captain on the bridge... Kirk and Spock (William Shatner and Leonard Nimoy) on the **USS Enterprise.**

The phenomenon that is *Star Trek* was launched in 1966. The show reached three series (79 episodes) before it was cancelled in 1969 because of dramatically declining ratings.

When the programme was repeated, its cult status and popularity grew to such an extent that the adventures of Captain Kirk, Bones, Spock, Scotty and the rest of the crew of the *Starship Enterprise* were re-run over and over again all around the world.

This led to a box-office hit movie, *Star Trek: The Motion Picture*, a new series, *Star Trek: The Next Generation* (177 episodes), *Star Trek: Voyager* and *Star Trek: Deep Space Nine*, an animated series, more films (a total of nine so far), hundreds of books and several computer games, CD-ROM encyclopedias and both official and unofficial *Star Trek* Internet sites.

● Beam me up, Scottie!

The motion picture *Star Trek: Generations* featured James T Kirk (the T stands for Tiberius) and other characters from the original series. It brought Kirk and his successor Captain Jean Luc Picard together to combat Dr Soran, who will stop at nothing in his efforts to regain entry to a magical and timeless place called 'The Nexus'. This is just one of a library of *Star Trek* titles that have been transformed into multimedia computer games.

These games are either based on specific movies or are original stories set in the *Star Trek* universe. There are also *Star Trek* simulations that let you walk the decks of various *Star Trek* vessels and even sit in the Captain's chair.

Massive *Star Trek* reference works are available on CD-ROM and, whether as games or reference sources, the whole *Star Trek* universe is embraced, from the original to the series produced most recently, such as *Star Trek: Deep Space Nine* and *Star Trek: Voyager*.

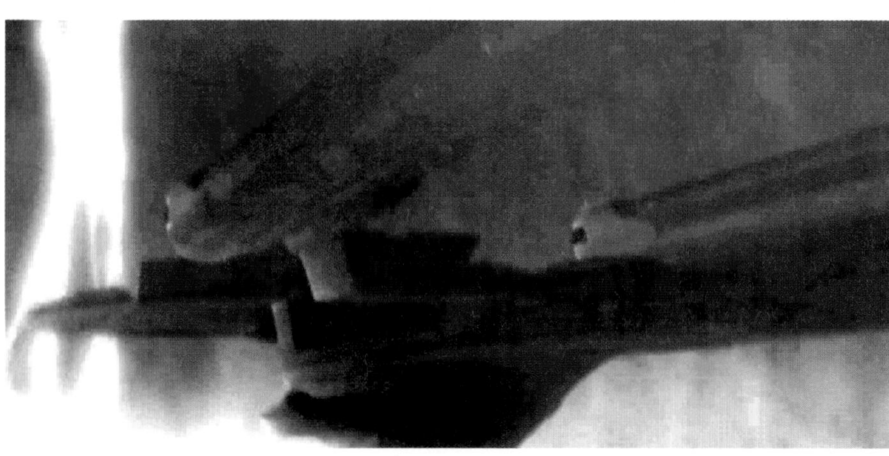

'A wagon train to the stars' was how the **Star Trek** *producer Gene Roddenberry pitched his original script in 1964. Over the next 35 years, no other science fiction series has caught the public imagination quite as much.*

● My generations

Star Trek: Generations, from Microprose, has a story line linked to the movie. When first released it was regarded as an authentic *Star Trek* game and it certainly brings the look and feel of the movie to your PC.

It has the character voices of William Shatner (Captain Kirk), Patrick Stewart (Captain Picard) and Malcolm McDowell (Dr Soran), along with realistic graphics, music and sound effects, plus sequences from the original movie. As a game, *Generations* involves trying to find the evil Dr Soran by solving puzzles, finding objects and killing enemies on various planets and space stations.

The Star Trek Encyclopedia ***(top) is a comprehensive reference work, while*** **Star Trek: Captain's Chair** ***places you at the helm of a virtual-reality*** **USS Enterprise.**

Star Trek: Generations ***from Microprose (background picture) mixes specially filmed live action with computer game play.***

● Klingons on the starboard bow

The ultimate guide to almost everything about *Star Trek* has to be *The Star Trek Encyclopedia*. It is a two-CD-ROM set that records the whole *Star Trek* history. It answers every question you have ever had about *Star Trek* – and also all the ones you never even thought to ask.

Information covers all the main and supporting characters, events, races, planets, stars, weapons, tools and medical equipment; in fact, all that has appeared in every season of the original series, every season of *Star Trek: The Next Generation*, seasons 1–5 of *Star Trek: Deep Space Nine*, all of *Star Trek: Voyager* and all the films from the 1979 version of *Star Trek: The Motion Picture* to date.

● Make it so

Star Trek CLASSIC: Captain's Chair puts you in the driving seat of the *USS Enterprise* – not just the NCC-1701 of the original series, but the different models encountered in *Star Trek: The Next Generation*, the NCC-1701-E of *Star Trek: First Contact*, the *USS Defiant* of *Star Trek: Deep Space Nine* and the *USS Voyager* of *Star Trek: Voyager*.

With *Captain's Chair* you can explore the *Star Trek* vessel of your choice, see how the technology has changed and developed, look behind the panels, respond to authentic Starfleet commands and come as close as possible to knowing what it is like to be James T Kirk, Jean Luc Picard, Kathryn Janeway and Captain Benjamin Sisko.

If you are one of the many people who have wondered what it would be like to stand on the bridge of the *USS Enterprise*, you now have the chance to find out.

TREKKER FACTS

- *Star Trek* is seen in 100 countries.
- There are more than 63 million *Star Trek* books in print.
- *Star Trek* books have been translated into more than 15 languages, among them Chinese, Norwegian, Hungarian and Hebrew.
- 'Trekkies' are now called 'Trekkers'.
- The first US Space Shuttle, *The Enterprise*, was given its name after NASA received over 400,000 requests.

SITES TO @ VISIT

There are so many *Star Trek* and *Star Trek*-related sites on the Internet that it would be impossible to list them all. One to make sure you visit is the Official Star Trek Site: www.startrek.com.

There are *Star Trek* fan sites covering everything from props used in the original series to lessons in Klingon. Just type in 'Star Trek' in a search engine such as Yahoo! (www.Yahoo.co.uk) and browse the results.

Learn more about the *Star Trek: Generations* game direct from the makers at Microprose: www.microprose.com

The Star Trek Encyclopedia and *Star Trek CLASSIC: Captain's Chair* are supplied by Zablac in the UK: www.ablac.co.uk/zablac.htm

See the plans of every *Star Trek* craft at the Starship Schematics page: www.shipschematics.net

Platform games

For pure fun and enjoyment, it's hard to beat the colourful and challenging world of the platform game.

Throughout computer history, some of the most popular games have been based on one simple action: not shooting or punching, but simply jumping. Programs that feature such action are known as platform games and have been around almost as long as computer games themselves.

Despite their apparent simplicity, such games have proved that jumping skills have just as much entertainment value in the computer's virtual reality world as they do on the athletics field.

● A slow start

In the early days, platform games used to be static, non-scrolling affairs. The ultimate goal might simply be to get across to the other side of the screen, but it often involved collecting a few objects on the way.

To add extra jeopardy to the proceedings, the screen was made up of several free-standing platforms, often no more sophisticated than flat horizontal lines. These were placed in increasingly awkward positions, so you had to use your expertise to judge when to jump from one to another. Usually, monsters would move around the area through which you had to jump, meaning that you had to get your timing exactly right, while accurately judging the distance and height you had to leap.

WHAT IT MEANS

SUPERCONSOLES

Just as the PC has evolved and improved over the years, so too have video game machines – to the point where they can often pack graphical power to match even a top-of-the-range PC. The previous earth-shattering games consoles, such as the Sega MegaDrive and Nintendo's SNES, have now given way to a new group, collectively known as superconsoles, which includes the Sony PlayStation and Sega Dreamcast. Increasingly, games originally written for consoles are re-programmed to run on PCs.

Oddworld: Abe's Oddyssee ***(above) and*** **Earthworm Jim 3D** ***(top) make great use of your computer's graphics ability, while providing fun and challenging game play.***

● Digging for victory

Early home computer titles, such as *Manic Miner* and *Jet Set Willy*, gave way to more skill-based (as opposed to purely reflex-based) titles such as *Super Mario Bros*. The platform game continued to evolve and change but the basic concept remained: to get from one end of a game world to the other without falling off a platform or getting killed by the monsters.

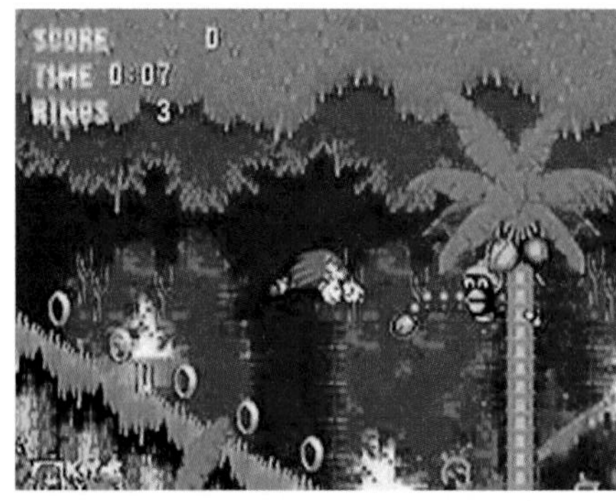

Sonic the Hedgehog ***might have begun life on dedicated games consoles, but you can now find him on the PC.***

Until quite recently, all platform games were two-dimensional. However, with the advent of modern superconsoles, platform games have seen the rise of *Sonic the Hedgehog* and have gained another dimension. Before Windows, PCs had a great deal of trouble displaying such graphics, but the PC, too, has begun to receive its fair share of these running, jumping, all-action games, including the game sensation of recent years – *Tomb Raider*.

● Top of the charts

The blockbusting *Tomb Raider* series has become one of the most famous

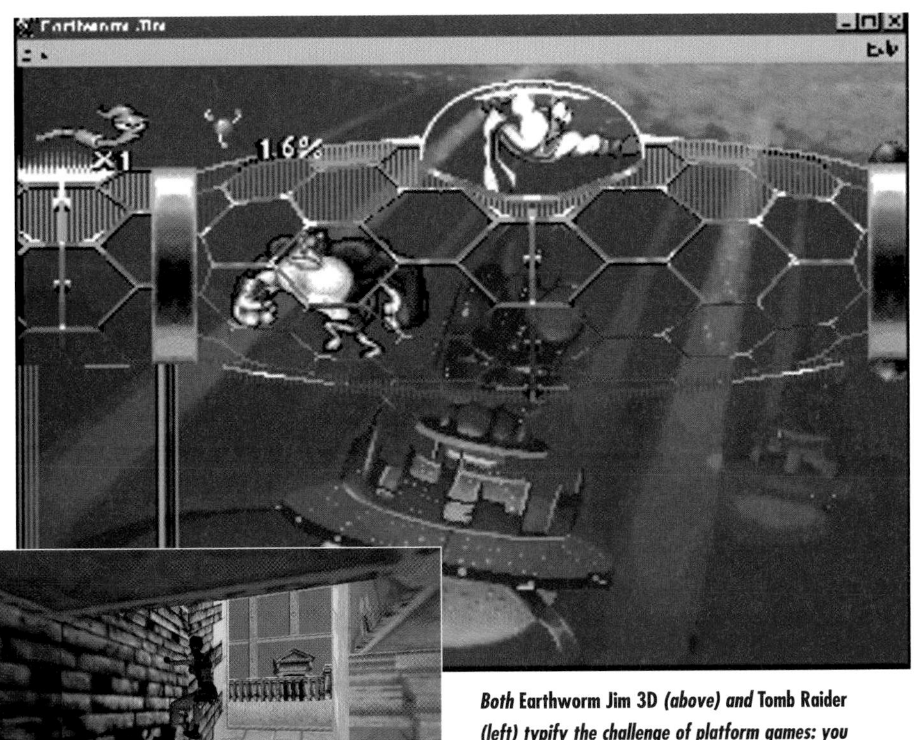

Both* Earthworm Jim 3D *(above) and* Tomb Raider *(left) typify the challenge of platform games: you learn how to get a bit further each time, until you can complete the task in one go.

PC games of all time, thanks largely to its central character Lara Croft – the world's first cyber-celebrity pin-up. While the game is thoroughly modern in terms of its superb graphics, complexity of gameplay and marketing hype, at heart it is really just a good, old-fashioned platform game. The first and fourth titles, in particular, feature very little shooting or puzzle-solving, but an awful lot of jumping onto awkwardly placed window ledges or rock outcrops (depending on the level).

This doesn't mean to say that the game is in any way poor or unexciting – it is, after all, one of the best-selling games ever; it's simply that its roots are rather more historic than the lovely Lara would have you believe. Of course, the combination of Lara and state-of-the-art 3D graphics makes the game's ancestry largely irrelevant.

Although it is little mentioned nowadays, the original *Tomb Raider* games were based very closely on an old 2D game called *Prince of Persia*. This game featured a similar control system and an almost identical mix of platform jumping and simple combat.

Somewhat ironically, *Prince of Persia 3D* was released later and manages to look very much like an Arabian Nights version of *Tomb Raider*. It's nevertheless quite good, and a pleasing break from the occasionally repetitive adventures of Ms Croft.

Tomb Raider: The Last Revelation *puts pneumatic heroine Lara Croft in a dangerous landscape of palaces and ruins. The excellent 3D graphics, and the charms of Lara, made this fourth game in the series another smash hit.*

For those totally immune to the charms of Lara, or for parents who feel she's a little on the adult side for their children, a number of similar titles aimed at a lower age group are beginning to appear. *Earthworm Jim 3D* is based on a popular cartoon, albeit one with a rather warped sense of humour. Like many platform heroes, Jim has also appeared in older 2D games, but this is his first jaunt in a full 3D world. Jim is still up to his usual nonsense, though, such as saving kidnapped cows and racing across breakfast tables on a surfboard-like salami.

3D or not 3D?

Despite the attraction of 3D worlds, 2D platform games just won't go away – perhaps because they still provide simple, straightforward fun.

Oddworld: Abe's Oddyssee, for example, is the first of a four-part series. It features some extremely detailed and well-animated 2D graphics. *Abe's Oddyssee* tries to add variety, depth and humour to the proceedings by including character interaction. You can speak with friendly creatures and get them to help you with your goals, or capture enemy creatures and use their skills and weapons.

Despite the success of *Abe's Oddyssee* and its sequel, *Oddworld: Abe's Exoddus*, the third game in the series will be in full 3D.

CONTACT POINTS

Tomb Raider
Price: £14.99*
Tomb Raider II
Price: £14.99*
Tomb Raider III
Price: £14.99*
Tomb Raider: The Last Revelation
Price: £29.99*
Eidos Interactive
Tel: 0121 332 4647

Prince of Persia 3D
Mattel Interactive
Price: £29.99*
Tel: 01664 481 563

Earthworm Jim 3D
Interplay Productions
Price: £19.99*
Tel: 01628 423723

Oddworld: Abe's Oddyssee
Price £9.99*
Oddworld: Abe's Exoddus
Price £14.99*
Infogramme
Tel: 020 8222 9700

*UK prices

http

The Internet

Easy Web browsing

There is a place for everything and almost everything has a place on the Internet. No matter how diverse your interests, they will be catered for. We show you where to look.

The single reason for the Internet becoming so popular is the World Wide Web; this is a collection of millions of pages of fun, programs and information stored on computers all around the world. Before the Web came along, the Internet was hard to use and only experts really gained much value from it.

With the World Wide Web (often abbreviated to WWW), the Internet became as easy to use as Windows itself. You can just point and click your way from page to page across the world. Each Web page can contain text, images, sound, video clips and animation – just like a multimedia CD-ROM.

Your browser helps you find what you want from the vast mass of information on the Internet. You can use your browser to find Web sites you already know or for making general searches.

● Browsing around

To view a page you need to use a program called a Web browser. This converts the special HTML codes that are used to create a Web page and displays the text and images in the intended format. Moving around Web pages and using hyperlinks is called browsing, or sometimes 'surfing'. However, before you can start browsing the pages on the Web, you need to get connected to the Internet and sign up with an Internet service provider (see Stage 1, pages 134–137).

● Browser connection

When you start your Web browser, it checks to see if you are already connected to the Internet. If you are not, it will start the software that dials up and connects you – you'll see a dialog box that asks you to confirm that you want to connect. Press the OK button and you'll hear your modem dial out.

Once it establishes a connection with your Internet service provider, you'll be able to start browsing.

There are two main types of browser available – Microsoft's Internet Explorer and Netscape's Communicator/Navigator. One of them is usually supplied to new users by the Internet service provider when it sends the start-up software needed for a Web connection. Although there are differences between the two, they will both allow you to move around the Web, viewing pages, images, video and animation.

WHAT IT MEANS

HTML

A Web page is created using a language called hypertext mark-up language, or HTML, which defines the way text is displayed. HTML is used for all parts of a Web page, from bold text to hyperlinks. For example, the code <b> will display text in bold. Your browser displays Web pages without showing the HTML code.

Changing your start-up Web address

After a while, you might notice that the site at which your Web browser starts isn't very interesting. Save time and money by choosing your own favourite site as your start-up Web address.

EACH TIME you start your Web browser, it will automatically display the initial welcome page from the same Web site – usually one created by the Web browser maker, or your ISP. Many ISPs have made their home pages into gateways – 'portals' – to the Web that offer news and services, together with links to a wealth of selected content. If you use such an ISP you may well be happy to stick with it as your home page.

● Saving money

However, if you have to wait for a relatively uninteresting page to load, you are wasting both time and money. In this case it might be worth changing your home page. There is a significant financial benefit to cutting down on waiting time. For example, if your family starts the browser three times a day on average, and this welcome page takes 30 seconds to load, you are wasting 630 seconds per week. That's 546 minutes a year, at a cost of £22 at peak rates. You can easily change the first page to a favourite one or leave it blank for a faster start-up.

Microsoft Internet Explorer

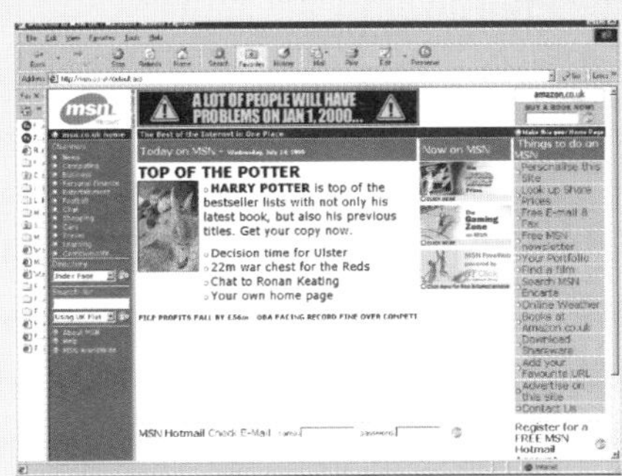

The Internet Explorer start-up page is the Microsoft Network, which contains all sorts of links to news and features. But it might not be the right mix for you.

To change the Internet Explorer start-up page, go to the Tools menu and select Internet Options. Click the General tab if that page is not already on screen. The top box refers to the home page. Select the current Web address and type in the new one, such as www.football365.co.uk. Click OK to save the changes and restart the browser. For a blank page, just click the Use Blank button.

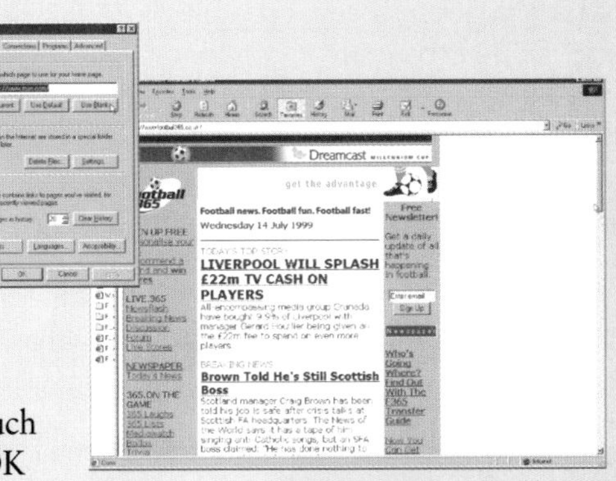

If you can't get enough of football, try making your home page an up-to-the minute soccer site like Football365 (www.football365.co.uk).

Netscape Communicator/Navigator

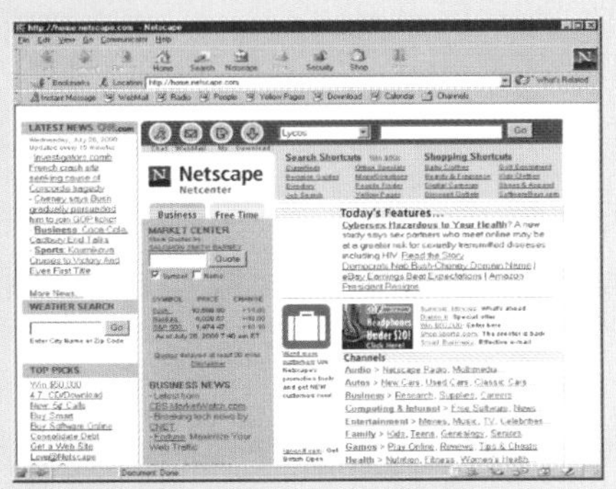

Netscape's Netcenter has links to all kinds of news and services – perhaps too many to make it an ideal home page.

To change your start-up page in Netscape Communicator or Navigator, choose Preferences from the Edit menu. In the Home Page box select the currently displayed address and type in the new one you want. Click OK and then restart the browser for the changes to take effect.

If you prefer a blank page, simply click the Blank page option at the top of the page.

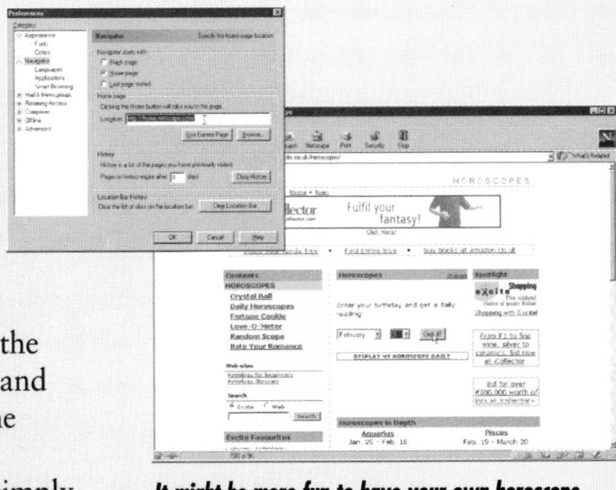

It might be more fun to have your own horoscope displayed each time you log on. Try www.excite.co.uk/horoscopes for a daily forecast.

Searching for information

The best way to navigate the millions of sites on the World Wide Web is to use a search engine. Just enter your enquiry and the search engine will give you a list of sites that match it.

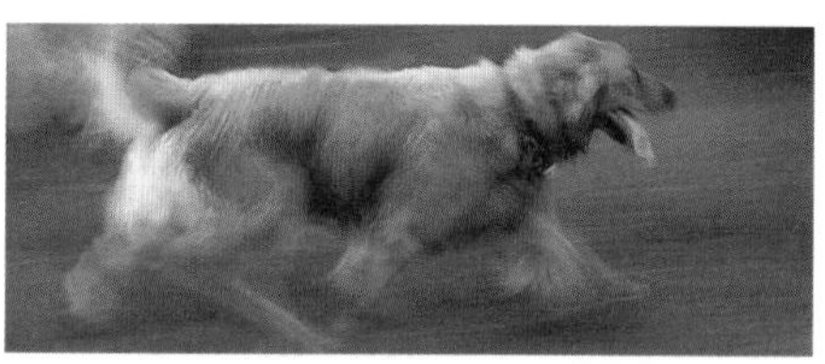

Asking a search engine to fetch the Internet pages that interest you is easy – and it doesn't expect a reward!

IF YOU ALREADY know where you want to go on the Internet and you have the address of the Web site, then you can type it directly into your browser. To find a site to answer a particular question, or to find information on a special subject, you first need to find the address of a site that holds the answer. Search engines are Web sites dedicated to finding addresses for practically any query imaginable.

Search engines are rather like huge telephone directories. You enter key words instead of flicking through pages and the search engine responds with addresses instead of telephone numbers. For example, if you want to find out about bee-keeping in New York, you could type in the search words 'bee-keeping' and 'New York' to see if the search engine has any Web pages that contain these terms. If there are any matches, or 'hits', you will see a summary of the contents of the Web page and a hyperlink so you can jump directly to the page.

Selecting a search engine

There are several search engines that are worth using to find information. One is Yahoo! – one of the most comprehensive search engines and certainly one of the best known. Yahoo! organizes information into categories that make it easier to find a Web site. Yell is provided by the Yellow Pages directory in the UK and is a good choice if you want UK Web sites. Excite is comprehensive and provides specialized advanced search features, while AltaVista is one of the most powerful and comprehensive search engines available. See pages 142–145 for further details on searching the Web.

HOW A SEARCH ENGINE WORKS

A search engine tries to index the text contained in every single page on the World Wide Web. Since there are millions of Web pages and many change almost every day, this is no mean feat. Some search engines try to provide the most exhaustive directory of Web pages, while others provide reviews to help you choose the best sites to visit. Try several of the Web search engines listed in the Sites To Visit box on the opposite page to see which works best for you.

When researching a work or school project, you don't need to know the exact address of any sites. Entering specific keywords such as 'biology frog lifespan' will usually provide some suggested sites to visit.

ADDRESSES ON THE WORLD WIDE WEB

Every page on the Web has a unique address. Wherever you are in the world, just typing the address into your browser takes you directly to it. In computer jargon, this address is called the Uniform Resource Locator or URL.

Often a URL looks something like: www.disney.com. The 'www' part signifies that you are looking for a Web page; the second part shows the name of the Web site (Disney); and the third part identifies the type of Web site (.com is a commercial site). To say the URL aloud, read it as 'w-w-w-dot-disney-dot-com'.

To view this page, just type the address into your browser's URL line. When you press the [Enter] key, your browser goes direct to the Disney Web site. When the first page has finished loading, you can see individual pages on the site by clicking on the links on the page (often marked in blue).

As you click on these links, look to see what happens to the URL line: it changes to show another URL. The first part looks the same but the whole URL is longer and refers to other pages on the Disney site.

Using Yahoo! to find a Web site

The World Wide Web has answers to many of life's tricky questions – if you know where to go. Let's look for information on how to mend the indicator light on an MG Midget, with the help of Yahoo!

1 Enter the Yahoo! URL (www.yahoo.com) into your Web browser to display its welcome page (right). It may not look very exciting, but it might soon become a favourite port of call. You can type search words (sometimes called keywords) into the box provided or use the ready-made categories to narrow down your search. You can enter just one keyword or a specific query that includes several.

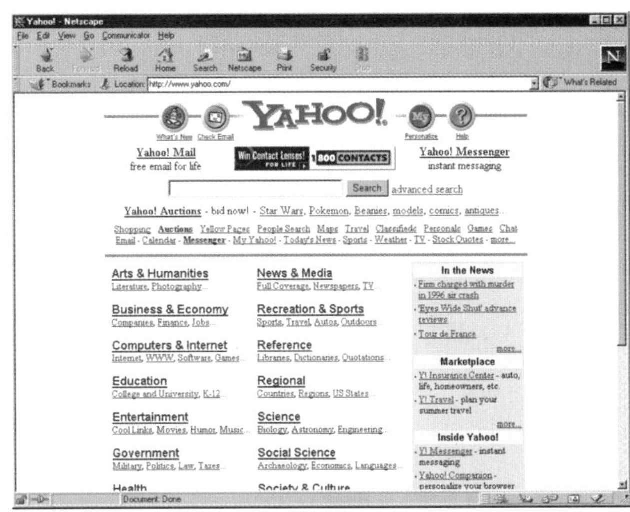

2 Clicking on Recreation & Sports takes us to this screen, which you can scroll down using your mouse to reveal the next possible choices, listed alphabetically.

3 As we are looking for information about cars, we select the Automotive category. Some 56 further options appear. We know the MG was a British car, so this will be our next choice.

4 As you can see, searching on the Internet with a search engine is like following a trail of clues. This not only makes it easy to find what you want, it also makes it a lot more fun. Here are the options which are listed under British Cars. Now we need to select the MG category.

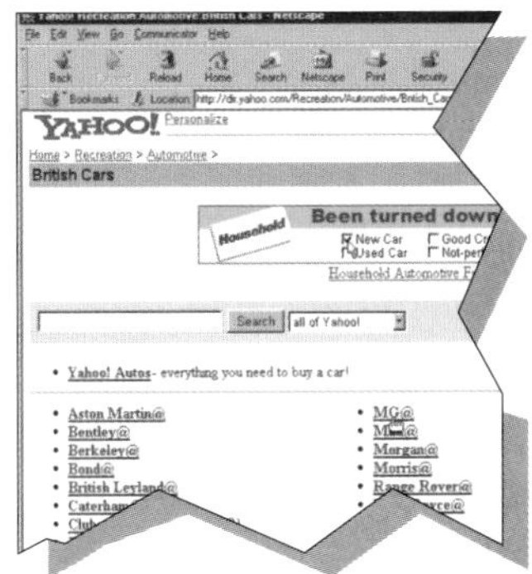

5 Now we see a list of the Web sites relating to MG cars. Scrolling down the page brings up a site which specializes in technical tips for MG owners. Clicking on the title of the site takes you straight there, with no need to type in the address. Then it's a matter of looking around the pages of the site by clicking on links and looking for the information you need (inset).

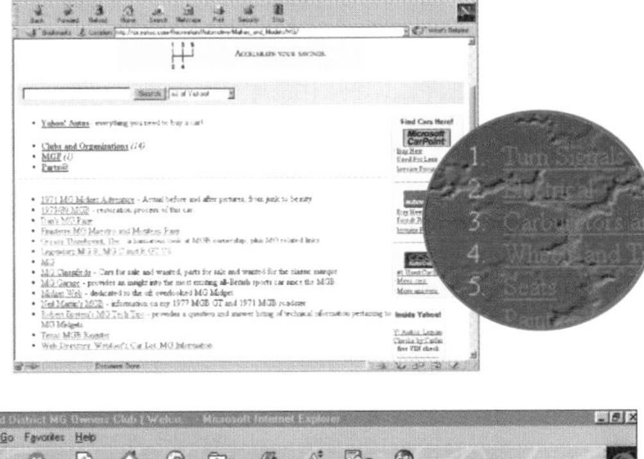

6 One of the exciting things about looking for something on the Internet is the huge amount of information that is available. There were many distractions on the way to our MG technical tips page, so we could easily have wandered off track and taken a look at MG motor racing or found an MG owners club – or even bought another MG.

Among the most popular sites on the Internet are the search engines. Internet users visit these sites to search for other sites. Here are some of the most popular search engines:

GONetwork: www.go.com
Yahoo!: www.yahoo.com
Lycos: www.lycos.co.uk
Yell: www.yell.co.uk
Excite!: www.excite.co.uk
AltaVista: www.altavista.com
UKPlus: www.ukplus.co.uk
Yahoo! UK: www.yahoo.co.uk
Google: www.google.com
WebCrawler: www.webcrawler.com

Smoother Web browsing

Searching for information or a specific site on the World Wide Web often seems like a struggle. We show you how error messages and registration forms are not always the dead ends they seem.

Imagine an ideal Web-browsing world, where you would enter the name of a Web site, press [Enter] and go straight to the site. We don't live in an ideal world and, as you explore the Web, you'll encounter a range of browsing obstacles, including error messages, announcements that a 'site has not been found', access restrictions and suggestions that you subscribe to a site. In the next few pages, we show you some common browsing obstacles and how to overcome them.

● Registration form

As you browse the Web, you'll come across requests to register with a site. In many cases, you can gain access to the site by filling in an on-screen form with your name, address and a few personal details. The company running the site asks for the details so that they can compile a profile of the type of visitor to the site. This information is used to persuade advertisers to promote their products on the Web site.

For other Web sites, such as those providing real-time share prices or business services (online company searches, for example), you will need to pay a subscription or enter your credit card details before you can access the site. On the following pages, you will see how to register for *Loot*'s classified advertising site. It contains thousands of adverts for all sorts of goods – and it's free.

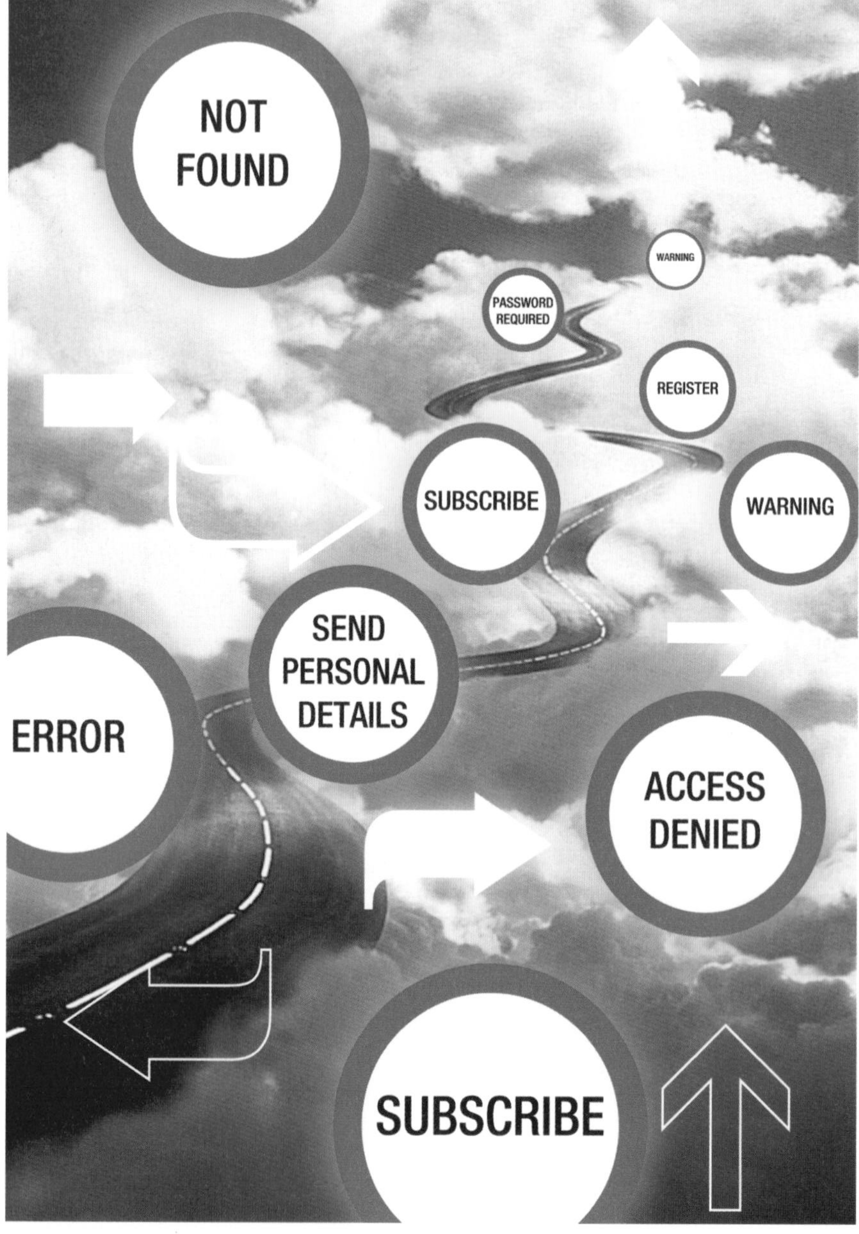

● Bells and whistles

Many Web sites use sophisticated techniques that provide video, sound and animation on the pages. Don't worry if your browser doesn't have the latest software needed to view and hear the latest multimedia sites – it's easy to download and install plug-ins (see page 141) that allow your browser to show these new features.

● Top two browsers

There are two main Internet browsers – Microsoft's Internet Explorer and Netscape's Communicator/ Navigator – and each has different features. If you have access to both browsers, you will notice that they sometimes display the same Web page in a slightly different way. For example, you may find that text and pictures sometimes line up differently on the screen. However, this is only a matter of concern to the purists and the content is generally the same.

HOW A BROWSER WORKS

A browser works by interpreting the special programming codes that are used to create a page. These codes – called HTML (see page 134) – describe the way that a page is set out, the format of the text and other aspects of the presentation.

Browser developments

The browser developers are always working on techniques to improve the way information is presented on screen. Problems arise because the latest additions to one browser might not be used by the other. So, if a Web site designer wants to use new extensions to the HTML codes (see How A Brower Works, above) developed by Microsoft, then these can often only be seen if you view the Web site with the latest Microsoft Explorer browser. If you use the Netscape browser (or an older version of Explorer), the Web page will not look as it is intended.

Security and warnings

Security on the Internet is essential to protect your personal details. When you move around a site, you are not sending any sensitive information – you are only using your browser to view and jump from page to page. However, many sites ask you to type in information such as your name and other personal details. In such cases, you are sending details about yourself over the Net to another computer.

Both the Microsoft and Netscape Web browsers will warn you when you are about to send personal information. Sometimes this warning is not necessary. If you type a word into a search engine, for example, this isn't sensitive information and there is no problem. In other circumstances, however, you might not appreciate the consequences of sending your credit card or other personal details across the Internet, so your computer reminds you to be cautious.

Error messages

While browsing the Web, you might also encounter an array of warning messages. Any messages containing a warning triangle will usually have an explanation of the problem your

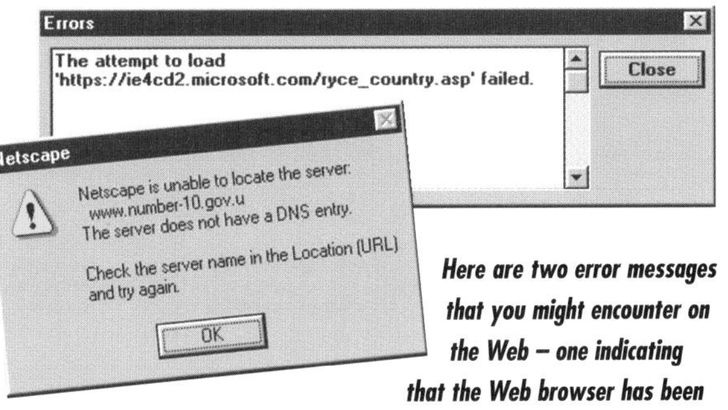

Here are two error messages that you might encounter on the Web – one indicating that the Web browser has been unable to access your chosen Web site without giving a reason (top), the other suggesting that you have typed an incorrect Web address into your browser.

Just like the roads, the Internet can come to a halt due to heavy traffic. If the Web site you are trying to visit is congested, your browser will suggest you visit it later.

browser is experiencing. It might be asking you to confirm your request to open a file over the Internet or it might be telling you it was unable to download a file you requested.

Some of the most common error messages are those which announce that a Web site you want to visit is busy and that you should try again later. This is usually caused by congestion – many other people are trying to visit the site at the same time. You might also encounter warning messages saying that a Web page you have requested does not exist. This happens if the Web site has been updated and old pages have been deleted.

Shopping with security on the Internet

Amazon.com is an Internet success story. This online bookshop has tapped a worldwide market of book-buyers using the Internet.

Retailers don't want potential customers to be scared off by security worries. Amazon.com has addressed this problem so successfully that it now has over 20 million customers. The company is a well-known and respected retailer that recognized concern over Internet security.

Using a secure server ensures that credit card details have an uninterrupted path from your PC direct to Amazon's computer. Once the details are in their computer, Amazon cannot be accessed from the outside world. If people still don't trust the Internet, they can email Amazon the first half of their credit card number and fax the rest – or just post a cheque!

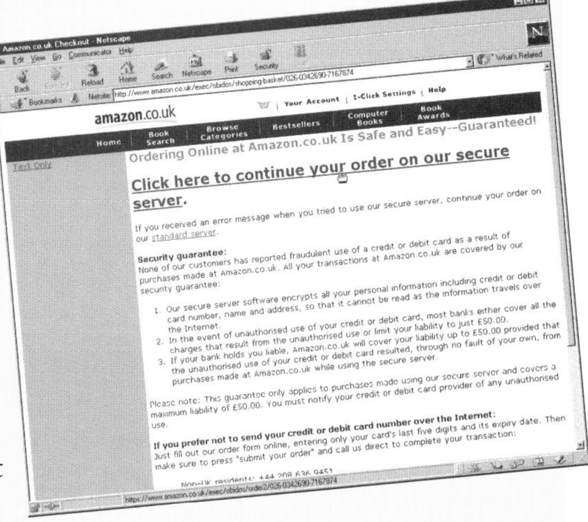

Signing up to a Web site

Don't be afraid of telling the provider of an Internet site a few things about yourself. Here we show you what a simple process it is.

1 Registering with a Web site is easy and is usually free. A good example is *Loot*'s free classified advertising site (www.loot.com). You can browse and search the ads immediately, but to advertise you must first register. Click the Register Now link on *Loot*'s home page.

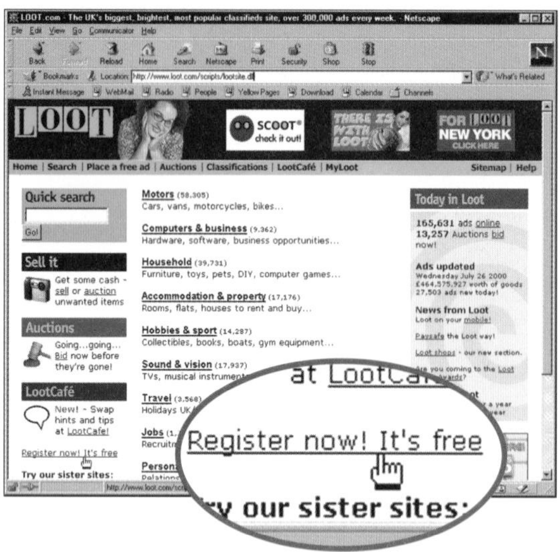

2 On the next page, start by typing in your email address and then select a password (make sure it's not the same as your email password, however).

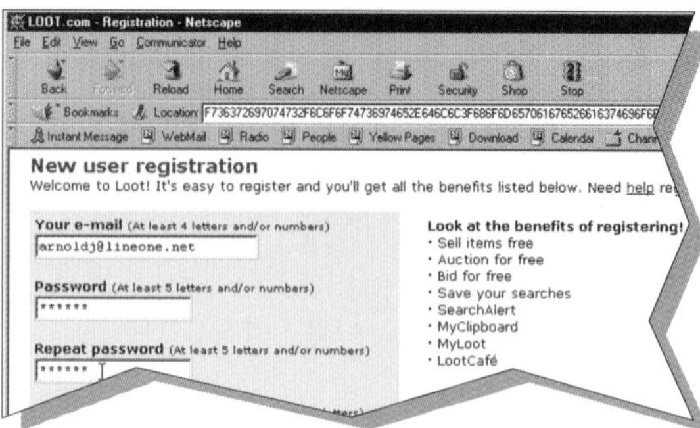

3 The registration form also asks you for some personal details, such as your name, age and occupation. You must fill in all the fields or your registration will not be accepted.

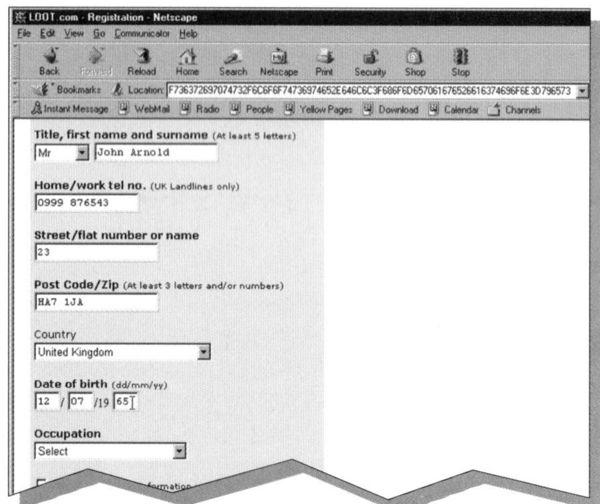

4 Many sites have a tick box that lets you opt out of mailing lists. When you have filled in all the details, click the Register now! button (inset) to submit the form.

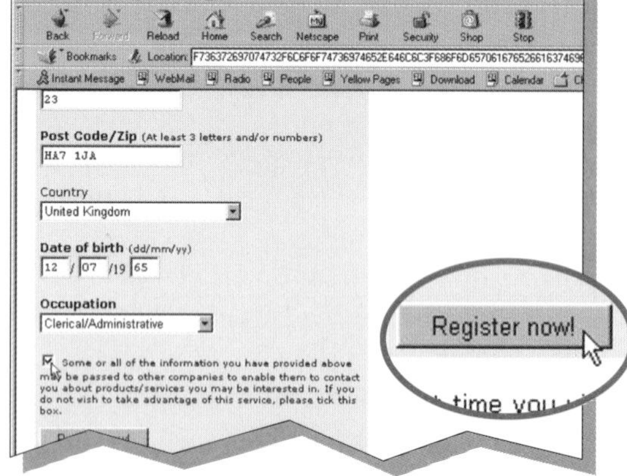

5 Now that you have registered, you can place classified ads for free. Go to *Loot*'s home page and click on the Place a free ad link.

6 You can now use *Loot*'s step-by-step advertising forms. These are stored in your own space on *Loot*'s computers so that you can renew the ad at a later date.

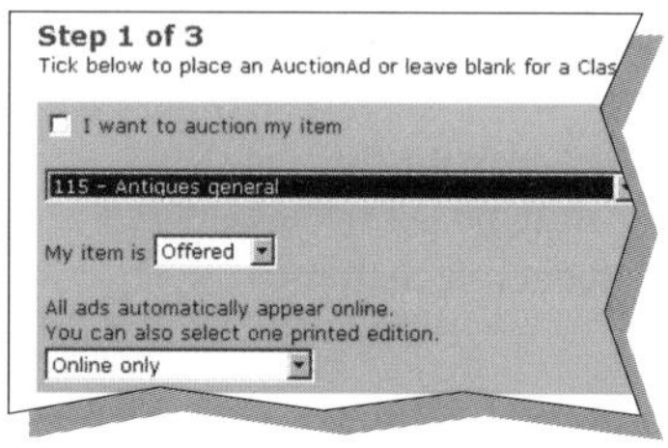

TAKING DOWN YOUR DETAILS

Many Web sites ask you to complete a registration form before you are allowed to use the site. The sites requiring registration may have thousands of pages of information on them. These pages have to be kept up to date and therefore require a lot of work to keep them running efficiently. Knowing what kind of people (their age, country and interests, for example) visit the site will help the site attract advertising revenue to pay for this work. Some sites that don't charge visitors, such as Yahoo!, have a multi-million dollar turnover as a result of the advertising that appears on its pages.

How to add an animation plug-in

Macromedia's Shockwave and Flash players are Web browser plug-ins that will breathe life into pictures and previously blank screens on Web sites. Here we show how to download these plug-ins.

1 When you visit a Web site for the first time, you are often given information about how to view the site at its best. The official Simpsons site (www.thesimpsons.com) looks best with the Macromedia Flash plug-in, which, amongst other things, displays animation. To illustrate how to add a plug-in, click the Cancel button when your Web browser asks if you want to download the plug-in automatically.

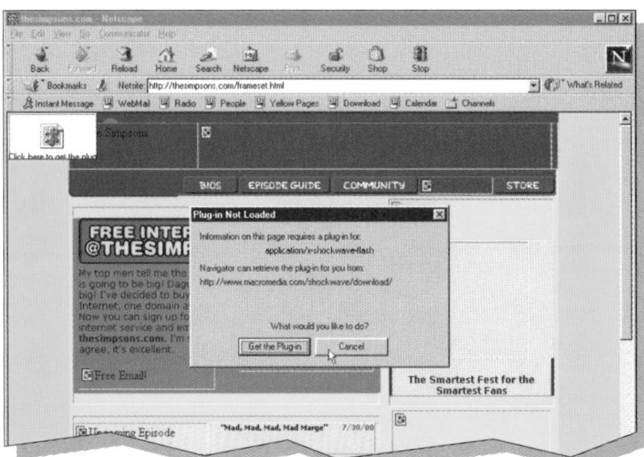

2 Visit the Macromedia home page (www.macromedia.com). Click on the Downloads link and then click on the Macromedia Shockwave and Flash Players link. Then click the Download Now! link and save the file on your Desktop.

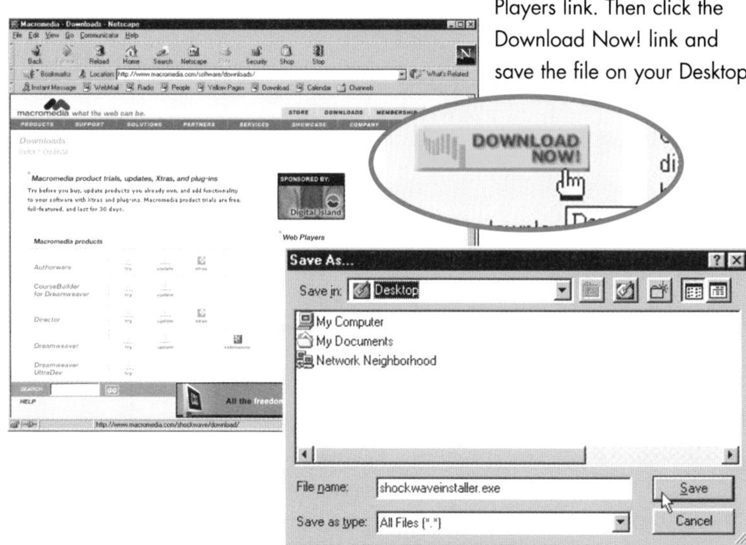

3 When the download is complete, disconnect from the Internet and double-click on the downloaded file. Follow the on-screen instructions to install the software.

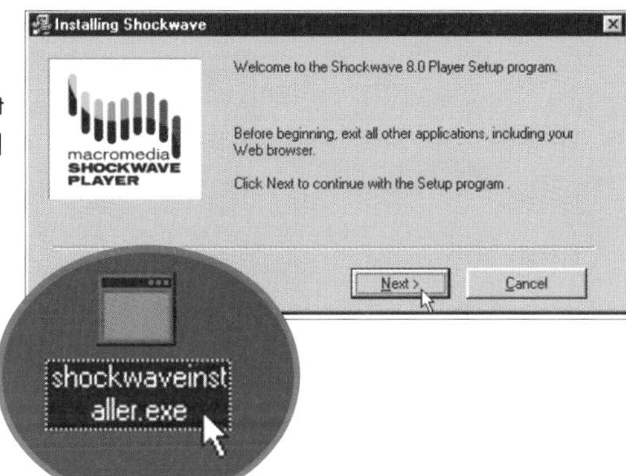

4 After setting up your computer, the software connects to the Internet to download the final component. As it does so, fill in the screen with your details so you can get regular news updates from Macromedia. Click Next to proceed.

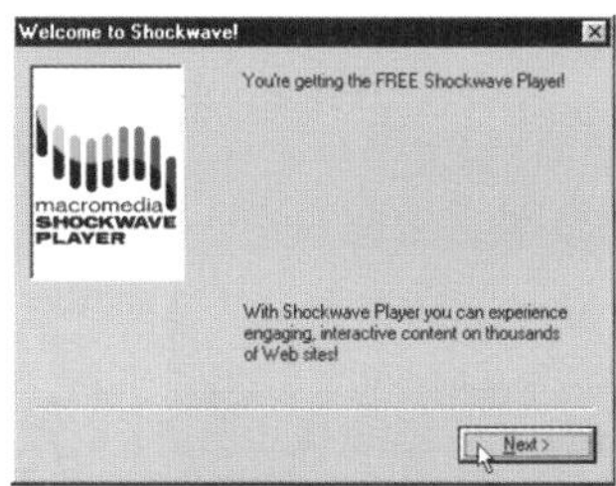

5 When the program has finished downloading (it should take 5–10 minutes with a 56k modem), your Web browser shows a selection of Shockwave animations to verify that the software is working.

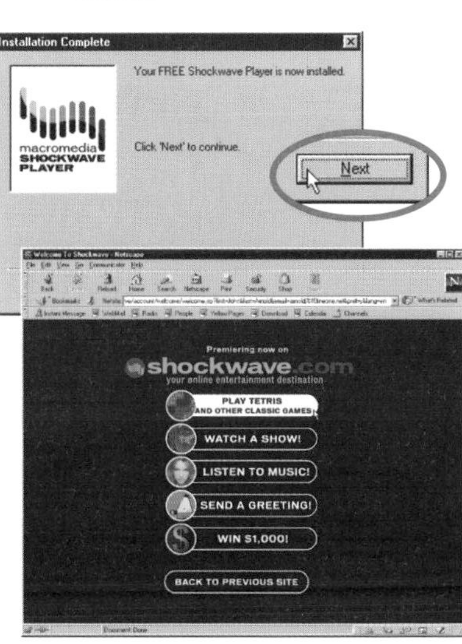

6 With this new software installed, you'll see the Simpsons site as its creators intended, with all the animations in place.

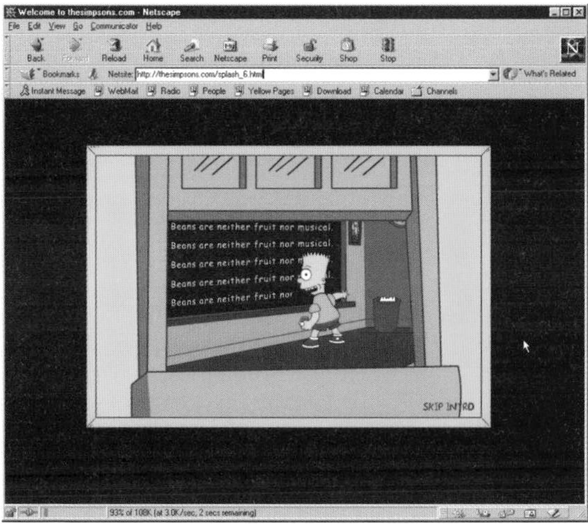

Effective Web searching

Finding precisely what you want on the ever-expanding World Wide Web isn't easy. But if you use one of the many search engines available, you'll soon be able to locate a needle in a haystack.

The more you use the Web, the more you'll become aware that you need help to get to what you want. It's okay if you know the full addresses, or URLs, of the sites you want to visit; you just type them into your Web browser. However, while it's possible to limit yourself to the few trusty sites you know, you would be ignoring the true power of the Web if you did not cast your net wider.

For Web browsing where you don't know the address but you have a good idea of the type of information you want, you need to use a search engine. These are powerful Internet sites that exist purely to help you find other sites based on a few key words.

A search engine has two parts. The first, which you don't see, continuously trawls through millions of Web pages and creates a huge index of the words contained in them. The second is the Web page, which you use to search the index that's been created by the first part. It reports back with the relevant Web addresses, and all you do is click on the list of links to go to the Web site.

● Search engine choices

The search engines on the Web can be divided into two broad categories: those organized by subject or topic, and those which use text searches.

Yahoo! (www.yahoo.co.uk) is a good example of the first type. When you visit the site, you can click through a series of subject headings to see more specific categories (see page 137). With this type of site, you needn't type anything at all – just search, point and click.

PC TIPS

Searching for specific sites on the Web can be tricky. Sometimes you have to think laterally in order to come up with some useful search criteria. If you don't know the name of a site, search for a few unusual words that are closely associated with it. For example, if you are looking for *Batman* sites, also try 'Gotham City' and 'Bruce Wayne'.

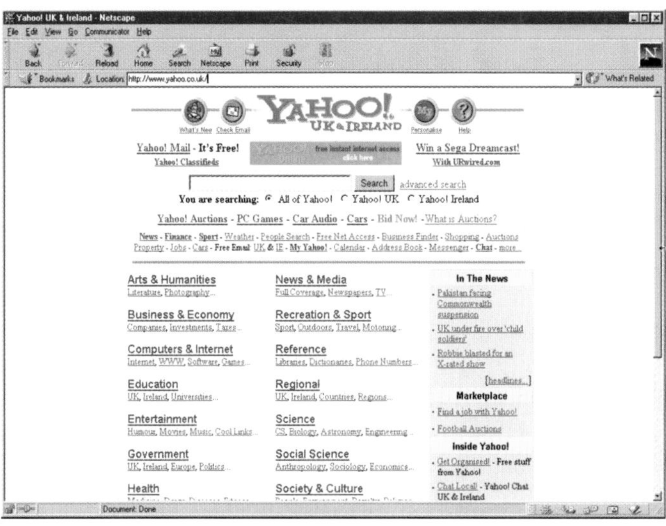

With Yahoo!, you need only point and click your way through a series of subject categories to find a list of Web sites you may want to visit.

The weakness of this type of searching, however, is that it can take a lot of clicking and loading of successive Web pages to find sites you are interested in. And to find very specific information, it's better to take advantage of text searches.

● Text-based searches

AltaVista (www.altavista.com) is one of the most popular text-based search engines. When the Web page loads you will see a simple text box into which you can type anything you like. When you press the Search button, AltaVista searches its index for the words you have typed.

Try the search engine and you will find that the more general the words that you type – 'dinosaur', 'fishing', etc. – the longer the list of sites it finds. It will present them in chunks of 20 sites at a time, and you will have to check through the descriptions, or even visit the sites themselves, to see if any contain the information you want.

For this reason, it's better to be as specific as possible with your search. Searching for 'triceratops', for instance, will yield fewer pages than searching for 'dinosaur'. In fact, the key to getting to relevant sites quickly (minimizing time and costs) is to exploit the way in which text-based search engines work.

There are special characters and phrases you can use to improve your search. While they might seem a little daunting at first sight, they are fast and extremely powerful once you know how to get the most out of them.

● Special commands

Search engines use many tricks, but among the more powerful are those known as 'Boolean operators'. The name is a mathematical phrase for what are simply logical words that can be used to define your search. The four most commonly used operators are AND, OR, NOT and NEAR.

● Using the operators

These operators work just as they sound. For example, you would type 'fishing AND bass' to locate Web pages which had both (thereby avoiding general fishing pages and those that cover bass guitars).

The other operators are just as useful. For instance, the OR operator works in the opposite way to AND. Thus you might search for 'Mercedes OR Porsche OR Jaguar' to find Web pages that contain information on any of these makes of car. Note, however, that you will also locate pages about the jaguar wild cat, too.

The NOT operator is used if you want to exclude a subject. This is very useful if the search word has more than one meaning. For example, 'windows NOT computer' is a good way to find pages about windowpanes instead of Microsoft Windows.

WHAT IT MEANS

SYNTAX

This refers to the grammatical structure of a search. Just like words in plain English, the order of commands in a search is important; it must be in a form the computer can understand.

The last of the four most common operators is NEAR, which is more rarely used than the other three. It can be useful if you are not sure how to describe the subject you are looking at, but can think of some specific words a page of interest should contain.

For example, 'ant NEAR nest NEAR society' could be a useful way to search for a scientific piece about ants if you didn't know that the study of ants is called myrmecology.

● Other text functions

The special text functions are just as easy to use. These are function words that work using a special syntax. They always end in a colon (:), followed by the word or phrase for which you are searching.

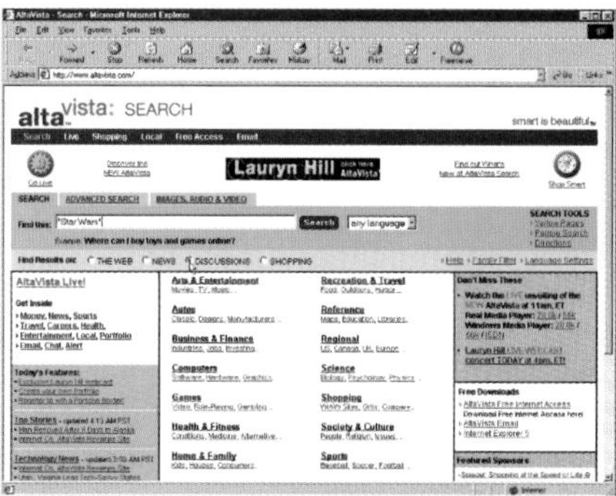

AltaVista is one example of a text-based search engine; if you type in a word or phrase, it will produce a list of all the sites it has found that contain the text.

For example, 'anchor:boat' will search for pages that contain the word 'boat' in a link (or anchor, as links are known in AltaVista).

Other function words include 'domain' (for specific domain names such as .org or .uk) and 'image' (useful for locating pictures with specific words in their names).

There are others that you will find detailed on the search engines' help pages.

● Fine-tuning your searches

With these simple additions to your text searches you will narrow the field considerably. This means that you're less likely to be confronted by hundreds of Web pages – any one of which may include the information you want, but most of which will be a waste of time.

Using different search engines

To illustrate how difficult a specific search can be, we'll try to find Steven Spielberg's first film, using Lycos and Yahoo!

SEARCH ENGINES proper – such as AltaVista and Lycos – can turn up thousands of pages. Directory-based search engines, such as Yahoo!, pre-select certain sites. We show how either approach can get what you want – in this case, the first film Steven Spielberg ever made.

Just typing in 'Steven Spielberg' isn't going to be too much use here, as it will turn up literally thousands of Web pages. We'll look for the information using two different search engines. Lycos will search the Web and report back with as many sites as it can find containing your search term. Yahoo!, on the other hand, is a directory service; its human staff select sites. This can cut out a lot of rubbish and can sometimes be a quicker way to search.

1 Go to the Lycos search engine by typing 'www.lycos.co.uk' in your browser's URL line. Select the option to search the whole Web rather than just UK sites. Then type in 'Steven Spielberg' in the Search for: box and click on the Go Get It! button.

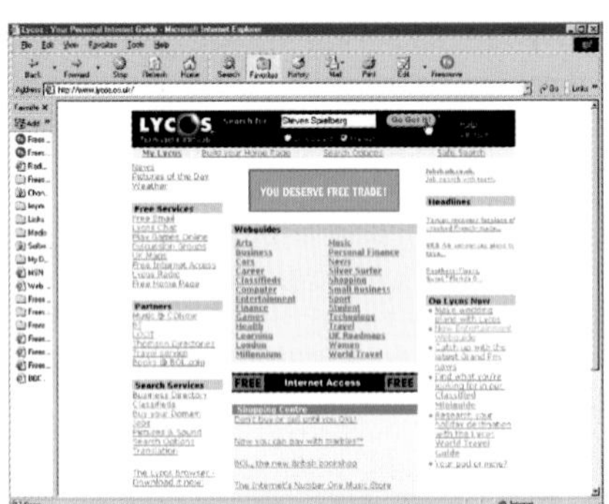

2 Lycos finds well over 12,000 pages. The information we want is in there somewhere, but it could take a long time to find it.

3 We need to refine our search. Type in the name, but now followed by three of Spielberg's films separated by the ampersand (&) symbol – which is short for the Boolean operator AND. This will, we hope, come up with sites listing Spielberg's films.

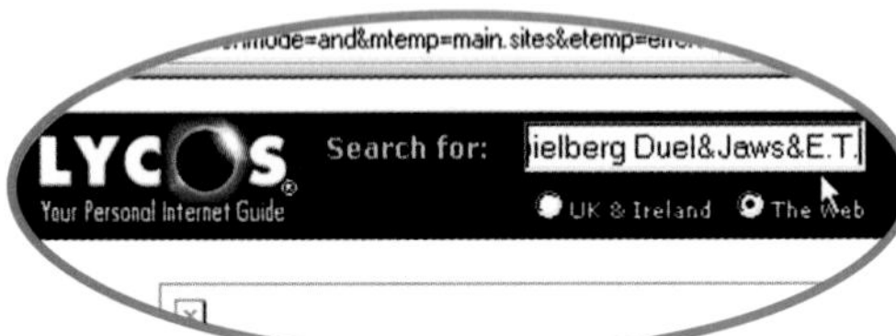

4 Now five web sites are returned. A scan suggests that the Steven Spielberg Encyclopedia could be good for us. Clicking on it takes us there, where we find that Spielberg won an award for his first film, a short war film called *Escape to Nowhere*.

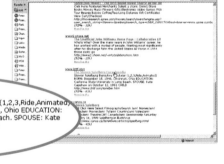

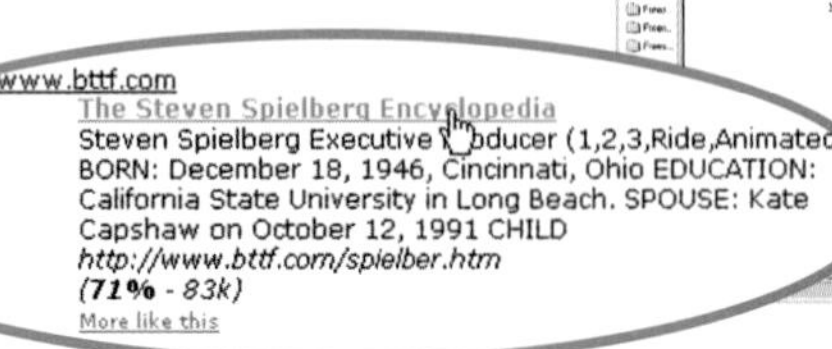

www.bttf.com
The Steven Spielberg Encyclopedia
BORN: December 18, 1946, Cincinnati, Ohio EDUCATION:
California State University in Long Beach. SPOUSE: Kate
Capshaw on October 12, 1991 CHILD
http://www.bttf.com/spielber.htm
(71% - 83k)
More like this

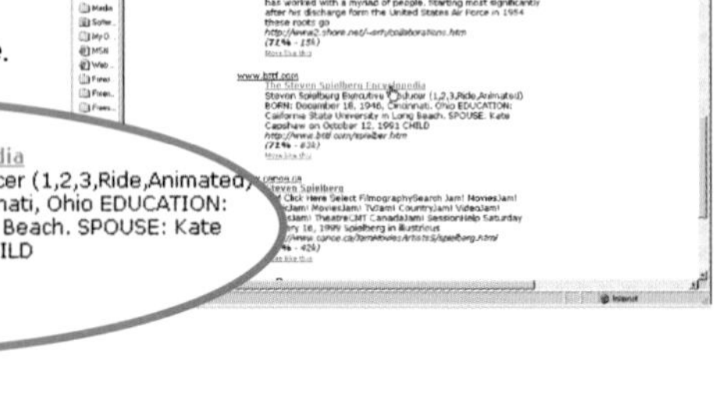

5 Now let's try Yahoo! (www.yahoo.com or www.yahoo.co.uk). We don't need to type anything in the Search box at first; instead, click on the Movies link in the Entertainment category.

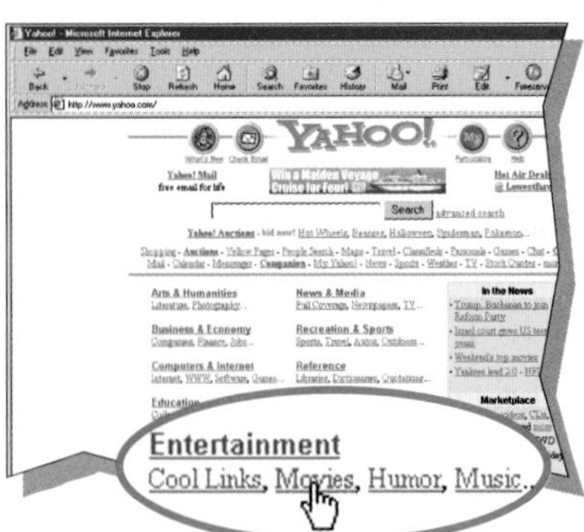

6 This brings up a number of movie-related sub-categories. Now we can refine our search. Type in the director's name in the Search box, then select the just this category option on the right. Now click on the Search button.

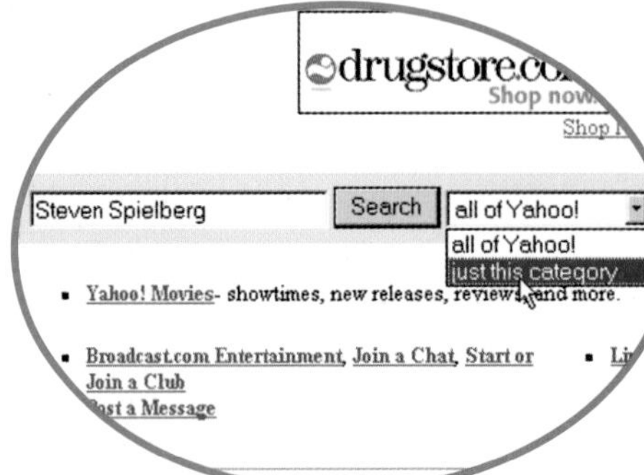

7 This brings up a list of sites specifically dealing with Spielberg's work. Very quickly we find a number of sites that contain the information we want.

Searching for pictures, links and newsgroups

Sometimes you will want to search for things other than specific words used in the text of a Web page. This is where special text search functions come in.

BY USING the special text search functions you will be able to find items that a Web search would normally miss. For example, you can find particular pictures or links – both parts of a Web page that a search engine would not normally look in.

These functions are also very useful for searching on Usenet, that part of the Internet used to host newsgroups (we'll cover this later in the course).

AltaVista has a useful option to search on Usenet, and it also has some special text functions for specifically searching Usenet rather than the Web.

What's more, you won't have to open up a special Newsgroup program to see the pages: AltaVista will simply display the pages themselves in your Web browser.

1 To search AltaVista for Usenet sites, first select the Discussion Groups option below the Find this: box.

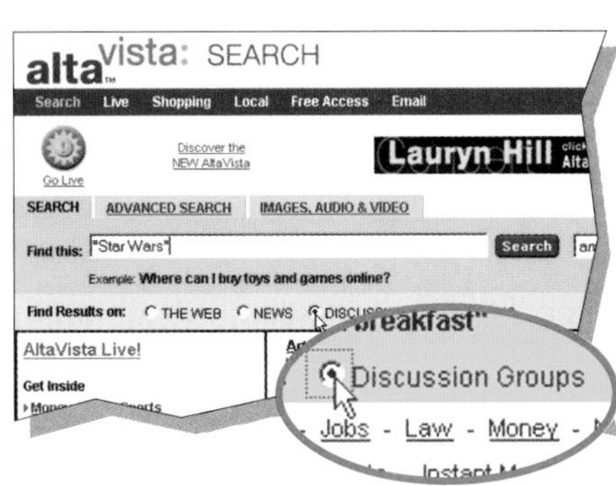

2 Now type in the subject and press Search. We're looking for Star Wars, and we've enclosed the phrase in quotation marks to make sure that AltaVista looks only for the two words next to each other.

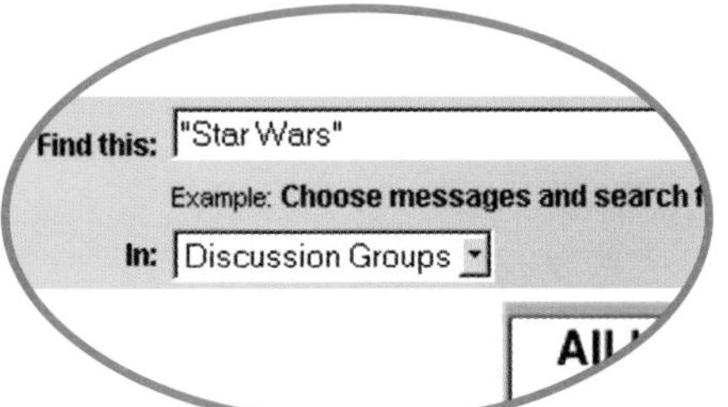

3 AltaVista then lists the matches it finds. Click on any one to see the individual message. Here someone is asking for information on the official status of the Dark Jedi.

4 To find pages that contain a specific word or phrase in the text of a link, you need to type the command 'anchor:' before the word. Here we're looking for links that contain the word 'dinosaur'.

5 The matches are all dinosaur pages, all of which seem pretty interesting.

6 You can use a similar approach if you want to find an image with a specific phrase in its file name. To find images of Elvis Presley you could type 'image: elvis' into AltaVista's search box. And within the matches results we find the Elvis Photo Gallery.

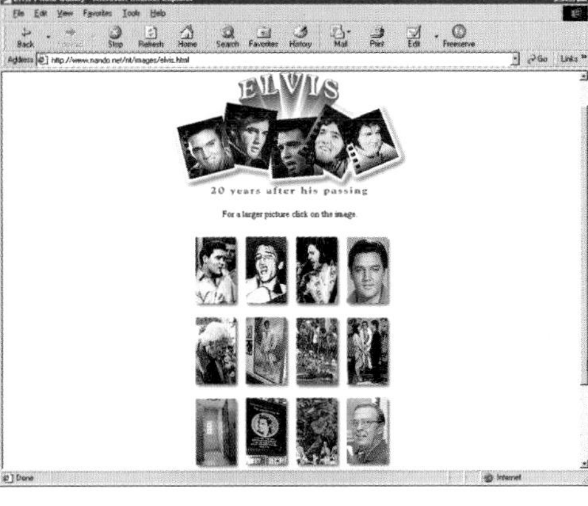

METASEARCHING

Whether you're using a 'classic' search engine or a directory-style site, it can't possibly report all the pages that might be relevant. And since each search engine uses its own technology and tricks, they will not all be equally accurate or comprehensive. If you want to do a really thorough search and cover all the bases, you might consider using what is called 'metasearch' software. These programs do not search the Web themselves, but take your query and get a number of different search engines to do it. The results can be impressively thorough.

Downloading software

The Internet is not only a great resource for information and entertainment, it also allows you to copy – or download – new programs and other useful software directly onto your computer.

The World Wide Web can be seen as a giant warehouse containing computer programs, text, photographs, video graphics and sound – all of which can be downloaded onto your home computer.

The Internet contains information on almost every subject, but it also has files that store programs, games, video footage, images and sounds. These files are stored on computers that are linked to the Internet, but you can copy a file onto your hard disk in order to use it. This process, called downloading, means that you can access new information or try out new programs quickly and cheaply.

Many Web pages have links that lead to a downloadable file, rather than to another Web page. If you click on one of these download links, your browser will automatically start to copy the file onto your computer's hard disk.

● What you can download

There is a wide range of different types of software that you can download and use at home. For example, many of the large software companies have trial versions of new or popular software for you to download and use before deciding whether to buy the full program.

There are demonstration versions of games that work for a few days or have a limited number of levels. New Internet technologies usually require new software and this is often available to download free of charge – for example, the QuickTime MoviePlayer Software, which allows you to run small video sequences on your PC. If you want to view 3D worlds or listen to music over the Internet, you will need to add software to your Web browser to allow it to use this feature. This software – called a plug-in – is made available as the new technologies are developed and can be downloaded free to keep your Web browser up to date (see page 141 for details on downloading animation plug-ins).

WHAT IT MEANS

PLUG-IN

A plug-in is a piece of software that extends the functions of a Web browser. Plug-ins are sometimes required for new Multimedia features in Web sites, such as video, audio, 3D graphics and animation. Plug-ins are supplied free and install automatically.

Software, called plug-ins, can be downloaded onto your computer to make your Web browsing more exciting.

The Internet also allows you to download the latest drivers for graphics hardware and modems; if you have a problem with a software program, you can often find and download a special program, called a patch, that fixes the fault.

If you want new software, there are thousands of shareware programs to download. If you like a program and use it regularly, you pay a registration fee to the program developer. Shareware programs include drawing and painting programs, word processors and business tools.

Find fantastic fonts

If you want to add new fonts (typefaces) to your computer or enhance a presentation with exciting graphic images, look on the Internet. There are thousands of different fonts created by professional designers – some are available to download free, while others can be tried out for free.

Download the QuickTime software (www.apple.com/quicktime) and you will be able to run both movie and video clips on your PC.

Lastly, the Internet started as a way of sharing information and now there are hundreds of millions of files that contain useful information covering just about every subject you can imagine. Information files from the telephone number of a local plumber to the population statistics of a country can be viewed, downloaded or printed.

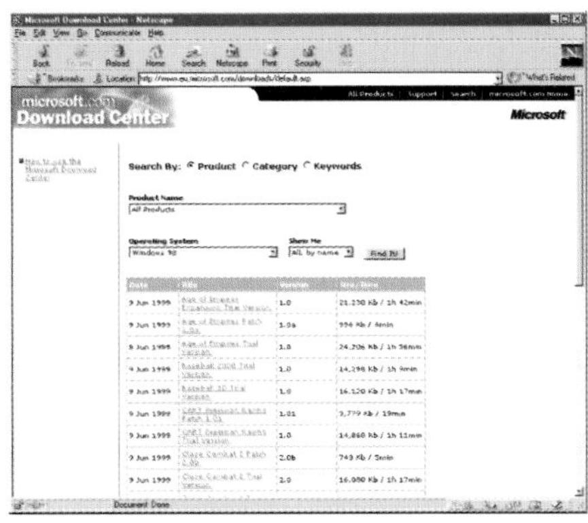

The Microsoft Web site (http//www.microsoft.com) is the place to go if you want updates and patches for Windows software.

Download drawbacks

The main drawback in downloading information is that the bigger the file, the longer it takes to download. For example, a full trial version of a Microsoft product, such as Internet Explorer 5.5, is stored in a file that is over 8MB in size. Even with a high-speed modem, this would take an hour or so to transfer to your PC. In some countries, local phone calls are free, but where local calls are charged, the cost of the software is inflated by the phone charges.

Taking time

There are many factors that affect the time it takes to transfer a file to your computer. If there are a lot of other users also trying to download the same file as you, then this will cause delays. If the file is stored on a slow computer, it will slow down the process. And if the file is stored on a computer in another country, then you are relying on the speed of the links between your Internet service provider and the other country.

You will find that, on average, a 1MB file will take around 5–10 minutes to download if you have a 56K modem (10–20 minutes if you have an older modem). Sometimes, however, you will pick a file stored on a high-speed computer at a quiet moment on the Internet and it will download quite quickly.

Watch out for viruses

Many users worry that they might introduce a virus to their PC. Most popular Web sites are regularly scanned for viruses and software that you download is also scanned. However, there is a chance of picking up a virus if you download files, so it's a good idea to install a virus detector on your PC, which you can download from the Internet (see page 148).

SITES TO @ VISIT

Some Web sites are dedicated to providing a store of files that you can download to your computer.

This site has a powerful search facility to help you find the software you are looking for:
www.shareware.com

With categories such as Education, Games, Kids and Home & Personal, this site is a vast resource of downloadable software:
www.download.com

Finding a virus detector to download

You may have heard about computer viruses - programs that can cause havoc on your computer. Virus detectors can protect your PC from infection and they're easy to download from the Internet.

IF YOU LOVE the idea of being able to download free software from the Internet, you might be reluctant to go ahead because of worries over a virus attack. A virus can, very occasionally, be transferred to your computer if you download software from the Internet and it could then damage files on your hard disk. The good news is that the threat is slight and there are special programs that can spot a virus and delete it before it does any damage.

Installing a virus detector program on your computer is a good idea and, as this type of program can be downloaded from the Internet, it provides the perfect opportunity to show the various steps involved in downloading software. Once you have downloaded the virus detector and installed the software, you can be safe in the knowledge that your computer will be protected against most future virus threats. The software will check every file on your hard disk, and any floppy disks or CD-ROMs, to make sure that there are no viruses present.

● Norton AntiVirus

One of many trial versions of virus detection programs that you can download is Norton AntiVirus from the software firm Symantec. Once you have downloaded and installed the software, it can be used for 30 days before it stops working. Thirty days is plenty of time to use the software to see if you like it. If you do like it and want to continue using it, you will need to buy the full program.

> **WHAT IT MEANS**
>
> VIRUS
>
> *A virus is a software program that buries itself within another program. It will then emerge and try to damage your data or delete your files. The problem with a virus is that if you copy a file, the virus will try and copy itself at the same time, so it can soon infect all your disks. The people who create a virus try to make it as destructive and hard to find as possible. One of the main ways you can 'catch' a virus is by downloading unchecked software from the Internet.*

In order to download the virus detector (and any other file type) you first need to be connected to the Internet and have started your Web browser. Go to Symantec's home page (the company that developed the Norton AntiVirus software) by typing their Web address in the address panel below the browser toolbar. The full address is: www.symantec.com.

1 The Symantec home page lets you choose the region of the world you are located in. Select the United Kingdom, and then on the next page click on Consumer/Home User as your visitor type.

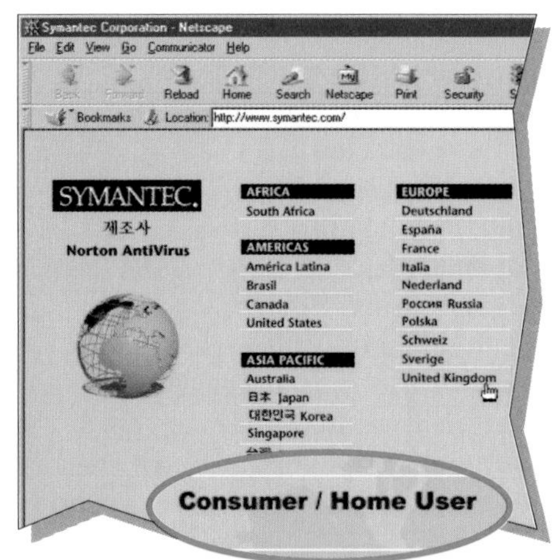

2 The next page offers links to the various services and products Symantec offer. We want to download a trial version of Norton AntiVirus, so move the pointer over the Trial Products icon and click once.

3 On the left of the next page, a list of the various software packages that you can download for trial from the site is displayed. Move your pointer over Norton AntiVirus and click once.

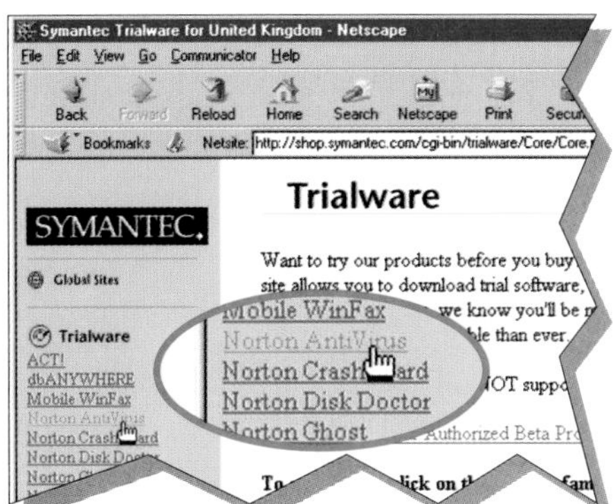

4 You now see a page listing the various versions of the program. We want the Windows 98 version – the second one down in the grid. Move your pointer down to the link labelled for Windows 98 and click once.

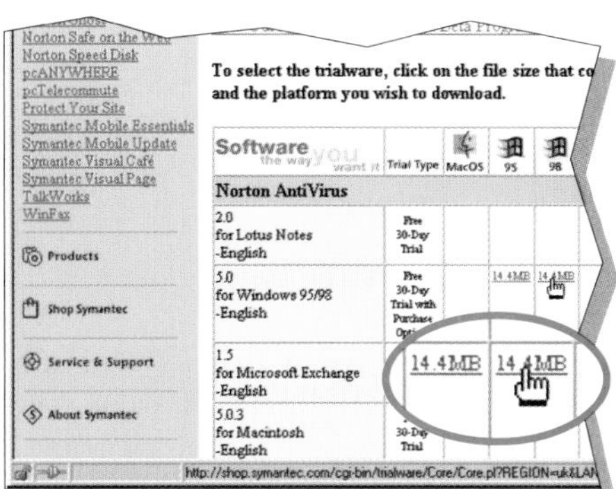

5 The next screen asks for user information. Many companies will ask you to fill in a questionnaire before allowing you to download software. Fill in the required sections and press the Continue button. (Your answers will normally be used by the company to send you details of new products.)

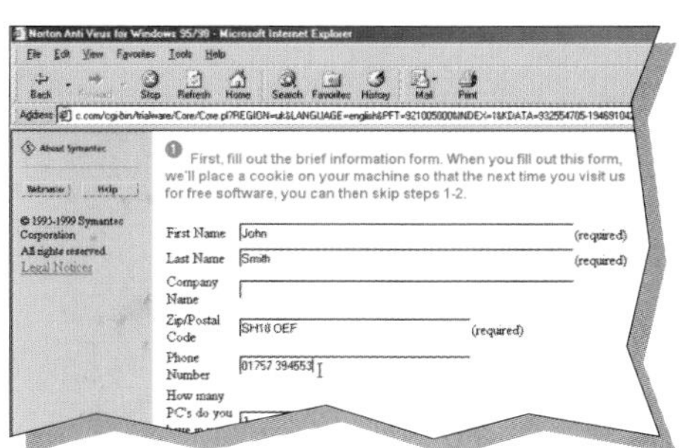

6 A license agreement is also displayed that covers the use of the product. Read through this carefully and, if you agree to the terms, press the Accept button at the bottom of the screen to proceed.

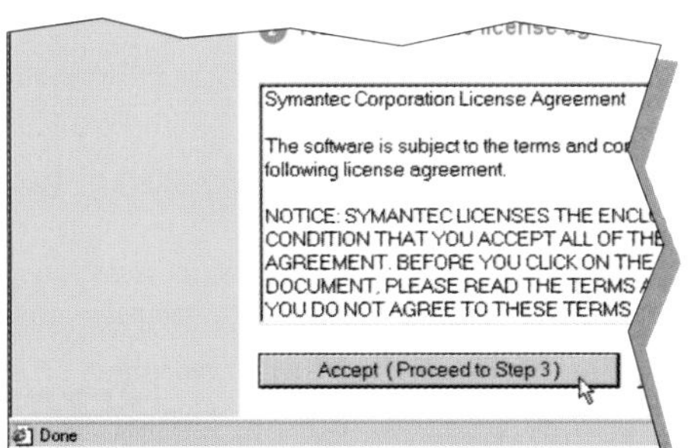

7 You then see the screen that allows you to download the software, with information about the hardware requirements needed to run it. Click on the download link (inset) to start downloading the program.

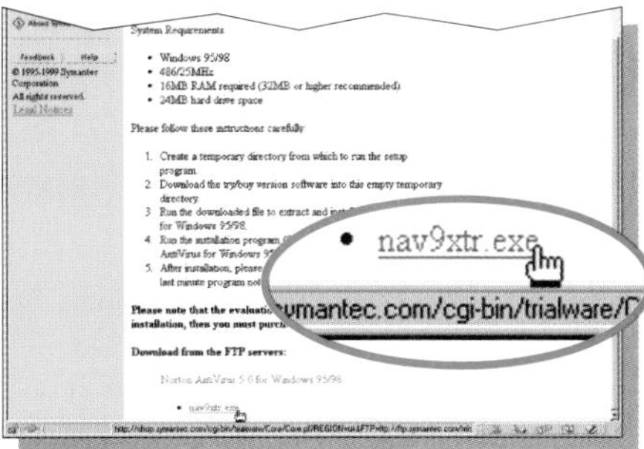

8 Your Web browser recognizes that you want to download the program and displays a dialog box asking where you want to save the file. Save it to your hard disk (C:). Click on Save to start the download process.

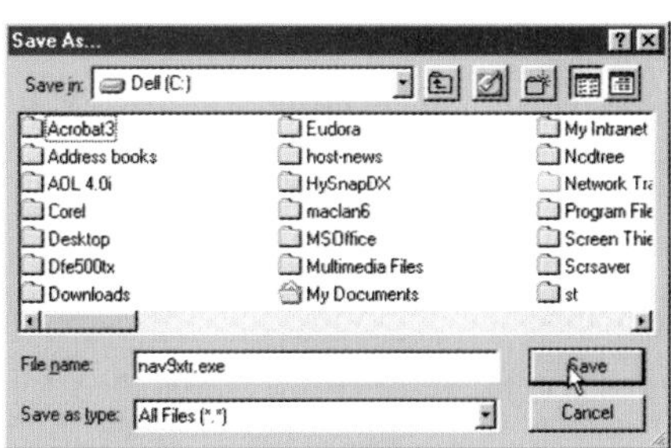

9 The browser starts to download the file. The dialog box may display the size of the file and an estimate of the time that it will take to download. You might also be given an idea of how the download is progressing. The speed of the file transfer depends on various factors (see page 147 – Taking time).

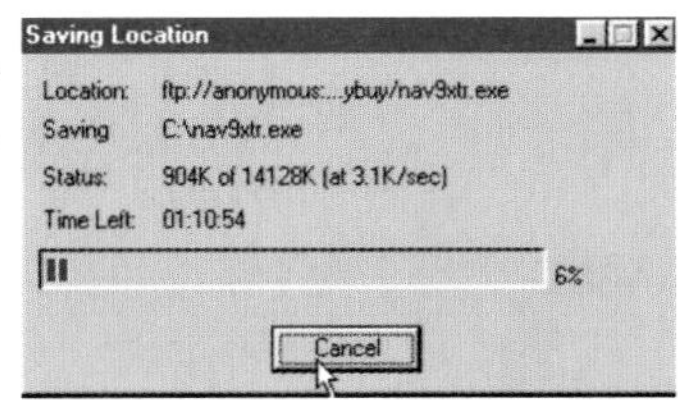

10 When the program has downloaded, you can install the software by running the program. To run the program, click on the Start menu, select the Run command and type the path to the downloaded file in the Open: box.

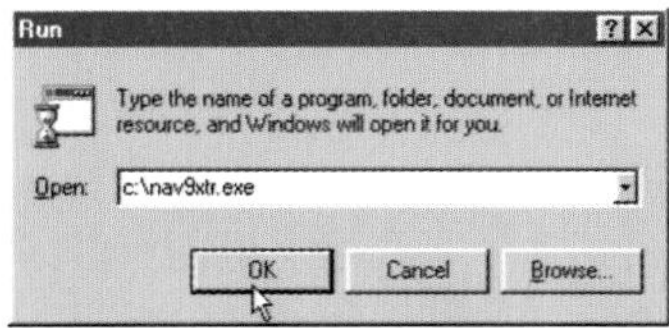

11 The trial version of Norton AntiVirus is a self-extracting program. This means that when you run the program, it expands the files that make it up (the file sizes are compressed so that they download more quickly). Click on Setup. The software will now start to install itself onto your hard disk. Follow the instructions on the screen. You will soon have your own virus detection software – downloaded from the Internet!

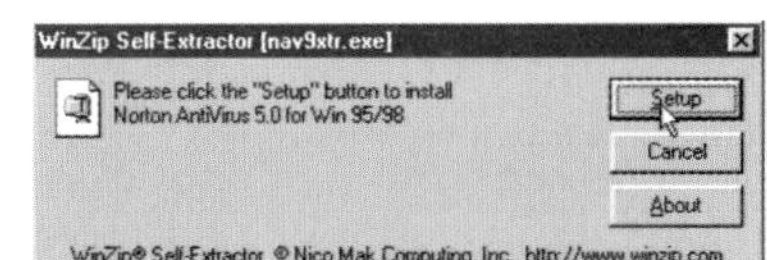

12 A screen welcomes you to the Norton AntiVirus setup program. There is now a simple series of instructions to work through before the program is up and running. All you have to do is click through the screens and you will soon have the program that protects your computer from the damaging viruses.

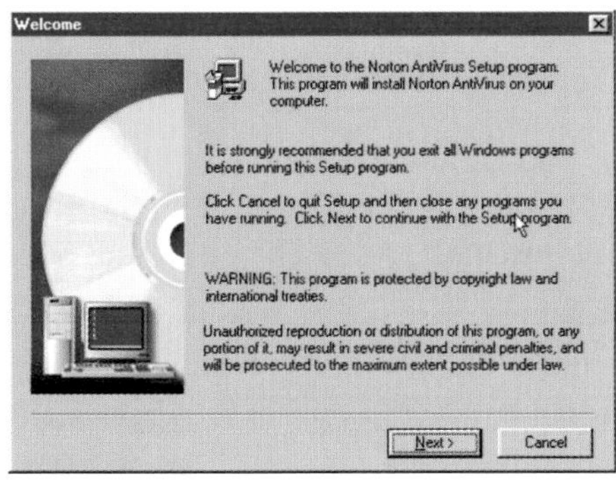

AFTER 30 DAYS

If, after 30 days, you decide that you do not want to keep the Norton AntiVirus software, you can remove it from your computer. To do this, click on the Start button, then Settings, then Control Panel and double-click on the Add/Remove Software icon. There is a list of installed software – select Norton AntiVirus and select Add/Remove. The software will be safely removed from your computer.

Hot news on the Web

If you want to keep in touch with the latest news as it breaks or follow up a particular story in depth, why not explore the Web's fast-growing news sites?

News flashes around the Web in seconds and many sites make it freely available. Today, increasingly more newspapers have associated Web sites that feature constantly updated news stories.

News stories can break anywhere in the world, at any time, and conventional media can't always provide up-to-date coverage until the following day. Newspapers won't appear until the morning after and television and radio will only give so much air-time to particular stories. If you want to find out more, try the Web, where news can be kept as up-to-the-minute as television and radio – if not more so – yet it's you who chooses how much time you spend on each item.

● News online

Everybody, from the major media giants and trade organizations to enthusiastic hobbyists, is creating and maintaining Web sites that offer extensive, up-to-the-minute news on all subjects, from major international stories to purely local items.

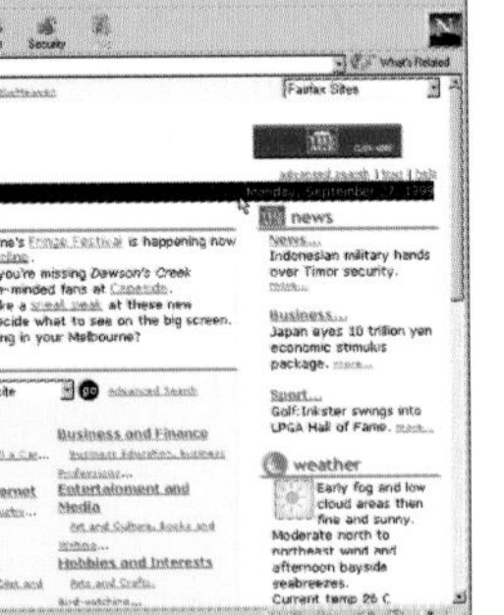

It can be just as easy to get the latest news from the other side of the world as it is to discover more information about local issues.

Many newspapers and broadcasting companies have Web sites to provide news coverage round the clock. For example, the BBC, *The Times* and CNN have Web sites and there are plenty of other newspapers, television and radio stations across the globe with Web-based news services.

● Keeping in touch

Web technology means that news sites can add video and sound clips to compete with television and radio. They often have room to provide enormous amounts of background or archive data and can further extend the information with links to other relevant Web sites.

News Web sites are perfect for anyone who wants to research topical or current affairs issues, whether for homework, business or general interest. Many sites include search tools to help you find particular stories or provide help with researching online news archives.

If you're interested in specialist or local news, there's probably a Web site that can cater for you, too. Subjects such as sport, entertainment, science and technology are particularly well served.

SITES TO  VISIT

World news

The Web is a great way to stay in touch with news that you might not see in your local media. Here's a selection of some of the bigger national news sites:

ABC
www.abcnews.com

24-hour Italian news site
www.ilsole24ore.it

The New York Times
www.nytimes.com

Japan's *Mainichi* newspapers
www.mainichi.co.jp/english

Le Monde
www.lemonde.fr

Die Welt
www.welt.de

The Sydney Morning Herald
www.smh.com.au/

Great news sites

There is a large – and rapidly growing – range of news sites on the Internet. Here's our guide to some of the best around.

A NEWS WEB site isn't worth its salt unless it's updated frequently enough to be topical. For general news, that means daily – and preferably more frequently, such as on the hour. However, more specialized news sites might only need to be updated once a week to give top-quality coverage. There is a huge range of fascinating sites, but not all are equally reliable. The sites featured on this page all give an excellent service.

ITN www.itn.co.uk
Independent Television News' Web site opens with a page of frequently updated headlines – usually with sound and video clips. Bulletins are brought up to date several times a day. There are sections for UK news, world news and business news, but perhaps the most interesting area is called News on Demand. Here you can choose from a selection of recent ITN video clips or watch a full news bulletin. But beware of the download times – they can be very long and you are paying the telephone bill.

Sky Television www.sky.com/news
The strength of this satellite television's news coverage is in sports, especially football, rugby union, rugby league, golf and tennis stories. Short, snappy reports are updated every day and, not surprisingly, there is in-depth coverage of events where Sky has exclusive live broadcast rights, such as the Ryder Cup golf tournament.

BBC News news.bbc.co.uk
This richly informative site draws on the immense television and radio reporting resources of the BBC. The front page's headlines are updated frequently and there are in-depth sections, including sport, science/technology and business. Each story comes with a set of links to other Web sites and many stories include sound and video clips from BBC television and radio reports.

CNN Interactive www.cnn.com
America's global television news service offers an extensive Web site, including sections for US news, world news, science/technology, sport and weather. But there is some light relief with sections about travel, style and show business. Ecology and health are also covered.

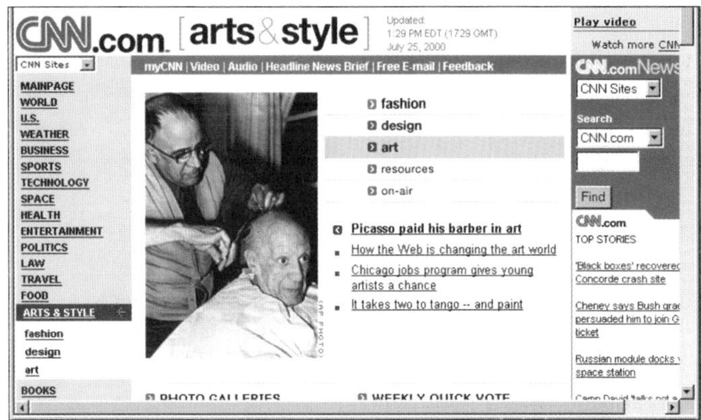

The Independent www.independent.co.uk
The news pages of *The Independent* are updated every day and include sections for UK news, international news, business and sport. There are also areas featuring the paper's columnists, leader articles and letters from readers. If you want to have your say on topical issues, you can follow the Argument link to join in *The Independent*'s own forums.

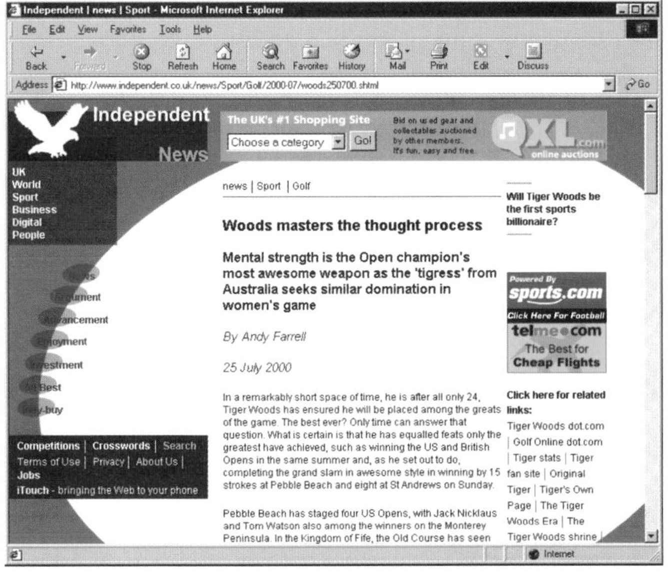

The Guardian
www.guardianunlimited.co.uk
This umbrella site gives you access to both *The Guardian* and *The Observer* newspapers, including their weekly supplements and their Web-only offshoots. Of particular interest if you want to keep up with Web developments is *The Guardian*'s weblog section. If you're more interested in sport, then there are daily updated pages for football and cricket. You can also subscribe to daily electronic newsletters to get the latest news delivered to your PC every afternoon. In addition, there are comprehensive archive and search facilities.

USA Today
www.usatoday.com
The *USA Today* site is the ideal way to catch up with the national headlines in the United States. There are also regular updates covering international news, plus a money section, the latest weather reports and very comprehensive US sports coverage. This is an excellent place to keep track of all the very latest American football, baseball, basketball and ice hockey results.

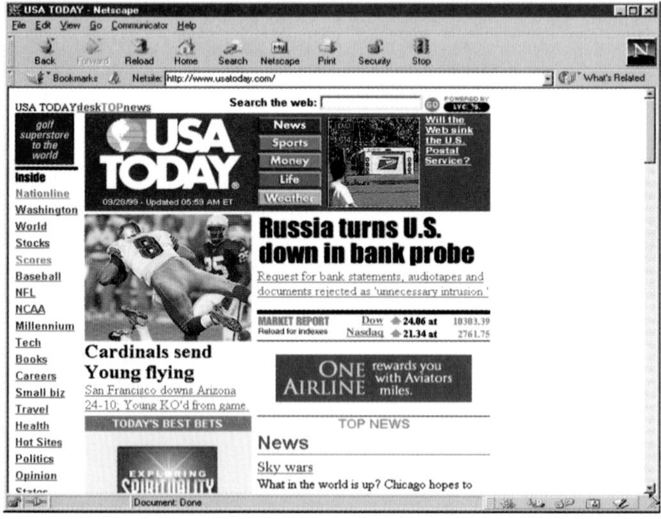

The Electronic Telegraph
www.telegraph.co.uk
The Daily Telegraph's Web site is one of the most complete of any UK newspaper. Its home page gives you links to the day's lead stories. There are special sections for UK, international and City news, as well as weather, sport and appointments. You can see today's Matt cartoon online and even try your hand at *The Telegraph*'s crossword, filling in the answers with your keyboard.

The Times
www.the-times.co.uk
This Web site gives you access to online versions of *The Times*, *The Sunday Times* and the three weekly publications comprising *The Times Education Supplement*, *The Times Higher Education Supplement* and *The Times Literary Supplement*. It has its own Resources area, too, which lets you search through their archives of online news articles from the present day to the start of 1996.

CNet
www.cnet.com
This US-based Web-only magazine is one of the best places to get the latest computing news. There's extensive coverage of PC, Apple Macintosh and Internet technology – with reports that are updated every day. It's also worth checking out the reviews of software and hardware and the terrific tips and tutorials. Watch out for all sorts of useful downloads in CNet's Software Central area.

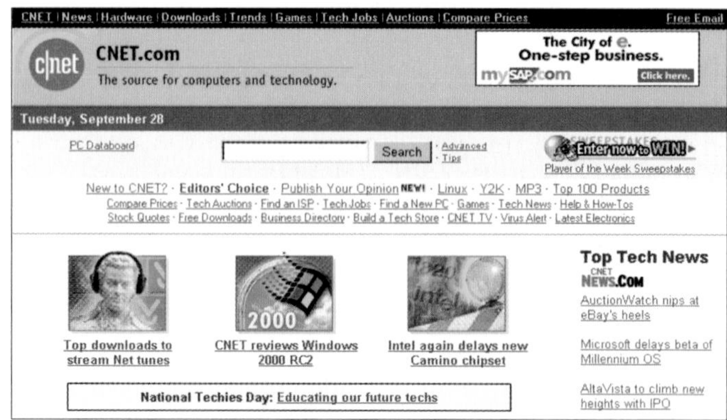

Dotmusic
www.dotmusic.com
Dotmusic is put together by the team that publishes *Music Week*, the UK's leading trade music magazine. If you want to find out about the latest chart news, get information about new releases before your friends and keep up with the dance music scene, then this is the place for you. There are music industry stories, the latest gossip and lots of sound and video downloads.

New Scientist
www.newscientist.co.uk
The New Scientist site provides authoritative science and technology news coverage. It features some of the best articles from the magazine, covering current topics from genetically modified crops to the safety of mobile phones, in a clear and accessible style. You'll also find Web-only material, archives and supplements to the magazine articles.

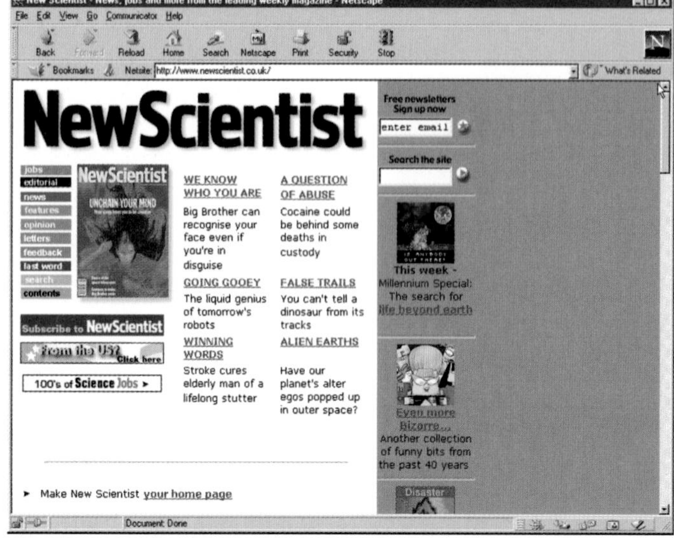

Sports.Com

www.sports.com

This dedicated sports news Web site concentrates on football and rugby, with player profiles, team news and all the stats and fixture details you could hope to find. There are also sections for other European leagues. Information for the sports gambler is a key element of the site, with betting advice on English and Italian matches.

The Hollywood Reporter

www.hollywoodreporter.com

This is the Web version of the famous LA-based film and entertainment magazine. Every day sees newly updated film, television and music stories. The site also includes an archive section and, if you're a member, you can use this terrific area to find out the latest status of films and television programmes currently in production.

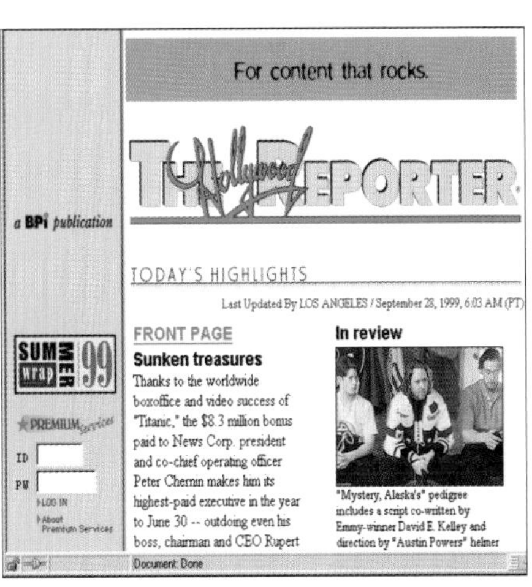

PC TIPS

How to find local news

In many places, local and regional newspapers have their own Web sites. Some local radio stations also maintain Web sites but these rarely carry much news. For this reason it's best to concentrate on finding out if your local paper is on the Net. The best tactic is to use an Internet search engine, preferably a regionally based one. If you know the name of your local newspaper, make a search using that name. If you don't, you could look in news sections using the name of your town or locality to instigate the search. Use your browser software to get to the Yahoo! UK home page at www.yahoo.co.uk. Here you'll notice a number of predefined sections – click on the Newspapers link in the News and Media section. Simply scroll down the screen and you'll find a comprehensive list of links to UK regional and national papers, from the *Aberdeen Independent* to the *Yorkshire Post*.

FINANCIAL NEWS

The finance industry is in the process of being revolutionized by the Internet, as companies bypass the middlemen and go straight to the wired consumers, who then take their destiny into their own hands by using the rich information sources that the Internet can supply.

However, savings and investments are inherently complex matters, so it helps if you can get your news – and advice – in a clear and comprehensible form. The Motley Fool UK (www.fool.co.uk) is the British offshoot of its US parent. Its motto is 'educate, amuse, enrich', providing financial news and background in a clear, amusing manner. There's frequently updated news from the money markets and plenty of informed background comment.

Times-Money (www.times-money.co.uk) is the Web offshoot of *The Times*' personal finance pages. The site gives you the latest news, online share prices and plenty of how-to-do-it advice in a straightforward way.

If your investment interests range globally, then Bloomberg.com is worth a look. This is the free Internet outpost of the professional investor's electronic news feed. As such, it is packed full of information on all aspects of global markets, with enough charts and graphs to keep you happy for hours.

And, if the hot new technology sector excites you, then you could do much worse than check out the Red Herring Online site (www.redherring.com), the Web version of a US magazine that is dedicated to technology news, research and analysis. This site has a snappy design with authoritative and quickly digestible content.

Sport on the Web

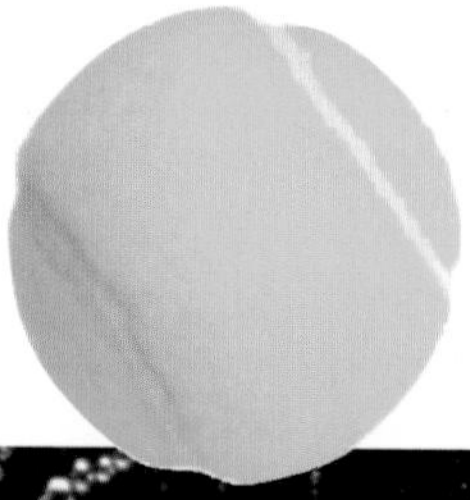

The Internet is a fabulous resource for sports fans. Wherever you are in the world, you can keep up with your favourite team, exchange gossip and make sure you know your idol's latest score.

It's easy to take advantage of the wealth of sports information on the Internet. You can keep up to date with a Sumo wrestling competition in Japan as easily as discovering the score of a local football match.

If you are a sports fan, you will find the Internet an amazing treasure trove of news, results and gossip. It doesn't really matter what your sport is – soccer or squash, bass fishing or boules, table tennis or ten-pin bowling – there is likely to be a site out there for you. Such sites are run by both official and unofficial organizations, and most are kept constantly up to date with the latest information.

For many sports, there is a huge range of different sites to choose from. There might well be a specific area devoted to your favourite league, your local club, or even your favourite individual player.

● By the fans, for the fans

The low cost of putting information on the Internet means that a huge number of sports sites are created and run by enthusiastic amateurs.

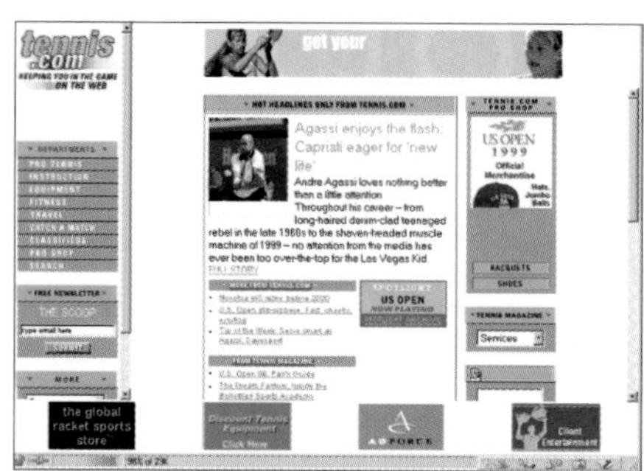

There's always a tennis tournament on somewhere in the world, and you can follow events as they happen.

This works well, because anyone who believes they have something interesting to tell the world about their love and knowledge of, say, speed skating is limited only by the time they have to devote to it.

● Instant results

News and results are the core of any good sports site on the Web, closely followed by chat and opinion. The speed of computers means that the slicker sites will have results, match reports – and often even pictures – only minutes after the events or games finish. This is long before you read about them in the newspaper or see them on the television news.

Great sports sites

To help you get the most out of sporting information available on the Internet, here's a rundown of some of the best sports sites.

SPORTS NEWS needs to be, above all, up to date, accurate and well-informed. All of the sites selected fit the bill in all these respects.

There is a range of commercial and official sites here, from the Carling Premier League site to the world's rugby union news, plus a selection of unofficial sites to give you a flavour of what's on offer. All the sites quoted are worth a visit if you're a general sports fan, but you will find many others if you browse the Internet, following up links.

You can rely on large publishers and official organizations for professional design and accuracy, but they are only likely to present the official line.

Club sites will also present an image that is beneficial to the club and might attempt to sell you memorabilia imprinted with the club logo as well as entrance tickets, season tickets and supporters' club membership.

For interesting, off-beat opinions and hot gossip, you might find the unofficial sites, run by enthusiasts, much more rewarding, although they cannot necessarily be relied on for either accuracy or slick design.

Sporting Life

www.sporting-life.com

This is the online version of the now defunct horse-racing enthusiast's daily newspaper. It is an excellent general sports site, covering a huge range of sports and is updated throughout the day. There's lots of hard news and a full results service.

The Sporting Life site has the latest news and results from a wide range of sports – including horse racing!

Football on the World Wide Web

There are countless football sites on the Internet. Here's a taster to kick off your footie browsing.

Chelsea Football Club

www.chelseafc.co.uk

This is the official site of Chelsea Football Club. As you would expect, it is smart and slick. There is news and feedback, opportunities to submit questions during an 'ask the players' session, online shopping from the club shop and the Chelsea Chat area, where the fans have their say. Like many big club sites, this is an excellent site.

Football 365

www.football365.co.uk

If you want a UK-wide view of soccer, try this site, part of the 365 network of Web sites that covers lots of entertainment subjects. In addition to the serious news stories covering all the top clubs, there's a look at the lighter side of football, containing look-alikes and recording the gaffes that soccer stars and pundits would rather forget about. Football 365 also offers plenty of ways of keeping up with what's going on if you don't want to visit every day: you can sign up for free email newsletters by typing in your email address.

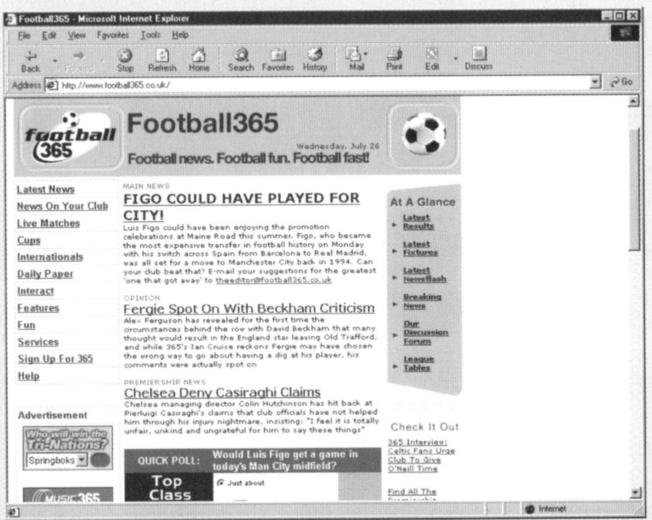

Australian Coarse Angling

www.coarsefishing.ws

There are plenty of fishing sites on the Internet, but few that are as sparky and entertaining as this one, which describes itself as 'the humorous alternative to uptight, over-serious fishing around the world'. The site is comprehensive, with sections covering everything from bait to floats and rods.

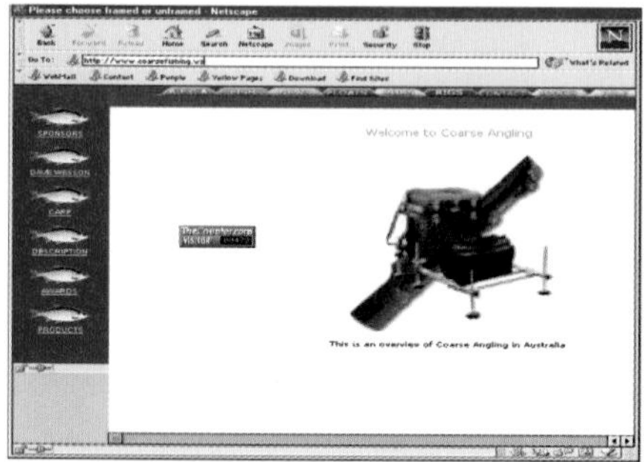

GolfWeb

www.golfweb.com

This US site is a huge compendium of everything you could want to know about the world of golf. There is opinion, latest tournament news, fun stuff, such as fantasy golf and voting for the players of the year, and sections on individual players and equal rights for the women's game.

Tennis Magazine Online

www.tennis.com

The Internet outpost of the US magazine *Tennis* has loads of news and feature material, as well as detailed archive sections on the year's Grand Slam events.

Cricket

www.uk.cricket.org

You'll find just about everything of interest in the world of cricket on this site. There are current test match scores and reports, player information, a breakdown of news from the main cricket-playing countries, interactive surveys (for example, find out who will bat first in the next test against New Zealand) and even live coverage of far-flung test cricket.

Tennis is well represented on the Net. Other popular sports with plenty of sites include golf and cricket. Most sports sites offer a huge range of information which is much more up to date than you could expect from a conventional magazine.

THE 2004 OLYMPIC GAMES

The Olympics is the mega-event of the sporting calendar. The 2004 games are to be held in Athens, which is the birthplace of the Olympics. The official site (www.olympics.org) gives you lots of information about the venues and competitions, as well as online ticketing and merchandise sales. There's also plenty of local information for those visiting in person. For a look at the leading contenders in the run-up to the games, it's worth checking out the NBC Olympics site (www.nbcolympics.com). Although focused on US contenders, it's extremely well done and informative.

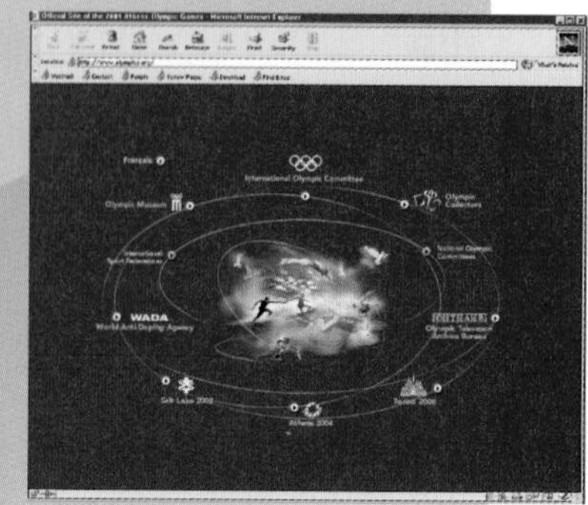

Scrum.com

www.scrum.com

This round-up of the world's rugby union news is updated daily. There is masses of comment from every conceivable angle on all the current talking points, and an excellent collection of links to other rugby union sites.

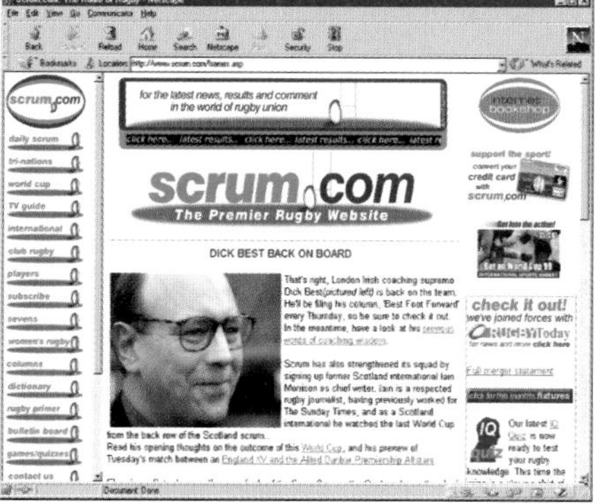

NZRugby.com

www.nzrugby.com

The awesome All Blacks have a suitably impressive Web presence, cleverly designed and packed with information on everything you want to know, including the famous Haka.

Ski central

www.skicentral.com

This site is one of the best for skiing and snowboarding aficionados, and has plenty of links to related winter sports sites.

Sportquest

www.sportquest.com

SIRC is a sports research organization distributing information on virtually any sport you can think of to coaches, sportsmen and women and fitness institutes. The site has an exhaustive list of sport-related links.

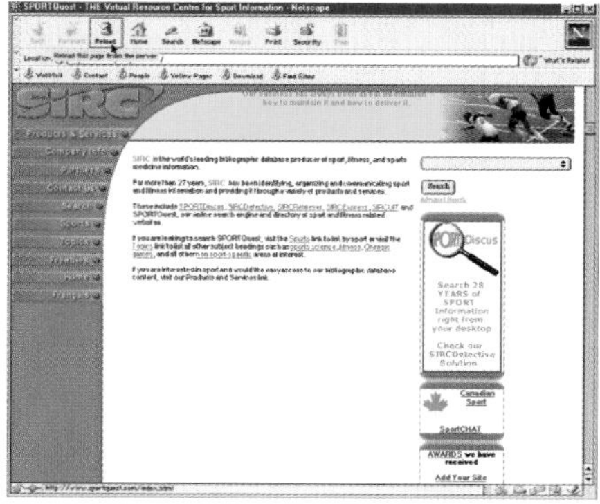

SumoWeb!

www.sumoweb.com

Sumo wrestling has a large presence on the Internet. Start by getting to grips with this excellent site.

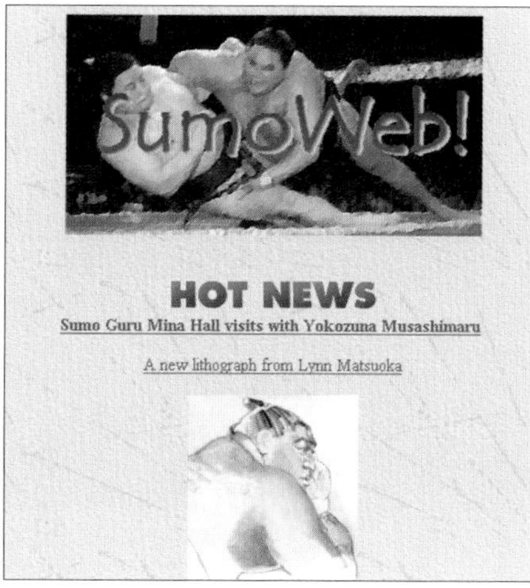

Carling Premiership

www.magicsponge.com

There's always space for more footie sites and the official site of England's Premier League is one of the best and most comprehensive of all.

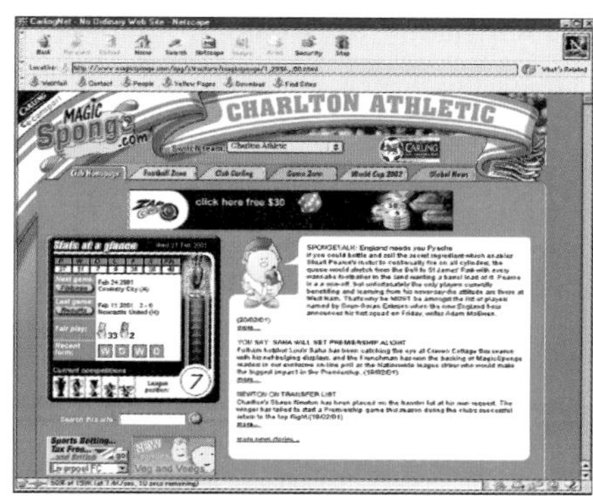

FIFA

www.fifa.com

This excellent site is the official Internet home of FIFA, the governing body of world football. It's got everything from world rankings (joint last are Anguilla and Monserrat) to updates on changes to the rules. It also features fascinating news and views for football fans worldwide.

SITES TO @ VISIT

Even if you're not a major fan of any one sport, there may be links that will help you discover a new hobby.

Boomerangs

www.flight-toys.com/boomerangs.html

A special-interest site, this has an exhaustive choice of links to sites dealing with boomerangs.

Yachting

www.yacht.co.uk

This contains information on UK yachting clubs, weather conditions and satellite pictures, plus links to other nautical sites.

● About the index

Text in italics is used for cross-references within the index (as in *see also...*). Page numbers in bold type denote the main entries for a topic.

Acknowledgments

Abbreviations: t = top; b = bottom; r = right; l = left; c = centre; bkg = background.
All cartoons are by Chris Bramley

8 Steve Bartholomew/De Agostini
10 Steve Bartholomew/De Agostini
12 Steve Bartholomew/De Agostini
14 De Agostini
15 Steve Bartholomew/De Agostini
18 De Agostini
22 De Agostini
23tl Steve Bartholomew/De Agostini
24 De Agostini
26 Steve Bartholomew/De Agostini
26 (Beethoven) AKG
27 (Prodigy) Redferns
30 (computer)De Agostini
30 (Shakespeare) Getty One Stone
32 Steve Bartholomew/De Agostini
33 Steve Bartholomew/De Agostini
34 Steve Bartholomew/De Agostini
36 Getty One Stone
40t Steve Bartholomew/De Agostini
40b Steve Bartholomew/De Agostini
41bl Steve Bartholomew/De Agostini
41br Steve Bartholomew/De Agostini
44 Lyndon Parker
46 De Agostini
50 De Agostini
54 Steve Bartholomew/De Agostini
56 Steve Bartholomew/De Agostini
58 Lyndon Parker
60 Lyndon Parker
60 (planets) NASA
61tl NASA
62 Lyndon Parker
64 Barratt East London
66 Images Colour Library
68 De Agostini
72 De Agostini
76 De Agostini
78 Lyndon Parker
82 Lyndon Parker
84 De Agostini
88 De Agostini
92t Steve Bartholomew/De Agostini
92c Labtec (courtesy)
92cl Labtec (courtesy)
92cr Steve Bartholomew/De Agostini
92b Sony (courtesy)
93 Steve Bartholomew/De Agostini
94t Steve Bartholomew/De Agostini
94b De Agostini
95b Steve Bartholomew/De Agostini
96t Steve Bartholomew/De Agostini
97all Steve Bartholomew/De Agostini
98 Lyndon Parker
99all Lyndon Parker
100t Images Colour Library
100b Lyndon Parker
104all Steve Bartholomew/De Agostini
105all Steve Bartholomew/De Agostini
106all Steve Bartholomew/De Agostini
107all Warrender Grant
108t Lyndon Parker
108b Microsoft PR (courtesy)
110 Steve Bartholomew/De Agostini
111all Plus Group PR
114tr Getty One Stone
115tr Getty One Stone
116cl Getty One Stone
118tr NASA
118b NASA
119tl NASA
119tr NASA
119bkg NASA
122 Quadrant Picture Library
123 Image Bank
124 Steve Bartholomew/De Agostini
126tr Steve Bartholomew/De Agostini
126c Image Bank
128tr Kobal Collection (courtesy MGM)
128tl NASA
129t Kobal Collection (courtesy Paramount Television)
134 Steve Bartholomew/De Agostini
134 (Tony Blair) Rex Features
136tr Image Bank
136b Steve Bartholomew/De Agostini
138 Image Bank
139tr Getty One Stone
142 De Agostini
146l Steve Bartholomew/De Agostini
146r Getty One Stone
147 Image Bank
148 (computer) Steve Bartholomew/De Agostini
148 (syringe) Telegraph Colour Library
150 (computer) Lyndon Parker
150 (globe) Stockmarket
153 Hulton Getty
154 (sports people) Allsports
154 (globe & web) The Imagebank
155 (football) De Agostini
156t,b De Agostini
157 (rugby ball) De Agostini